Lecture Notes in Artificial Intelligence   4870

Edited by J. G. Carbonell and J. Siekmann

Subseries of Lecture Notes in Computer Science

Jaime Simão Sichman   Julian Padget
Sascha Ossowski   Pablo Noriega (Eds.)

Coordination, Organizations, Institutions, and Norms in Agent Systems III

COIN 2007 International Workshops
COIN@AAMAS 2007, Honolulu, HI, USA, May 14, 2007
COIN@MALLOW 2007, Durham, UK, September 3-4, 2007
Revised Selected Papers

 Springer

Series Editors

Jaime G. Carbonell, Carnegie Mellon University, Pittsburgh, PA, USA
Jörg Siekmann, University of Saarland, Saarbrücken, Germany

Volume Editors

Jaime Simão Sichman
Escola Politécnica da Universidade de São Paulo (USP)
Lab. de Técnicas Inteligentes (LTI)
Av. Prof. Luciano Gualberto, tv. 3, 158, 05508-970 São Paulo, SP, Brazil
E-mail: jaime.sichman@poli.usp.br

Julian Padget
University of Bath
Department of Computer Science
Bath BA2 7AY, UK
E-mail: jap@cs.bath.ac.uk

Sascha Ossowski
Universidad Rey Juan Carlos
Grupo de Inteligencia Artificial
Campus de Móstoles, Calle Tulipán s/n, 28933 Móstoles, Spain
E-mail: sascha.ossowski@urjc.es

Pablo Noriega
Institut d'Investigació en Intel.ligència Artificial (IIIA)
Consejo Superior de Investigaciones Científicas (CSIC)
Campus UAB, Bellaterra, 08193 Barcelona, Spain
E-mail: pablo@iiia.csic.es

Library of Congress Control Number: 2008923934

CR Subject Classification (1998): I.2.11, I.2, D.2, F.3, D.1, C.2.4, D.3

LNCS Sublibrary: SL 7 – Artificial Intelligence

ISSN   0302-9743
ISBN-10   3-540-79002-0 Springer Berlin Heidelberg New York
ISBN-13   978-3-540-79002-0 Springer Berlin Heidelberg New York

This work is subject to copyright. All rights are reserved, whether the whole or part of the material is
concerned, specifically the rights of translation, reprinting, re-use of illustrations, recitation, broadcasting,
reproduction on microfilms or in any other way, and storage in data banks. Duplication of this publication
or parts thereof is permitted only under the provisions of the German Copyright Law of September 9, 1965,
in its current version, and permission for use must always be obtained from Springer. Violations are liable
to prosecution under the German Copyright Law.

Springer is a part of Springer Science+Business Media

springer.com

© Springer-Verlag Berlin Heidelberg 2008
Printed in Germany

Typesetting: Camera-ready by author, data conversion by Scientific Publishing Services, Chennai, India
Printed on acid-free paper   SPIN: 12251803   06/3180   5 4 3 2 1 0

Preface

In recent years, social and organizational aspects of agency have become major research topics in MAS. Current applications of MAS in Web services, grid computing and ubiquitous computing highlight the need for using these aspects in order to ensure social order within such environments. Openness, heterogeneity, and scalability of MAS, in turn, put new demands on traditional MAS interaction models and bring forward the need to investigate the environment wherein agents interact, more specifically to design different ways of constraining or regulating agents' interactions. Consequently, the view of coordination and control has been expanding to entertain not only an agent-centric perspective but societal and organization-centric views as well. The overall problem of analyzing the social, legal, economic and technological dimensions of agent organizations and the co-evolution of agent interactions pose theoretically demanding and interdisciplinary research questions at different levels of abstraction. The MAS research community has addressed these issues from different perspectives that have gradually become more cohesive around the four concepts that give title to this workshop series: *coordination, organization, institutions* and *norms*.

The COIN@AAMAS 2007 and COIN@MALLOW 2007 events belong to a workshop series that started in 2005, and since then has continued with two editions per year. The main goal of these workshops is to bring together researchers from different communities working in theoretical and/or practical aspects of coordination, organization, institutions and norms, and to to facilitate a more systematic discussion of these themes that have until lately been considered from different perspectives.

In 2007, the COIN workshops were hosted by AAMAS 2007 (May 14, Honolulu, USA) and by MALLOW 2007 (September 3–4, Durham, UK). The papers contained in this volume are the revised versions of a selection of the papers presented in these workshops. In COIN@AAMAS 2007, 9 papers were presented at the workshop out of 15 submissions, while from 23 submissions to COIN@MALLOW 2007, 15 were accepted for presentation.

We want to express our gratitude to the Program Committee members and additional reviewers of both events, to the participants of the workshops and most particularly to the authors for their original contributions and further revisions for this volume. We also want to thank the organizers of the 6th International Joint Conference on Autonomous Agents and Multiagent Systems (AAMAS 2007) and of the MALLOW 2007 event for hosting and supporting the organization of the COIN workshops. Finally, we would also like to acknowledge the encouragement and support from Springer, in the person of Alfred Hofmann, for the publication of the COIN workshops since the first edition.

December 2007   COIN@AAMAS 2007: Sascha Ossowski
                                                        Jaime Simão Sichman
                                         COIN@MALLOW 2007: Pablo Noriega
                                                               Julian Padget

Organization

Organizing Committees

COIN@AAMAS 2007

Sascha Ossowski	Universidad Rey Juan Carlos (Spain)
Jaime Simão Sichman	University of São Paulo (Brazil)

COIN@MALLOW 2007

Pablo Noriega	Intitut d'Investigació en Intelligència Artificial (Spain)
Julian Padget	University of Bath (UK)

COIN Steering Committee (2005-2007)

Andrea Omicini	University of Bologna (Italy)
Guido Boella	University of Turin (Italy)
Jaime Simão Sichman	University of São Paulo (Brazil)
Julian Padget	University of Bath (UK)
Olivier Boissier	ENS Mines Saint-Etienne (France)
Pablo Noriega	Intitut d'Investigació en Intelligència Artificial (Spain)
Sascha Ossowski	Universidad Rey Juan Carlos (Spain)
Victor Lesser	University of Massachusetts (USA)
Virginia Dignum	Utrecht University (The Netherlands)

Program Committees

COIN@AAMAS 2007

Alessandro Provetti	Università degli Studi di Messina (Italy)
Andrea Omicini	University of Bologna (Italy)
Anja Oskamp	Free University Amsterdam (The Netherlands)
Carl Hewitt	MIT (USA)
Catherine Tessier	ONERA (France)
Christian Lemaître	Universidad Autónoma Metropolitana (Mexico)
Danny Weyns	Katholieke Universiteit Leuven (Belgium)
Eric Matson	Wright State University (USA)
Eugénio Oliveira	Universidade do Porto (Portugal)

Fabiola López y López   Benemérita Universidad Autónoma
de Puebla (Mexico)

Frank Dignum   Utrecht University (The Netherlands)

Gabriela Lindemann   Humboldt University Berlin (Germany)

Guido Boella   University of Turin (Italy)

Holger Billhardt   University Rey Juan Carlos, Madrid (Spain)

Jaime Simão Sichman   University of São Paulo (Brazil)
(**Co-chair**)

Javier Vázquez-Salceda   Universitat Politècnica de Catalunya (Spain)

Jomi Fred Hübner   FURB Blumenau (Brazil)

Juan A. Rodríguez-Aguilar   Intitut d'Investigació en Intelligència
Artificial (Spain)

Julian Padget   University of Bath (UK)

Leendert van der Torre   University of Luxembourg (Luxembourg)

Liz Sonenberg   University of Melbourne (Australia)

Mario Verdicchio   Politecnico di Milano (Italy)

Michael Luck   University of Southampton (UK)

Nicoletta Fornara   Università della Svizzera Italiana
(Switzerland)

Olivier Boissier   ENS Mines Saint-Etienne (France)

Olivier Gutknecht   LPL (France)

Pablo Noriega   Intitut d'Investigació en Intelligència
Artificial (Spain)

Pinar Yolum   Bogazici University (Turkey)

Sascha Ossowski   Universidad Rey Juan Carlos (Spain)
(**Co-chair**)

Stephen Cranefield   University of Otago (New Zealand)

Ulises Cortés   Universitat Politècnica de Catalunya (Spain)

Vicent Botti   Universitat Politècnica de Valencia (Spain)

Victor Lesser   University of Massachusetts-Amherst (USA)

Virginia Dignum   University of Utrecht (The Netherlands)

Wamberto Vasconcelos   University of Aberdeen (UK)

Yves Demazeau   Leibniz Institute (France)

COIN@MALLOW 2007

Andrea Omicini   University of Bologna (Italy)

Carl Hewitt   MIT (USA)

Carles Sierra   Intitut d'Investigació en Intelligència
Artificial (Spain)

Christian Lemaître   Universidad Autónoma Metropolitana
(Mexico)

Cristiano Castelfranchi   Istituto di Scienze e Tecnologie della
Cognizione (Italy)

Eric Matson   Wright State University (USA)

Eugénio Oliveira   Universidade do Porto (Portugal)

Fabiola López y López   Benemérita Universidad Autónoma
de Puebla (Mexico)

Gabriela Lindemann   Humboldt University Berlin (Germany)

Guido Boella   University of Turin (Italy)

Jaime Simão Sichman   University of São Paulo (Brazil)

Javier Vázquez-Salceda   Universitat Politècnica de Catalunya (Spain)

Juan A. Rodríguez-Aguilar   Intitut d'Investigació en Intelligència
Artificial (Spain)

Julian Padget   University of Bath (UK)
(**Co-chair**)

Marc Esteva   University of Technology Sydney (Australia)

Marek Sergot   Imperial College (UK)

Marina de Vos   University of Bath (UK)

Mario Verdicchio   Politecnico di Milano (Italy)

Michael Luck   University of Southampton (UK)

Nicoletta Fornara   Università della Svizzera Italiana
(Switzerland)

Olivier Boissier   ENS Mines Saint-Etienne (France)

Pablo Noriega   Intitut d'Investigació en Intelligència
Artificial (Spain) (**Co-chair**)

Sascha Ossowski   Universidad Rey Juan Carlos (Spain)

Stephen Cranefield   University of Otago (New Zealand)

Tim Norman   University of Aberdeen (UK)

Victor Lesser   University of Massachusetts-Amherst (USA)

Virginia Dignum   University of Utrecht (The Netherlands)

Wamberto Vasconcelos   University of Aberdeen (UK)

Additional Reviewers

Andrés García-Camino   Henrique Lopes Cardoso

Arianna Tocchio   Holger Billhardt

Dimitri Melaye   Jelle Herbrandy

Grégory Bonnet   Luca Tummolini

Guillaume Piolle   Maite López-Sánchez

Table of Contents

Coordination

Organizations and Institutions

Norms

Towards a Framework for Agent Coordination and Reorganization, AgentCoRe*

Mattijs Ghijsen, Wouter Jansweijer, and Bob Wielinga

Human Computer Studies Laboratory, Institute of Informatics,
University of Amsterdam
{mattijs,jansw,wielinga}@science.uva.nl

Abstract. Research in the area of Multi-Agent System (MAS) organization has shown that the ability for a MAS to adapt its organizational structure can be beneficial when coping with dynamics and uncertainty in the MASs environment. Different types of reorganization exist, such as changing relations and interaction patterns between agents, changing agent roles and changing the coordination style in the MAS. In this paper we propose a framework for agent **Co**ordination and **Re**organization (AgentCoRe) that incorporates each of these aspects of reorganization. We describe both declarative and procedural knowledge an agent uses to decompose and assign tasks, and to reorganize. The RoboCupRescue simulation environment is used to demonstrate how AgentCoRe is used to build a MAS that is capable of reorganizing itself by changing relations, interaction patterns and agent roles.

1 Introduction

The quality of organizational design of a MAS has a large influence on its performance. However, this is not the only factor that determines MAS performance. It is the combination of the organizational design together with the nature of the task performed by the MAS and the characteristics of the environment in which the MAS is embedded that determines the performance of a MAS [1]. A MAS that operates in a dynamic environment can mitigate or reduce negative effects of dynamics in this environment by changing its organization [2].

Existing research on the design of adaptive MAS organizations [3], [4] and [5], focuses on the organizational design while the issue of the design of agents in such dynamic organizations remains largely untouched. In this paper we address this issue by presenting AgentCoRe, a framework that enables agents to make decisions in dynamic multi-agent organizations. AgentCoRe provides a set of decision making modules that enables agents to make decisions about dynamic selection of coordination mechanisms, task decomposition, task assignment and adaptation of the MAS organizational structure. The description of the reasoning

---

* The research reported in this paper is part of the Interactive Collaborative Information Systems (ICIS) project, supported by the Dutch Ministry of Economic Affairs, grant BSIK03024.

J.S. Sichman et al. (Eds.): COIN 2007, LNAI 4870, pp. 1–14, 2008.
© Springer-Verlag Berlin Heidelberg 2008

processes as well as the input and output of those processes is at the knowledge level [6] to ensure a generic, domain independent design.

Although the focus of the framework is on providing capabilities for reorganizing, we have also included capabilities for coordinating work in the organization. This is because we view structuring and restructuring an agent organization as an essential part of a coordination mechanism. As shown in the research by Mintzberg, the structure of human organizations and the type of coordination mechanism used by its managers are closely related [7]. We emphasize that the goal of the AgentCoRe framework is not to improve existing work on coordination but rather to extend capabilities of agents by integrating capabilities for coordinating and reorganizing into a single framework.

Before we describe the AgentCoRe framework we discuss theory and related work on MAS reorganization. After a description of AgentCoRe, we will show how AgentCoRe is used to design and implement agents in the RoboCupRescue simulator [8]. We end with discussion, conclusions and directions for future work.

2   Theory and Related Work

In this paper we use definitions based on [9] and [10]. A task is defined as an activity performed by one or more agents to achieve a certain effect or goal in the environment. A task can be decomposed into subtasks and, in the case a task cannot be decomposed any further, it is called a primitive task. We define a role as a set of tasks that an agent is committed to perform when it is enacting that role. Capabilities are defined as a set of roles the agent is capable of enacting.

We define a MAS organization as a group of distributed agents, pursuing a common goal. The design of a MAS organization consists of relationships and interactions between the agents [11], agent roles [10] and coordination style [12]. Thus we define reorganization of a MAS as changing one or more of these organizational aspects. We assume that reorganization is triggered by the agents of the MAS, and not by a system designer or "human in the loop" as in [13].

A generic definition of coordination is given by [14] who define coordination as managing dependencies between activities. Research in the area of coordination in MAS has resulted in frameworks such as GPGP/TÆMS [15] and COM-MTDP [16] and both have been used in research on reorganization.

Nair et al. [17] extend [16] and change the composition of teams of agents to perform a rescue task in a highly dynamic environment where tasks can (de)escalate in size and new tasks are formed. Horling and Lesser change the relations and interaction patterns between agents in TÆMS structures but do not allow for role changes [18]. Their work is recently being extended by Kamboj and Decker [19] who use agent cloning [20] to allow for role changes in the organization. Martin and Barber present dynamic adaptation of coordination mechanisms as a mechanism for dealing with a dynamic environment [21].

The approaches described above all involve different aspects of reorganization; changing relations and interactions, changing agent roles and changing coordination style. In the next section we present the AgentCoRe framework which gives a knowledge level description of a framework for coordination and reorganization. We extend existing work by incorporating all aspects of reorganization described above into a single framework. By giving a knowledge level description, we refrain from computational details and focus on the required knowledge and reasoning for combined coordination and reorganization.

3   The AgentCoRe Framework

The AgentCore framework consists of 4 decision making modules that can be used independently from each other. An overview of these modules and their input and output is shown in figure 1. The oval shapes depict the decision making modules, the rectangles depict the input and output of these processes.

   The first module enables the agents to dynamically select the coordination mechanism that is being used. Being able to change to another coordination mechanism is an important aspect of organizational adaptation and it is an effective mechanism for a MAS to adapt to changes in the environment [22], [21] and [23]. Selection of the coordination mechanism is based on the current state of the environment and strategy rules which prescribe the use of a coordination strategy in a certain situation. A task-decomposition strategy, an assignment strategy and a reorganization strategy together form a coordination mechanism. Each of these strategies is used as input for the decision making modules in figure 1.

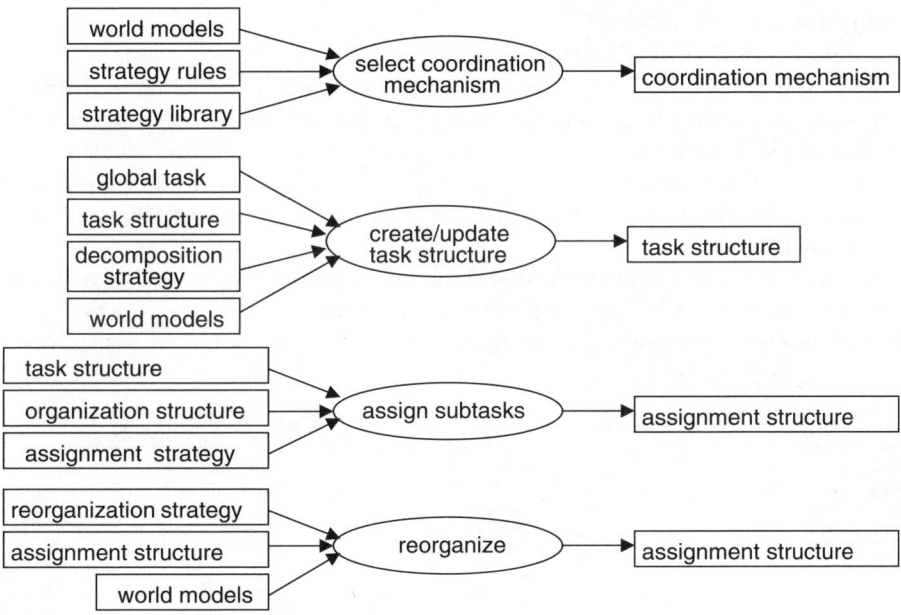

Fig. 1. AgentCoRe Modules

The next module of the framework takes care of creating and updating the task structure. Based on sensory input – which can be observations by the agent and messages from other agents – the agent will decompose the global task into subtasks. The structure of decomposed tasks is called a task structure which is a simplified version of the goal trees in the TÆMS framework [15]. A domain specific decomposition strategy describes how the global task decomposes into subtasks.

Relations and interaction patterns between agents and agent roles in the MAS are described in the organization structure. In the task assignment module, subtasks of the task structure are connected to the agents in the organization structure. The task structure combined with the organization structure by means of assignments is called the assignment structure. Which agents are assigned to which tasks is determined by the assignment strategy that is used.

When assignment is completed, the agent can reorganize the assignment structure (which contains the task structure as well as the organization structure). A reorganization strategy describes when and how reorganization takes place. These changes can be changes in team composition [17], agent relations [18] or agent roles [24].

3.1 Declarative Ingredients

The basic declarative components of the framework (see figure 2) are `task`, `agent` and `assignment`. A `task` has a set of subtasks and a description of the goal that is to be achieved by performing the task. Furthermore each `task` has a priority. Using the `task` concept, task structures can be created that show how tasks are decomposed into subtasks.

An `agent` has a set of roles the agent is currently enacting (in section 2 a role is defined as a set of tasks) and a set of capabilities which is the set of all roles the agent is capable of enacting. Furthermore, `agent` has relations with other agents. These relations describe which other agents the agent knows, communicates with, is boss of and which agent is its boss. Using the `agent` concept an organization structure can be created where agents have relations with each other, have roles and capabilities.

An `assignment` is a reified relation between `task` and `agent`. It has a timestamp that indicates when the assignment is created, a report frequency that defines when status reports on the progress of the task should be sent, and a

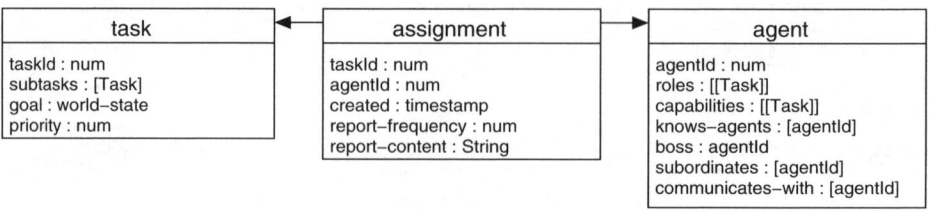

Fig. 2. Basic AgentCoRe declarative concepts

specification of the content of the reports. The `assignment` concept connects task structures and organization structures to form assignment structures.

The decomposition, assignment and reorganization strategies are mostly domain specific procedural descriptions of how a specific task should be decomposed or what types of roles should be assigned when reorganizing. Examples of these strategies are given in section 4 of this paper.

3.2   AgentCoRe Modules

A knowledge level description of the internal structure of the decision making modules shown in figure 1 is given by using the CommonKADS notation of inference structures [25]. Rectangles depict dynamic information, ovals represent elementary reasoning processes and arrows indicate input-output dependencies. Two thick horizontal lines depict static information used as input for the reasoning processes. For clarity purposes we depict the starting point of the inference structure by a thick squared rectangle.

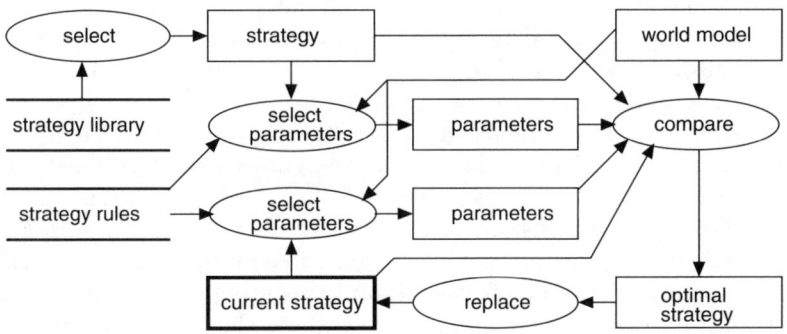

Fig. 3. Strategy selection inference structure

Figure 3 shows the inference structure of strategy selection in which the current coordination strategy is compared to other available strategies in the strategy library. To obtain the most optimal strategy, parameters are used which represent selection criteria of a coordination strategy (e.g. "required time", "required resources" or "required capabilities"). Strategy rules define in which situation a coordination strategy is optimal by indicating which parameters should be used to compare the strategies. Examples of strategy rules are; "always use the cheapest strategy" and "use the cheapest strategy but when lives are at stake, use the fastest strategy". In the first case, the parameter that indicates cost will be selected. In the second case, the parameters for cost and required time will be selected. The value of a parameter is determined by the current state of the world.

Figure 4 shows the inference structure for task decomposition. First, one of the tasks is selected from the task structure and based on the current model

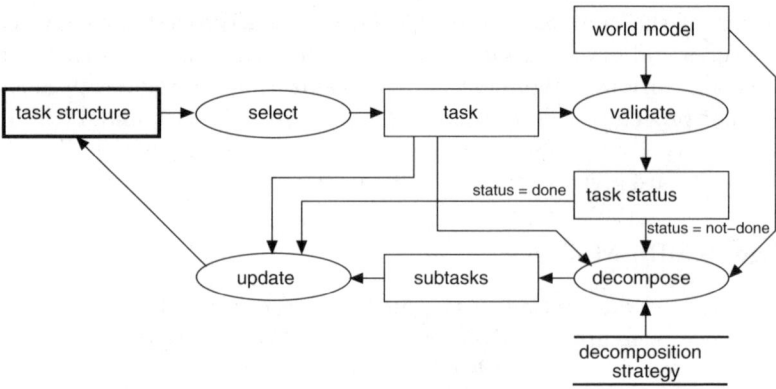

Fig. 4. Task decomposition inference structure

of the world, it is determined whether the task is still valid; is the goal still a valid goal or has a report been received that the task is finished. In the case the task is not valid, the task structure is updated immediately. Otherwise, the task is decomposed as prescribed by the decomposition strategy. The task and the generated subtasks are then used to update the task structure. This continues until each task in the task structure has been validated and decomposed.

In figure 5 the task assignment inference structure (based on the assignment inference structure in [25]) is shown. The assignment strategy determines selection of a set of tasks and a set of agents based on the current assignment structure. Grouping of tasks and agents can be used if multiple agents are assigned to a single task, or one agent is assigned to a group of tasks, or a group of agents is assigned to a group of tasks. If and how grouping is done, depends on the assignment strategy. If no grouping takes place the assign inference will use the task and agent sets that have been selected. The assign inference couples the sets or groups of tasks to the agents which results in a set of new assignments. This continues until all agents are assigned or no tasks are left to perform.

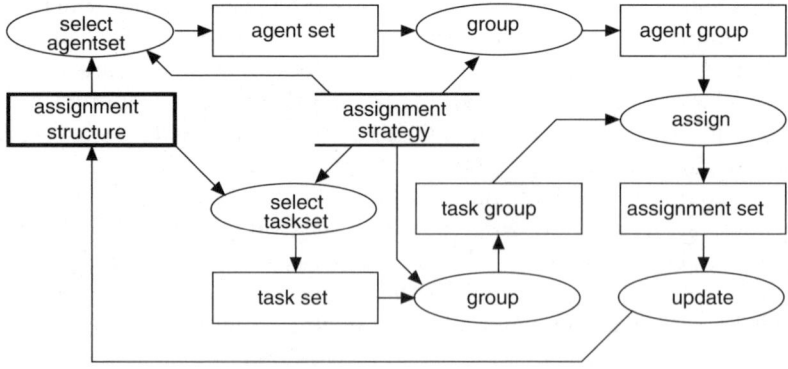

Fig. 5. Task assignment inference structure

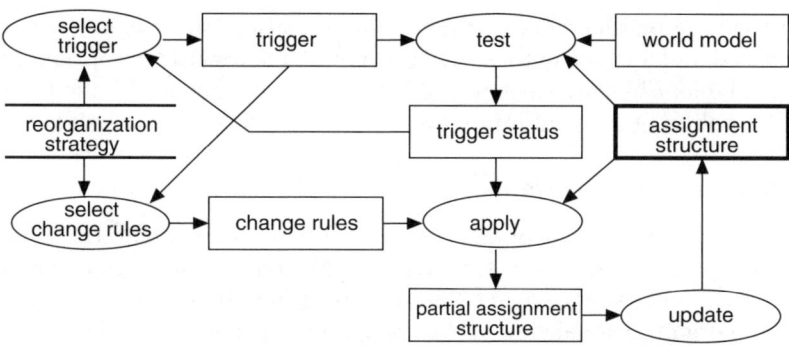

Fig. 6. Reorganize inference structure

In the reorganize inference structure in figure 6, a reorganization strategy gives a set of available triggers. Triggers are rules that initiate change in organization. Some examples of triggers are detecting an unbalanced workload over the agents, sudden changes in priority of one of the unassigned subtasks while all available agents are already allocated to other tasks, or an event in the environment that requires two teams to work together. Triggers are tested on the assignment structure and if they fire, a set of matching change rules is selected and applied to the assignment structure. Possible change rules are to assign agents to different roles and creating and/or removing relations between agents, but also taking an agent away from the task it is currently performing and assigning it to a task with a higher priority. Applying change rules results in a partial new assignment structure which is used to update the current assignment structure. Trigger selection continues until all triggers have been tested on the assignment structure.

4   A MAS Implementation Using AgentCoRe

In this section we demonstrate how the AgentCoRe modules can be used in an agents design and how the input and output of the modules are defined. As an example we use the "standardization of skills[1] extended with reorganization" approach which is one of the mechanisms for coordination and reorganization used in [26].

The environment in which the MAS is embedded is the RobuCupRescue Simulation System (RCRSS) [8]. In this environment, agents are deployed that jointly perform a rescue operation. When the simulation starts, buildings collapse, civilians get injured and buried under the debris, buildings catch fire and fires spread to neighboring buildings. Debris of the collapsed buildings falls on the roads

---

[1] The name of this decomposition strategy is based on "coordination by standardization of skills" described by Mintzberg [7]. Coordination by standardization of skills can be characterized by assignment of large and complex tasks to the operator agents.

causing roads to be blocked. For this rescue operation, three main tasks can be distinguished and for each of these tasks a type of agent with appropriate capabilities is available. Fires are extinguished by fire brigade teams, blocked roads are cleared by police agents and injured civilians are rescued by ambulance teams.

4.1   Organizational Design

Before we show the design of the agents, we first discuss how the agents are organized. The organization of the MAS in [26] consists of 9 `Ambulance` agents and one `AmbulanceManager` agent. The organizational structure shown in figure 7 is the initial organizational view of the `AmbulanceManager` agent. The initial view of the `Ambulance` agents contains only themselves and the `AmbulanceManager` agent. The lines between objects depict authority relations, `communicates-with` relations and `knows-agent` relations. The tasks for this MAS are the following:

- `SearchAndRescueAll` is the main task of searching the complete map and rescuing all injured civilians. This task has no additional attributes.
- `SearchAndRescueSector`, is the same task as the main task but is restricted to a single sector on the map (the map is divided into 9 sectors). The additional attribute for this task is a `sectorId`.
- `CoordinateWork` is the task of coordinating (by means of the AgentCoRe framework) another task. The additional attribute for this task is a `taskId` of the task that is to be coordinated.

Based on these tasks, we define the following roles in the MAS organization:

- `AmbulanceRole`: [SearchAndRescueSector]
- `GlobalManagerRole`: [CoordinateWork]
- `LocalManagerRole`: [CoordinateWork, SearchAndRescueSector]

The `AmbulanceManager` always performs the `GlobalManagerRole`. Intially all `Ambulance` agents will perform the `AmbulanceRole` however these agents can also perform the `LocalManagerRole` when ordered by their direct superior. An agent with the `LocalManagerRole` is able to assign tasks and order role changes to its direct subordinates.

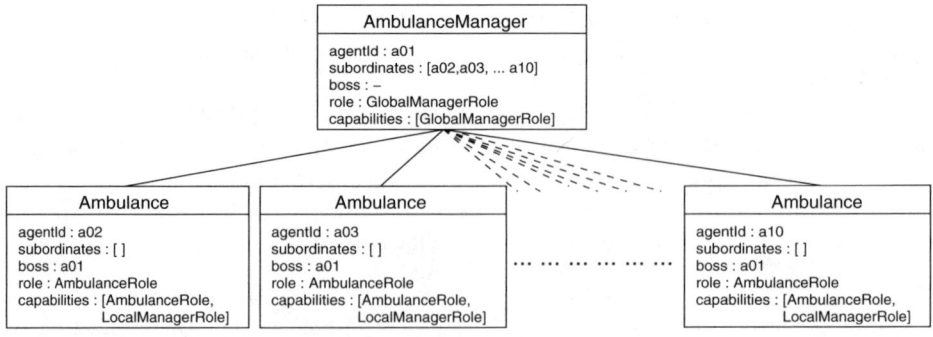

Fig. 7. Initial organizational structure as viewed by the `AmbulanceManager` agent

4.2   Agent Design

The global design of an agent is shown in figure 8. The agent first processes its input (sensory input and messages from other agents) and updates its knowledge base. This knowledge base consists of a model of the RCRSS environment

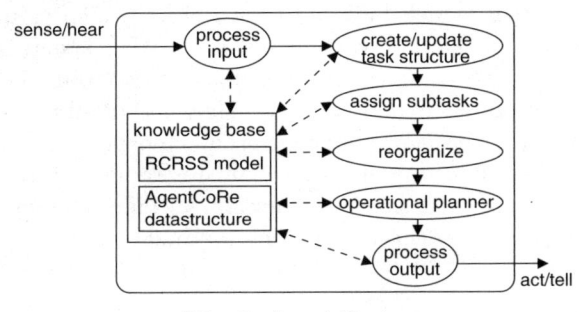

Fig. 8. Agent Design

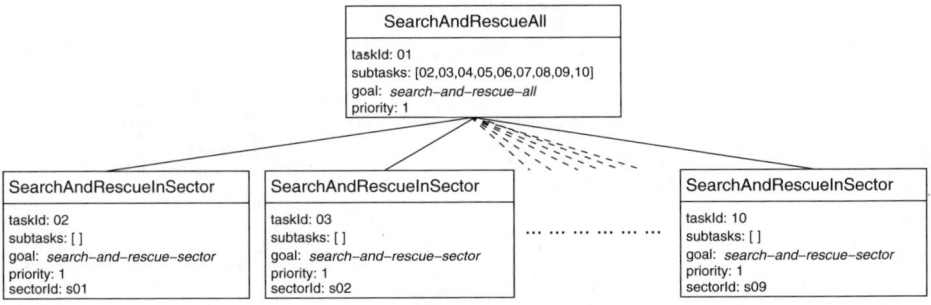

Fig. 9. Task structure in the knowledge base of the `AmbulanceManager`

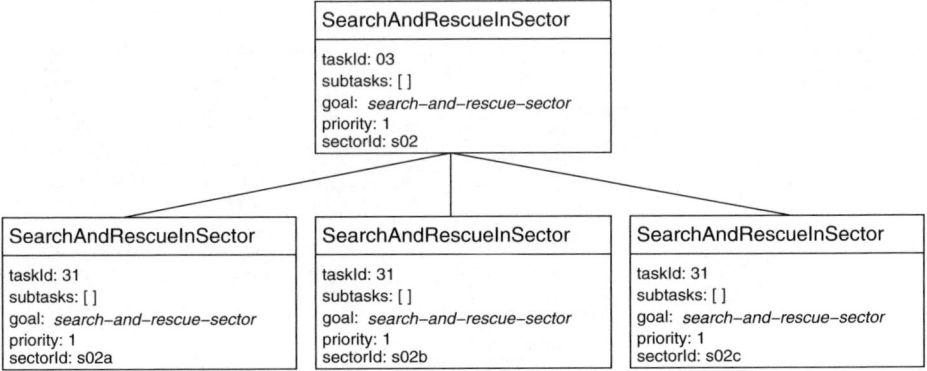

Fig. 10. Task structure in the knowledge base of an `Ambulance` agent with a `LocalManagerRole`

and the AgentCoRe related knowledge shown as input and output in figure 1. Knowledge from the knowledge base is used by and adapted by the remaining processes which is depicted by the dotted-arrows. In the next two steps, tasks are decomposed and assigned. Based on the resulting assignment structure, the reorganize module decides whether the organization needs to be changed. When the AgentCoRe related decisions have been made, the agent starts to plan its operational actions (e.g. which building to search or which civilian to rescue). The final step is to send the necessary messages to other agents and to perform the planned actions. Note that this design does not contain the select coordination mechanism module. In [26] we have shown that different coordination mechanisms perform differently under different environmental conditions but the dynamic selection of coordination mechanisms remains future work. In the remainder of this section we describe the domain specific strategies that are used as input of the AgentCoRe decisions making modules.

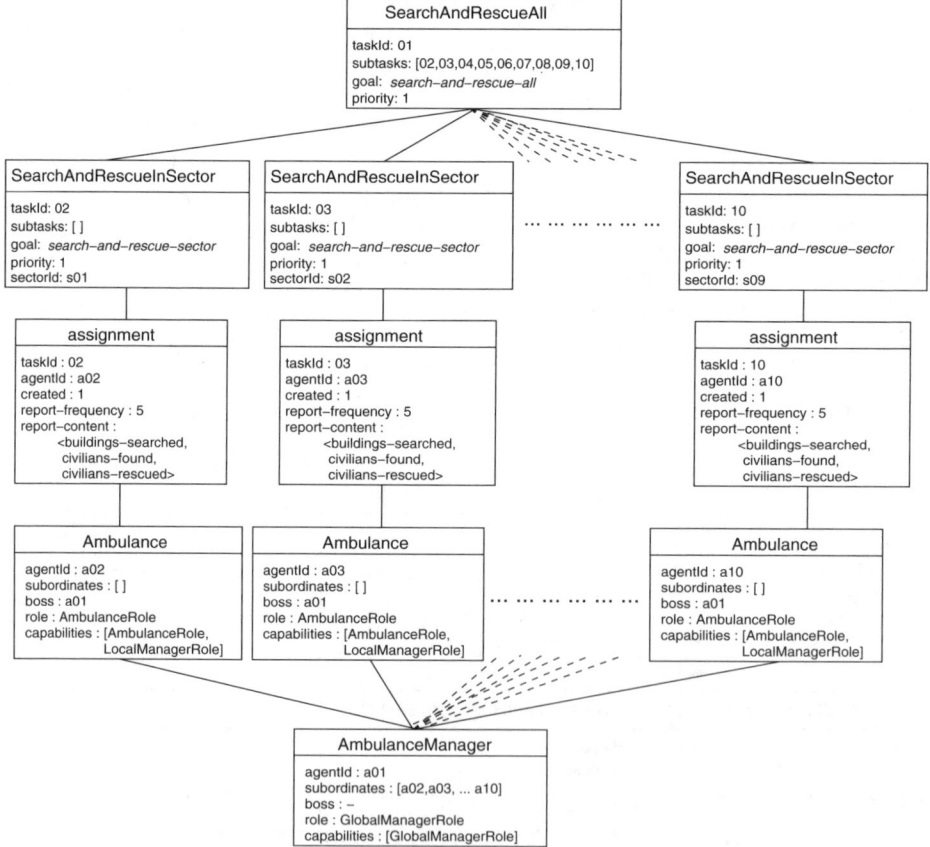

Fig. 11. Assignment structure in the knowledge base of the `AmbulanceManager` agent

The task decomposition strategy decomposes the `SearchAndRescueAll` into 9 `SearchAndRescueSector` tasks which results in a task structure as in figure 9. This task structure resides in the knowledge base of the `AmbulanceManager` agent. When an `Ambulance` agent is performing the `AmbulanceRole` there is no task to decompose and the agent does not make any decisions. Also for the other two modules, assign subtasks and reorganize, the agent does not make any decisions. However when an `Ambulance` agent performs the `LocalManagerRole`, the agent decomposes the `SearchAndRescueSector` into a number of smaller `SearchAndRescueSector` tasks and assigns these smaller tasks to its direct subordinates and to itself. This results in a task structure as shown in figure 10.

For the assignment process we have implemented a strategy that selects tasks from the assignment structure that have not yet been assigned to an agent. From that subset, the tasks with the highest priority are selected. The strategy also selects the agents from the assignment structure that are not assigned to a task. The strategy does not include grouping of agents or tasks. This results in an assignment structure as shown in figure 11.

A reorganization strategy has been implemented with one trigger and a set of change rules that are used when the trigger fires. The trigger fires if two conditions both hold; (1) there is at least one agent that has not been assigned to a task and (2) there is at least one task that is still being executed. The change rules specify that the `Ambulance` agent that is already working on that task has to switch from the `AmbulanceRole` to the `LocalManagerRole` (role change) and

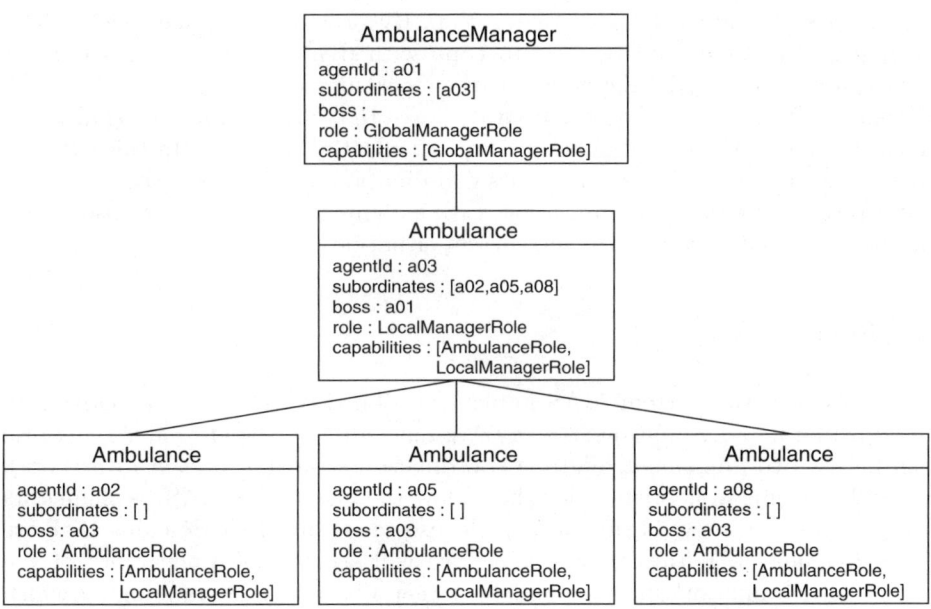

Fig. 12. Organizational structure in the knowledge base of `Ambulance` agent a03 with a `LocalManagerRole`

that the other agent will become a subordinate agent of the agent with the `LocalManagerRole` (structural change). The rationale behind this is that the first agent assigned to a task has acquired the most information on that task and is therefore most suited to coordinate work on this task when other agents are assigned to the same task. For the agent with the `LocalManagerRole` this results in an organizational structure as shown in figure 12. Each agents organizational structure will only contain its direct superior and its direct subordinates. An agent that is a subordinate of an agent with a `LocalManagerRole` can no longer "see" the superior agent of that agent with the `LocalManagerRole`.

5   Discussion and Conclusions

In the previous section we have described an implementation of a MAS in the RoboCupRescue environment using the AgentCoRe framework. By using a re-organization strategy, the MAS is capable of adapting agent relations and agent roles. The example in this paper shows only how one of the three coordination mechanisms in [26] was implemented. However, the other two coordination mechanisms in [26] have also been implemented using the AgentCoRe decision making modules.

The design of the AgentCoRe framework enables an agent to use strategies for task-decomposition, task-allocation and reorganization. By using these strategies as input in the inference structures we have been able to distinguish domain dependent strategies from the domain independent reasoning for task decomposition, task assignment and reorganization. By providing the agent with these strategies, the agent will be able to cope with dynamics in the environment [26]. However, it may be the case that the environment or the nature of its task changes in such a way that these strategies – that are designed to enable the agent to cope with these dynamics – are not effective anymore. In this case the agent has the possibility to change its coordination strategy by selecting different strategies for task decomposition, task assignment and reorganization, that are better suited to cope with the current situation.

6   Future Work

As mentioned, the current MAS implementation does not have the capability of adjusting its coordination strategy. We have already shown that AgentCoRe can be used to implement multiple coordination strategies and in future work we will implement strategy rules that allow the agent in a MAS to change its coordination strategy. Future work will also focus on other domains that are more dynamic in nature. Furthermore we will study the applicability of the AgentCoRe framework in these domains to get a better understanding for which types of problem domains AgentCoRe is suited or not.

As also recognized by Dignum et al. [27], different reasons for reorganization exist. Our future research will continue to focus on the questions of *when* a

MAS should reorganize and if such a situation occurs, *how* the MAS should reorganize. The first question involves identifying appropriate triggers for strategy selection and reorganization. The second question involves the identification of appropriate change-operators on a MAS organization and determine how these change-operators should be used by the agents in a MAS to achieve a more optimal organization structure.

References

1. So, Y., Durfee, E.: Designing organizations for computational agents. In: Prietula, M., Carley, K., Gasser, L. (eds.) Simulating Organizations, pp. 47–64. AAAI Press/MIT Press, Menlo Park (1998)
2. Carley, K.: Computational and mathematical organization theory: Perspectives and directions. Journal of Computational and Mathematical Organizational Theory (1995)
3. Cernuzzi, L., Zambonelli, F.: Dealing with adaptive multi-agent organizations in the gaia methodology. In: Müller, J.P., Zambonelli, F. (eds.) AOSE 2005. LNCS, vol. 3950, pp. 109–123. Springer, Heidelberg (2006)
4. Bernon, C., Gleizes, M., Peyruqueou, S.: Adelfe: A methodology for adaptive multi-agent systems engineering (Revised Papers). In: Petta, P., Tolksdorf, R., Zambonelli, F. (eds.) ESAW 2002. LNCS (LNAI), vol. 2577, Springer, Heidelberg (2003)
5. Hübner, J.F., Sichman, J.S., Boissier, O.: S-MOISE$^+$: A middleware for developing organised multi-agent systems. In: Boissier, O., Padget, J.A., Dignum, V., Lindemann, G., Matson, E.T., Ossowski, S., Sichman, J.S., Vázquez-Salceda, J. (eds.) AAMAS Workshops. LNCS, vol. 3913, pp. 64–78. Springer, Heidelberg (2006)
6. Newell, A.: The Knowledge Level. Artificial Intelligence 18(1), 87–127 (1982)
7. Mintzberg, H.: Structures in fives: Designing effective organizations. Prentice Hall, Englewood Cliffs (1993)
8. Kitano, H., Tadokoro, S., Noda, I., Matsubara, H., Takahashi, T., Shinjou, A., Shimada, S.: Robocup-rescue: Search and rescue for large scale disasters as a domain for multi-agent research. In: Proceedings of IEEE Conference on Man, Systems, and Cybernetics(SMC-1999) (1999)
9. Uschold, M., King, M., Moralee, S., Zorgios, Y.: The enterprise ontology. The Knowledge Engineering Review (1998)
10. Zambonelli, F., Jennings, N.R., Wooldridge, M.: Organisational abstractions for the analysis and design of multi-agent systems. In: 1st International Workshop on Agent-Oriented Software Engineering at ICSE 2000 (2000)
11. Carley, K., Gasser, L.: Computational organization theory. In: Weiss, G. (ed.) Multi-Agent Systems, A Modern Approach to Distributed Artificial Intelligence, pp. 299–330. MIT Press, Cambridge (1999)
12. Jennings, N.: Coordination techniques for distributed artificial intelligence. In: O'Hare, G., Jennings, N. (eds.) Foundations of Distributed Artificial Intelligence, pp. 187–210. Wiley, Chichester (1996)
13. Tambe, M., Pynadath, D.V., Chauvat, N.: Building dynamic agent organizations in cyberspace. IEEE Internet Computing 4(2), 65–73 (2000)
14. Malone, T.W., Crowston, K.: The interdisciplinary study of coordination. ACM Computing Surveys 26(1) (March 1994)

15. Lesser, V., Decker, K., Wagner, T., Carver, N., Garvey, A., Horling, B., Neiman, D., Podorozhny, R., Prasad, M.N., Raja, A., Vincent, R., Xuan, P., Zhang, X.Q.: Evolution of the GPGP/TAEMS domain-independent coordination framework. Autonomous Agents and Multi-Agent Systems 9, 87–143 (2004)
16. Pynadath, D.V., Tambe, M.: Multiagent teamwork: Analyzing key teamwork theories and models. In: First Autonomous Agents and Multiagent Systems Conference (AAMAS) (2002)
17. Nair, R., Tambe, M., Marsella, S.: Team formation for reformation. In: Proceedings of the AAAI Spring Symposium on Intelligent Distributed and Embedded Systems (2002)
18. Horling, B., Benyo, B., Lesser, V.: Using self-diagnosis to adapt organization structures. In: Proceedings of the 5th International Conference on Autonomous Agents, June 2001, pp. 529–536. ACM Press, New York (2001)
19. Kamboj, S., Decker, K.: Organizational self-design in semi-dynamic environments. In: 2007 IJCAI workshop on Agent Organizations: Models and Simulations (AOMS@IJCAI 2007) (2007)
20. Shehory, O., Sycara, K., Chalasani, P., Jha, S.: Agent cloning: An approach to agent mobility and resource allocation. In: IEEE Communications
21. Martin, C., Barber, K.S.: Adaptive decision-making frameworks for dynamic multi-agent organizational change. Autonomous Agents and Multi-Agent Systems 13(3), 391–428 (2006)
22. Excelente-Toledo, C.B., Jennings, N.R.: The dynamic selection of coordination mechanisms. Autonomous Agents and Multi-Agent Systems 9(1–2), 55–85 (2004)
23. Rosenfeld, A., Kaminka, G.A., Kraus, S., Shehory, O.: A study of mechanisms for improving robotic group performance. Artificial Intelligence (in press)
24. Kamboj, S., Decker, K.: Organizational self-design in semi-dynamic environments. In: Proceedings of the Sixth International Joint Conference on Autonomous Agents and Multiagent Systems (AAMAS 2007), pp. 1220–1227 (May 2007)
25. Schreiber, G., Akkermans, H., Anjewierden, A., de Hoog, R., Shadbolt, N., van de Velde, W., Wielinga, B.: Knowledge Engineering and Management: The CommonKADS Methodology. MIT Press, Cambridge (2000)
26. Ghijsen, M., Jansweijer, W., Wielinga, B.: The effect of task and environment factors on M.A.S. coordination and reorganization. In: Proceedings of the Sixth International Joint Conference on Autonomous Agents and Multi-Agent Systems, short paper (to appear, 2007)
27. Dignum, V., Dignum, F., Sonenberg, L.: Towards dynamic reorganization of agent societies. In: Proceedings of CEAS: Workshop on Coordination in Emergent Agent Societies at ECAI 2004, pp. 22–27 (September 2004)

Ignoring, Forcing and Expecting Simultaneous Events in Electronic Institutions

Andrés García-Camino

IIIA, Artificial Intelligence Research Institute
CSIC, Spanish National Research Council
Campus UAB, 08193 Bellaterra, Spain
andres@iiia.csic.es

Abstract. Norms constitute a powerful coordination mechanism among heterogeneous agents. We propose means to specify open environments regulated using the notions of ignoring, forcing, expecting and sanctioning events and prevention of unwanted states. These notions make explicit and clear the stance of institutions about forbidden and obligatory behaviour. Our rule-based language calculates the effects of concurrent events generated by agents given a set of norms based on the deontic notions previously mentioned. Our formalism has been conceived as basis for an implementation of Electronic Institutions.

1   Introduction

Ideally, open multi-agent systems (MAS) involve heterogeneous and autonomous agents whose concurrent interactions ought to conform to some shared conventions. The challenge is how to express and enforce such conditions so that truly autonomous agents can adscribe to them. One way of addressing this issue is to look at MAS as environments regulated by some sort of normative framework.

There are many examples of languages for regulating agent behaviour (for example, [1,2,3,4,5]). However, very few of them regulate concurrent events taking into account the rest of events that occur at an instant of time. The few that exist (e.g. [3]) are not conceived to deal with open MAS.

Furthermore, in the literature we find that almost all these languages are based on deontic logic [6] that establishes which actions are permitted, forbidden or obligatory. However, it does not establish which is the semantics of these modalities with respect to a computational system. For instance, when an action is claimed to be forbidden, does it means that it is prevented to happen, or that the agents that bring it about must be sanctioned or that the effects of that action are just ignored?

Instead, we propose a language, called $\mathcal{I}$, and one implementation of it that uses the notions of ignoring, forcing, and expecting events along with the notion of preventing a state, in the computation of the effects of concurrent agent behaviour in a regulated open MAS. The main contribution of $\mathcal{I}$ is the management of sets of events that occur simultaneously and the distinction between norms that can be violated or not. For instance, an obligation that may be violated

J.S. Sichman et al. (Eds.): COIN 2007, LNAI 4870, pp. 15–26, 2008.
© Springer-Verlag Berlin Heidelberg 2008

to perform a set of simultaneous events is represented as the expectation of the attempts to perform them. However, the enforcement of an obligation that may not be violated to perform a set of events is carried out by the system by taking these events as performed even they are not. We denote such enforcement as forcing events.

The paper is structured as follows. Section 2 introduces $\mathcal{I}$, a rule language for electronic institutions. A basic example illustrating the expressiveness of $\mathcal{I}$ is shown in section 3. In section 4, we introduce the formulae that we use for modelling electronic institutions. An example of a bank institution is presented in section 5. In section 6 we contrast our approach with a sample of other contemporary work. Finally, we draw conclusions and outline future work in section 7.

2 $\mathcal{I}$: A Rule Language for Electronic Institutions

In this section we introduce a rule language for the regulation and management of concurrent events generated by a population of agents. Our rule-based language allows us to represent norms and changes in an elegant way.

The building blocks of our language are first-order terms and implicitly, universally quantified atomic formulae without free variables. We shall make use of numbers and arithmetic functions to build terms; arithmetic functions may appear infix, following their usual conventions[1]. We also employ arithmetic relations (*e.g.*, $=$, $\neq$, and so on) as predicate symbols, and these will appear in their usual infix notation with their usual meaning.

$$
\begin{aligned}
ECA\text{-}Rule &::= \textbf{on } events \textbf{ if } conditions \textbf{ do } actions \\
if\text{-}Rule &::= \textbf{if } conditions \textbf{ do } actions \\
ignore\text{-}Rule &::= \textbf{ignore } events \textbf{ if } conditions \\
prevent\text{-}Rule &::= \textbf{prevent } conditions \textbf{ if } conditions \\
force\text{-}Rule &::= \textbf{force } events \textbf{ on } events \textbf{ if } conditions \textbf{ do } actions \\
events &::= list\_of\_events \,|\, \emptyset \\
list\_of\_events &::= atomic\_formula, list\_of\_events \,|\, atomic\_formula \\
conditions &::= conditions \wedge conditions \,|\, \neg(conditions) \,|\, atomic\_formula \\
actions &::= action \bullet actions \,|\, action \\
action &::= \oplus atomic\_formula \,|\, \ominus atomic\_formula
\end{aligned}
$$

Fig. 1. Grammar for $\mathcal{I}$

One goal of the $\mathcal{I}$ language is to specify which are the effects of concurrent events and this is achieved with Event-Condition-Action (ECA) rules. Intuitively, an ECA-rule means that whenever the events occur and the conditions hold then the actions are applied. These actions consist in the addition and removal of

---

[1] We adopt Prolog's convention using strings starting with a capital letter to represent variables and strings starting with a small letter to represent constants.

atomic formulae from the state of affairs. ECA-rules are checked in parallel and they are executed only once without chaining.

If-rules are similar to rules in standard production systems, if the conditions hold then the actions are applied. They are implemented with a forward chaining mechanism: they are executed sequentially until no new formula is added or removed.

Ignore-rules are used for ignoring events when the conditions hold in order to avoid unwanted behaviour. Similarly, prevent-rules are used for preventing some conditions to hold in the situations given. In order to prevent unwanted states, events causing such unwanted states are ignored. Force-rules generate events and execute actions as consequence of other events and conditions.

Sanctions over unwanted events can be carried out with ECA-rules. For instance, we can decrease the credit of one agent by 10 if she generates certain event.

We add an additional kind of rules, expectation-rules, that generate and remove expectations of events. If the expectation fails to be fulfilled then some sanctioning or corrective actions are performed.

$$expectation\text{-}Rule ::= \textbf{expected } event \textbf{ on } events \textbf{ if } conditions$$
$$\textbf{fulfilled-if } conditions' \textbf{ violated-if } conditions''$$
$$\textbf{sanction-do } actions$$

Each expectation rule can be translated into three ECA-rules:

$$\textbf{on } events \textbf{ if } conditions \textbf{ do } \oplus exp(event) \tag{1}$$
$$\textbf{if } exp(event) \wedge conditions' \textbf{ do } \ominus exp(event) \tag{2}$$
$$\textbf{if } exp(event) \wedge conditions'' \textbf{ do } \ominus exp(event) \bullet actions \tag{3}$$

Rules 1 and 2 respectively adds and removes an expectation whenever the events have occurred and the conditions hold. Rule 3 cancels the unfulfilled expectation and sanctions an agent for the unfulfilled expectation by executing the given *actions* whenever some *conditions* hold.

2.1 Semantics

Instead of basing the $\mathcal{I}$ language in the standard deontic notions, two types of prohibitions and two types of obligations are included. In our language, ECA-rules determine what is possible to perform, i.e. they establish the effects (including sanctions) in the institution after performing certain (possibly concurrent) events. ECA-rules might be seen as conditional count-as rules: the given events count as the execution of the actions in the ECA-rule if the conditions hold and the event is not explicitly prohibited. As for the notion of permission, all the events are permitted if not explicitly prohibited. The notion of an event being prohibited may be expressed depending on whether that event has to be ignored or not. If not otherwise expressed, events are not ignored. Likewise, the notion of a state being prohibited may be specified depending on whether that state has to be prevented or not. By default, states are not prevented. Obligations are differentiated in two types: expectations, which an agent may not fulfill, and forced (or obligatory) events, which the system takes as institutional events even they are not really performed by the agents.

Each set of ECA-rules generates a labelled transition system $\langle S, E, R \rangle$ where each state S is a set of atomic formulae, E is a set of events, and R is a $S \times 2^E \times S$ relationship indicating that whenever a set of events occur in the former state, then there is a transition to the subsequent state.

Ignore-rules avoid to execute any transition that contains in its labelling all the events that appear in each ignore-rule. For instance, having a rule **ignore** α_1 **if** *true* would avoid to execute the transitions labelled as $\{\alpha_1\}$, $\{\alpha_1, \alpha_2\}$ and $\{\alpha_1, \alpha_2, \alpha_3\}$. However, having a rule **ignore** α_1, α_2 **if** *true* would avoid to execute $\{\alpha_1, \alpha_2\}$ and $\{\alpha_1, \alpha_2, \alpha_3\}$ but not $\{\alpha_1\}$.

Prevent-rules ignore all the actions in an ECA-rule if it brings the given formulae about. For example, suppose that we have

$$\textbf{prevent } q_1 \textbf{ if } \textit{true}$$

along with ECA-rules 4, 5 and 6. After the occurrence of events α_1 and α_2 and since q_1 is an effect of event α_2, all the actions in ECA-rule 5 would be ignored obtaining a new state where p and r hold but neither q_1 nor q_2.

$$\textbf{on } \alpha_1 \textbf{ if } \textit{true} \textbf{ do } \ \oplus p \tag{4}$$
$$\textbf{on } \alpha_2 \textbf{ if } \textit{true} \textbf{ do } \ \oplus q_1 \bullet \oplus q_2 \tag{5}$$
$$\textbf{on } \alpha_1, \alpha_2 \textbf{ if } \textit{true} \textbf{ do } \ \oplus r \tag{6}$$

Force-rules generate events during the execution of the transition system. However, the effects of such events are still specified by ECA-rules and subject to prevent and ignore-rules.

2.2   Operational Semantics

In the definitions below we rely on the concept of *substitution*, that is, the set of values for variables in a computation [7,8]:

We now define the semantics of the conditions, that is, when a condition holds:

Definition 1. *Relation* $\mathbf{s}_l(\Delta, C, \sigma)$ *holds between state* Δ, *a condition* C *in an* **if** *clause and a substitution* σ *depending on the format of the condition:*

1. $\mathbf{s}_l(\Delta, C \wedge C', \sigma)$ *holds iff* $\mathbf{s}_l(\Delta, C, \sigma')$ *and* $\mathbf{s}_l(\Delta, C' \cdot \sigma', \sigma'')$ *hold and* $\sigma = \sigma' \cup \sigma''$.
2. $\mathbf{s}_l(\Delta, \neg C, \sigma)$ *holds iff* $\mathbf{s}_l(\Delta, C, \sigma)$ *does not hold.*
3. $\mathbf{s}_l(\Delta, seteq(L, L2), \sigma)$ *holds iff* $L \subseteq L2$, $L2 \subseteq L$ *and* $|L| = |L2|$.
4. $\mathbf{s}_l(\Delta, true, \sigma)$ *always holds.*
5. $\mathbf{s}_l(\Delta, \alpha, \sigma)$ *holds iff* $\alpha \cdot \sigma \in \Delta$.

Case 1 depicts the semantics of atomic formulae and how their individual substitutions are combined to provide the semantics for a conjunction. Case 2 introduces the negation by failure. Case 3 compares if two lists have the same elements possibly in different order. Case 4 gives semantics to the keyword *"true"*. Case 5 holds when an atomic formulae α is part of the state of affairs.

We now define the semantics of the actions of rules:

Definition 2. *Relation* $s_r(\Delta, A, \Delta')$ *mapping a state* Δ, *the action section of a rule and a new state* Δ' *is defined as:*

1. $s_r(\Delta, (A \bullet As), \Delta')$ *holds iff both* $s_r(\Delta, A, \Delta_1)$ *and* $s_r(\Delta_1, As, \Delta')$ *hold.*
2. $s_r(\Delta, \oplus\alpha, \Delta')$ *holds iff*
   (a) $\alpha \notin \Delta$ *and* $\Delta' = \Delta \cup \{\alpha\}$ *or;*
   (b) $\Delta' = \Delta$.
3. $s_r(\Delta, \ominus\alpha, \Delta')$ *holds iff*
   (a) $\alpha \in \Delta$ *and* $\Delta' = \Delta \setminus \{\alpha\}$ *or;*
   (b) $\Delta' = \Delta$.

Case 1 decomposes a conjunction and builds the new state by merging the partial states of each update. Cases 2 and 3 cater respectively for the insertion and removal of atomic formulae α.

We now define relation $check_{prv}$ that checks if there is no prevent-rule that has been violated, i.e., not all the conditions hold in the state of affairs Δ'. It checks whether Δ' contain all the conditions of each prevent-rule or not, if Δ also contain the given conditions.

Definition 3. *Relation* $check_{prv}(\Delta, \Delta', PrvRules)$ *mapping* Δ, *state before applying updates,* Δ', *state after applying updates, and a sequence* $PrvRules$ *of prevent-rules holds iff an empty set is the largest set of conditions* C *such that prevent-rule* $p = $ **prevent** C **if** C', $p \in PrvRules$, $s_l(\Delta, C')$ *and* $s_l(\Delta', C)$ *hold.*

Definition 4. *Relation* $fire(\Delta, PrvRules,$ **if** C **do** $A, \Delta')$ *mapping a state* Δ, *a sequence* $PrvRules$ *of prevent-rules, an if-rule and a new state* Δ' *holds iff* $assert(fired(C))$, $s_r(\Delta, A, \Delta')$ *and* $check_{prv}(\Delta, \Delta', PrvRules)$ *hold.*

Relation *can_fire* checks whether the conditions of a given if-rule hold and the rule after applying substitution σ has not been already fired.

Definition 5. *Relation* $can\_fire(\Delta,$ **if** C **do** $A, \sigma)$ *mapping a state* Δ *an if-rule and a substitution* σ *holds iff* $s_l(\Delta, C, \sigma)$ *holds and* $fired(C \cdot \sigma)$ *does not hold.*

Relation *resolve* determines the rule that will be fired by selecting the first rule in the list.

Definition 6. *Relation* $resolve(RuleList, SelectedRule)$ *mapping a list of if-rules and a selected if-rule holds iff*

1. $RuleList = \emptyset$ *and* $SelectedRule = \emptyset$; *or*
2. $RuleList = \langle r_1, \ldots, r_n \rangle$ *and* $SelectedRule = r_1$.

Relation *select_rule* determines the rule that will be fired by selecting all the rules that can fire and resolving the conflict with relation *resolve*.

Definition 7. *Relation select_rule(Δ, IfRulesList, SelectedRule) mapping a state of affairs Δ a list of if-rules and a selected if-rule holds iff Rs is the largest set of rules $R \in IfRulesList$ such that can_fire(Δ, R, σ); resolve(Rs, SR) hold and SelectedRule = $SR \cdot \sigma$.*

Relation s_{if} determines the new state of affairs after applying a set of if-rules to a initial state of affairs taking into account a set of prevent-rules.

Definition 8. *Relation $s_{if}(\Delta, IfRules, PrvRules, \Delta')$ mapping a state of affairs Δ, a list of if-rules, a list of prevent-rules and a new state of affairs holds iff*

1. *select_rule(Δ, IfRules, R) hold, $R \neq \emptyset$, fire(Δ, PrvRules, R, Δ'') and $s_{if}(\Delta'', IfRules, PrvRules, \Delta')$ hold; or*
2. *select_rule(Δ, IfRules, R) hold, $R = \emptyset$; or*
3. *$s_{if}(\Delta, IfRules, PrvRules, \Delta')$ hold.*

Relation *ignored* determines a set of events that occurred have to be ignored taking into account a list of ignore-rules.

Definition 9. *Relation ignored($\Delta, \Xi, E, IgnRules$) mapping a state of affairs Δ, a list Ξ of events that occurred, a list of events in a ECA-rule and a list of ignore-rules holds iff $i = $ **ignore** E' **if** C, $i \in IgnRules$, $E' \subseteq \Xi$, E intersects with E' and $s_l(\Delta, C)$ holds.*

Relation s'_r applies s_r first and then s_{if} in order to activate the forward chaining.

Definition 10. *Relation $s'_r(\Delta, IfRules, PrvRules, ActionList, \Delta')$ mapping a state of affairs Δ, a list of if-rules, a list of prevent-rules, a list of actions and a new state of affairs holds iff*

1. *ActionList = $\emptyset$ and $\Delta' = \Delta$; or*
2. *ActionList = $\langle a_1, \ldots, a_n \rangle$, $s_r(\Delta, a_1, \Delta'')$, $check_{prv}(\Delta, \Delta'', PrvRules)$, $s_{if}(\Delta'', IfRules, PrvRules, \Delta''')$ and $s'_r(\Delta''', IfRules, PrvRules, \langle a_2, \ldots, a_n \rangle, \Delta')$ hold; or*
3. *$s'_r(\Delta, IfRules, PrvRules, \langle a_2, \ldots, a_n \rangle, \Delta')$.*

Relation s_{on} calculates the new state of affairs Δ' from an initial state Δ and a set Ξ of events that occurred applying a list of ECA-rules, if-rules, ignore-rules and prevent-rules.

Definition 11. *Relation $s_{on}(\Delta, \Xi, ECARules, IfRules, IgnRules, PrvRules, \Delta')$ mapping a state of affairs Δ, a list Ξ of events that occurred, a list of ECA-rules, a list of if-rules, a list of ignore-rules, a list of prevent-rules, and a new state of affairs holds iff As is the largest set of actions $A' = A \cdot \sigma$ in a ECA-rule $r = $ **on** E **if** C **do** A such that $R \in ECARules$, $E \cdot \sigma' \subseteq \Xi$, $s_l(\Delta, C, \sigma'')$ hold, ignored($\Delta, \Xi, E, IgnRules$) does not hold and $\sigma = \sigma' \cup \sigma''$; and $s'_r(\Delta, IfRules, PrvRules, As, \Delta')$ hold.*

Relation s_f calculates the new state of affairs Δ' and the new set Ξ' of occurred events from an initial state Δ and a set Ξ of events that occurred applying a list of if-rules, ignore-rules, prevent-rules and force-rules.

Definition 12. *Relation* $\mathsf{s}_f(\Delta, \Xi, IfRules, IgnRules, PrvRules, FrcRules,$ $\Xi', \Delta')$ *mapping a state of affairs* Δ, *a list* Ξ *of events that occurred, a list of if-rules, a list of ignore-rules, a list of prevent-rules, a list of force-rules, a new list of events that occured and a new state of affairs holds iff EAs is the largest set of tuples* $\langle FE \cdot \sigma, A \cdot \sigma \rangle$ *of forced events and actions in a force rule* $fr =$ **force** FE **on** E **if** C **do** A *such that* $fr \in FrcRules$, $E \cdot \sigma' \subseteq \Xi$, $\mathsf{s}_l(\Delta, C, \sigma'')$ *holds,ignored*($\Delta, \Xi, E, IgnRules$) *does not hold and* $\sigma = \sigma' \cup \sigma''$; *Es is the largest set of forced events Ev such that* $\langle Ev, A \rangle \in EAs$; $\Xi' = \Xi \cup Es$; *As is the largest set of actions A such that* $\langle Ev, A \rangle \in EAs$; *and* $\mathsf{s}'_r(\Delta, IfRules, PrvRules, As, \Delta')$ *holds.*

Relation s^* calculates the new state of affairs Δ' from an initial state Δ and a set Ξ of events that occurred applying a list of ECA-rules, if-rules, ignore-rules, prevent-rules and force-rules.

Definition 13. *Relation* $\mathsf{s}^*(\Delta, \Xi, ECARules, IfRules, IgnRules, PrvRules,$ $FrcRules, \Delta')$ *mapping a state of affairs* Δ, *a list* Ξ *of events that occurred, a list of ECA-rules, a list of if-rules, a list of ignore-rules, a list of prevent-rules, a list of force-rules and a new state of affairs holds iff Cs is the largest set of conditions C such that retract(fired(C)) holds; assert(fired(false))*, $\mathsf{s}_{if}(\Delta,$ $IfRules, PrvRules, \Delta'')$, $\mathsf{s}_f(\Delta'', \Xi, IfRules, IgnRules, PrvRules, FrcRules,$ $\Xi', \Delta''')$ *and* $\mathsf{s}_{on}(\Delta''', \Xi', ECARules, IfRules, IgnRules, PrvRules, \Delta')$ *hold.*

3 Example of Concurrency: Soup Bowl Lifting

In this section we present an example on how to use the $\mathcal{I}$ language in order to specify a variation of a problem about concurrent action: the Soup Bowl Lifting problem [9]. Picture a situation where a soup bowl has to be lifted by two (physical) agents; one lifting from the right-hand side and the other one from the left-hand side. If both sides are not lifted simultaneously then the soup spills.

The order in which the rules are declared is important since they are executed in the order they are declared. We do not obtain the same effect with rules 7, 8 and 9 (finally *spilled* does not hold after lifted from both sides simultaneously) than with rules 9, 7 and 8 (finally *spilled* holds even after lifted from both sides simultaneously).

$$\textbf{on } pushLeft \textbf{ if } true \textbf{ do } \oplus spilled \qquad (7)$$

$$\textbf{on } pushRight \textbf{ if } true \textbf{ do } \oplus spilled \qquad (8)$$

$$\textbf{on } pushLeft, pushRight \textbf{ if } true \textbf{ do } \ominus spilled \bullet \ominus onTable \qquad (9)$$

Rules 7 and 8 specify that the soup is spilled whenever the bowl is lifted either from the right-hand side or the left-hand side. However, rule 9 removes the spill effect whenever both events are done simultaneously. However, with rules 9, 7 and 8, we do not obtain the desired result since the *spilled* formula may be added after executing the rule that removes *spilled* formula.

To prevent the bowl from spilling, we may add the next rule to rules 7–9:

$$\textbf{prevent } spilled \textbf{ if } true \qquad (10)$$

However, adding the following rules instead would also prevent the bowl to be lifted since ignoring one event will prevent all the combined events to be considered.

$$\textbf{ignore } pushLeft \textbf{ if } true \qquad (11)$$
$$\textbf{ignore } pushRight \textbf{ if } true \qquad (12)$$

Contrarily, if we add rule 13 to rules 7-9, we prevent the bowl to be lifted from both sides simultaneously but not to be only lifted from one side since we are only ignoring the events if they occur together.

$$\textbf{ignore } pushLeft, pushRight \textbf{ if } true \qquad (13)$$

This basic example give us a sample of the expressiveness of $\mathcal{I}$. In the next section, we introduce electronic institutions and the meaning of the formulae needed for representing them in $\mathcal{I}$.

4   Electronic Institutions

Our work extends *electronic institutions* (EIs) [10][2], providing them with a normative layer specified in terms of ignore, prevent and force rules. There are two major features in EIs: the *states* and *illocutions* (*i.e.*, messages) uttered (*i.e.*, sent) by those agents taking part in the EI. The states are connected via edges labelled with the illocutions that ought to be sent at that particular point in the EI. Another important feature in EIs are the agents' *roles*: these are labels that allow agents with the same role to be treated collectively thus helping engineers abstract away from individuals. We define below the class of illocutions we aim at – these are a special kind of term:

Definition 14. *Illocutions* I *are terms* $ill(p, ag, r, ag', r', \tau)$ *where* p *is a performative (*e.g. inform *or* request*); ag, ag' *are agent identifiers;* r, r' *are role labels; and* τ *is a term with the actual content of the message.*

We shall refer to illocutions that may have uninstantiated (free) variables as *illocution schemes*, denoted by $\bar{I}$.

An institutional state is a state of affairs that stores all utterances during the execution of a MAS, also keeping a record of the state of the environment, all observable attributes of agents and all the expectations associated with the agents.

We differentiate three kinds of events, with the following intuitive meanings:

1. I – an agent uttered illocution I.
2. $newtick(t)$ – a new tick of the clock occurred at time t.
3. the rest of events expressed as an atomic formula.

---

[2] EI scenes are basically covered with ECA rules.

We shall use event 2 above to obtain the time with which illocutions and expectations are time-stamped.

We differentiate two kinds of atomic formulae in our institutional states Δ, with the following intuitive meanings:

1. $inst(event, t)$ – $event$ was accepted as an institutional event at time t.
2. $exp(event, t)$ – $event$ is expected to occur since time t.

We allow agents to declare whatever they want to bring about (via events). However, the unwanted events may be discarded and/or may cause sanctions, depending on the deontic notions we want or need to implement via our rules. The $inst$ formulae are thus *confirmations* of events. We shall use formula 2 above to represent expectations of agents within EIs.

5   Applied Example: Bank

In this section we introduce an example of banking institution where agents are allowed to do certain operations with money. The operations in our bank are depositing, withdrawing and transferring. In our example we have two types of accounts called a and b owned by two different agents. In order to perform an operation in one of these accounts both agents have to *simultaneously* make the proper request.

Type a accounts have the limitation that no withdrawing, transferring from and debiting is allowed having a negative credit. If it is the case and there is enough money in a type b account of the same agent then necessary credit is automatically transferred to the account with negative credit and a fee is debited.

Type b accounts have the following limitations:
1. They cannot be in red. All the transactions that would finish in negative credit are rejected.
2. Withdrawing from or depositing to these accounts is not allowed.

Rule 14 specify the effects of opening an account of type T to agents $A1$ and $A2$ with an amount M of credit if another account of the same type with the same owners is not already opened.

$$
\begin{aligned}
&\textbf{on } \; newtick(Time), open\_account(Id, A1, A2, T, M) \\
&\textbf{if } \; \neg account(Id, A1, A2, T, \_) \wedge \neg account(Id, A2, A1, T, \_) \\
&\textbf{do } \; \oplus account(Id, A1, A2, T, M) \bullet \\
&\qquad \oplus inst(open\_account(Id, A1, A2, T, M), Time)
\end{aligned} \tag{14}
$$

Rule 15 specify the effect of withdrawing a given quantity M_q of money from a given account due to the simultaneous request of both owners of the account. The rules in the action section calculate the new credit for the account and modifies its value by removing the old credit and adding the new one. Likewise, a rule for the effects of depositing may also be specified.

$$
\begin{aligned}
&\textbf{on } \; newtick(Time), withdraw(A1, Id, M_q), withdraw(A2, Id, M_q) \\
&\textbf{if } \; account(Id, A1, A2, T, M) \\
&\textbf{do } \; M2 = M - M_q \bullet \ominus account(Id, A1, A2, T, M) \bullet \\
&\qquad \oplus account(Id, A1, A2, T, M2) \bullet \oplus inst(withdraw(A1, A2, Id, M_q), Time)
\end{aligned} \tag{15}
$$

Rule 16 specifies the effect of transferring from one account (of an agent and of a certain type) to another account possibly as payment of a certain concept C: the source account is reduced and the destination account is increased by the stated amount.

on $newtick(Time), transfer(A1, Id_s, Id_d, C, M), transfer(A2, Id_s, Id_d, C, M)$
if $account(Id_s, A1, A2, T_s, M_s) \land account(Id_d, A3, A4, T_d, M_d)$
do $M2_s = M_s - M \bullet \ominus account(Id_s, A1, A2, T_s, M_s) \bullet$
$\qquad \oplus account(Id_s, A1, A2, T_s, M2_s) \bullet M2_d = M_d + M \bullet \qquad\qquad (16)$
$\qquad \ominus account(Id_d, A3, A4, T_d, M_d) \bullet \oplus account(Id_d, A3, A4, T_d, M2_d) \bullet$
$\qquad \oplus inst(transfer(A1, A2, Id_s, Id_d, C, M), Time)$

To avoid concurrent actions affecting the same account, we use rule 17. In this case, only the first action is taken into account and the rest of concurrent actions are ignored.

prevent $account(I, A_1, A_2, T, M) \land account(I, A_1, A_2, T, M_2)$ **if** $M \neq M_2$ (17)

In our example, accounts of type a have the restriction that agents are not allowed to withdraw or transfer from a accounts with negative credit. This is achieved with rules like:

$\qquad$ **ignore** $withdraw(A, Id, \_)$ **if** $account(Id, A, \_, a, M) \land M < 0$ $\qquad$ (18)
$\qquad$ **ignore** $transfer(A, Id_s, \_, \_, \_)$ **if** $account(Id_s, A, \_, a, M) \land M < 0$ $\qquad$ (19)

Accounts of type b also have some restrictions. First, they cannot go into negative numbers. This is achieved with the following rule:

$\qquad$ **prevent** $account(Id, A1, A2, b, M)$ **if** $M < 0$

Second, agents are not allowed to withdraw from accounts of type b. This is achieved by rule 20.

$\qquad$ **ignore** $withdraw(\_, Id, \_)$ **if** $account(Id, \_, \_, b, \_)$ $\qquad\qquad$ (20)

Furthermore, if an account of type a goes into the negatives then the necessary amount to avoid this situation is transferred from an account of type b. Rule 21 forces this type of events. Notice that a similar rule but with the order of the owners of the accounts reversed is also necessary since the owners may not appear in the same order.

$\qquad$ **force** $\quad transfer(A, Id_b, Id_a, a\_negative, C), transfer(A2, Id_b, Id_a, a\_negative, C)$
$\qquad$ **if** $\qquad account(Id_a, A, A2, a, C2) \land C2 < 0 \land C = -C2$ $\qquad\qquad\qquad$ (21)

6   Related Work

In the model of Electronic Institutions of [10], agent interaction is brought about by uttering illocutions and it is decomposed in a set of scenes where only one illocution is accepted as legal simultaneously. As for norms, agents may be expected to utter certain illocutions under given conditions. However, there is no notion of prevention of a state or force of events. Furthermore, only events that are not part of the protocol are ignored, not allowing to write further conditions in which an illocution is ignored.

The work presented in this paper is the result of the evolution of our previous work on norm languages for electronic institutions [1]. In that work, we presented a rule language that does not use forward chaining to calculate the effects of events and to explicitly manage normative positions (i.e. permissions, prohibitions and obligations). For the present work, we use those rules in the form of event-condition-action rules. Then, we added standard condition-action rules that use forward chaining. Furthermore, we changed our standard deontic notions that only regulated one illocution into more institutional-centred notions as ignoring, forcing or expecting concurrent events or preventing an institutional state.

nC_+ [3] is a language for representing and reasoning about action domains that include some normative notions. Its semantics is based on labelled transition systems. The language allows to make queries about the transition system generated from an action description allowing to pre-dict, post-dict, or plan. In the normative aspect, nC_+ only labels states and actions as green or red without including our notion of prevention that ignores actions that lead to an unwanted state. We can obtain this labeling by adding $green$ to the initial state and rules of the form "**on** $events$ **if** $conditions$ **do** $\ominus green \bullet \oplus red$" or "**if** $condition$ **do** $\ominus green \bullet \oplus red$". Instead of using ignore-rules, nC_+ may label events as non-executable obtaining no solution when this kind of events occur. Since we want to maintain the state of the multi-agent system, we would need to ignore all the actions that occurred in that moment even the ones that does not lead to an unwanted state.

The implementation of nC_+ loads the full transition system in order to resolve the queries. When dealing with fluents with large numeric values, the implementation suffers from a state explosion increasing the load and resolution time. As mentioned above, we are aiming at monitoring and maintaining the state of the enactment of open regulated multi-agent systems. To use the implementation of nC_+ in this setting, we would have to add the new agents to the action description file and reload it again. However, the long time that elapses to complete this operation makes unviable the use of the implementation for our purposes and motivated this work.

7   Conclusions and Future Work

In this paper we have introduced a formalism for the management and regulation of concurrent events generated by agents in open MAS. Ours is a rule language in which concurrent events may have a combined effect and may be ignored, forced, expected or sanctioned. The semantics of our formalism relies on transition systems conferring it a well-studied semantics.

We have explored our proposal in this paper by specifying an example of concurrency: soup bowl lifting problem and an example of bank as Electronic Institution.

Although our language is not as expressive as the language of [3] since we cannot post-dict or plan about an action description, our language is not a language for checking properties of a transition system but for specifying its behaviour.

As a proof of concept, an interpreter of $\mathcal{I}$ were implemented in Prolog. As future work, we would like to embed this interpreter in a real MAS and include the distributed management of normative positions introduced in [11].

Acknowledgements. This work was partially funded by the Spanish Education and Science Ministry as part of the projects TIN2006-15662-C02-01 and 2006-5-0I-099 and it was partially done during a stay of the author in Imperial College London. The author wants to thank Marek Sergot for his advise and hospitality. He also thanks Juan-Antonio Rodríguez-Aguilar and Pablo Noriega for their comments and reviews. García-Camino enjoys an I3P grant from the Spanish National Research Council (CSIC).

References

1. García-Camino, A., Rodríguez-Aguilar, J.A., Sierra, C., Vasconcelos, W.: Norm Oriented Programming of Electronic Institutions. In: Proceedings of 5th International Joint Conference on Autonomous Agents and Multiagent Systems (AAMAS 2006) (2006)
2. Artikis, A., Kamara, L., Pitt, J., Sergot, M.: A Protocol for Resource Sharing in Norm-Governed Ad Hoc Networks. In: Leite, J.A., Omicini, A., Torroni, P., Yolum, P. (eds.) DALT 2004. LNCS (LNAI), vol. 3476, Springer, Heidelberg (2005)
3. Sergot, M., Craven, R.: The deontic component of $n\mathcal{C}+$. In: Goble, L., Meyer, J.-J.C. (eds.) DEON 2006. LNCS (LNAI), vol. 4048, pp. 222–237. Springer, Heidelberg (2006)
4. Alberti, M., Gavanelli, M., Lamma, E., Mello, P., Sartor, G., Torroni, P.: Mapping deontic operators to abductive expectations. In: Proceedings of 1st International Symposium on Normative Multiagent Systems (NorMAS 2005), AISB 2005, Hertfordshire, Hatfield, UK (2005)
5. Minsky, N.: Law Governed Interaction (LGI): A Distributed Coordination and Control Mechanism (An Introduction, and a Reference Manual). Technical report, Rutgers University (2005)
6. von Wright, G.H.: Norm and Action: A Logical Inquiry. Routledge and Kegan Paul, London (1963)
7. Apt, K.R.: From Logic Programming to Prolog. Prentice-Hall, Englewood Cliffs (1997)
8. Fitting, M.: First-Order Logic and Automated Theorem Proving. Springer, New York (1990)
9. Gelfond, M., Lifschitz, V., Rabinov, A.: What are the limitations of the Situation Calculus? In: Essays in Honor of Woody Bledsoe, pp. 167–179 (1991)
10. Esteva, M.: Electronic Institutions: from specification to development. PhD thesis, Universitat Politecnica de Catalunya, Number 19 in IIIA Monograph Series (2003)
11. Gaertner, D., García-Camino, A., Noriega, P., Rodríguez-Aguilar, J.A., Vasconcelos, W.: Distributed Norm Management in Regulated Multi-agent Systems. In: Proceedings of 6th International Joint Conference on Autonomous Agents and Multiagent Systems (AAMAS 2007) (2007)

A Contract Model for Electronic Institutions

Henrique Lopes Cardoso and Eugénio Oliveira

LIACC – NIAD&R, Faculdade de Engenharia, Universidade do Porto
R. Dr. Roberto Frias, 4200-465 Porto, Portugal
{hlc,eco}@fe.up.pt

Abstract. Electronic institutions are software frameworks integrating normative environments where agents interact to create mutual commitments. Contracts are formalizations of business commitments among a group of agents, and comprise a set of applicable norms. An electronic institution acts as a trusted third-party that monitors contract compliance, by integrating in its normative environment the contractual norms, which are applicable to the set of contractual partners. In this paper we present and explore a contract model that facilitates contract establishment by taking advantage of an institutional normative background. Furthermore, the model is flexible enough to enable the expansion of the underlying normative framework, making it applicable to a wide range of contracting situations.

1 Introduction

Research on norms and multi-agent systems has grown the Electronic Institution (EI) concept as the basis for the development of appropriate normative environments. Such environments are created to establish some kind of social order [4] that allows successful interactions among heterogeneous and autonomous entities.

As with any recent discipline, however, differences exist between the conceptual views of the "institutional environment". Some authors [1] advocate in favor of a restrictive "rules of the game" approach, where the EI fixes what agents are permitted and forbidden to do and under what circumstances. In this case norms are a set of interaction conventions that agents are willing to conform to. Other researchers [2] take a different standpoint, considering the institution as an external entity that ascribes institutional powers and normative positions, while admitting norm violations by prescribing appropriate sanctions. Others still [9] focus on the creation of institutional reality from speech acts, regarding an agent communication language as a set of conventions to act on a fragment of that reality.

A common element in each of these approaches is the *norm*, which enables us to control the environment, making it more stable and predictable. Arguably, one of the main distinguishing factors among researchers using norms in institutions is the level of control one has over agents' autonomy.

Our own view of electronic institutions (as initiated in [14] and developed in [13]) has got two main features that motivate the present paper. Firstly, the institution includes a set of services that are meant to assist (not only regulate) agent interaction and the creation of new normative relationships. This means we do not take the

J.S. Sichman et al. (Eds.). COIN 2007, LNAI 4870, pp. 27–40, 2008.
© Springer-Verlag Berlin Heidelberg 2008

environment as static from a normative point of view (as seems to be the case in [1]). New commitments may be established among agents, through contract negotiation (as also noted by [3]); the resulting contracts comprise a set of applicable norms. Additionally, part of the aforementioned assistance is achieved by enriching the institutional environment with a supportive normative framework. This will allow contracts to be underspecified, relying on default norms that compose the institution's normative environment where the contract will be supervised.

In this paper we present and explore the definition of a contract model that takes advantage of an institutional normative framework. The model is flexible enough to encompass contracts of varying degrees of complexity. A contract is established with support of the normative background and relying on a model of institutional reality.

The paper is organized as follows. Section 2 briefly describes the institutional environment supporting the contract model. Section 3 addresses the contract model itself, including its motivation and detailing its constituent parts. The model tries to take advantage of the underlying environment while at the same time enabling the expansion of the normative framework. Section 4 explains contract handling within our electronic institution framework, focusing on the representation of contracts in a computational way. A sample contract is provided for illustration purposes. Finally, section 5 concludes by highlighting the main features of our approach.

2 Institutional Environment

The notion of multi-agent systems assumes the existence of a common environment, where agent interactions take place. Recently more attention is being given to the environment as a first-class entity [17]. In the case of electronic institutions, they provide an environment whose main task is to support governed interaction by maintaining the normative state of the system, embracing the norms applicable to each of the interacting agents.

In order to accomplish such task, in our approach [13] the EI is responsible for recording events that concern *institutional reality*. This reality is partially constructed by attributing institutional semantics to agent interactions.

As mentioned before, we seek to have an EI environment with a supportive normative framework. For this, norms are organized in a hierarchical structure, allowing for norm inheritance as "default rules" [5].

2.1 Elements of Institutional Reality

The institutional environment embraces a set of events composing a reality based on which the normative state of the system is maintained. Norm compliance is monitored consistently with those events, which can be grouped according to their source:

- *Agent-originated events*: in our approach, norm compliance detection is based on the assumption that it is in the best interest of agents to publicize their abidance to commitments. They do so by provoking the achievement of corresponding *institutional facts* (as described in [13]), which represent an institutional recognition of action execution.
- *Environment events*: norms prescribe *obligations* when certain situations arise. In order to monitor norm compliance, the institutional environment applies a set of

rules that obtain certain elements of institutional reality, including the *fulfillment* and *violation* of obligations. While fulfillment acknowledgement is based on institutional facts, violations are detected by keeping track of *time*, using appropriate time ticks. Both norms and rules may use institutional facts as input. Rules also allow obtaining new institutional facts from older ones.

These events are the elements of institutional reality summarized in Table 1.

Table 1. Elements of institutional reality

Element	Structure
institutional fact	ifact(*<IFact>*, *<Timestamp>*)
obligation	obligation(*<Agent>*, *<IFact>*, *<Deadline>*)
fulfillment	fulfilled(*<Agent>*, *<IFact>*, *<Timestamp>*)
violation	violated(*<Agent>*, *<IFact>*, *<Timestamp>*)
time	time(*<Timestamp>*)

Because of the normative framework's organization (as explained in the next section), elements of institutional reality are *contextualized*, that is, they report to a certain context defined inside the institutional background.

Our norm definition is equivalent to the notion of conditional obligation with deadline found in [8]. In particular, an *Ifact* (an atomic formula based on a predefined ontology) as included in an obligation comprises a state of affairs that should be brought about, the absence of which is the envisaged agent's responsibility; intuitively, only an achievement of such state of affairs before the deadline fulfills the obligation. The *Deadline* indicates a temporal reference at which an unfulfilled obligation will be considered as violated. Fulfilled or violated obligations will no longer be in effect. Monitoring rules capture these semantics, by defining causal links (as described in [7]) between achievements and fulfillments, and between deadlines and violations.

There is a separation of concerns in norm definition and norm monitoring. The latter is seen as a context-independent activity. Also, the detection of norm (or, strictly speaking, obligation) fulfillment or violation is distinguished from repair measures, which may again be context-dependent (e.g. through contrary-to-duty obligations). This approach differs from [16], where norms include specific violation conditions, detection and repair measures.

2.2 Normative Framework

Our view of the EI concept [13] considers the institution as an environment enforcing a set of institutional norms, but also allowing agents to create mutual commitments by voluntarily adhering to a set of norms that make those commitments explicit. The EI will act as a trusted third-party that receives contracts to be monitored and enforced.

Furthermore, with the intent of facilitating contract formation, we approach the normative framework using a hierarchical approach, enabling the adoption of contract law concepts such as the notion of "default rules" [5]. These enable contracts to be underspecified, relying instead on an established normative background. The grouping of predefined norms through appropriate contexts also mimics the real-world organization of legislations applicable to specific activities. These norms will be imposed when the activity they regulate is adhered to by agents.

Our approach consists of organizing norms through *contexts*. Each contractual relationship is translated into a new context specifying a set of norms while inheriting others from the context within which it is raised. The top-level context is the EI itself.

A context definition includes the information presented in Table 2. The *super-context* (which may often be the EI itself) indicates where the current context may inherit norms from, while the *context type* dictates what kinds of norms are applicable (those that govern this type of relationship).

Table 2. Context definition information

Component	Description
super-context	the context within which this context was created
type	the type of context
id	the context identifier
when	the starting date of the underlying contract
who	the participants of the underlying contract

The components described in the table are meant to provide structure to our normative framework. It is the normative environment's responsibility to use this structured context representation in order to find applicable norms in each situation.

The specificity of norms will require further information regarding the contract to which they apply. For this, we consider the explicit separate definition of contextual-information, which will be dependent on the type of context at hand. For instance, in a simple purchase contract, the delivery and payment obligations will need information about who are the vendor and customer, what item is being sold and for what price.

3   Contract Model

This section will provide a description of our proposed contract model. We will start by providing the main assumptions that guided the approach, and proceed with the details of each contract piece. The figures illustrating contract sections were obtained using Altova® XMLSpy®.

3.1   Guidelines

When devising our contract model, we considered the main principles that should guide this definition. On one hand, as stated before we wanted a model that could take advantage of an established normative environment; therefore, each contract should be obtainable with little effort, and with as few information as possible. On the other hand, we also wanted to make the contract model as expansible as possible, allowing for the inclusion of non-predefined information and norms, while still keeping it processable by the EI environment. This requirement will allow us to apply the EI platform to different business domains.

The contract model should therefore allow us to:

– Include information necessary for context creation, and additionally any contract-type-dependent information to be used by institutionally defined norms.

- Add contract-specific details that are meant to override default institutional norms, e.g. by defining contract-specific norms.
- Expand the predicted contract scenarios by enriching the environment's rules for institutional fact generation.

The next sections describe how each of these purposes is handled.

3.2 Contract Header

Although, in general, a contract may include rules and norms, in the extreme case a contract that is to be monitored by the EI may be composed only of its header. Everything else (including the applicable norms) may be inherited from the EI. This minimalist case is illustrated in Figure 1, where dotted lines indicate optional components that we will refer to later. The rounded rectangle with ellipses is a compositor indicating a sequence of components.

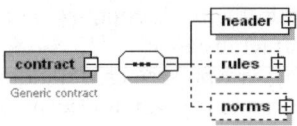

Fig. 1. Generic contract

The contract header (Figure 2) includes mandatory information that is needed for context definition, namely: the contract *id*, the creation date (*when*), and the participants' identification (*who*). The *type* of contract is optional; if not defined, a generic context type will be assumed. The *super-context* is also optional; if omitted, the general EI context is assumed.

Depending on the contract type, some foundational information may need to be provided (e.g. role definitions and goods specification). This information can be included in a frame-based approach: each peace of *contractual-info* (Figure 3) has a name and a set of slots (name/value pairs).

Finally, each contract may indicate the state-of-affairs according to which the contract shall be terminated. The structure of *ending-situation* is analogous to the situation component of a norm definition (as described in the following section).

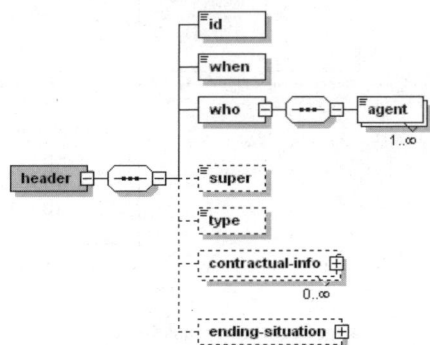

Fig. 2. Contract header

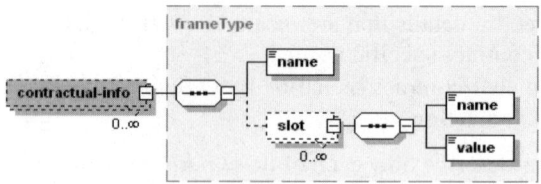

Fig. 3. Contract-type-dependent contractual-info

3.3 Adding Contract-Specific Norms

One way of escaping the default institutional normative setting is by defining norms that are to be applied to a particular contract instance. This is irrelevant of the contract having or not a type as indicated in its heading. A contract of a certain type will inherit institutional norms that are applicable to that type of contract as long as no other contract-specific norms override them. A contract with no type at all will need its norms to be defined in the contract instance.

In our conceptualization, a *norm* prescribes obligation(s) when a certain state-of-affairs is verified (Figure 4). A name is given for norm identification purposes.

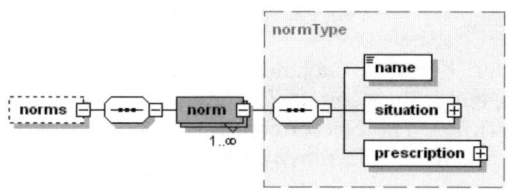

Fig. 4. Contractual norm

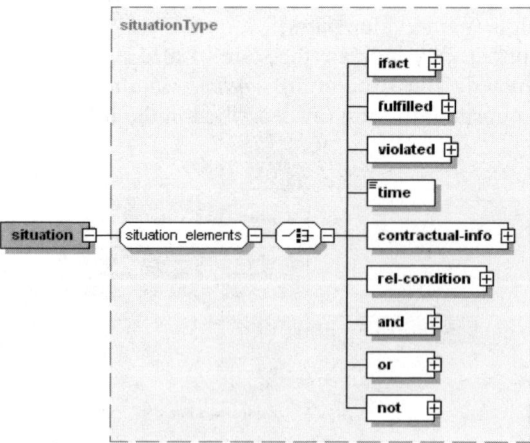

Fig. 5. Situation assessment

The *situation* may be described by institutional reality elements (except obligations) and access contractual-info. Figure 5 includes a choice compositor for situation elements, which may be combined by the logical connectives *and*, *or*, and *not*.

The situation elements *ifact*, *fulfilled* and *violated* match the corresponding institutional reality elements (see Figure 6 and Table 1), as does *time*.

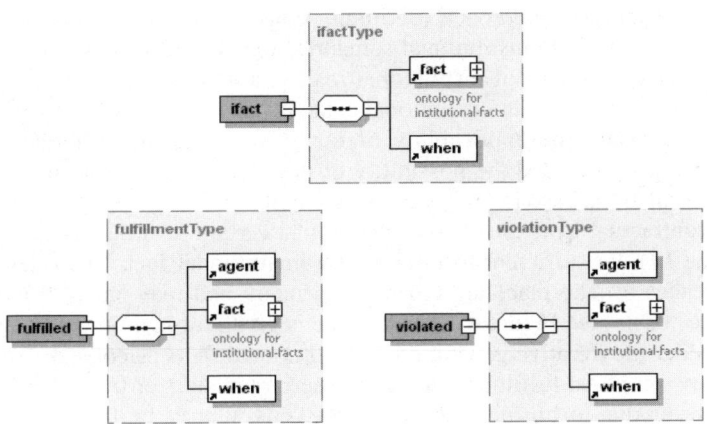

Fig. 6. Situation elements from institutional reality

The inclusion of institutional reality elements and contractual-info inside norms is allowed to use variables for each element's value, such that they can be referred to in other norm components as bounded variables (namely in the prescription part). For that, each element that can hold a variable has an attribute for indicating if the content is a variable name or a value (this approach is adapted from JessML [10]). In order to exploit the institutional ontology, the *fact* element has a frame-like structure similar to that of *contractual-info*. Variables may be used to match slot values inside both of these elements. Restrictions may be imposed through relational conditions that can combine expressions using variables.

The *prescription* of norms includes *obligations* (Figure 7), which have a similar structure to the corresponding institutional reality element. The deadline can be obtained with a numeric expression involving time variables bound in the situation part.

When including norms in a contract-specific way, the normative environment will consider as applicable the most specific norms, that is, those with a narrower scope.

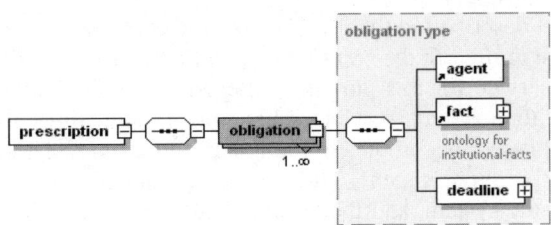

Fig. 7. Obligation prescription

This allows a contract to override predefined norms from a super-context (if specified). The same approach is taken when defining a contract-specific ending situation (in the contract header), which may also be predefined for certain context types.

3.4 Expanding the Creation of Institutional Facts

Following a "counts-as" approach (defining "constitutive rules" [15] or "empowerments" [12]), we attribute institutional semantics to agent illocutions. That is, institutional facts, which are part of institutional reality, are created from these illocutions. This process takes place at an institutional context.

In order to assure the applicability of our environment to different contracting situations, we also included the possibility of iterating through institutional facts (although this is also the case in [15], we take a slightly different perspective [13]). That is, certain contractual situations may consider that certain institutional facts (as recognized by the EI) are sufficient to infer a new institutional fact. The rules that allow these inferences to take place are context-dependent and may be specified in a contract-instance basis (see Figure 8). A rule name is given for identification purposes.

We consider the iterative generation of institutional facts as context-dependent because it allows contract fulfillment to be adjusted by matters of trust between contractual partners or due to business specificities. Thus, it may be the case that only in specific contractual relationships some institutional fact(s) count as another one.

This approach also enhances the expansibility of the system, not restricting norm definition to the institutional fact ontology defined in the preexistent fact-generating rules. It may be the case that a contract defines new institutional facts through these rules and also incorporates norms that make use of them.

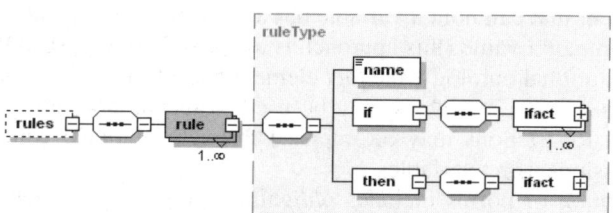

Fig. 8. Rule definition for institutional facts

4 Contract Handling in the Electronic Institution

The contract model described in the previous section comprises an XML schema from which contracts are drafted in the contract negotiation phase. The EI provides a negotiation mediation service for this purpose. After this, the negotiation mediator hands over the contract to a notary service, who collects signatures from the involved agents. After this process is completed, the notary requests the EI to include the contract in its normative environment. The contractual norms will then be part of the normative state of the system, and the normative environment will be responsible for maintaining this state by monitoring the compliance of the involved agents. Figure 9 illustrates this process.

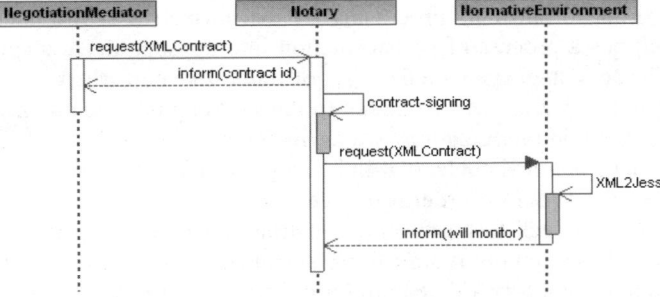

Fig. 9. Contract handling

The figure admittedly underestimates the need for contract validation, which we assume to be implicitly done by the notary and/or the EI. We find this step to be especially relevant when using predefined contract types, which may require the inclusion of foundational information.

As to the contractual norms themselves, in non-electronic practice parties are afforded a considerable degree of freedom in forming contractual relations [6]. Along with this line, our original aim is not to impose predefined regulations on agents, but instead to help them in building contractual relationships by providing a normative background. We therefore do not address for now the issue of predefined norms that are not to be overridden.

4.1 From XML to a Computational Contract Representation

In order to achieve a computational normative environment, a declarative language was chosen for norm representation and processing. Furthermore, in order to facilitate communication with the rest of the agents, the EI includes an agent personifying the normative environment itself. This agent includes an instance of a Jess rule-engine [10], which is responsible for maintaining the normative state of the system and to apply a set of procedures concerning the system's operation.

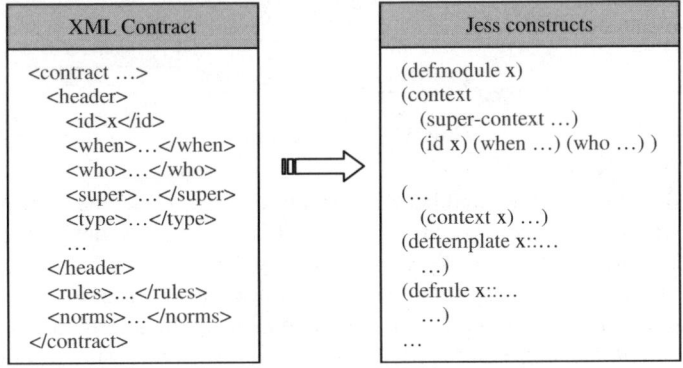

Fig. 10. From XML to Jess

Hence, in order to allow its processing by the normative environment, the XML contract undergoes a process of transformation into appropriate Jess constructs. (see Figure 10). The Jess language includes a set of frame-like constructs.

The generated Jess code will be added to the Jess engine, and comprises information regarding the contract creation (which includes a Jess *module* definition and a context construct), optional contextual-info (and associated Jess *template* definitions), and applicable rules and norms (defined as Jess *rules*).

A rule-based approach to norm representation and monitoring is also pursued in [11]. However, those authors seem to implement in a backward-chaining logic program the semantics of a forward-chaining production system. We follow a more intuitive approach by employing a forward-chaining shell.

4.2 Example

In this section we sketch a simple example of a minimalist contract that illustrates our approach. Figure 11 shows, on the left side, a portion of an XML-contract based on the presented schema. The contract, established by two agents, is a *supply-agreement*; agent *smith* will supply resource *wheel* for a unit price of *10.00*. The right side of Figure 11 shows the resulting Jess code that is generated when adding the contract to the normative environment.

```
<contract>
  <header>
    <id>sa_117</id>
    <when>2007-05-10T15:13:18.328Z</when>
    <who>
      <agent>adam</agent><agent>smith</agent>
    </who>
    <type>supply-agreement</type>
    <contractual-info>
      <name>supply-info</name>
      <slot><name>agent</name><value>smith</value></slot>
      <slot><name>resource</name><value>wheel</value></slot>
      <slot><name>unit-price</name><value>10.00</value></slot>
    </contractual-info>
    <contractual-info>
      <name>wheel</name><slot>...</slot>...
    </contractual-info>
  </header>
</contract>
```

```
(defmodule sa_117)

(supply-agreement
  (id sa_117)
  (when 1178810004375)
  (who adam smith) )

(supply-info
  (context sa_117)
  (agent smith)
  (resource wheel)
  (unit-price 10.00) )

(deftemplate sa_117::wheel
  (slot context) (slot ...) ... )
(wheel
  (context sa_117) ... )
```

Fig. 11. Sample contract

Taking advantage of the established normative framework, the contract does not specify any norms of its own. It will inherit whatever norms are defined at the normative environment regarding *supply-agreement*s. Figure 12 shows such an applicable norm, together with definitions that make up the normative structure. The upper definitions define the notions of *context* and *contextual-info*; the middle definitions define *supply-agreement* and *supply-info*, which were used in the right side of Figure 11. The lower part of Figure 12 shows a norm applicable to all *supply-agreement*s. Briefly,

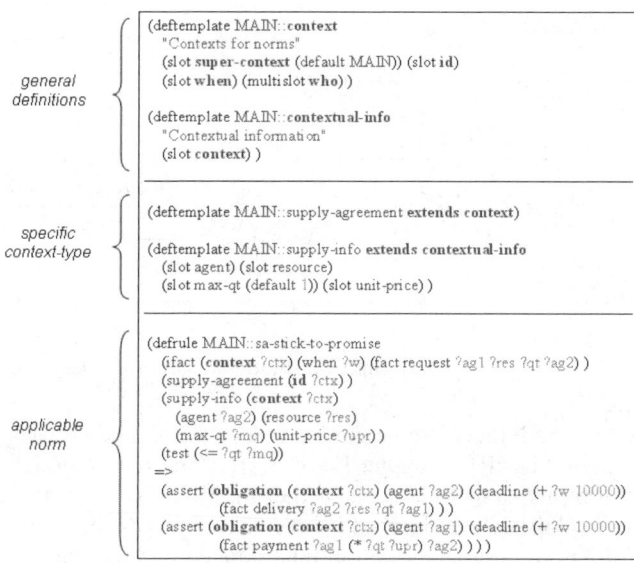

general
definitions

```
(deftemplate MAIN::context
  "Contexts for norms"
  (slot super-context (default MAIN)) (slot id)
  (slot when) (multislot who) )

(deftemplate MAIN::contextual-info
  "Contextual information"
  (slot context) )
```

specific
context-type

```
(deftemplate MAIN::supply-agreement extends context)

(deftemplate MAIN::supply-info extends contextual-info
  (slot agent) (slot resource)
  (slot max-qt (default 1)) (slot unit-price) )
```

applicable
norm

```
(defrule MAIN::sa-stick-to-promise
  (ifact (context ?ctx) (when ?w) (fact request ?ag1 ?res ?qt ?ag2) )
  (supply-agreement (id ?ctx) )
  (supply-info (context ?ctx)
    (agent ?ag2) (resource ?res)
    (max-qt ?mq) (unit-price ?upr) )
  (test (<= ?qt ?mq))
  =>
  (assert (obligation (context ?ctx) (agent ?ag2) (deadline (+ ?w 10000))
    (fact delivery ?ag2 ?res ?qt ?ag1) ) )
  (assert (obligation (context ?ctx) (agent ?ag1) (deadline (+ ?w 10000))
    (fact payment ?ag1 (* ?qt ?upr) ?ag2) ) ) )
```

Fig. 12. A predefined norm

that norm states that a request for the furnishing of the promised resource implies an obligation of the supplier to deliver that resource and an obligation of the requester to pay for it.

For lack of space, the example shows only one edge of the spectrum of ways in which the normative environment can be exploited. Contracts can be established that make a partial use of the predefined normative structure, by defining their own specific norms, while still being processable (in terms of monitoring and enforcement activities) by the normative environment. The next section describes the process of norm applicability.

4.3 Norm Monitoring and Inheritance

The module definition and the structured context representation (using *super-context* relations), are the cornerstones for enabling norm inheritance. Norms are defined inside the module representing the contract's context (in the right side of Figure 10, that is what the "*x::*" after *defrule* stands for, where *x* is the module/context name). When applying rules, the Jess engine looks at a focus stack containing modules where to search rules for firing. When no rules are ready to fire in the module at the top of the stack, that module is popped and the next one becomes the focus module.

Exploiting this mechanism, we implemented rules that manage the focus stack and thereby enable the application of the most specific norms in the first place. The event that triggers these rules is the occurrence of a new institutional reality element (IRE), which as explained before pertains to a certain context. Together with the Jess rule engine, our context management rules somewhat implement the algorithm depicted in the flowchart of Figure 13.

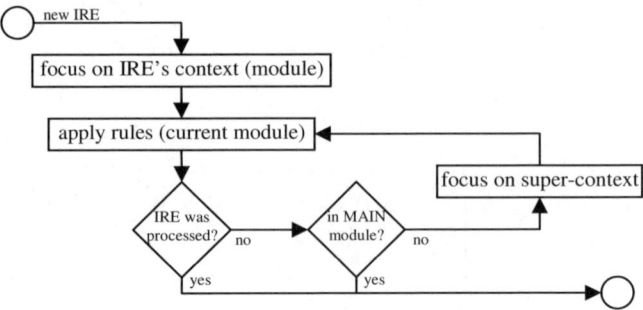

Fig. 13. Processing an institutional reality element

The Jess engine will therefore be guided to look for a module where there is an applicable rule taking the IRE as input. It will start at the IRE's module, and go up one level until the top (*main*) module is reached or the IRE is processed.

This initial exploitation of Jess's features enabled us to start building a proof-of-concept regarding our approach to norm inheritance in a hierarchical normative structure. Further refinements will allow us to configure the system concerning monitoring responsiveness and the integration of social extensions like reputation mechanisms.

5   Conclusions

The EI concept has been approached from different perspectives. Considering the increasing importance of multi-agent system environments [17], the EI can be seen as an interaction-mediation infrastructure maintaining the normative state of the system.

One of the most important principles of our approach is the assumption of a non-static normative environment; this means that we depart from a more conservative view of norms seen as a set of preexistent interaction conventions that agents are willing to comply with (as in the *adscription* approach of [1]). We pursue an EI that provides a supportive normative framework whose main purpose is to facilitate the establishment of further commitments among a group of contracting agents.

The possibility of having an underlying normative framework, from which norms may be inherited, is a distinguishing feature of our approach, as is the "loose coupling" between norms and contrary-to-duties. Also, the institution includes norm monitoring policies that span all created contracts. This is in contrast with other approaches, namely [16], where these policies and repair measures are spread among the norms themselves.

The hierarchical organization of norms takes inspiration in the real-world. The most useful case for "default rules" [5] is in defining contrary-to-duty situations, which typically should be not likely to occur. For this reason, such situations are not dealt with in each contractual agreement, and parties usually recur to law systems that include default procedures [6].

In this paper we presented our approach towards the definition of a contract model that can exploit such an environment. The model was devised taking into account two aims: it should be easy to compose a new contract, by taking advantage of an institutional normative background; and it should be possible to improve on the EI's environment in order to make it applicable to different business domains.

We are confident that we have met both these goals. In our model, a minimalist contract may be limited to header information including the contract participants and contractual-info describing foundational information. On the other hand, a complex unnoticed contractual relationship may be defined using our contract model, by exploiting the whole structure including contract-specific norms and institutional fact generating rules. The next steps of this work include exploring the developed contract model through different contracting scenarios.

Acknowledgments. This project is supported by FCT (Fundação para a Ciência e a Tecnologia) under Project POSC/EIA/57672/2004. Henrique Lopes Cardoso enjoys the FCT grant SFRH/BD/29773/2006.

References

[1] Arcos, J.L., Esteva, M., Noriega, P., Rodríguez-Aguilar, J.A., Sierra, C.: Environment engineering for multiagent systems. Engineering Applications of Artificial Intelligence 18, 191–204 (2005)

[2] Artikis, A., Pitt, J., Sergot, M.: Animated specifications of computational societies. In: Castelfranchi, C., Johnson, W.L. (eds.) International Joint Conference on Autonomous Agents and Multi-Agent Systems. Association for Computing Machinery, New York 10036-5701, United States, Bologna, Italy, pp. 1053–1062 (2002)

[3] Boella, G., van der Torre, L.: Contracts as Legal Institutions in Organizations of Autonomous Agents. In: Jennings, N.R., Sierra, C., Sonenberg, L., Tambe, M. (eds.) Third International Joint Conference on Autonomous Agents & Multi Agent Systems, pp. 948–955. ACM Press, New York (2004)

[4] Castelfranchi, C.: Engineering Social Order. In: Omicini, A., Tolksdorf, R., Zambonelli, F. (eds.) ESAW 2000. LNCS (LNAI), vol. 1972, pp. 1–18. Springer, Heidelberg (2000)

[5] Craswell, R.: Contract Law: General Theories. In: Bouckaert, B., De Geest, G. (eds.) Encyclopedia of Law and Economics, pp. 1–24. Edward Elgar, Cheltenham (2000)

[6] Daskalopulu, A., Maibaum, T.: Towards Electronic Contract Performance. In: 12th International Conference and Workshop on Database and Expert Systems Applications, pp. 771–777. IEEE Computer Society Press, Los Alamitos (2001)

[7] Dignum, F., Broersen, J., Dignum, V., Meyer, J.-J.: Meeting the deadline: Why, when and how. In: Hinchey, M.G., Rash, J.L., Truszkowski, W.F., Rouff, C.A. (eds.) FAABS 2004. LNCS (LNAI), vol. 3228, pp. 30–40. Springer, Heidelberg (2004)

[8] Dignum, V., Meyer, J.-J.C., Dignum, F., Weigand, H.: Formal Specification of Interaction in Agent Societies. In: Hinchey, M.G., Rash, J.L., Truszkowski, W.F., Rouff, C.A., Gordon-Spears, D.F. (eds.) FAABS 2002. LNCS (LNAI), vol. 2699, pp. 37–52. Springer, Heidelberg (2003)

[9] Fornara, N., Viganò, F., Colombetti, M.: Agent Communication and Institutional Reality. In: van Eijk, R.M., Huget, M.-P., Dignum, F.P.M. (eds.) AC 2004. LNCS (LNAI), vol. 3396, pp. 1–17. Springer, Heidelberg (2005)

[10] Friedman-Hill, E.: Jess in Action, Manning Publications Co. (2003)

[11] García-Camino, A., Rodríguez-Aguilar, J.A., Sierra, C., Vasconcelos, W.: Norm-Oriented Programming of Electronic Institutions: A Rule-Based Approach. In: Noriega, P., Vázquez-Salceda, J., Boella, G., Boissier, O., Dignum, V., Fornara, N., Matson, E. (eds.) COIN 2006. LNCS (LNAI), vol. 4386, pp. 177–193. Springer, Heidelberg (2007)

[12] Jones, A., Sergot, M.: A Formal Characterisation of Institutionalised Power. Logic Journal of the IGPL 4, 427–443 (1996)

[13] Lopes Cardoso, H., Oliveira, E.: Electronic Institutions for B2B: Dynamic Normative Environments, Artificial Intelligence and Law (in press)

[14] Lopes Cardoso, H., Oliveira, E.: Virtual Enterprise Normative Framework within Electronic Institutions. In: Gleizes, M.-P., Omicini, A., Zambonelli, F. (eds.) ESAW 2004. LNCS (LNAI), vol. 3451, pp. 14–32. Springer, Heidelberg (2005)

[15] Searle, J.R.: The Construction of Social Reality. Free Press, New York (1995)

[16] Vázquez-Salceda, J., Aldewereld, H., Dignum, F.: Implementing norms in multiagent systems. In: Lindemann, G., Denzinger, J., Timm, I.J., Unland, R. (eds.) MATES 2004. LNCS (LNAI), vol. 3187, pp. 313–327. Springer, Heidelberg (2004)

[17] Weyns, D., Omicini, A., Odell, J.: Environment as a first class abstraction in multiagent systems. Journal of Autonomous Agents and Multi-Agent Systems 14, 5–30 (2007)

Embedding Landmarks and Scenes in a Computational Model of Institutions

Owen Cliffe, Marina De Vos, and Julian Padget

Department of Computer Science
University of Bath, BATH BA2 7AY, UK
{occ,mdv,jap}@cs.bath.ac.uk

Abstract. Over the last decade, institutions have demonstrated that they are a powerful mechanism to make agent interactions more effective, structured, coordinated and efficient. Different authors have tackled the problem of designing and verifying institutions from different angles. In this paper we propose a formalism that is capable of unifying and extending some of these approaches, as well as providing the necessary tools to assist in the design and verification processes. We demonstrate our approach with a non-trivial case-study.

1 Introduction

The concept of landmarks appears in [27] where they are used to identify a set of semantic properties relating to the state of a conversation, and which may furthermore be organized into sequences or patterns, while transition between landmarks is made by an appropriate sequence of one or more speech acts. A more detailed discussion follows in [21], where they are presented as propositions that are true in the state represented by the landmark (sic). The value of landmarks, and more specifically, their partial ordering into landmark patterns, is how they permit the identification of phases in a conversation protocol corresponding to the achievement of goals (and subgoals). Additionally, they form an integral part of realizing joint intention theory [11] as participants in a conversation interact with one another, *via* speech acts, to follow a common protocol and satisfy common goals. The utility of landmarks, from the electronic institution designer's perspective is their potential role in building a bridge [13, 1] between the rigidity of the protocols that feature in bottom-up design and the (relative) flexibility of norms that characterize top-down design.

The formal model put forward in [9] and its corresponding operationalization through Answer Set Programming (ASP) [5] aims to support the top-down design of electronic institutions through the provision of a domain-specific action language [26], called InstAL, tailored to the specification of institutions. Tools have been developed to translate InstAL into the SMODELS [23] syntax for processing by the answer set solver and furthermore the soundness and completeness of the institutional programs with respect to the formal model have been proven [8]. In this paper we explore the consequences of the correspondence between landmarks, as described in the literature, and the institutional states of our (executable) model, argue that the stronger logical framework of our formalism is advantageous and demonstrate the expressiveness of the Inst*AL* language through a non-trivial case-study.

J.S. Sichman et al. (Eds.): COIN 2007, LNAI 4870, pp. 41–57, 2008.
© Springer-Verlag Berlin Heidelberg 2008

2   The Institutional Framework

In this section we provide a brief description of our framework, starting with the formal model and following with the semantics. We then turn our attention to ASP as the underlying computational mechanism and the mapping from action language to ASP.

The Formal Model: Our model of an institution is a quintuple, $\mathcal{I} := \langle \mathcal{E}, \mathcal{F}, \mathcal{C}, \mathcal{G}, \Delta \rangle$, comprising three disjoint sets:

- events $\mathcal{E}$, which can be either institutional (generated within the institution) or exogenous (caused by events outside of the scope of the institution). In particular, we define a subset of the exogenous events as *creation events*, $\mathcal{E}_+$, which contain events which account for the creation of an institution and a subset of the institutional events as *dissolution events*, $\mathcal{E}_\times$.
- fluents $\mathcal{F}$, being the four distinguished sets of fluents — powers $\mathcal{W}$, permissions $\mathcal{P}$, obligations $\mathcal{O}$, domain-specific fluents $\mathcal{D}$ — that constitute the state of the institution and hence the basis for reasoning about the institution.
- and an initial state Δ comprising the initial set of fluents in the institution

and two relations $\mathcal{C}$ and $\mathcal{G}$ over $\mathcal{X} \times \mathcal{E}$, where $\mathcal{X} = 2^{(\mathcal{F} \cup \neg \mathcal{F})}$ and $\phi \in \mathcal{X}$ represents a set of conditions which must be met in a given state in order for either relation to have an effect.

- $\mathcal{C}$ defines under which circumstances fluents are initiated and terminated.
- $\mathcal{G}$ implements the *count-as* operation and defines under which conditions in the institutional state the occurence of a given event will result in the generation of one or more new events.

Semantics: The semantics of this framework are defined by traces of exogenous events. Each trace induces a sequence of institutional states, called a model. Starting from the initial state, the first exogenous event will, using the $\mathcal{G}$, generate a set of events. Each of these events will possibly affect the next state by means of the $\mathcal{C}$ relation. The combined effect results in the next state of the model. This process continues until all exogenous events in the trace have taken place.

ASP: In *answer set programming* ([5]) a logic program is used to describe the requirements that must be fulfilled by the solutions of a certain problem. The answer sets of the program, usually defined through (a variant/extension of) the stable model semantics [17], then correspond to the solutions of the problem. The programs consist of a set clauses with negation-as-failure in the body. Assumptions are verified by eliminating negation from the program using the Gelfond-Lifschitz reduction and to check if this new positive program sustains the assumptions made. Tools for obtaining answers sets are called answer set solvers. For our system we use the SMODELS [23] solver.

The Mapping: The mapping of each actual institution $\mathcal{I}$ into an answer set program consists of two parts: (i) P_{base} which is identical for each institution and handles the occurrence of observed events, the semantics of obligations and rules to maintain the commonsense inertia of fluents , and (ii) $P_{\mathcal{I}}^*$ which is specific to the institution being

modelled and represents the translation of it rules (norms and action semantics). Together they form the answer set program $P_\mathcal{I}$. In order to be able to use this program to
reason about the institution, it is then combined with two other ASP programs: a trace
program, containing a contraint on the length of traces of events being considered, and
a query program expressing some constraint over the answer sets that shall be generated
— the property or properties of the model that we wish to investigate.

InstAL : Our primary objective in this work is to be able to specify the behaviour
of an institution in terms of its norms, and then to be able to test properties of the
model of the institution thus defined. Consequently, we need a machine-processable
representation. The engine for the verification is an answer set solver, so one approach
would be to require the specification to be written in the input syntax for such a system,
such as SMODELS, as outlined in [9]. However, while it may be useful for the designer to
examine the code given to the answer set solver occasionally, it also necessarily contains
low level support details that are less relevant to the task of institutional design. For this
reason and because of the event-oriented nature of the specification, a domain-specific
event language seems an appropriate medium, hence InstAL.

We define the language InstAL in order to simplify the process of specifying institutions. Individual institution specifications and multi-institution specifications are written as single InstAL programs in a human-readable text format. These files can then be
translated automatically into answer set programs that directly represent the semantics
of the institutions specified in the original descriptions.

The language supports a simple set-based type system and syntax for the declara-
tion of fluents, events, and institutions (bearing in mind the model also supports multi-
institutional models as discussed in [10]). Normative fluents are pre-defined for power,
permission and obligation. The designer may also specify static properties of an institution, that are initiated when the institution is created and never change. This provides
a straightforward way to associate roles with institutions. Rather than give a formal
syntax specification, for which there is not room here, we put forward and extended example in section 4 to illustrate the language features in a use-case. A detailed discussion
of the InstAL language can be found in [10, 8].

An InstAL reasoning problem consists of the following:

1. One or more InstAL institution descriptions each of which describes a single institution or a multi-institution.
2. A domain definition that grounds aspects of the descriptions. This provides the
   domains for types and any static properties referenced in the institution and multi-
   institution definitions.
3. A *trace program* which defines the set traces of exogenous events to investigate.
4. A *query program* which describes the desired property to validate with the InstAL
   reasoning tool.

The reasoning process can be summarised as follows:

1. The InstAL to ASP translator takes one or more single or multi-institution descriptions (in the InstAL syntax described below), and domain definition files (described

below) as input. Using these files, the translator generates a set of answer set programs which describe the semantics of the input institutions.

2. The translated institution programs along with a trace program and query program are then grounded by the LPARSE program (part of the SMODELS toolkit).

3. This grounded program description is then given as input to the SMODELS answer set solver. This produces zero or more answer sets. Each answer set corresponds to a possible model of the input institution for a given trace described by the trace program that matches the given query.

4. These answer sets may then be visualised and interpreted by the designer.

3   Landmarks and Scenes

As already discussed in the introduction, the essence of a landmark is a condition on a state in order for an action in some protocol to have effect. The relative sophistication of a landmark specification can be affected by the logic that is used to define the condition, but in many respects this is a technicality. For example [27] use first order logic augmented with modal operators for propositional attitudes and event sequences, [21] use dynamic propositional logic with modal operators from the previous work, while [13] (p.126) has atoms, implying the conjunction of positive values, within a Kripke model and [1] uses linear-time temporal logic. More important is the actual purpose of landmarks, as [21] states:

> Besides contributing to formal analyses of protocol families, the landmark-based representation facilitates techniques similar to partial order planning [22] for dynamically choosing the most appropriate action to use next in a conversation, allows compact handling of protocol exceptions, and in some cases, even allows short circuiting a protocol by opportunistically skipping some intermediate landmarks.

This highlights the relationship between agent actions and conventional AI planning and leads to the observation of the correspondence between landmarks and scenes (also mentioned in [13]). By scenes, we refer to the components of performative structure identified by Noriega [24] that are essentially sub-protocols of the larger institution or viewed bottom-up, an institution *may* be seen as the composition of numerous protocols that help agents achieve various sub-goals. What it is important to observe about Noriega's (and later in [25]) definition of the performative structure is how various conditions are imposed on the transitions from one scene to another, typically constraining the number and role of the agents that may move. A scene essentially encapsulates a self-contained protocol whose purpose is to achieve some sub-goal of the institution contributing to the objective of using the institution in the first place.

From this perspective, we can now turn to the relationship between our formalism and both landmarks and scenes, having established that both concepts serve to identify some (final) state in which a condition (capturing some institutional sub-goal) has been satisfied. Returning to the relations that drive our formalism (see section 2), the event generation function serves to create institutional facts, while the consequence relation focuses attention on the initiation and termination of fluents. The function is expressed as $C : \mathcal{X} \times \mathcal{E} \rightarrow 2^{\mathcal{F}} \times 2^{\mathcal{F}}$. Where the first set in the range of the function describes which fluents are initiated by the given event and the second set represents those fluents terminated by the event. We use the notation $C^{\uparrow}(\phi, e)$ to denote the fluents that are initiated by the event e in a state matching ϕ and the notation $C^{\downarrow}(\phi, e)$ to denote those terminated by event e in a state matching ϕ.

From the description of event generation and the consequence relation, it can be seen that fluents are initiated and terminated in respect of an event and some conditions on the state of the institution. This corresponds exactly with the notion of landmark, in that an event takes the institution into a new state *but* this is predicated on the current state — that is, a condition. Thus landmarks arise naturally from our formalization and furthermore, the condition language would appear to be richer than in some earlier work because the condition may contain both positive and negative information, including the use of negation as failure and hence non-monotonic reasoning, since these are basic properties of answer set semantics. Our conclusion therefore is that our formalism provides landmarks for free and, thanks to ASP semantics, enriches the landmark description language over earlier examples.

In the literature cited above, landmarks appear to be restricted to speech acts, that is messages from participating agents. Our model goes further, as we also consider exogenous events that do not originate from participating agents or from institutional events. This makes our approach a convenient tool for reasoning with scenes, where the transition between the various scenes does not necessarily depend on agents' actions. Instead the transition markers could be linked to exogenous events which are taken into account when the institution reaches a certain state. At this point the consequence relation could be used to set the powers and permissions (and so the behaviour) of the participating agents. The Dutch auction protocol detailed in the next section uses this technique to distinguish between the various phases/scenes of the protocol.

4   The Dutch Auction Protocol

Informal Description of Dutch Auction: In this protocol a single agent is assigned to the role of auctioneer, and one or more agents play the role of bidders. The purpose of the protocol as a whole is either to determine a winning bidder and a valuation for a particular item on sale, or to establish that no bidders wish to purchase the item. The protocol is summarised as follows:

1. Round starts: The auctioneer selects a starting price for the item and informs each of the bidders present of this price. The auctioneer then waits for a given period of time for bidders to respond.
2. Upon receipt of the starting price, each bidder has the choice as to whether to send a message indicating their desire to bid on the item at that price, or to send no message indicating that they do not wish to bid on the item.
3. At the end of the prescribed period of time, if the auctioneer has received a single bid from a given agent, then the auctioneer is obliged to inform each of the participating agents that this agent has won the auction.
4. If no bids are received at the end of the prescribed period of time, the auctioneer must inform each of the participants that the item has not been sold.

5. If more than one bid was received then the auctioneer must inform each agent that a conflict has occurred.
6. In the case where the item is sold the protocol is finished.
7. In the case that no bids are received then the auctioneer may either start a new round of bidding at a lower price, or withdraw the item from sale.
8. In the case where a conflict occurs then the auctioneer must re-open the bidding at a higher price and start the round again in order to resolve the conflict.

We focus on the protocol for the round itself (items 1-6). In our description below we omit from the messages a definition of the item in question and the starting price. While the inclusion of these aspects in the protocol is possible, their inclusion does not change the structure of the protocol round so we leave them out for simplicity.

In the following paragraphs we go through the Inst*AL* code step by step. The full listing can be found in Figures 1 and 2. Each line of Inst*AL* code is labelled with DAR-FigureNr-LineNr for ease of reference.

The first lines indicate the name of the institution (DAR-1-1) and the types of agents, Bidder (DAR-1-2) and Auctioneer (DAR-1-3) that may participate in the institution. These types are used as placeholders in the Inst*AL* rules for the agents participating in a particular instance of the institution, then when instantiated all rules are grounded appropriately. The institution is created by one creation event `createdar` as specified by rule DAR-1-4.

Based on the protocol description above, the following agent messages are defined (DAR-1-8 – DAR-1-12): the auctioneer announces a price to a given bidder (`annprice`), the bidder bids on the current item (`annbid`), the auctioneer announces a conflict to a given bidder (`annconf`) and the auctioneer announces that the item is sold (`annsold`) or not sold (`annunsold`) respectively. Each exogenous action has a corresponding institutional event (DAR-1-16 – DAR-1-20 which accounts for a valid execution of the physical action performed. In all cases the two events are linked by an unconditional generates statement in the description (DAR-2-29, DAR-2-32, DAR-2-37, DAR-2-38, DAR-2-39).

In addition to the agent actions we also include a number of time-outs indicating the three external events (which are independent of agents' actions) that affect the protocol. For each time-out we define a corresponding institutional event suffixed by `dl` indicating a deadline in the protocol:

`priceto`, `pricedl`: A time-out indicating the deadline by which the auctioneer must have announced the initial price of the item on sale to all bidders. (DAR-1-5 and DAR-1-13).
`bidto`, `biddl`: A time-out indicating the expiration of the waiting period for the auctioneer to receive bids for the item (DAR-1-6 and DAR-1-14).
`desto`, `desdl`: A time-out indicating the deadline by which the auctioneer must have announced the decision about the auction to all bidders (DAR-1-7 and DAR-1-15).

We assume that the time-outs will occur in the order specified (that is, due to their durations it is impossible for this to be otherwise). We use the corresponding institution events in the protocol description and constrain the order in which they are empowered in the institution to ensure that while the exogenous events may occur in any order,

```
institution dutch;                                 (DAR-1-1)

type Bidder;                                       (DAR-1-2)
type Auct;                                         (DAR-1-3)

create event createdar;                            (DAR-1-4)

exogenous event priceto;                           (DAR-1-5)
exogenous event bidto;                             (DAR-1-6)
exogenous event desto;                             (DAR-1-7)

exogenous event annprice(Auct,Bidder);             (DAR-1-8)
exogenous event annbid(Bidder,Auct);               (DAR-1-9)
exogenous event annconf(Auct,Bidder);              (DAR-1-10)
exogenous event annsold(Auct,Bidder);              (DAR-1-11)
exogenous event annunsold(Auct,Bidder);            (DAR-1-12)

inst event pricedl;                                (DAR-1-13)
inst event biddl;                                  (DAR-1-14)
inst event desdl;                                  (DAR-1-15)

inst event price(Auct,Bidder);                     (DAR-1-16)
inst event bid(Bidder,Auct);                       (DAR-1-17)
inst event conf(Auct,Bidder);                      (DAR-1-18)
inst event sold(Auct,Bidder);                      (DAR-1-19)
inst event unsold(Auct,Bidder);                    (DAR-1-20)

dest event badgov;                                 (DAR-1-21)
dest event finished;                               (DAR-1-22)

inst event alerted(Bidder);                        (DAR-1-23)

fluent onlybidder(Bidder);                         (DAR-1-24)
fluent havebid;                                    (DAR-1-25)
fluent conflict;                                   (DAR-1-26)

initially pow(price(A,B)), perm(price(A,B)),
          perm(annprice(A,B)),
          perm(badgov),pow(badgov),
          perm(pricedl),pow(pricedl),
          perm(priceto),
          perm(biddl),
          perm(bidto),
          perm(desto);                             (DAR-1-27)
```

Fig. 1. InstAL for the Dutch Auction Round Institution Part 1

the institution event may only occur once in each iteration and in the order specified (DAR-2-52 to DAR-2-59).

We define a single additional institution event `alerted(Bidder)` (DAR-1-23) that represents the event of a bidder being validly notified of the result of the auction. We additionally specify a dissolution event `finished` (DAR-1-22) that indicates the end of the protocol.

```
initially obl(price(A,B),pricedl,badgov);                              (DAR-2-28)
annprice(A,B) generates price(A,B);                                    (DAR-2-29)
price(A,B) terminates pow(price(A,B));                                 (DAR-2-30)
price(A,B) initiates pow(bid(B,A)),perm(bid(B,A)),perm(annbid(B,A));   (DAR-2-31)

annbid(A,B) generates bid(A,B);                                        (DAR-2-32)
bid(B,A) terminates pow(bid(B,A)),perm(bid(B,A)),perm(annbid(B,A));    (DAR-2-33)
bid(B,A) initiates havebid,onlybidder(B) if not havebid;              (DAR-2-34)
bid(B,A) terminates onlybidder(_) if havebid;                          (DAR-2-35)
bid(B,A) initiates conflict if havebid;                                (DAR-2-36)

annsold(A,B) generates sold(A,B);                                      (DAR-2-37)
annunsold(A,B) generates unsold(A,B);                                  (DAR-2-38)
annconf(A,B) generates conf(A,B);                                      (DAR-2-39)
biddl terminates pow(bid(B,A));                                        (DAR-2-40)
biddl initiates pow(sold(A,B)),pow(unsold(A,B)),
       pow(conf(A,B)), pow(alerted(B)),perm(alerted(B));               (DAR-2-41)
biddl initiates perm(annunsold(A,B)),perm(unsold(A,B)),
       obl(unsold(A,B),desdl,badgov) if not havebid;                   (DAR-2-42)
biddl initiates perm(annsold(A,B)),perm(sold(A,B)),
       obl(sold(A,B), desdl, badgov) if havebid, not conflict;         (DAR-2-43)
biddl initiates perm(annconf(A,B)),perm(conf(A,B)),
       obl(conf(A,B), desdl, badgov) if havebid, conflict;             (DAR-2-44)
unsold(A,B) generates alerted(B);                                      (DAR-2-45)
sold(A,B) generates alerted(B);                                        (DAR-2-46)
conf(A,B) generates alerted(B);                                        (DAR-2-47)
alerted(B) terminates pow(unsold(A,B)), perm(unsold(A,B)),
  pow(sold(A,B)), pow(conf(A,B)), pow(alerted(B)),
  perm(sold(A,B)), perm(conf(A,B)), perm(alerted(B)),
  perm(annconf(A,B)),perm(annsold(A,B)),perm(annunsold(A,B));          (DAR-2-48)
desdl generates finished if not conflict;                              (DAR-2-49)
desdl terminates havebid,conflict,perm(annconf(A,B));                  (DAR-2-50)
desdl initiates pow(price(A,B)), perm(price(A,B)),
  perm(annprice(A,B)), perm(pricedl),pow(pricedl),
  obl(price(A,B),pricedl,badgov) if conflict;                          (DAR-2-51)
priceto generates pricedl;                                             (DAR-2-52)
pricedl terminates pow(pricedl);                                       (DAR-2-53)
pricedl initiates pow(biddl);                                          (DAR-2-54)

bidto generates biddl;                                                 (DAR-2-55)
biddl terminates pow(biddl);                                           (DAR-2-56)
biddl initiates pow(desdl);                                            (DAR-2-57)

desto generates desdl;                                                 (DAR-2-58)
desdl terminates pow(desdl);                                           (DAR-2-59)
```

Fig. 2. InstAL for the Dutch Auction Round Institution Part 2

For the sake of simplicity, we do not focus in detail on the effects of the auction-eer violating the protocol. Instead we define a dissolution institutional event badgov (DAR-1-21) that accounts for *aany* instances in which the auctioneer has violated the protocol. Once an auctioneer has violated the protocol, we choose to treat the remainder of the protocol as invalid and dissolve the institution.

Once the institution has been created, the auctioneer will receive power and permission to announce prices. We also provide empowerment and permission for the dissolution event `badgov`. Furthermore all deadlines are permitted but only pricing is empowered. This is specified by DAR-1-27.

The rules of the institution are driven by the occurrence of the time-outs described above and hence may be broken down in to three phases as follows:

1. In the first phase of the protocol the auctioneer must issue price statements to each of the bidders. We represent this in the protocol by defining an initial obligation on the auctioneer to issue a price to each bidder before the price deadline (DAR-2-28). Once this has taken place, the auctioneer is no longer permitted to issue a price (DAR-2-30).

   Once a price has been sent to the bidder, the bidder is empowered and permitted to bid in the round (note that we permit both the action of validly bidding itself, `bid(B,A)`, as well as the action of sending the message which may count as bidding, `annbid(B,A)` (DAR-2-31).

2. In the second phase of the protocol, bidders may choose to submit bids. These must be sent before the bid time-out event. In order to account for the final phase of the protocol, we must capture the cases when one bid, no bids or multiple bids (a conflict) occur. In addition, in a given round, we must also take into account that bids may be received asynchronously from different agents over a period of time. In order to capture which outcome of the protocol has occurred we use three domain fluents (DAR-1-24 – DAR-1-26) to record the state of the bidding: `onlybidder(Bidder)`, `havebid`, `conflict`.

   The first of these fluents denotes the case where a single bid has been received and no others (and records the bidder which made this bid), the second fluent records cases where one or more bids have been received and the third records cases where more than one bid has been received.

   These fluents are determined in the second phase of the protocol using DAR-2-34, DAR-2-35 and DAR-2-36. The first rule accounts for the first bid that is received, and is only triggered if no previous bids have been made. The second rule accounts for any further bids and terminates the `onlybidder` fluent when a second bid is received. The final rule records a conflict if a bid is received and a previous bid has occurred.

   Once a bid has been submitted we do not wish to permit an agent to submit further bids, or for those further bids to be valid. In order to account for this we have line DAR-2-33.

3. In the third and final phase of the protocol the auctioneer must notify the bidding agents of the outcome of the auction. This phase is brought about by the occurrence of the `biddl` event which denotes the close of bidding. In order to account for this, we terminate each agents' capacity to bid further in the auction (DAR-2-40) and correspondingly initiate the auctioneer's power to bring about a resolution to the auction (DAR-2-41). To do so, we create an obligation upon the auctioneer to issue the right kind of response (`sold`, `unsold`, `conflict`) depending on outcome of the previous phase (`havebid`, `conflict`) before the next deadline (`desdl`) is announced. This is encoded by DAR-2-42 – DAR-2-43. For

each outcome, the auctioneer is obliged and permitted to issue the appropriate response to every bidding agent before the decision deadline. If an auctioneer fails to issue the correct outcome to any agent before the final deadline then a violation will occur. The protocol follows these notifications using DAR-2-45 – DAR-2-46.

Once an agent has been notified we wish to prohibit the auctioneer from notifying that agent again. We do this by introducing a rule which terminates the auctioneer's power and permission to issue more than one notification to any one agent (DAR-2-48).

Finally, when the deadline expires (the exogenous event `desto` triggers `desdl`) and either the protocol ends or the bidders have created a conflict. In the former case, DAR-2-49 ensures dissolution of the institution. In the conflict case, the auctioneer must re-open the bidding using a new round. We represent this by adding two lines. The first terminates the intermediate fluents which were used to represent the outcome of the protocol (`havebid` and `conflict`). This is established by DAR-2-50.

The second (DAR-2-51), initiates the obligation for the auctioneer to re-open the round by issuing a price to the bidders and all associated powers and permissions.

Verification: Once we have the Inst*AL* description of our institution, we can obtain an ASP program as described in Section 2. This program may then be combined with a trace program and query, allowing us to query properties and determine possible outcomes of this protocol.

The simplest type of verification procedure is to execute the program with no query. In this case all possible traces of the protocol will be provided as answer sets of the translated program.

Each answer set represents all possible sequences of states which may occur in the model and these may in turn be used to visualise all reachable states of the protocol (for a given number of agents). In order to execute the protocol we need to ground it with an auctioneer a and a bidder b. We could execute the translated program as is, however the answer sets of the program would include *all* traces of the protocol, including those containing actions which have no effect. Transitions of this kind may be of interest in some cases (we may be interested in the occurrence of associated violations for instance) however in this case we choose to omit them in order to reduce the number of answer sets to analyse. This can be achieved by specifying a query program which limits answer sets only to those containing traces in which a change of state occurs. For the technical details on this query program, see [8].

Solving the translated program with the associated query program yields a total of 60 answer sets corresponding to each possible trace where an effect occurs in each transition. By extracting the states from the answer set we may generate a graphical representation of the transition system which the protocol creates.

In order to include all possible states of the protocol we must select a large enough upper bound for the length of traces such that all possible states are reached. In general the selection of this upper bound depends on the program and query in question and it should be noted that the answer sets of the program represent *only* those solutions to the query which can be found in the given trace length.

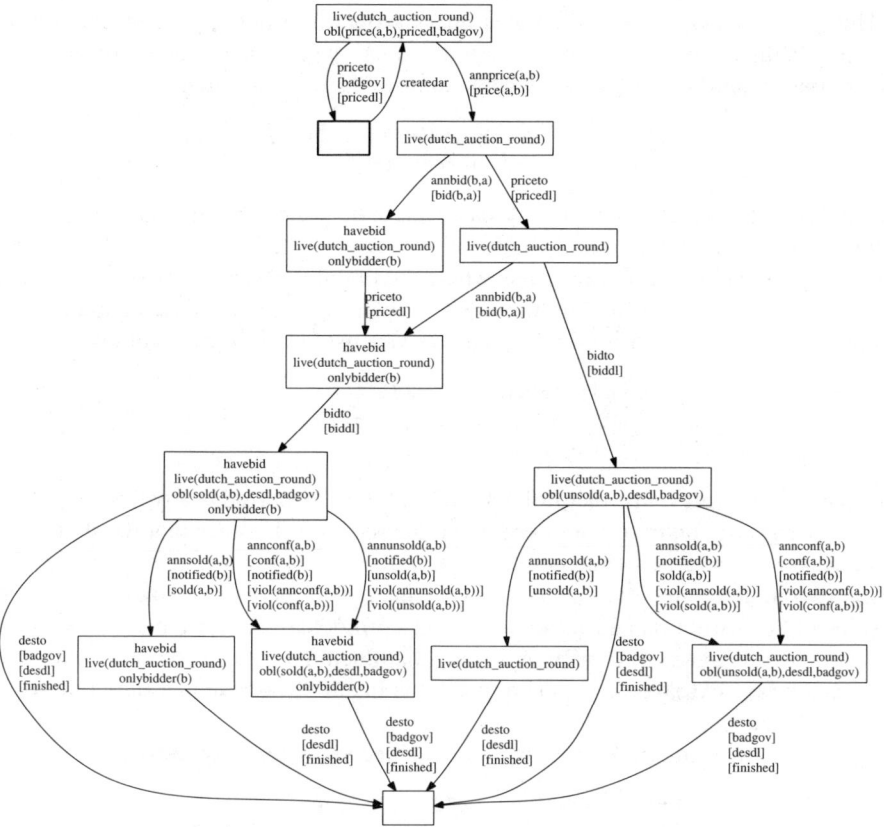

Fig. 3. States of the auction round for a single bidder

In the case of the auction protocol examined here we had to establish this upper bound by the somewhat unsatisfactory process of iterating the solver process and determining the number states until no more states were found. For the example above, with only two agents, the longest traces which yield new states are of length 7, resulting in 33 answer sets.

Figure 3 illustrates all possible states for a single round of the protocol with one bidder (for a larger number of bidders, the state space will be considerably larger, growing exponentially with their number). Note that as there is only one bidder participating in the protocol conflicts cannot occur. For the sake of clarity we omit fluents relating to powers and permissions from the figure.

Further Verification: In the above protocol we stated that when there was a conflict in the bidding for the protocol (that is, when two or more bidders issue valid bids) that the bidding should re-open. In order to ensure that this new round continues as before we must ensure that the institutional state at the beginning of a re-opened round is the same as the institutional state when the original round opened.

This property may be specified as a query program in our framework, as we now describe. In this case we are only interested in traces where a conflict has occurred. We specify this by adding the following constraints to the query program:

$$\text{hadconflict} \leftarrow \text{holdsat}(\text{conflict}, \text{I}), \text{instant}(\text{I}).$$
$$\bot \leftarrow \text{not hadconflict}.$$

The first rule states that if there is any state where the conflict fluent occurs, then the literal hadconflict should be included in the answer set. The second rule states that we should not include any answer sets where the literal hadconflict is not included.

We are also only interested in traces where the protocol is re-started and bidding is re-opened. We add this constraint in a similar way, using two rules as follows:

$$\text{restarted} \leftarrow \text{occurred}(\text{desdl}, \text{I}),$$
$$\text{holdsat}(\text{conflict}, \text{I}), \text{instant}(\text{I}).$$
$$\bot \leftarrow \text{not restarted}.$$

The first of these rules state that if the desdl event has occurred at any time we include the literal restarted in our answer set and the second rule states that we should only include answer sets where this literal is included.

In order to determine the fluents (if any) which differ between a state following the creation of the institution and a state following a protocol re-start, we mark these fluents using the literals startstate(F) indicating that fluent F is true in the start state of this trace, and restartstate(F) indicating that the fluent F was true in a state following a protocol re-start.

Literals of the form startstate(F) are defined using the following rule:

$$\text{startstate}(\text{F}) \leftarrow \text{holdsat}(\text{F}, \text{I1}),$$
$$\text{occurred}(\text{createdar}, \text{I0}),$$
$$\text{next}(\text{I0}, \text{I1}), \text{ifluent}(\text{F}).$$

Which states that F is a fluent in the start state, if F holds at time instant I1 and creation event createdar occurred at instant I0 and that instant I1 immediately follows instant I0.

We similarly define the fluents that hold in the re-start state with the rule:

$$\text{restartstate}(\text{F}) \leftarrow \text{holdsat}(\text{F}, \text{I1}), \text{occurred}(\text{desdl}, \text{I0}),$$
$$\text{holdsat}(\text{conflict}, \text{I0}), \text{next}(\text{I0}, \text{I1}), \text{ifluent}(\text{F}).$$

which states that F holds in the restart state, if it held in the state I1 which immediately followed the occurrence of the decision deadline desdl when a conflict held in that state.

We then define the following rules which indicate the differences between the start state and the re-start state:

$$\text{missing}(\text{F}) \leftarrow \text{startstate}(\text{F}), \text{notrestartstate}(\text{F}), \text{ifluent}(\text{F}).$$
$$\text{added}(\text{F}) \leftarrow \text{restartstate}(\text{F}), \text{notstartstate}(\text{F}), \text{ifluent}(\text{F}).$$

These rules indicate that a fluent is present in the start state, but missing from the restart state (indicated by missing(F)), or missing in the start state, but present in the restart state (indicated by added(F)) respectively.

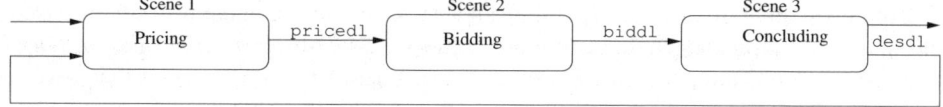

Fig. 4. Landmarks in the Dutch Auction round

Finally we define the query constraint, in this case we are only interested in traces where a difference occurs between the start state and the restart state. We add these constraints using following rules:

$$\text{invalid} \leftarrow \text{missing}(F), \text{ifluent}(F).$$
$$\text{invalid} \leftarrow \text{added}(F), \text{ifluent}(F).$$
$$\perp \leftarrow \textbf{not } \text{invalid}.$$

The first two rules state that if a fluent F is either `missing` or `added`, then the literal `invalid` is true. The third rule constrains answer sets of the program to only those containing the literal `invalid`.

These rules, when combined with the translated program of the institution allow us to determine which fluents have changed between the start state and end state of the protocol.

Given the translated program and the query program described above, we obtain no answer sets for the protocol as defined, indicating that it is indeed the case that there are no fluents which differ in the state following a protocol restart and the state following the creation of the institution. This result is consistent with the original description of the protocol and will permit subsequent rounds following a conflict to continue in the same way as the original round. The same query holds true for auctions including three or four bidders.

The Scene Perspective: Although the InstAL language does not explicitly allow for the definition of scenes (i.e. no special constructs are available), it is straightforward to achieve this with the available language constructs. The auction protocol discussed above, can be seen as composed of three scenes each marked by the occurrence of a deadline (except for the start of the protocol). Figure 4 provides the scene transition diagram. Each of these deadlines is the result of an exogenous event generated by the environment (e.g. DAR-2-52). The occurrence of such a deadline, changes the empowerment and permissions of the agents involved in the protocol (e.g. DAR-2-50). Rules are provided to assure the correct transition through the scenes (e.g. DAR-2-53).

5   Discussion

In this article we have demonstrated that the formal system described in [9] can easily deal with non-trivial institutions. Furthermore, we have shown that our characterisation can deal directly with landmarks and scenes, thus linking it more clearly with earlier work on institutional specification.

Much recent and contemporary work on modelling norms and violations has chosen temporal logics as a starting point, as we now discuss.

Colombetti et al in [16, 12, 29] outline an abstract model for agent institutions based on social commitments, where institutions comprise a set of *registration rules* that capture agents' entry into and exit from institutions, a set of *interaction rules* that govern commitment creation and satisfaction, a set of *authorisations* that describe agents' capabilities and an *internal ontology* that describes a model for the interpretation of terms relevant to the institution. Their approach builds on the CTL± extension of CTL[7], which includes past tense modalities for reasoning about actions which have already occurred. Dignum in [14] also uses an extension of CTL to describe her language for representing contracts in the building of agent organisations.

The Event Calculus (EC) [19, 20] is a declarative logic that reinterprets the Situation Calculus to capture when and how states change in response to external events. EC has been used to model both the behaviour of commitments [31] among agents in order to build interaction protocols, corresponding to the regulatory aspects of the work described above, as well as more general social models such as those described in [18]. From a technical point of view, our approach essentially has a kind of duality compared to EC, in that the basis for the model is events rather than states. In itself, this offers no technical advantage although we believe that being able to express violations in terms of events rather than states better captures their nature. More significant are the consequences of the grounding in ASP:

- For the most part the state and event models are equivalent with respect to properties such as induction and abduction, but non-monotonicity is inherent in ASP and so resort to the tricky process of circumscription is avoided.
- Likewise, reasoning about defaults requires no special treatment in ASP.
- The consequence rules of our specification have equivalents in EC, but the event generation rules do not.
- The state of a fluent is determined by its truth-value in the ASP interpretation, whereas EC (typically) has to encode this explicitly using two predicates.
- Inertia in EC is axiomatic, whereas in our approach it follows from the application of the TR operator—although there is a strong syntactic similarity (perhaps compounded by using the same terminology!) the philosophy is different.
- ASP allows a wider variety of queries than is typically provided in EC implementations but space constraints do not allow the full illustration of this aspect here.

Artikis et al. in [2, 3, 4, 18] describe a system for the specification of normative social systems in terms of power, empowerment and obligation. This is formalized using both the event calculus [19] and a subset of the action language $C+$ [15]. The notions of power and empowerment are equivalent in both systems, but additionally we introduces violation as events and our modelling of obligations differs in that (i) they are deadline-sensitive, and (ii) can raise a violation if they are not met in time. Violations greatly improve the capacity to model institutions, but it should be remembered that institutional modelling was (apparently) not Artikis's goal. Likewise, although the interpretation of $C+$ using the CCalc tool gives rise to similar reasoning capabilities (with similar complexity) to ASP, we believe our approach, including violations, provides a more intuitive and natural way of expressing social constraints involving temporal aspects. A further advantage is in the formulation of queries, where ASP makes it possible to encode queries similar to those found in (bounded) temporal logic model checking, whereas, as noted above, queries on action languages are constrained by the action language implementation. The other notable difference is once again our focus on events rather than states.

Viganò and Colombetti [30] focus on two key elements: a language for the definition and the verification of social aspects of MAS in respect of normative systems and electronic institutions, building on Colombetti's work on ontological decomposition of institutions and on Searle's model of constructed social reality. The basis for the work is the concept of status functions that capture institutional facts (including roles, such as buyer and refinement of roles, such as auction winner) and deontic positions (sic). Status functions are only reified when needed to verify the legitimacy of an action and as such constitute institutional objects, rather than observables, in contrast to the event-based approach described here. The authors use model checking to verify offline.

Apart from ASP, a number of other techniques could be applied to the problem of reasoning about institution specifications. One of these techniques, which has had considerable attention in field of multi-agent systems is symbolic model checking. Symbolic temporal logic model checking is a technique for verifying finite state systems with a large number of states. The technique was first described in [7]. While model checking may be applied to much larger state spaces than those which can be studied using ASP, model-checkers are limited to queries that can be expressed in temporal logic used by the underlying model checker: in the case of CTL [6] for instance, they are limited to formulae that are quantified over all future paths — making some queries impossible to specify.

References

[1] Aldewereld, H.: Autonomy vs. Conformity: an Institutional Perspective on Norms and Protocols. PhD thesis, Utrecht (2007)

[2] Artikis, A.: Executable Specification of Open Norm-Governed Computational Systems. PhD thesis, Department of Electrical & Electronic Engineering, Imperial College London (September 2003)

[3] Artikis, A., Sergot, M., Pitt, J.: An executable specification of an argumentation protocol. In: Proceedings of conference on artificial intelligence and law (icail), pp. 1–11. ACM Press, New York (2003)

[4] Artikis, A., Sergot, M., Pitt, J.: Specifying electronic societies with the Causal Calculator. In: Giunchiglia, F., Odell, J.J., Weiss, G. (eds.) AOSE 2002. LNCS, vol. 2585, Springer, Heidelberg (2003)

[5] Baral, C.: Knowledge Representation, Reasoning and Declarative Problem Solving. Cambridge Press, Cambridge (2003)

[6] Cimatti, A., Clarke, E.M., Giunchiglia, F., Roveri, M.: NUSMV: A new symbolic model checker. International Journal on Software Tools for Technology Transfer 2(4), 410–425 (2000)

[7] Clarke, E.M., Emerson, E.A., Sistla, A.P.: Automatic verification of finite-state concurrent systems using temporal logic specifications. ACM Transactions on Programming Languages and Systems 8(2), 244–263 (1981)

[8] Cliffe, O.: Specifying and Analysing Institutions in Multi-Agent Systems Using Answer Set Programming. PhD thesis, Dept. Computer Science, University of Bath (June 2007)

[9] Cliffe, O., De Vos, M., Padget, J.A.: Answer set programming for representing and reasoning about virtual institutions. In: Inoue, K., Satoh, K., Toni, F. (eds.) CLIMA 2006. LNCS (LNAI), vol. 4371, pp. 60–79. Springer, Heidelberg (2007)

[10] Cliffe, O., De Vos, M., Padget, J.A.: Specifying and reasoning about multiple institutions. In: Noriega, P., Vázquez-Salceda, J., Boella, G., Boissier, O., Dignum, V., Fornara, N., Matson, E. (eds.) COIN 2006. LNCS (LNAI), vol. 4386, pp. 63–81. Springer, Heidelberg (2007)

[11] Cohen, P.R., Levesque, H.: Intention is choice with commitment. Artificial Intelligence 42, 213–261 (1990)

[12] Colombetti, M., Verdicchio, M.: An analysis of agent speech acts as institutional actions. In: Alonso, E., Kudenko, D., Kazakov, D. (eds.) AAMAS 2000 and AAMAS 2002. LNCS (LNAI), vol. 2636, pp. 1157–1164. Springer, Heidelberg (2003)

[13] Dignum, V.: A Model for Organizational Interaction. PhD thesis, Utrecht (2004)

[14] Dignum, V., Meyer, J.-J., Dignum, F., Weigand, H.: Formal Specification of Interaction in Agent Societies. In: Hinchey, M.G., Rash, J.L., Truszkowski, W.F., Rouff, C.A., Gordon-Spears, D.F. (eds.) FAABS 2002. LNCS (LNAI), vol. 2699, pp. 37–52. Springer, Heidelberg (2003)

[15] Giunchiglia, E., Lee, J., Lifschitz, V., McCain, N., Turner, H.: Nonmonotonic causal theories. Artificial Intelligence 153, 49–104 (2004)

[16] Fornara, N., Colombetti, M.: Operational specification of a commitment-based agent communication language. In: Alonso, E., Kudenko, D., Kazakov, D. (eds.) AAMAS 2000 and AAMAS 2002. LNCS (LNAI), vol. 2636, pp. 536–542. Springer, Heidelberg (2003)

[17] Gelfond, M., Lifschitz, V.: The stable model semantics for logic programming. In: Proc. of fifth logic programming symposium, pp. 1070–1080. MIT Press, Cambridge (1988)

[18] Kamara, L., Artikis, A., Neville, B., Pitt, J.: Simulating computational societies. In: Petta, P., Tolksdorf, R., Zambonelli, F. (eds.) ESAW 2002. LNCS (LNAI), vol. 2577, pp. 53–67. Springer, Heidelberg (2003)

[19] Kowalski, R., Sergot, M.: A logic-based calculus of events. New Gen. Comput. 4(1), 67–95 (1986)

[20] Kowalski, R.A., Sadri, F.: Reconciling the event calculus with the situation calculus. Journal of Logic Programming 31(1–3), 39–58 (1997)

[21] Kumar, S., Huber, M.J., Cohen, P.R., McGee, D.R.: Toward a formalism for conversation protocols using joint intention theory. Computational Intelligence 18(2), 174–228 (2002)

[22] Minton, S., Bresina, J., Drummond, M.: Total order and partial order planning: A comparative analysis. Journal of Artificial Intelligence Research 2, 227–262 (1994)

[23] Niemelä, I., Simons, P.: Smodels: An implementation of the stable model and well-founded semantics for normal LP. In: Fuhrbach, U., Dix, J., Nerode, A. (eds.) LPNMR 1997. LNCS, vol. 1265, pp. 420–429. Springer, Heidelberg (1997)

[24] Noriega, P.: Agent mediated auctions: The Fishmarket Metaphor. PhD thesis, Universitat Autonoma de Barcelona (1997)

[25] Rodríguez-Aguilar, J.A.: On the Design and Construction of Agent-mediated Institutions. PhD thesis, Universitat Autonoma de Barcelona (2001)

[26] Sergot, M. (C+)++: An Action Language For Representing Norms and Institutions. Technical report, Imperial College, London (August 2004)

[27] Smith, I., Cohen, P., Bradshaw, J., Greaves, M., Holmback, H.: Designing conversation policies using joint intention theory. In: Proceedings of International Conference on Multi Agent Systems, pp. 269–276 (1998), doi:10.1109/ICMAS.1998.699064

[28] Vázquez-Salceda, J., Noriega, P. (eds.): Coordination, Organizations, Institutions, and Norms in Agent Systems II. In: Noriega, P., Vázquez-Salceda, J., Boella, G., Boissier, O., Dignum, V., Fornara, N., Matson, E. (eds.) COIN 2006. LNCS (LNAI), vol. 4386, Springer, Heidelberg (2007)

[29] Verdicchio, M., Colombetti, M.: A logical model of social commitment for agent communication. In: AAMAS 2003: Proceedings of the second international joint conference on Autonomous agents and multiagent systems, pp. 528–535. ACM Press, New York (2003)

[30] Viganò, F., Colombetti, M.: Specification and verification of institutions through status functions. In: Noriega, P., Vázquez-Salceda, J., Boella, G., Boissier, O., Dignum, V., Fornara, N., Matson, E. (eds.) COIN 2006. LNCS (LNAI), vol. 4386, Springer, Heidelberg (2007)

[31] Yolum, P., Singh, M.P.: Flexible protocol specification and execution: applying event calculus planning using commitments. In: AAMAS 2002: Proceedings of the first international joint conference on Autonomous agents and multiagent systems, pp. 527–534. ACM Press, New York (2002)

Coordination and Sociability for Intelligent Virtual Agents

Francisco Grimaldo, Miguel Lozano, and Fernando Barber

Computer Science Department, University of Valencia,
Dr. Moliner 50, (Burjassot) Valencia, Spain
{francisco.grimaldo,miguel.lozano,fernando.barber}@uv.es

Abstract. This paper presents a multi-agent framework designed to simulate synthetic humans that properly balance task oriented and social behaviors. The work presented in this paper focuses on the social library integrated in BDI agents to provide socially acceptable decisions. We propose the use of ontologies to define the social relations within an artificial society and the use of a market based mechanism to reach sociability by means of task exchanges. The social model balances rationality, to control the global coordination of the group, and sociability, to simulate relations (e.g. friendliness) and reciprocity among agents. The multi-agent framework has been tested successfully in dynamic environments while simulating a virtual bar, where groups of waiters and customers can interact and finally display complex social behaviors (e.g. task passing, reciprocity, planned meetings).

1 Introduction

Multi-agent systems are sometimes referred to as societies of agents and provide an elegant and formal framework to animate synthetic humans. When designing such agents, the main concern has normally been with the decision-making mechanism, as it is the responsible for the actions that will be finally animated. Virtual actors normally operate in dynamic resource bounded contexts; thus, multi-agent simulations require group coordination, as self-interested agents easily come into conflicts due to the competition for the use of shared resources (i.e. objects in a virtual environment). These obstructions produce low quality animations where characters do not act realistically. Moreover, virtual humans represent roles in the scenario (e.g. a virtual guide, a waiter, a customer, etc.) and the social network formed by the relations among the members of the society should also be considered when animating their behaviors.

This paper presents a multi-agent simulation framework to produce good quality animations where the behavior of socially intelligent agents better imitates that of real humans. We aim at incorporating human style social reasoning in virtual characters. Therefore, we have developed a market based social model [1] which coordinates the activities of groups of virtual characters and incorporates social actions in the agent decision-making. Our approach is inspired in reciprocal task exchanges between agents [2] and uses ontologies to define the

J.S. Sichman et al. (Eds.): COIN 2007, LNAI 4870, pp. 58–70, 2008.
© Springer-Verlag Berlin Heidelberg 2008

social relations within an artificial society. According with the main parameter of the model, that is sociability, the agents can balance their task-oriented behaviors (e.g. a virtual waiter should serve customers) and their social skills (e.g. negotiate with other waiters to gain access to a resource, assume external actions/favors, or simple chats).

The structure of the paper is as follows: in section 2 we describe briefly some previous literature on the field. In section 3 we present the multi-agent simulation framework and the main components of the social model. Section 4 describes an illustrative example modeled to test our framework. Lastly, section 5 summarizes the first results extracted and analyzes them.

2   Related Work

Many interactive games and virtual communities put human users together with synthetic characters. In this context, some research has been done on the believability issues of virtual actors, usually centred on the interactions either between a human user and a single character [3] or among the synthetic characters themselves [4]. These interactive scenarios often present tasks to the participants that must be solved collaboratively [5]. Therefore, behavioral animation has broadly been tackled from the field of coordinated multi-agent systems (e.g. Generalized Partial Global Planning (GPGP) [6], the TAEMS framework [7] or the RETSINA system [8]). Moreover, task coordination has been applied to HSP-based (Heuristic Search Planning) virtual humans in [9] and [10] to adapt better to the dynamism of shared environments.

Social reasoning has also been extensively studied in multi-agent systems in order to incorporate social actions to cognitive agents [11]. As a result of these works, agent interaction models have evolved to social networks that try to imitate the social structures found in reality [12]. Social dependence networks in [13] allow agents to cooperate or to perform social exchanges attending to their dependence relations (i.e. social dependence and social power). Trust networks in [14] are used to define better delegation strategies by means of a contract net protocol and fuzzy cognitive representations of the other agents as well as of the dynamic environment. In preference networks, such as the one presented in this paper, agents express their preferences using utility functions and their attitude towards another agent is represented by the differential utilitarian importance they place on that agent's utility.

Semantic information can be of great value to the agents inhabiting a virtual world. As demonstrated in [15], the use of semantics associated to objects can enhance the interaction of virtual humans in complex environments. Environment-based approaches are also emerging to provide semantic interoperability among intelligent agents through the use of coordination artifacts [16]. Furthermore, ontologies are very useful to model the social relations between the agents involved in graphical and interactive simulations [17]. In MOISE+ [18], ontological concepts join roles with plans in a coherent organizational specification. Another example can be found in [19] where a functional ontology for reputation is proposed.

Although the results obtained by the previous approaches show realistic simulations for many task-oriented behaviors, synthetic characters should also display pure social behaviors (e.g. interchanging information with their partners or grouping and chatting with their friends). MAS-SOC [20] aims at creating a platform for multi-agent based social simulations with BDI agents, which is also our purpose. In this context, work is ongoing in order to incorporate social-reasoning mechanisms based on exchange values [21]. The multi-agent framework presented here is oriented to simulate socially intelligent agents able to balance their rationality and sociability, a key point to finally display high quality behavioral animations.

3   Multi-agent Simulation Framework

The multi-agent simulation framework presented in figure 1 has been developed over Jason [22], which allows the definition of BDI agents using an extended version of AgentSpeak(L). The animation system (virtual characters, motion tables, etc) is located at the 3D engine, which can run separately. The environment is handled by the *Semantic Layer*, which acts as an interface between the agent and the world. It is in charge of perceiving the state of the world and executing the actions requested by the agents, while ensuring the consistency of the *World Model*. Ontologies define the world knowledge base using two levels of representation: the *SVE Core Ontology* is a unique base ontology suitable for all virtual environments and it is extended by different *Domain Specific Ontologies* in order to model application-specific knowledge.[1]

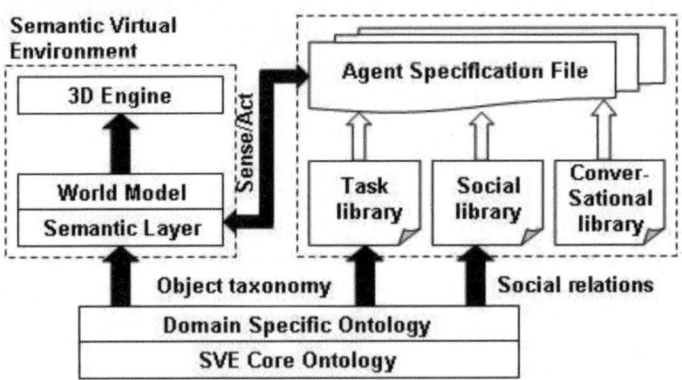

Fig. 1. Multi-agent simulation framework

The agent decision-making is defined in the *Agent Specification File*. This file contains the initial beliefs as well as the set of plans that make up the agent's finite state machine. The *Task library* contains the set of plans that sequence

---

[1] See [15] for details on ontologies and their use to enhance agent-object interaction.

the actions needed to animate a task. For instance, a virtual waiter serving a coffee will go to the coffee machine to get the coffee and will give it to the customer afterwards. Here, modularity is guaranteed since the *Task library* can be changed depending on the environment and the roles being simulated. As stated above, only rational behaviors are not enough to simulate agent societies. Therefore, we have extended the ontologies to define the possible social relations among the agents of a society and we have included a *Social library* to manage different types of situations. This library is based on an auction model and uses social welfare concepts to avoid conflicts and allow the agents to behave in a coordinated way. The *Social library* also incorporates a reciprocity mechanism to promote egalitarian social interactions. Finally, the *Conversational library* contains the set of plans that handle the animation of the interactions between characters (e.g. ask someone a favor, planned meetings, chats between friends...).

3.1 Social Ontology

The set of possible social relations among the agents within an artificial society can be ontologically represented in the form of interrelations between classes of agents. Figure 2 shows the extensions made to the object ontology previously presented in [15] in order to hold agent relations. We distinguish two basic levels of social relations: the level of individuals (i.e. *agentSocialRelations*) and the institutional level (i.e. *groupSocialRelations*). When one agent is related with another single agent, an *agentSocialRelation* will link them. Different application domains can need specific relations; thus, Domain Specific Ontologies are used to inherit particular relations from the core ontology. For instance, the property *workFriend* is used by the waiters in the virtual bar presented in section 4 to model the characteristic of being a friend of a workmate. Other examples of individual relations are family relations such as to be parent of or to be married with another agent. In this case, there is not only semantic but also structural difference, since *parent* is a unidirectional relation whereas *marriedWith* is bidirectional.

On the other hand, *groupSocialRelations* can be used to represent an agent belonging to a group. The social network created by this type of relation can be explored to get the rest of the agents of the same group, thus modeling a one-to-many relation. The *Group* class is an abstraction of any kind of aggregation. Therefore, we can model from physical groups such as the players of a football team to more sophisticated mental aggregations such as individuals of a certain social class or people of the same religious ideology. Although not considered in this paper, many-to-many relations between groups could also be created using this ontological approach. The dynamics of how these relations are created, modified and terminated falls out of the scope of this paper. Thus, at the moment relations are set off-line and do not change during the simulation.

3.2 Social Library

The simulation of worlds inhabited by interactive virtual actors normally involves facing a set of problems related to the use of shared limited resources and the

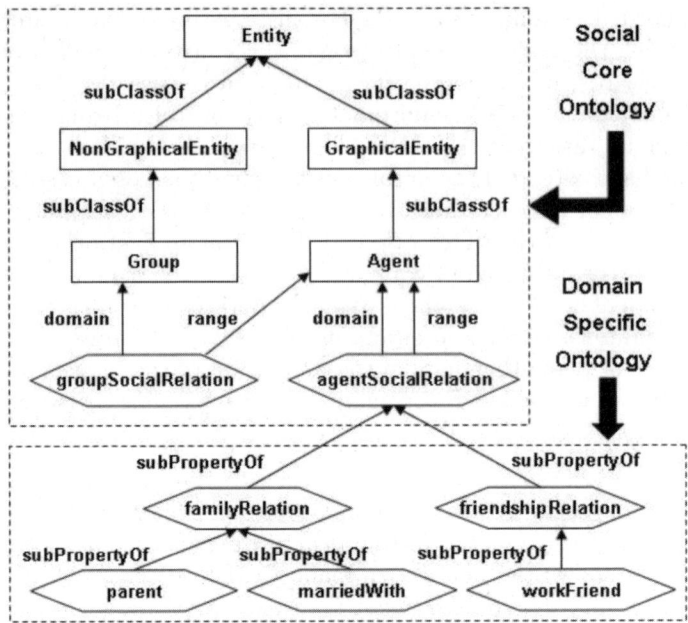

Fig. 2. Social Ontology

need to animate pure social behaviors. Both types of problems are managed by the *Social library* by using a Multi-agent Resource Allocation approach [1]. This library allows any agent to auction tasks in order to reallocate them so that the global social welfare can be increased. Tasks are exchanged between agents using a first-price sealed-bid (FPSB) auction model where the agents express their preferences using *performance and social utility functions*.

The performance utility function $U^i_{perf}(\langle i \leftarrow t \rangle)$ of a bidder agent i reflects the efficiency achieved when the task t is allocated to the agent i ($\langle i \leftarrow t \rangle$). There can be many reasons for an agent to be more efficient: it may perform the task faster than others because of his know-how or it may be using a resource that allows several tasks to be performed simultaneously (e.g. a coffee machine in a virtual bar can be used by a waiter to make more than one coffee at the same time). The utility function has to favor the performance of the agents, but high performances can also be unrealistic for the animation of artificial human societies. For example, if all agents work as much as they can, they will display unethical or robotic behaviors. Furthermore, agents should also show pure social behaviors to animate the normal relations between the members of a society.

Whereas the performance utility function modelled the interest of an agent to exchange a task from an efficiency point of view, we introduce two additional social utilities to represent the social interest in exchanging a task. The aim of social utilities is to promote task allocations that lead the agents to perform social interactions with other agents (e.g. planned meetings with their friends). Therefore, these functions take into account the social relations established between the agents and defined in the ontology to compute the value that expresses their social preferences. Negotiation of long sequences of actions is not very interesting for interactive characters, as plans are likely to be thwarted due to the dynamism of the environment and to other unpredictable events. Thus, we define the following social utility functions:

- Internal social utility $(U_{int}^i(\langle i \leftarrow t, j \leftarrow t_{next}\rangle))$: is the utility that a bidder agent i assigns to a situation where i commits to do the auctioned task t so that the auctioneer agent j can execute his next task t_{next}.
- External social utility $(U_{ext}^i(\langle j \leftarrow t\rangle))$: is the utility that a bidder agent i assigns to a situation where the auctioneer agent j executes the auctioned task t while i continues with his current action.

The winner determination problem has two possible candidates coming from performance and sociability. In equation 1 the welfare of a society is related to performance, hence, the winner of an auction will be the agent that bid the maximum performance utility. On the other hand, equation 2 defines the social winner based on the maximum social utility received to pass the task to a bidder (see $U_{int}^*(t)$ in equation 3) and the maximum social utility given by all bidders to the situation where the task is not exchanged but performed by the auctioneer j (see $U_{ext}^*(t)$ in equation 4). To balance task exchange, social utilities are weighted with a reciprocity matrix (see equations 3 and 4). We define the reciprocity factor w_{ij} for two agents i and j, as the ratio between the number of favors (i.e.tasks) that j has made to i (see equation 5).

$$winner_{perf}(t) = \left\{ k\epsilon Agents | U_{perf}^i(t) = \max_{i\epsilon Agents} \{U_{perf}^i(\langle i \leftarrow t\rangle)\} \right. \tag{1}$$

$$winner_{soc}(t) = \begin{cases} j\ U_{ext}^*(t) >= U_{int}^*(t) \\ i\ U_{ext}^*(t) < U_{int}^*(t) \wedge U_{int}^i(t) = U_{int}^*(t) \end{cases} \tag{2}$$

$$U_{int}^*(t) = \max_{i\epsilon Agents} \{U_{int}^i(\langle i \leftarrow t, j \leftarrow t_{next}\rangle) * w_{ij}\} \tag{3}$$

$$U_{ext}^*(t) = \max_{i\epsilon Agents} \{U_{ext}^i(\langle j \leftarrow t\rangle) * w_{ji}\} \tag{4}$$

$$w_{ij} = \frac{Favours_{ji}}{Favours_{ij}} \tag{5}$$

At this point, agents can decide whether to adopt this kind of social allocations or to be only rational as explained previously. They choose between them in accordance with their *Sociability* factor, which is the probability to select the social winner instead of the rational winner. *Sociability* can be adjusted in the range [0,1] to model intermediate behaviors between efficiency and total reciprocity. This can provide great flexibility when animating characters, since *Sociability* can be dynamically changed thus producing different behaviors depending on the world state.

4   Application Example

In order to test the presented social multi-agent framework, we have created a virtual university bar where waiters take orders placed by customers (see figure 3a). The typical locations in a bar (e.g. a juice machine) behave like resources that have an associated time of use to supply their products (e.g. 2 minutes to make an orange juice) and they can only be occupied by one agent at a time. Agents can be socially linked using the concepts defined in the *Social Ontology*. According to them, all waiters are related through a *groupSocialRelation* to *Waiters*, a group representing their role (see figure 3b). Moreover, they can be individually related with other waiters through *workFriend*. This relation semantically means that the agents are friends at work and, in this application, it has been modeled as bidirectional but not transitive. For example, in figure 3b, Albert is friend of Dough and John but these later ones are not friends of each other. Moreover, we have also specified three possible groups of customers: teachers, undergraduates and graduates. The social network specified by them is used to promote social meetings among customers in the university bar.

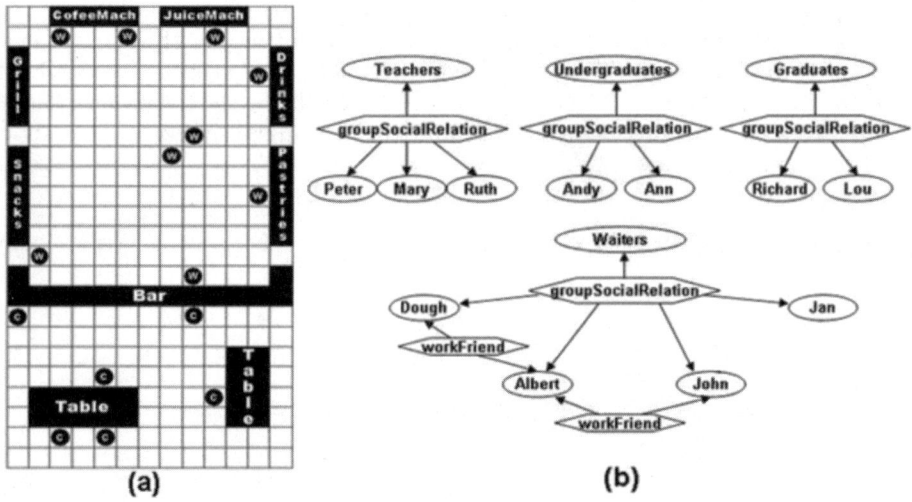

Fig. 3. (a) Virtual university bar environment, (b) Social relations between agents

The waiters are governed by the finite state machine[2] shown in figure 4a, where orders are served basically in two steps: first, using the corresponding resource (e.g. the grill to produce a sandwich) and second, giving the product to the customer. Tasks are always auctioned before their execution in order to find good social allocations. Equations 6 and 7 define the utility values returned by the performance utility function for these tasks. This function aims at maximizing

---

[2] Specified by means of plans in Jason's extended version of AgentSpeak(L).

the number of tasks being performed at the same time and represents the waiters' willingness to serve orders as fast as possible. Social behaviors defined for a waiter are oriented to animate chats among his friends at work. Therefore, waiters implement the internal and external social utility functions detailed in equations 8 and 9, where *Near* computes the distance between the agents while they are executing a pair of tasks. These functions evaluate social interest as the chance to meet a *workFriend* in the near future, thus performing a planned meeting.

$$U^i_{perf}(\langle i \leftarrow \text{'Use'}\rangle) = \begin{cases} 1 \text{ if } [(i = Auctioneer) \wedge IsFree(Resource)] \vee \\ \quad [IsUsing(i, Resource) \wedge not(IsComplete(Resource))] \\ 0 \text{ Otherwise} \end{cases}$$
(6)

$$U^i_{perf}(\langle i \leftarrow \text{'Give'}\rangle) = \begin{cases} 1 \text{ if } [(i = Auctioneer) \wedge nextAction = NULL] \vee \\ \quad [currentTask = \text{'Give'} \wedge not(handsBusy < 2)] \\ 0 \text{ Otherwise} \end{cases}$$
(7)

$$U^i_{int}(\langle i \leftarrow t, j \leftarrow t_{next}\rangle) = \begin{cases} 1 \text{ if } IsWorkFriend(i,j) \wedge Near(t, t_{next}) \wedge \\ \quad ExecTime(t_{next}) > RemainTime(currentTask) \\ 0 \text{ Otherwise} \end{cases}$$
(8)

$$U^i_{ext}(\langle j \leftarrow t\rangle) = \begin{cases} 1 \text{ if } IsWorkFriend(i,j) \wedge Near(currentTask, t) \\ 0 \text{ Otherwise} \end{cases}$$
(9)

On the other hand, customers place orders and consume them when served. At the moment, we are not interested in improving customer performance but in animating interactions between the members of a social group (i.e. teachers,

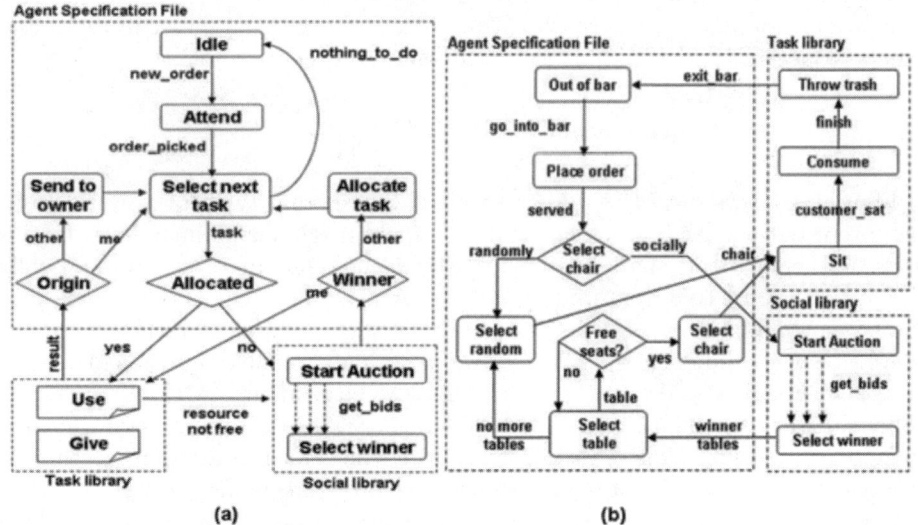

Fig. 4. (a)Waiter specification, (b) Customer specification

undergraduates and graduates). The finite state machine in figure 4b governs the actuation of customers that use auctions to solve the problem of *where to sit*. Depending on his or her sociability factor, a customer can randomly choose a chair or start an auction to decide where to sit and consume. This auction is received by all customers in the bar, which use the external social utility function defined in equation 10 to promote social meetings. This function uses the *groupSocialRelations* to determine if two individuals belong to the same group. We define the performance and the internal social utility functions as 0 since task passing is not possible in this case (i.e. no-one can sit instead of another customer). Finally, when a social meeting emerges, both waiters and customers use the plans in the *Conversational Library* to sequence the speech-acts needed to animate commitments, greetings or simple conversations.

$$U^i_{ext}(\langle j \leftarrow \text{'Sit'}\rangle) = \begin{cases} 1 \text{ if } IsSameGroup(i,j) \wedge IsConsuming(i, auctionedTable) \\ 0 \text{ Otherwise} \end{cases}$$

$$(10)$$

5   Results

To illustrate the effects of the social techniques previously defined we have simulated the virtual university bar example with up to 10 waiters serving 100 customers, both with different sociability factors. We estimate the social welfare of our society using two metrics explained along this section: *Throughput* and *Animation*. *Throughput* is an indicator in the range $[0, 1]$ that estimates how close a simulation is to the ideal situation in which the workload can be distributed among the agents and no collisions arise. Thus, equation 11 defines *Throughput* as the ratio between this ideal simulation time (T^*_{sim}) and the real simulation time (T_{sim}), where N_{tasks} and N_{agents} are the number of tasks and agents respectively and $\overline{T_{task}}$ is the mean time to execute a task.

$$Throughput = \frac{T^*_{sim}}{T_{sim}} = \frac{N_{tasks} * \overline{T_{task}}/N_{agents}}{T_{sim}}$$

$$(11)$$

Figure 5a shows the *Throughput* obtained by different types of waiters versus self-interested agents (i.e. agents with no social mechanisms included). In this first social configuration, all waiters are friends and customers are automatically assigned a group (teacher, undergraduate or graduate) when they come into the scenario. Self-interested agents collide as they compete for the use of the shared resources and these collisions produce high waiting times as the number of agents grows. We can enhance this low performance with elitist agents (*Sociability* = 0) which coordinately exchange tasks with others that can carry them out in parallel, thus reducing the waiting times for resources. Nevertheless, they produce unrealistic outcomes since they are continuously working if they have the chance, leaving aside their social relationships (in our example, chats between friends). The *Sociability* factor can be used to balance rationality and sociability. Therefore, the *Throughput* for the sort of animations we are pursuing should be placed somewhere in between elitist and fully reciprocal social agents (*Sociability* = 1). On the other hand, figure 5b demonstrates that the higher the *Sociability* factor is, the larger the number of social meetings that will be performed by the customers when they sit at a table.

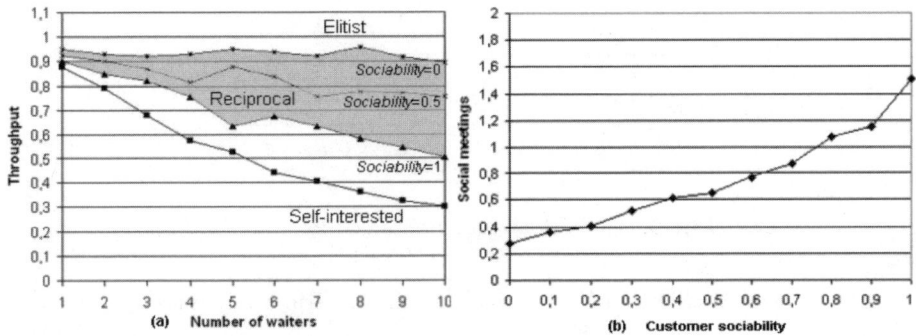

Fig. 5. (a) Waiter *Throughput*, (b) Customer social meetings

Throughput is an estimator for the behavioral performance but, despite being a basic requirement when simulating groups of virtual characters, it is not the only criterion to evaluate when we try to create high quality simulations. Therefore, we have defined another estimator that takes into account the amount of time that the designer of the simulation wants to be spent in social interactions. According to this, we define the following simulation estimator:

$$Animation = \frac{T^*_{sim} + T_{social}}{T_{sim}},\qquad(12)$$

where T_{social} represents the time devoted to chatting and to animating social agreements among friends. In our virtual bar we have chosen T_{social} as the 35% of T^*_{sim}. Figure 6 shows the animation values for 10 reciprocal social waiters with 4 degrees of friendship: all friends, 75% of the agents are friends, half of the agents are friends and only 25% of the agents are friends. As we have already mentioned, low values of *Sociability* produce low quality simulations since the values obtained for the animation function are greater than the reference value (*Animation* = 1). On the other hand, high values of *Sociability* also lead to low quality simulations, especially when the degree of friendship is high. In these cases, the number of social conversations being animated is too high to be realistic and animation is far from the reference value. The animation function can be used to extract the adequate range of values for the *Sociability* factor, depending on the situation being simulated. For example, in our virtual bar we consider as good quality animations those which fall inside ±10% of the reference value (see shaded zone in figure 6). Hence, when all the waiters are friends, good animations emerge when *Sociability* ∈ [0.1, 0.3].

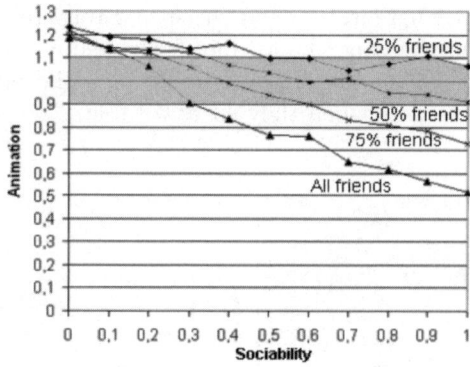

Fig. 6. Animation results obtained for waiters

Table 1. Time distribution for 10 waiters in the bar (time values are in seconds)

Agent	T_{wait}	T_{use}	T_{give}	Balance	T_{wait}	T_{use}	T_{give}	Balance
	\multicolumn{4}{Sociability = 0}			\multicolumn{4}{Sociability = 1}			
1	0	32	19	-6	16	69	34	-2
2	3	4	26	-3	18	58	24	-2
3	14	52	1	28	41	45	16	0
4	3	16	28	-3	48	60	27	3
5	0	7	30	-16	34	58	12	-1
6	3	37	17	-1	48	64	14	-2
7	0	67	4	21	18	48	24	1
8	0	45	17	1	33	45	24	4
9	7	5	23	-11	46	36	21	0
10	1	6	41	-10	27	56	20	-1

Finally, table 1 compares the amount of time devoted to executing each type of task in executions with 10 elitist waiters ($Sociability = 0$) and 10 fully reciprocal social waiters ($Sociability = 1$). The irregular values in the columns T_{use} and T_{give} on the left side of the table demonstrate how some agents have specialized in certain tasks. For instance, agents 2, 5, 9 and 10 spend most of their time giving products to the customers while agents 3 and 7 are mainly devoted to using the resources of the bar (e.g. the coffee machine, etc). Although specialization is a desirable outcome in many multi-agent systems, egalitarian human societies need also to balance the workload assigned to each agent. On the right side of the table, fully reciprocal social waiters achieve equilibrium between the time they are giving products and the time they are using the resources of the environment (see columns T_{use} and T_{give}). Furthermore, the reciprocity factor balances the number of favors exchanged among the agents (compare *Balance* columns). A collateral effect of this equilibrium is the increase in the waiting times, since social agents will sometimes prefer to meet his friends in a resource than to reallocate the task (compare columns T_{wait}).

6   Conclusions and Future Work

The animation of groups of intelligent characters is a current research topic with a great number of behavioral problems to be tackled. We aim at incorporating human style social reasoning in character animation. Therefore, this paper presents a technique to properly balance social with task-oriented plans in order to produce realistic social animations. We propose the use of ontologies to define the social relations within an artificial society and the use of a market based mechanism to reach sociability by means of task exchanges. The multi-agent animation framework presented allows for the definition of different types of social agents: from elitist agents (that only use their interactions to increase the global performance of the group) to fully reciprocal agents. These latter agents extend the theory of social welfare with a reciprocity model that allows the agents to control the emergence of social interactions among the members of a society.

Work is ongoing to provide the agents with mechanisms to self-regulate their *Sociability* factor depending on their social relations and on their previous intervention. Thus, agents will be able to dynamically adjust to the situation in order to stay within the boundaries of good quality animations at all times.

Acknowledgements

This work has been jointly supported by the Spanish MEC and European Commission FEDER funds under grants Consolider Ingenio-2010 CSD2006-00046 and TIN2006-15516-C04-04.

References

1. Hogg, L.M., Jennings, N.: Socially intelligent reasoning for autonomous agents. IEEE Transactions on System Man and Cybernetics 31(5), 381–393 (2001)
2. Piaget, J.: Sociological studies. Routledge (1995)
3. Bickmore, T., Cassell, J.: Relational agents: A model and implementation of building user trust. In: Proc. of CHI 2001: Conference on Human Factors in Computing Systems, ACM, New York (2001)
4. Tomlinson, B., Blumberg, B.: Social synthetic characters. In: Proc. of Computer Graphics. vol. 26 (2002)
5. Prada, R., Paiva, A.: Believable groups of synthetic characters. In: Proc. of AAMAS 2005: Autonomous Agents and Multi-Agent Systems, pp. 37–43. ACM, New York (2005)
6. Decker, K.S., Lesser, V.R.: Designing a family of coordination algorithms. In: Readings in Agents (1997)
7. Decker, K.: Environment Centered Analysis and design of Coordination Mechanisms. PhD thesis, University of Massachusetts, Amherst (May 1995)
8. Giampapa, J.A., Sycara, K.: Team-oriented agent coordination in the RETSINA multi-agent system. Tech. report CMU-RI-TR-02-34, Robotics Institute-Carnegie Mellon University (2002)
9. Ciger, J.: Collaboration with agents in VR environments. PhD thesis, École Polytechnique Fédérale de Lausanne (2005)

10. Grimaldo, F., Lozano, M., Barber, F., Orduña, J.: Integrating social skills in task-oriented 3D IVA. In: Panayiotopoulos, T., Gratch, J., Aylett, R.S., Ballin, D., Olivier, P., Rist, T. (eds.) IVA 2005. LNCS (LNAI), vol. 3661, Springer, Heidelberg (2005)
11. Conte, R., Castelfranchi, C.: Cognitive and Social Action. UCL Press, London (1995)
12. Hexmoor, H.: From inter-agents to groups. In: Proc. of ISAI 2001: International Symposium on Artificial Intelligence (2001)
13. Sichman, J., Demazeau, Y.: On social reasoning in multi-agent systems. Revista Ibero-Americana de Inteligencia Artificial 13, 68–84 (2001)
14. Falcone, R., Pezzulo, G., Castelfranchi, C., Calvi, G.: Why a cognitive trustier performs better: Simulating trust-based contract nets. In: Proc. of AAMAS 2004: Autonomous Agents and Multi-Agent Systems, pp. 1392–1393. ACM Press, New York (2004)
15. Grimaldo, F., Barber, F., Lozano, M.: An ontology-based approach for IVE+VA. In: Proc. of IVEVA 2006: Intelligent Virtual Environments and Virtual Agents (2006)
16. Viroli, M., Ricci, A., Omicini, A.: Operating instructions for intelligent agent co-ordination. The Knowledge Engineering Review 21, 49–69 (2006)
17. Kao, E.C.C., H-M., C.P., Chien, Y.H., Soo, V.W.: Using ontology to establish social context and support social reasoning. In: Panayiotopoulos, T., Gratch, J., Aylett, R.S., Ballin, D., Olivier, P., Rist, T. (eds.) IVA 2005. LNCS (LNAI), vol. 3661, Springer, Heidelberg (2005)
18. Giménez-Lugo, G., Sichman, J., Hübner, J.: Addressing the social components of knowledge to foster communitary exchanges. International Journal on Web Based Communities 1(2), 176–194 (2005)
19. Casare, S., Sichman, J.: Towards a functional ontology of reputation. In: Proc. of AAMAS 2005: Autonomous Agents and Multi-Agent Systems, ACM, New York (2005)
20. Bordini, R.H., da Rocha, A.C., Hübner, J.F., Moreira, A.F., Okuyama, F.Y., Vieira, R.: MAS-SOC: A social simulation platform based on agent-oriented programming. Journal of Artificial Societies and Social Simulation 8(3) (2005)
21. Ribeiro, M., da Rocha, A.C., Bordini, R.H.: A system of exchange values to support social interactions in artificial societies. In: Proc. of AAMAS 2003: Autonomous Agents and Multi-agent Systems, ACM Press, New York (2003)
22. Bordini, R.H., Hübner, J.F.: Jason (March 2007), Available at http://jason.sourceforge.net/

The Examination of an Information-Based Approach to Trust

Maaike Harbers[1], Rineke Verbrugge[2], Carles Sierra[3], and John Debenham[4]

[1] Institute of Information and Computing Sciences, Utrecht University, P.O. Box 80.089,
3508 TB Utrecht, The Netherlands
maaike@cs.uu.nl
[2] Institute of Artificial Intelligence, University of Groningen, Grote Kruisstraat 2/1,
9712 TS Groningen, The Netherlands
rineke@ai.rug.nl
[3] IIIA-CSIC, Campus UAB, 08193 Cerdanyola, Catalonia, Spain
sierra@iiia.csic.es
[4] Faculty of Information Technology, University of Technology, Sydney, P.O. Box 123,
Broadway, NSW 2007, Australia
debenham@it.uts.edu.au

Abstract. This article presents the results of experiments performed with agents based on an operalization of an information-theoretic model for trust. Experiments have been performed with the ART test-bed, a test domain for trust and reputation aiming to provide transparent and recognizable standards. An agent architecture based on information theory is described in the paper. According to a set of experimental results, information theory is shown to be appropriate for the modelling of trust in multi-agent systems.

1 Introduction

In negotiation, one tries to obtain a profitable outcome. But what is a profitable outcome: to pay little money for many goods of high quality? Although this seems to be a good deal, it might not always provide the most profitable outcome in the long run. If negotiation partners meet again in the future, it could be more rational to focus on the relationship with the other agents, to make them trust you and to build up a good reputation.

In computer science and especially in distributed artificial intelligence, many models of trust and reputation have been developed over the last years. This relatively young field of research is still rapidly growing and gaining popularity. The aim of trust and reputation models in multi-agent systems is to support decision making in uncertain situations. A computational model derives trust or reputation values from the agent's past interactions with its environment and possible extra information. These values influence the agent's decision-making process, in order to facilitate dealing with uncertain information.

Big differences can be found among current models of trust and reputation, which indicates the broadness of the research area. Several articles providing an overview of the field conclude that the research activity is not very coherent and needs to be more

J.S. Sichman et al. (Eds.): COIN 2007, LNAI 4870, pp. 71–82, 2008.
© Springer-Verlag Berlin Heidelberg 2008

unified [1,2,3,4]. In order to achieve that, test-beds and frameworks to evaluate and compare the models are needed.

Most present models of trust and reputation make use of game-theoretical concepts [1,5]. The trust and reputation values in these models are the result of utility functions and numerical aggregation of past interactions. Some other approaches use a cognitive model of reference, in which trust and reputation are made up of underlying beliefs. Castelfranchi and Falcone [6] developed such a cognitive model of trust, based on beliefs about competence, dependence, disposition, willingness and persistence of others. Most existing models of trust and reputation do not differentiate between trust and reputation, and if they do, the relation between trust and reputation is often not explicit [1,3]. The ReGreT system [7] is one of the few models of trust and reputation that does combine the two concepts. Applications of computational trust and reputation systems are mainly found in electronic markets. Several research reports have found that seller reputation has significant influences on on-line auction prices, especially for high-valued items [3]. An example is eBay, an online market place with a community of over 50 million registered users [2].

Sierra and Debenham [8] introduced an approach using information theory for the modeling of trust, which has been further developed in [9], [10]. The present article presents an examination of Sierra and Debenham's information-based approach to trust. Experiments have been performed with the ART test-bed [4], a test domain for trust and reputation. Section 2 introduces the trust model, section 3 describes the ART test-bed, and section 4 describes how the model has been translated into an agent able to participate in the ART test-bed. The remainder of the article gives an overview of the experiments (section 5) and the results (section 6), followed by a discussion (section 7). The article ends with conclusions and recommendations for further research (section 8).

2   The Information-Based Model of Trust

In Sierra and Debenham's information-based model, trust is defined as the measure of how uncertain the outcome of a contract is [8]. All possible outcomes are modelled and a probability is ascribed to each of them. More formally, agent α can negotiate with agent β and together they aim to strike a deal δ. In the expression $\delta = (a,b)$, a represents agent α's commitments and b represents β's commitments in deal δ. All agents have two languages, language C for communication and language L for internal representation. The language for communication consists of five illocutionary acts (Offer, Accept, Reject, Withdraw, Inform), which are actions that can succeed or fail. With an agent's internal language L, many different worlds can be constructed. A possible world represents, for example, a specific deal for a specific price with a specific agent.

To be able to make grounded decisions in a negotiation under conditions of uncertainty, the information-theoretic method denotes a probability distribution over all possible worlds. If an agent would not have any beliefs or knowledge, it would ascribe to all worlds the same probability to be the actual world. Often however, agents do have knowledge and beliefs which put constraints on the probability distribution. The agent's knowledge set K restricts *all worlds* to all *possible worlds*: that is, worlds that are consistent with its knowledge. Formally, a world v corresponds to a valuation function on the positive ground literals in the language, and is an element of the set of all possible worlds V. Worlds inconsistent with the agent's knowledge are not considered.

An agent's set of beliefs B determines its opinion on the probability of possible worlds: according to its beliefs some worlds are more probable to be the actual world than others. In a probability distribution over all possible worlds, W, a probability p_i expresses the degree of belief an agent attaches to a world v_i to be the actual world. From a probability distribution over all possible worlds, the probability of a certain sentence or expression in language L can be derived. For example the probability $P(executed \mid accepted)$ of whether a deal, once accepted, is going to be executed can be calculated. This derived sentence probability is considered with respect to a particular probability distribution over all possible worlds. The probability of a sentence σ is calculated by taking the sum of the probabilities of the possible worlds in which the sentence is true. For every possible sentence σ that can be constructed in language L the following holds: $P_{\{W|K\}}(\sigma) \equiv \Sigma_n\{p_n : \sigma$ is true in $v_n\}$. An agent has attached given *sentence probabilities* to every possible statement φ in its set of beliefs B.

A probability distribution over all possible worlds is consistent with the agent's beliefs if for all statements in the set of beliefs, the probabilities attached to the sentences are the same as the derived sentence probability. Expressed in a formula, for all beliefs φ in B the following holds: $B(\varphi) = P_{\{W|K\}}(\varphi)$. Thus, the agent's beliefs impose linear constraints on the probability distribution. To find the best probability distribution consistent with the knowledge and beliefs of the agent, *maximum entropy inference* (see [11]) uses the probability distribution that is maximally non-committal with respect to missing information. This distribution has maximum entropy and is consistent with the knowledge and beliefs. It is used for further processing when a decision has to be made.

When the agent obtains new beliefs, the probability distribution has to be updated. This happens according to the principle of *minimum relative entropy*. Given a prior probability distribution $\underline{q} = (q_i)_{i=1}^n$ and a set of constraints, the *principle of minimum relative entropy* chooses the posterior probability distribution $\underline{p} = (p_i)_{i=1}^n$ that has the least relative entropy with respect to $\underline{q}$, and that satisfies the constraints. In general, the relative entropy between probability distribution p and q is calculated as follows: $D_{RL}(p \parallel q) = \Sigma_{i=1}^n p_i \log_2 \frac{p_i}{q_i}$. The principle of minimum relative entropy is a generalization of the principle of maximum entropy. If the prior distribution $\underline{q}$ is uniform, the relative entropy of $\underline{p}$ with respect to $\underline{q}$ differs from the maximum entropy $H(\underline{p})$ only by a constant. So the principle of maximum entropy is equivalent to the principle of minimum relative entropy with a uniform prior distribution (see also [8]).

While an agent is interacting with other agents, it obtains new information. Sierra and Debenham [8] mention the following types of information from which the probability distribution can be updated:

- *Updating from decay and experience.* This type of updating takes place when the agent derives information from its direct experiences with other agents. It is taken into account that negotiating people or agents may forget about the behavior of a past negotiation partner.
- *Updating from preferences.* This updating is based on past utterances of a partner. If agent α prefers a deal with property Q_1 to a deal with Q_2, he will be more likely to accept deals with property Q_1 than with Q_2.

– *Updating from social information.* Social relationships, social roles and positions held by agents influence the probability of accepting a deal.

Once the probability distribution is constructed and up to date, it can be used to derive trust values. From an actual probability distribution, the trust of agent α in agent β at the current time, with respect to deal δ or in general, can be calculated. The trust calculation of α in β is based on the idea that the more the actual executions of a contract go in the direction of the agent α's preferences, the higher its level of trust. The relative entropy between the probability distribution of acceptance and the distribution of the observation of actual contract execution models this idea. For $T(\alpha, \beta, b)$, the trust of agent α in agent β with respect to the fulfillment of contract (a, b), the following holds:

$$T(\alpha, \beta, b) = 1 - \sum_{b' \in B(b)^+} P^t(b') \log \frac{P^t(b')}{P^t(b'|b)}$$

Here, $B(b)^+$ is the set of contract executions that agent α prefers to b. $T(\alpha, \beta)$, the trust of α in β in general, is the average over all possible situations. After making observations, updating the probability distribution and calculating the trust, the probability of the actual outcomes for a specific contract can be derived from the trust value and an agent can decide about the acceptance of a deal.

3   The ART Test-Bed

Participants in the ART test-bed [4] act as appraisers who can be hired by clients to deliver appraisals about paintings, each for a fixed client fee. Initially, a fixed number of clients is evenly distributed among appraisers. When a session proceeds, appraisers whose final appraisals were most accurate are rewarded with a larger share of the client base. Each painting in the test-bed has a fixed value, unknown to the participating agents. All agents have varying levels of expertise in different artistic eras (e.g. classical, impressionist, post-modern), which are only known to the agents themselves and which will not change during a game. To produce more accurate appraisals, appraisers may sell and buy opinions from each other. If an appraiser accepts an opinion request, it has to decide about how much time it wants to invest in creating an opinion. The more time (thus money) it spends in studying a painting, the more accurate the opinion.

However, agents might (on purpose) provide bad opinions or not provide promised opinions at all. Then without spending time on creating an opinion, the seller receives payment. So to prevent paying money for a useless opinion, the test-bed agents have to learn which agents to trust. To facilitate this process, agents can buy information about other agents' reputations from each other. Here again agents do not always tell the truth or provide valuable information.

Appraisers produce final appraisals by using their own opinion and the opinions received from other appraisers. An agent's final appraisal is calculated by the simulation, to ensure that appraisers do not strategize for selecting opinions after receiving all purchased opinions. The final appraisal $p*$ is calculated as a weighted average of received opinions: $p* = \frac{\sum_i (w_i \cdot p_i)}{\sum_i w_i}$. In the formula, p_i is the opinion p received from provider i and w_i is the appraiser's weight for provider i: the better α trusts an agent i, the higher the weight w_i attached to that agent and the more importance will be given to its opinion. Agent α determines its final appraisal by using all the opinions it received plus its own opinion. The true painting value t and the calculated final appraisal $p*$ are revealed by the simulation to the agent. The agent can use this information to revise its trust models of other participants.

4 An Information-Based Test-Bed Agent

The implemented test-bed agent ascribes probabilities to the accuracy of the opinions other agents provide. The agent maintains a probability distribution for each era of expertise with respect to each agent. The different possible worlds in a probability distribution represent the possible grades of the opinions an agent might provide in a specific era. An opinion of high grade means that the appraised value of a painting is close to the real value of the painting. A low grade means that the agent provides very bad opinions in the corresponding era or that the agent does not provide opinions at all. The quality of an opinion actually is a continuous variable, but to fit the model all possible opinions are grouped into ten levels of quality. The act of promising but not sending an opinion is classified in the lowest quality level.

The probability distributions are updated during the course of a session each time the agent receives new information, which can be of three types:

- Updating from direct experiences;
- Updating from reputation information;
- Updating from the evaporation of beliefs (forgetting).

Updating from reputation information corresponds to *Updating from social information* in Sierra and Debenham's model [8]. The other two types of updating are derived from *Updating from decay and experience* in the model.

Updating from direct experiences takes place when the agent receives the true values of paintings. The value of a constraint is obtained by taking the relative error of an opinion: the real value of a painting and an agent's estimated value of a painting are compared to each other. *Updating from reputation information* takes place when the agent receives witness information. The value of a constraint is derived by taking the average of the reputation values in all messages received at a specific time from trusted agents about a specific agent and era. *Updating from forgetting* is performed each time when a probability distribution is updated either from direct experiences or from reputation information.

Direct experiences and reputation information are translated into the same type of constraints. Such a constraint is for example: agent α will provide opinions with a quality of at least 7 in era e with a certainty of 0.6. This constraint is put to the probability distribution of agent α and era e. After updating from this constraint, the probabilities of the worlds 7, 8, 9 and 10 should together be 0.6. Constraints are always of the type opinions of *at least* quality x.

The value of a constraint (the quality grade) derived from a direct experience is obtained by comparing the real value of a painting to an agent's estimated value according to the equation: $constraintValue = 10 \cdot (1 - \frac{|appraisedValue - trueValue|}{trueValue})$. The outcome represents the quality of the opinion and a new constraint can be added to the set of beliefs. If a value lower than one is found, a constraint with the value of one is added to the set of beliefs. Reputation information is translated into a constraint by taking the average of the reputation values in all messages received at a specific time from trusted agents about a specific agent and era multiplied by ten: $constraintValue = 10 \cdot \Sigma_{r \in reps} \frac{r}{n_1}$, where r is a reputation value, $reps$ is the set of useful reputation values and n_1 is the size of $reps$.

With a set of constraints and the principle of maximum entropy, an actual probability distribution can be calculated. Therefore one general constraint is derived from all the stored constraints for calculating the probability distribution. The general constraint is a weighted average of all the constraints stored so far, calculated according to the following equation: $generalconstraintValue = \frac{1}{n_2} \cdot \Sigma_{c \in C} \frac{1}{(c(t_{obtained}) - t_{current}) + 1} \cdot c(value)$, where constraint c is an element of the set C of stored constraints and n_2 the total amount of constraints. Each constraint c consists of the time it was obtained $c(t_{obtained})$ and a quality grade $c(value)$, calculated with one of the formulas $constraintValue$ above. The outcome is rounded to get an integer value.

The constraints are weighted with a factor one divided by their age plus one (to avoid fractions with a zero in the denominator). Forgetting is modelled by giving younger constraints more influence on the probability distribution than older constraints. In this calculation, constraints obtained from reputation information are weighted with a factor which determines their importance in relation to constraints obtained from direct information. A ratio of 0.3:1, respectively, was taken because reputation info is assumed to have less influence than info from direct experiences. With the principle of maximum entropy, a new and updated probability distribution can be found.

Finally, when all information available has been processed and the probability distributions are up to date, trust values can be derived from the probability distributions. There are two types of trust, the trust of a particular agent in a specific era and the trust of a particular agent in general. The trust value of an agent in a specific era is calculated from the probability distribution of the corresponding agent and era. In an *ideal probability distribution*, the probability of getting opinions of the highest quality is very high and the probability of getting opinions with qualities lower than that is very low. Now trust can be calculated by taking one minus the relative entropy between the ideal and the actual probability distribution, as follows: $trust(agent, era) = 1 - \Sigma_{i=1}^{n_3} (P_{actual}(i) \cdot \log \frac{P_{actual}(i)}{P_{ideal}(i)})$, where n_3 is the number of probabilities. The trust of an agent in general is calculated by taking the average of the trust values of that agent in all the eras. At each moment of the game, the agent can consult its model to determine the trust value of an agent in general or the trust value of an agent with respect to a specific era. These trust values guide the behavior of the agent.

At the beginning of a new session the agent trusts all agents, so the probability distributions are initialized with all derived trust values (for each agent in each era) at 1.0. During the game the model is updated with new constraints and trust values change. The general behavior of the information-based agent is honest and cooperative towards the agents it trusts. The agent buys relevant opinions and reputation messages from all agents it trusts (with trust value 0.5 or higher). The agent only accepts and invests in requests from trusted agents, and if the agent accepts a request it provides the best possible requested information. If the agent does not trust a requesting agent, it informs the other agent by sending a decline message. If a trusted agent requests for reputation information, the agent provides the trust value its model attaches to the subject agent. If the agent trusts an agent requesting for opinions, it always highly invests in ordering opinions from the simulator for that agent. Finally, the agent uses the model for generating weights for calculating the final opinions. It weights each agent (including itself) according to the trust in that agent in that era.

5 Set-Up of the Experiments

To test the influences of the use of different types of information, four variations of an information-based agent have been made. The suffixes in the names of the agents indicate the information types they use for updating: *de* corresponds to direct experiences, *rep* to reputation information and *time* to forgetting.

- Agent *Info-de* only updates from direct experiences;
- Agent *Info-de-time* updates from direct experiences and from forgetting;
- Agent *Info-rep-time* updates from reputation information and forgetting;
- Agent *Info-de-rep-time* updates from all three types of information.

The performances of these agents in the ART test-bed are in the first place measured by their ability to make accurate appraisals, which is indicated by their client shares after the last game round. Besides, information about the agents' bank account balances will be presented. The use of each of the information types is expected to increase the average appraisal accuracy of an information-based test-bed agent. Moreover, the use of the combination of all three information types is expected to deliver the best results. In order to verify the correctness of these expectations, three test conditions have been designed and four extra agents have been implemented.

The **first condition** tests an agent's ability to distinguish between a cooperating and a non-cooperating agent. In this first part of the experiment, the agents *Info-de*, *Info-de-time* and *Info-de-rep-time* each participated in a game together with the test-agents *Cheat* and *Naive*. The test-agent *Cheat* never makes reputation or opinion requests itself, but when it receives requests it always promises to provide the requested reputation information or opinions. As its name suggests, the agent cheats on the other agents and it never sends any promised information. Its final appraisals are just based on its own expertise. The agent *Naive* bases its behavior on the idea that all agents it encounters are trustworthy and *Naive* keeps on trusting others during the whole course of a game. This agent always requests every other agent for reputation information and opinions, it accepts all requests from other agents and it highly invests in creating the requested opinions. Its final appraisals are based on its own expertise and on the (promised but sometimes not received) opinions of all other agents.

For the **second condition**, a third test-agent was developed to investigate other agents' ability to adapt to new situations. This agent *Changing* shows the same behavior as *Naive* during the first ten rounds of a game. Then it suddenly changes its strategy and from the eleventh game round till the end of the game it behaves exactly the same as the agent *Cheat*. The performances of the agents *Info-de* and *Info-de-time* in reaction to *Changing* have been examined.

The **third condition** was designed to examine the updating from reputation information. This type of updating is only of use if there are agents in the game that provide reputation information, so a reputation information providing agent *Providing* has been implemented. The only difference with *Info-de-time* is that the *Providing* agent always accepts reputation requests and provides the wished reputation information, whereas the agent *Info-de-time* only provides reputation to agents it trusts. The agents *Info-de-time*, *Info-rep-time* and *Info-de-rep-time* each participated in a game with *Providing*, *Cheat* and *Naive*.

6 Results

In the first experiment, each of the agents *Info-de*, *Info-de-time* and *Info-de-rep-time* participated in a test-bed game together with the agents *Cheat* and *Naive*. The graphics in Figure 1 show an example of a session with the agents *Info-de-time*, *Cheat* and *Naive*. Left the development of the agents' bank account balance during the whole game is shown. All agents have increasing balances, but *Info-de-time* ends the game with the most and *Naive* with the least money. The right part of the figure shows the average appraisal errors of the agents in each round. The appraisals of *Naive* are obviously less accurate than those of the other two agents. This can be explained by *Naive*'s behavior to keep on trusting the cheating agent during the whole game. *Info-de-time* provides its least accurate appraisals the first game round; there it still has to learn that it cannot trust the agent *Cheat*. After that, its appraisals are the most accurate: the errors are close to the zero line and show the least deviation. This can be explained by *Info-de-time* using the expertise of two agents (itself and *Naive*), whereas *Cheat* only uses its own expertise.

Table 1 shows the averages of 30 sessions for the three information-based agents in condition one. In the tables, Client refers to the final number of clients of an agent at

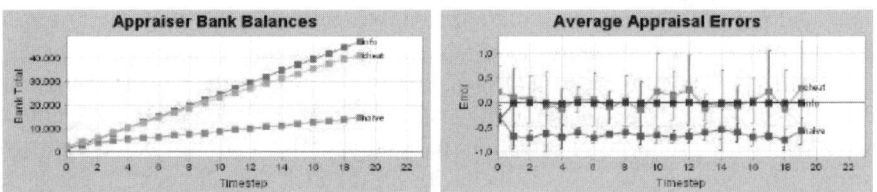

Fig. 1. Bank account balances and average appraisal errors of agents *Info-de-time* (black), *Cheat* (light grey) and *Naive* (dark grey) in the first test conditions

Table 1. Averages for three information-based agents in conditions of type one

	Cheat		Naive		Agent	
	Bank	Client	Bank	Client	Bank	Client
info-de	45957	24.5	14361	8.8	40700	26.4
info-de-time	47975	25.9	13552	8.8	40262	25.0
info-de-rep-time	46097	24.7	14073	8.2	41461	26.7

Table 2. Averages for the agent *Changing*

	Changing		Agent	
	Bank	*Client*	*Bank*	*Client*
info-de	44189	33.4	25817	6.6
info-de-time	36211	21.2	33864	18.8

Table 3. Averages for three information-based agents in the third set of conditions

	Cheat		Naive		Providing		Agent	
	Bank	*Client*	*Bank*	*Client*	*Bank*	*Client*	*Bank*	*Client*
info-de-time	43252	23.1	12986	10.6	34889	23.3	34245	22.7
info-rep-time	45337	22.3	15363	12.7	35337	23.5	28713	21.1
info-de-rep-time	41076	21.3	14089	10.8	34988	23.4	35099	24.5

the end of a session and Bank means its final bank account balance. The first row shows the average final bank account balance and average final number of clients of respectively, *Cheat*, *Naive* and *Info-de*, for the sessions in which the three of them participated together in the game. The second row displays the results of the sessions with *Cheat*, *Naive* and *Info-de-time*. Applying Student T-test (two-tailed, homoscedastic distribution) showed that with a significance level of 5% one can only conclude that *Info-de-rep-time* gathers a significantly bigger client share than *Info-de-time*. The differences in bank account balances between the different agents are not significant.

In the second condition *Info-de* and *Info-de-time* participate in a game with the agent *Changing*, which starts to cheat from the tenth round of the game. In contrast to *Info-de*, the agent *Info-de-time* does take forgetting into account. As time goes by, information gathered in the past becomes less and less important. The difference is clear: after a first big decrease in appraisal accuracy when the agent *Changing* starts cheating, *Info-de-time* learns from *Changing*'s new behavior and adjusts its trust values. Its past beliefs about a seemingly trustworthy agent *Changing* do not overrule the new information it gathers and it ends with higher scores. The averages of all the sessions with the agent *Changing* are presented in Table 2. Both client share and bank account balance of the two information-based agents are significantly different on a 5% level of significance according to the Student T-test. The results of the third condition, testing the update from reputation information, are shown in Table 3. A Student T-test demonstrates that all differences in client shares between the three tested agents are significant.

7   Discussion

It was expected that the experiments would show that each of the three types of updating would contribute to appraisal accuracy. Condition one shows that, except for *Info-de-time*, all agents updating from direct experiences provide more accurate appraisals than *Cheat* and *Naive*, which do not update from past experiences. The third condition of the experiment is even more convincing regarding the usefulness of information from experiences. Two information-based agents, one with and one without updating from direct experiences, were tested in the same condition. The agent that updated from direct experiences had a significantly larger final client share and therefore must have produced more accurate appraisals. Thus, the expectation that updating from direct experiences improves the appraisal accuracy is supported by the experimental results.

For evaluating updating from forgetting, the first two test conditions can be examined. Here two information-based agents updating from direct experiences, one of them also updating from forgetting, were tested in the same condition. In the condition with the agents *Cheat* and *Naive*, the agent *Info-de* scored better than *Info-de-time*, but the difference is not significant. In the condition with the agent *Changing*, the agent *Info-de-time* updating from forgetting, has a significant larger client share than *Info-de*. This supports the expectation that updating from forgetting would contribute to more accurate appraisals.

The last type of information, updating from reputation information, has been examined in the third condition. The participating agents are the information-based agent to be evaluated, combined with the three test-agents *Cheat*, *Naive*, and *Providing* which provides reputation information. The agent *Providing* performs very well, so the reputation information it provides is supposed to be useful. Agent *Info-rep-time* does not update from any of its own experiences, so its performance only depends on updating from reputation information. *Info-rep-time* ended with much larger client shares than *Naive*, so it seems to use *Providing*'s reputation information profitably. This observation supports the expectation that the use of reputation information would increase the average appraisal accuracy of an information-based test-bed agent. Of course this conclusion only holds when there is at least one agent in the game that is able and willing to provide useful reputation information.

The results show that all three types of updating contribute to appraisal accuracy, but do they also work well in combination? Updating from forgetting can be used in combination with the other two types of updating without hindering them. However, updating from information from direct experiences and from reputation information cannot be added to each other. When more reputation information is used, less information from direct experiences can be used and vice versa. The results show that in both condition one and three, the use of all available types of information yields the most accurate appraisals.

However, in the first condition *Naive* is the only agent providing reputation information and it assumes that each agent is trustworthy, so it always provides reputations with the value 1. So the good performance of the agent using reputation information in this condition cannot be due to its updating from reputation information. In the third condition however, useful reputation information is provided and the agent *Info-de-rep-time* seems to make good use of it. So the results support the expectation that all three types of updating contribute to providing more accurate appraisals, and the information-based agent using all three types of updating provides the most accurate appraisals.

The experiments performed are not exhaustive and when interpreting the results, some remarks should be kept in mind. First, an agent's performance depends a lot on the other participants in a test-bed game. For example, an agent with a very sophisticated model for dealing with reputation information only profits when other agents are prepared to provide reputation information. A cooperative agent functions very well with other cooperative participants, but it might perform very badly with non-cooperative participants. In the experiments, four test-agents were used, *Naive*, *Cheat*, *Changing* and *Providing*, which show quite simple and obvious behavior. The use of more complex test-agents would provide more information. Moreover, conditions with larger numbers of participants would create new situations and might yield extra information.

A second consideration is the choice of the ART test-bed. A general problem of all test-beds is *validity*: does the system test what it is supposed to test? Especially when complicated concepts are involved, it is difficult to prove that a test-bed just examines the performance of a model on that particular concept. The aim of the ART test-bed is to compare and evaluate trust- and reputation-modeling algorithms [4]. But what do the developers exactly understand by trust and reputation? The ART test-bed is quite complicated and allows so many variables that it is sometimes difficult to explain why something happened.

A final remark about the experiments is that in the translation of the trust model to a test-bed agent some adjustments and adaptations had to be made. Not every part of the model can be used in the ART test-bed. Sierra and Debenham's model [8] allows updating from preferences and different power relations between agents; these facets cannot be tested by the ART test-bed. On the other hand, the trust model lacks theory for some topics needed in the ART test-bed. The updating from reputation was not very elaborated in the model [8] and had to be extended. Besides, the information-based trust model does not provide a negotiation strategy: it is a system to maintain values of trust. The strategy used might have influenced the test results.

8 Conclusion and Further Research

The goal of this article is to examine Sierra and Debenham's information-based model for trust [8]. Therefore, an agent based on the model has been implemented and several experiments in the ART test-bed have been performed. The experiments showed that the information-based agent learned about its opponents during a game session and could distinguish between cooperating and non-cooperating agents. They also demonstrated that the three examined types of updating (from direct experiences, from reputation information and from the evaporation of beliefs as time goes by), all improved the agent. So in general expectations have been met: the results are promising and the information-based approach seems to be appropriate for the modeling of trust.

The diversity and the amount of the experiments could be extended. The information-based agent could be tested in more conditions with different test agents and with larger amounts of participating agents. It would also be interesting to pay more attention to the agent's strategy. Besides, the implementation of the agent could be improved. Some aspects of the trust model could be translated more literally to the implementation of the information-based agent. Even another test-bed could be used, as the ART test-bed is not able to evaluate all aspects of the theory. All these suggestions would deliver new information about the model and would justify making stronger statements about it.

As to Sierra and Debenham's trust model itself [8,9], its core seems to be robust and clear: they use a clear definition of trust and probability distributions are updated from a set of beliefs with the principle of minimum relative entropy. The experiments support the model. To further improve it, more work could be done on other concepts related to trust. For example, now it provides some initial ideas about how to deal with reputation and other types of social information. But social aspects are becoming more and more central in the field of multi-agent systems lately, so a contemporary model of trust should give a complete account of it. So, it can be said conclusively that the core of the model seems to be a good approach, but for a fully developed approach to trust and reputation more work should be done. This should not be a problem, because the model is flexible and provides ample space for extensions.

Acknowledgements. Carles Sierra's research is partially supported by the Open-Knowledge STREP project, sponsored by the European Commission under contract number FP6-027253, and partially by the Spanish project "Agreement Technologies" (CONSOLIDER CSD2007-0022, INGENIO 2010).

References

1. Sabater, J., Sierra, C.: Review on computational trust and reputation models. Artificial Intelligence Review 24, 33–60 (2005)
2. Jøsang, A., Ismail, R., Boyd, C.: A survey of trust and reputation systems for online service provision. Decision Support Systems 43, 618–644 (2007)
3. Mui, L., Mohtashemi, M., Halberstadt, A.: Notions of reputation in multi-agents systems: A review. In: AAMAS 2002: Proceedings of the First International Joint Conference on Autonomous Agents and Multiagent Systems, pp. 280–287. ACM Press, New York (2002)
4. Fullam, K., Klos, T., Muller, G., Sabater, J., Topol, Z., Barber, K.S., Rosenschein, J.: A specification of the agent reputation and trust (ART) testbed: Experimentation and competition for trust in agent societies. In: F.D. et al. (ed.) Fifth International Conference on Autonomous Agents and Multiagent systems (AAMAS 2005), Utrecht, The Netherlands, pp. 512–518 (2005)
5. Ramchurn, S.D., Huynh, D., Jennings, N.R.: Trust in multiagent systems. Knowledge Engineering Review 19, 1–25 (2004)
6. Castelfranchi, C., Falcone, R.: Principles of trust for MAS: Cognitive anatomy, social importance, and quantification. In: Demazeau, Y. (ed.) Proceedings of the Third International Conference of Multi-agent Systems (ICMAS 1998), pp. 72–79 (1998)
7. Sabater, J., Sierra, C.: REGRET: reputation in gregarious societies. In: AGENTS 2001: Proceedings of the Fifth International Conference on Autonomous Agents, pp. 194–195. ACM Press, New York (2001)
8. Sierra, C., Debenham, J.: An information-based model for trust. In: F.D. et al. (ed.) Fifth International Conference on Autonomous Agents and Multiagent systems (AAMAS 2005), Utrecht, The Netherlands, pp. 497–504 (2005)
9. Sierra, C., Debenham, J.: Trust and honour in information-based agency. In: Stone, P., Weiss, G. (eds.) Proceedings Fifth International Conference on Autonomous Agents and Multi Agent Systems (AAMAS 2006), Hakodate, Japan, pp. 1225–1232. ACM Press, New York (2006)
10. Sierra, C., Debenham, J.: Information-based agency. In: Proceedings of Twentieth International Joint Conference on Artificial Intelligence (IJCAI 2007), Hyderabad, India (2007)
11. MacKay, D.: Information Theory, Inference and Learning Algorithms. Cambridge University Press, Cambridge (2003)

A Dynamic Coordination Mechanism Using Adjustable Autonomy

Bob van der Vecht[1,2], Frank Dignum[2], John-Jules Ch. Meyer[2], and Martijn Neef[1]

[1] TNO Defence, Safety and Security, The Hague
{bob.vandervecht,martijn.neef}@tno.nl
[2] Department of Information and Computing Sciences, Universiteit Utrecht, Utrecht
{dignum,jj}@cs.uu.nl

Abstract. Agents in an organization need to coordinate their actions in order to reach the organizational goals. This research describes the relation between types of coordination and the autonomy of actors. In an experimental setting we show that there is not one best way to coordinate in all situations. The dynamics and complexity of, for example, crisis situations require a crisis management organization to work with dynamic types of coordination. In order to reach dynamic coordination we provide the actors with adjustable autonomy. Actors should be able to make decisions at different levels of autonomy and reason about the required level. We propose a way to implement this in a multi-agent system. The agent is provided with reasoning rules with which it can control the external influences on its decision-making.

1 Introduction

The motivation of this research lies in coordination challenges for crisis management organizations. Crisis situations in general are complex and share environmental features; there is no complete information, the evolvement of the situation is unpredictable and quick response is required. A crisis management organization should control the crisis as fast as possible, and therefore, it should be able to cope with such situations. For an adequate, quick response the organization needs high control. At the same time the organization needs to be able to adapt to unexpected events and therefore it needs to be dynamic and robust.

In this paper we describe different ways of coordination, and show that there is not one best way to coordinate in all situations. When modelling the decision-making process of the actors we see that there is always a trade-off between local autonomy and global control. In this paper we describe levels of autonomy in decision-making of actors, and we propose a way to implement adjustable autonomy in artificial actors in order to achieve a dynamic coordination mechanism.

In Sect. 2 we argue why we need dynamic coordination mechanisms in multi-agent systems. We describe the relation between types of coordination and the autonomy of actors. Using an experiment we point out the strong and the weak points

J.S. Sichman et al. (Eds.): COIN 2007, LNAI 4870, pp. 83–96, 2008.
© Springer-Verlag Berlin Heidelberg 2008

of different coordination types. In Sect. 3 we define agent autonomy and we introduce adjustable autonomy as a concept that allows dynamically switching between coordination types. Section 4 proposes a way to implement adjustable autonomy in agents. We extend the experiment with an implementation of adjustable autonomy. After that, Sect. 5 discusses our results and describes future research.

2   Why Dynamic Coordination?

In this section we argue why dynamic coordination mechanisms are relevant to achieve coordinated behavior in multi-agent systems. We discuss different types of coordination and their relation with the autonomy of the actors. Using an experiment we point out the weak and strong points of the coordination types and show that a static coordination mechanism is not optimal in all situations.

2.1   Autonomy and Coordination

All organizations designed for a certain purpose require coordinated behavior of the participants. There are several approaches to reach coordination, ranging from emergent coordination to explicit coordination by strict protocols. At the same time the actors in an organization are seen as autonomous entities that make their own decisions. In this paragraph we investigate the relation between autonomy of actors and coordination of behavior.

Autonomy is one of the key features of agents. It is often being used in the definition of agents [1]. In Jennings' use of the term, agent autonomy means that agents have control over both their internal state and over their behavior. The agent determines its beliefs and it decides by itself upon its actions. Multi-agent systems consist of multiple autonomous actors that interact to reach a certain goal. We will first take a closer look at coordination mechanisms for multi-agent systems.

One approach to reach coordinated group behavior is *emergent coordination*. Autonomous actors perform their tasks independently and the interaction between many of them leads to coordinated behavior. This approach is often used for agent-based social simulations. One characteristic of emergent coordination is that the actors have no awareness of the goals of the organization they are part of. The actors make their own local decisions and are fully autonomous. Although the actors have no organizational awareness, the designer of such a system has. The coordination principles are specified implicitly within the local reasoning of all actors. The organization is relatively flexible within the single task for which it has been designed. However, in the extreme case, the agents are fully autonomous, and there is no point of control that can force the organization to change its behavior if unexpected situations occur that cannot be solved by the local reasoning rules of the actors.

Where the fully emergent approach is one extreme type of coordination, the other extreme is fully *controlled coordination*. This is the case in a hierarchical organization, where there is a single point of control that determines the tasks all the others have to perform. The actors are autonomous in performing their task, but they do not make their own decisions. Therefore, the actors do not meet the autonomy definition as used in [1].

A characteristic of such a centralistic approach is that the task division is made from a global perspective. Therefore an organization can adapt quickly to changes in the environment by sending out new orders to all actors. However, such an organization is sensitive to incomplete information. Wrong information at the global level can lead to wrong decisions. Furthermore, the organization is highly dependent on the decision maker at the top of the hierarchy and it misses the flexibility at the local level. Fully controlled coordination can be a good solution if there is always complete information about the situation. Task specifications and interaction protocols can be defined for all possible cases.

In between the two extreme types there are several ways to achieve coordination. For example, the designer can allow the agents to communicate and exchange information. Or he can divide the organizational task in roles, and define the interaction in protocols. Several methodologies for multi-agent systems design, e.g. Opera [2], use this approach. Drawback here is that the specified coordination framework are static. There is no flexibility within the predefined roles and interactions.

2.2   Experiment

We have set up an experimental environment in which we can test the characteristics of coordination principles. A simple coordination task is performed by an organization, and different scenarios contain situational features that can reveal the strong and the weak points of each coordination mechanism.

Organizational Description. The basic setting is a Firefighter organization. The organization operates in a world where fires appear that need to be extinguished as fast as possible. In the organization we define two roles; *coordinator* and *firefighter*. The coordinator makes a global plan and tells the firefighters which fire they should extinguish. Therefore the coordinator has a global view of the whole world. The firefighters perform the actual tasks in the world; they move to a fire location and extinguish the fires. They have only local views.

There is a hierarchical relation between the two roles, the coordinator is superior of the firefighters and can send orders to the firefighters, which fire they have to extinguish. We want to show different forms of coordination within this organization. In our imlementation we achieve this by changing the autonomy level of the decision-making process of the firefighters. We have created different types of firefighters; obedient agents that follow the orders of their superior (no decision-making autonomy) and disobedient agents that ignore their superior and make their decisions only based on local observations. Now we can describe the coordination types:

- *Emergent coordination*: Disobedient firefighters, choices are made based on local information
- *Explicit coordination*: Obedient firefighters, choices are made based on global information

The performance of the organization should be measurable. In our experiment we can measure the time it takes to extinguish the fires for each of the coordination types. The best organizational performance has the lowest score.

Scenarios. We will describe the scenarios in more detail. The organization in our experiment has one coordinator and four firefighters. The start position of the firefighters in the world is equally distributed. We have one standard scenario, scenario A, in order to test whether both coordination types perform equally well. In this scenario four fires are distributed equally over the world. The start situation of scenario A is shown in Fig. 1.

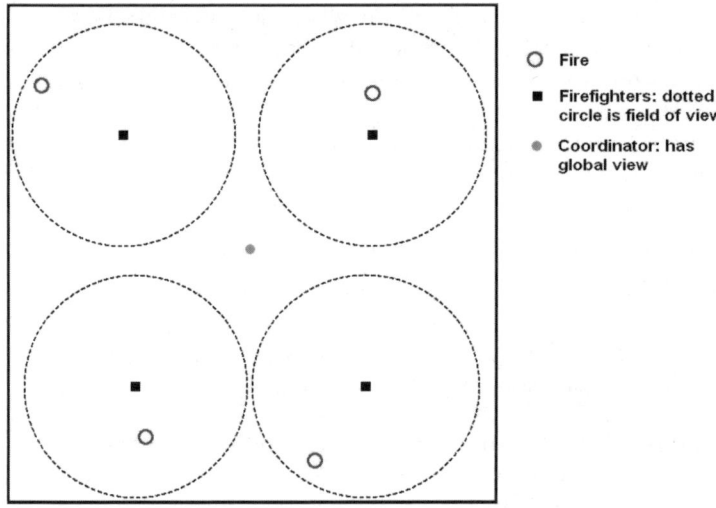

Fig. 1. Screenshot of the experimental environment: begin situation of scenario A

Two other scenarios have been created that make this situation more complex. They contain the features that also return in real world situations. Scenario B is a setting where the fires are distributed equally over the world, but the coordinator has no global view, he can only see half of the world at once. As result there is no complete information at the global level. The third scenario, Scenario C, reflects a situation where the fires are not distributed equally, such that some firefighters do not observe any fires, whereas others observe several fires.

Results. The results of the experiment are shown in Table 1. The score is calculated by thenumber of time steps it takes until all fires have been extinguished. It is measured per scenario and coordination type. Scenario A shows no significant difference in the performance of both organizations. This is our standard scenario that shows that both coordination mechanisms work. In scenario B the firefighters reach a better performance based on their local information than the

Table 1. Results of our Experiment; time (s) until all fires are extinguished per scenario and coordination type

	Explicit Coordination: No Autonomy	Emergent coordination: Full Autonomy
Scenario A: Standard scenario	38.7	36.8
Scenario B: No complete global information	66.6	36.8
Scenario C: No equal distribution of fires	69.8	93.8

coordinator based on its information. The coordinator has no complete knowledge, and therefore he might miss important information for his planning task. In scenario C the fires were not equally distributed. The global information of the coordinator was more useful than the local information of the firefighters, because the coordinator's commands sent the firefighters to the fires. In the emergent organization not all firefighters could see the fires, which made them inactive.

The difference between the two organizations was that the decisions were made at a different level of the organization and based on different information. Both perform well in specific situations, none of them proved to be sufficient for all situations. We can conclude that in a scenario with a dynamic environment in which the agents experience these situations successively, both coordination types perform badly because of the weak points that are pointed out in the previous scenarios. In that case the best organization would be one that dynamically switches between the coordination mechanisms.

2.3 Dynamic Coordination

From our experiment, we can conclude that a dynamic coordination mechanism can outperform the presented organizations in a dynamic environment. In each coordination mechanism mentioned in Sect. 2.1 the autonomy of the actors with respect to the organization is fixed. We want to achieve dynamic coordination by allowing the agents to make local decisions about their autonomy level. We want them to act following organizational rules, but also allow them to decide not to follow the rules in specific situations. We believe that organizations in complex environments can benefit from agents that show *adjustable autonomy*. In the next paragraph we define adjustable autonomy in more detail and propose a way to achieve this in artificial agents.

3   Adjustable Autonomy

In this section we explain the concept of adjustable autonomy. Recall the autonomy requirement for agents as it is used by [1]. It states that agents should have control over their internal state and their behavior. We have argued that this conflicts with the extreme form of explicit coordination. The agents just follow orders and they do not determine their own actions.

We will take a closer look at agent decision-making. We believe that the decision-making process can take place at different levels of autonomy. An autonomous agent should be able to select its style of decision-making. This process is what we call *adjustable autonomy*. In this section we define levels of autonomy in agent decision-making and we propose a way to implement adjustable autonomy in agents.

3.1 Autonomy Levels in Agent Decision-Making

The difference between the two agent types in the experiment, obedient and disobedient, was the knowledge they used for their own decision-making. With autonomous decision-making the agent makes its own decisions based on its own observations, disregarding information and orders from other agents. The other extreme is that agents perform only commands that are given, and do not choose their actions based on their own knowledge.

The degree of autonomy of decision making can be defined as the degree of intervention by other agents on the decision making process of one agent [3]. Using this definition, the disobedient agent from our experiment makes its decisions autonomously, whereas the obedient agent had no autonomy at all concerning the decision making. An agent that switches between different levels of autonomy of its decision-making shows adjustable autonomy. We propose a reasoning model in which different levels of autonomy can be implemented.

3.2 Controlling Autonomy

An agent's level of autonomy is determined by the influence of other agents on the decision-making process. Adjustable autonomy implies that the level of autonomy in the decision-making process can be adjusted. Therefore, an agent should control external influences that it experiences. The agent should choose which knowledge it uses for its decision-making. Figure 2 shows the reasoning process of an agent schematically. The module for event-processing precedes the actual decision making and it determines the level of autonomy of the decision-making process.

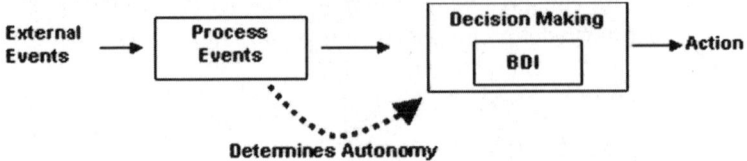

Fig. 2. The adjustable autonomy module within the reasoning process

In the reasoning model the agent is provided with a module that gives the agent control over external influences. These external influences are the agent's own observations and messages that it gets from other agents. The agent can make an explicit choice about the knowledge that it will use for its decision-making process.

3.3   Related Work on Adjustable Autonomy

The topics *agent autonomy* and *adjustable autonomy* have been subject of many studies. However, there is no common definition of autonomy. As a result, the approaches taken to describe its features are quite distinct. We discuss the concept of autonomy and the way it is used in related work. And we investigate what adjustability is in the different perspectives that are taken. We will relate the other views on autonomy with our own view.

Castelfranchi and Falcone, [4] [5], have investigated autonomy in the context of (social) relations between agents. Considering a hierarchical relation, the abstraction level of decision-making of the delegate determines the agent's level of autonomy with respect to the master. Levels of autonomy they distinguish are *executive autonomy* (agent is not allowed to decide anything but the execution of delegated task), *planning autonomy* (agent is allowed to plan (partially), the delegated task is not fully specified) and *goal autonomy* (agent is allowed to find its own goals). Verhagen, [6], has added *norm autonomy* as an extra level, where the agent is allowed to formulate its own organizational norms.

Adjustable autonomy is the process of switching between the abstraction levels of decision making. The autonomy levels as presented above concern goals, actions, plans and norms. We believe that also *beliefs* should be part of the autonomy definition, since beliefs are another concept used in the reasoning process. If an agent does not control its own beliefs, it can hardly be called autonomous. In our definition the autonomy level is gradually related to the influence an agent allows on its decision-making process. We propose reasoning rules to control external influences that capture explicit knowledge for reasoning about autonomy.

Schurr et al. [7] and Tambe et al. [8] use the term adjustable autonomy for the process in which a decision maker transfers the control of the decision-making process to another agent (or human). The researchers do not give a definition of autonomy, but it is related to decision-making control with respect to a certain goal. A coordination mechanism that runs independent of the agent's decision-making, handles the transfer-of-control (t-o-c) process. A t-o-c strategy consists of a list of decision makers and the constraints for transferring the control. An agent's position in the list of decision-makers determines an agent's level of autonomy with respect to the goal. They do not use autonomy as a gradual property of the decision-making process of the agent itself. Their reasoning mechanism for adjustable autonomy can only be used when there are more agents that have the capability to making the decision. The mechanism should make sure the optimal decision maker is selected.

In contrast, our approach focuses on the decision-making process of a single agent. The agent should select the optimal input (beliefs, goals, plans) for its own reasoning process. Those resources determine the autonomy level of a reasoning process. We look at adjustable autonomy as a process within an agent's reasoning, whereas they view it as a separate mechanism.

Barber and Martin, [9], look at the decision-making process of a group of agents. An agent's level of autonomy with respect to a task is measured as its share in the group decision-making process. In their context adjustable autonomy concerns different decision-making strategies for a group of agents. They present an Adaptive Decision-Making Framework, in which agents propose strategies to the group, and therewith change their own autonomy level. This way, adjustable autonomy becomes a group process, because other agents can accept or reject proposed decision-making strategies.

The focus of Barber and Martin is on the decision-making process of a group of agents. In contrast, our focus is on the decision-making of a single agent. In our work, adjustment of the autonomy is a local process within the agent's reasoning process. Furthermore Barber and Martin do not specify how an agent can determine the right decision-making strategies. In the experiments they conducted they provided the agents with knowledge about the best strategy for each situation. We want the agents to reason about what the best strategy is, based on local observations.

Dastani et al., [10], argue that the deliberation cycle of an agent determines autonomy of an agent as well. Autonomy levels can be viewed at as an agent's commitment to its own decisions. For example, one deliberation cycle makes that an agent commits to a goal until it has been fulfilled, whereas another cycle makes an agent to reconsider its goals every time it receives new information. They propose a meta-language to describe the deliberation cycle of an agent. The functions used in the deliberation cycle as well as their actual implementation are relevant for agent autonomy. Levels of autonomy can be constructed changing the deliberation cycle.

In their approach, levels of autonomy are determined by the deliberation cycle, and therefore by the way decisions are made. Our approach focuses on the sources that are used for decision-making and on the process of how an agent determines its autonomy level. The two approaches can exists next to each other and complement each other.

As we see in this discussion of related work there is not a single definition of agent autonomy and adjustable autonomy. Sometimes autonomy and adjustable autonomy is viewed in the context of group decision-making, whereas others look at single agent decision-making. Furthermore different aspects of agent decision-making are taken into account, such as decision-making control or abstraction levels of decision-making. Our approach is to give the agent control over the external influences it experiences.

4   Agent Reasoning Model

Here we present a reasoning model for agents that enables the agent to control its autonomy level. The level of autonomy depends on the influence of other agents on the reasoning process. In the reasoning-process we distinguish a phase for event-processing and a phase for decision-making, as shown in Fig. 2. The event-processing phase gives the agent control over its autonomy. The decision phase focuses on the decision on action. We describe the implementation of the two phases, starting with the latter one.

4.1 Decision Making

In the decide-phase the agent will decide upon the next action. A popular approach for goal-directed reasoning is to use of Beliefs, Desires and Intentions (BDI), introduced by Rao and Georgeff [11]. Several BDI reasoning-models have been proposed. For example, 3APL [12], [13] provides the designer with a formalized programming language which is designed for BDI-agent programming. A 3APL agent uses reasoning rules to create plans to reach a certain goal. Such reasoning rules have the following form:

```
<HEAD> <- <GUARD> | <BODY>
```

The head of a rule should match the goals of an agent. The guard should match the beliefs of the agent. The body of the agent contains sets of actions. If head and body match, the agent can commit to the plan in the body and start to execute it.

The firefighters in our experiment have been implemented using 3APL. They have a goal to fight fires and they have reasoning rules to make a plan in order to reach their goal. Figure 3 shows the source code of the decision phase. If a firefighter agent has a certain fire selected, it is going to extinguish that fire. Depending on the distance to this fire, they will perform either the action *GoTo* or *Extinguish*. If no fire is selected, the agent will wait.

```
GOALBASE:
    fightFires()
RULEBASE:
    fightFires() <- SelectedFire(Fire) | extinguishFire(Fire)
    fightFires() <- TRUE | Wait()

    extinguishFire(FIRE) <- distance(Fire, D) |
        BEGIN
            IF D < 20
            THEN Extinguihs(FIRE)
            ELSE GoTo(FIRE)
        END
```

Fig. 3. Source code of 3APL plan to fight fires

Each decision of the agent takes depends on its beliefs. The beliefs that are used in this plan are: *selectedFire* and *distance*. These beliefs are determined before the plan reasoning starts. Therefore we describe the event-processing phase, which prepares the actual decicion-making phase.

4.2   Event Processing

In the event-processing phase the agent prepares the decision-making phase. External influences are processed here. External influence can be an agent's observations or messages from other agents. We have chosen to implement the orient phase using 3APL rules as well. This gives us the opportunity to reason with semantic knowledge. The main process consists of three functions: *handle observations*, *handle messages*, and *prepare decision-making*.

The autonomy level of the decide phase is determined by those functions. Will the agent follow the commands from the coordinator, or will it create own goals? Does the agent adopt information from the coordinator, or does it use its own observations? We show how we can implement reasoning rules that provide the agent with choices. We will take the firefighters from our experiment as example.

Handle Observations. Reasoning rules can be added to make the agent choose to handle observations differently. We gave one rule to our firefighters, which states that is believes all its own observations:

```
handleObservations() <- TRUE | Observations2Beliefs()
```

Our firefighters use only this rule for observation processing. It is possible too add more rules that distinguish between different situations. To use the rule, the guard of the rule has to match with the beliefs of the agent. Adding rules with a specified guard, the agent handles its observations differently if that guard is true.

Handle Messages. Agents can receive messages from other agents. An agent can be programmed to handle messages in different ways by adding the same types of rules. If an agent functions in an organization, it needs to know how to deal with relations towards other agents. We have implemented the following rule for a hierarchical relation. When the agent gets a request from another agent who is his superior, he interprets the content as a command.

```
handleMessages() <- message(SENDER, request, CONTENT)
   AND superior(CONTENT) | AcceptCommand(SENDER, CONTENT)
```

The firefighters believe that the coordinator is their superior. They will process the requests of the coordinator as commands. In a similar manner other rules that can be defined. For example, an agent can have a rule to ignore all messages when it feels it is in danger.

```
handleMessages() <- danger() | ignoreMessages()
```

If an agent has both rules for message handling it is dependent on the agent whether it processes messages or not. Does the agent perceive danger or not? By adding such a rule, local beliefs of the agent can change the way it handles external influences, and therefore it can influence the autonomy level of the agents' decision-making.

Prepare Decision-Making. Finally, in the function *prepare decision-making* rules are specified that determine the autonomy level of the agent. The reasoning rules in the decide-phase use certain beliefs. Here we specify per goal what kind of belief processing should take place. Recall from Fig. 3 that the beliefs that are used for the goal to fight fires are *selectedFire* and *distance*. We have specified the following rules:

```
prepareDecisionMaking() <- goal(fightfires) AND
    command(FIRE) | SelectFire(FIRE); CalculateDistance(FIRE)

prepareDecisionMaking() <- goal(fightfires) AND noCommand()
    AND seeFire(FIRE) | SelectFire(FIRE); GetDistance(FIRE)
```

These two rules specify how the beliefs for the decision-making process are determined dependent on the situations. The *SelectFire* and *CalculateDistance* statements are capabilities of the agent that construct the selectedFire and the distance belief respectively. The variable given to those functions has a different origin in both cases. If the agent has a command, he will follow the command. If there is no command, but the agent sees a fire, it will use this observation for further reasoning.

5   Extending the Experiment

We have extended the experiment of Sect. 2. We have constructed a third organization with firefighters that show adjustable autonomy. They are at certain moments disobedient to the commands of the coordinator and at other moments they follow the orders, depending on their local beliefs. So, the organization can switch between explicit coordination and emergent coordination. We have implemented reasoning rules for event processing, we have used the same rules as presented in the Sect. 4.2. The rules ensure that the agents follow the commands, but if there are no commands they will pursue their goal using local observations.

5.1   Results

We have run all three scenarios as well with our dynamic coordination mechanism. Table 2 shows the results next to the static coordination mechanisms.

Table 2. Results of our Experiment, including adjustable autonomy

	Explicit Coordination: No Autonomy	Emergent coordination: Full Autonomy	Dynamic Coordination: Adjustable Autonomy
Scenario A	38.7	36.8	37.0
Scenario B	66.6	36.8	37.1
Scenario C	69.8	93.8	70.2

We can see that the organization with agents that use adjustable autonomy performs well in all scenarios compared to the other two organizations. The agents in the organization adapt the coordination mechanism based on the environmental features.

From the experiment we can conclude that dynamic coordination is powerful in agent organizations. The organization using dynamic coordination performs as good as the best of the other organizations. Furthermore the organization using adjustable autonomy will perform well in dynamic scenarios, since it continuously adapt its coordination mechanism.

The way we achieve a dynamic coordination mechanism, is by letting the agents adjust their autonomy level. The agents have reasoning rules to control external influences in the reasoning process. The agents decide locally on their autonomy level.

5.2   Discussion

We provide the agents with reasoning rules to control external influences. This gives the agents additional, task-unspecific knowledge that it can use in its reasoning process. It allows the agent to use its beliefs and its goals to reason about its openness towards other agents. The reasoning rules make use of criteria based on *introspection*, *social knowledge*, or *coordination requirements*.

Using introspection, the agent assesses its own mental state. Castelfranchi, [4], argues the importance of introspection in the reasoning process. For example, *relevance of information* can be determined by introspection. Certain information can be more or less relevant depending on an agent's goals. Therefore an agent may observe the world differently depending on its goals.

An agent may have a reasoning rule that makes the agent react differently to external input when it feels danger than when it feels at ease. To make such adaptive behavior possible, the agent also needs to have the capability to determine when it is in danger.

Social and organizational knowledge are other examples of criteria that can be used to control external influences. The importance of explicitly modelling organizational awareness for coordination is argued by Oomes [14]. For example, knowledge about the sender of a message is useful when deciding what to do with the content. If we assume that an organization is implemented following a methodology as Opera [2], organizational concepts are available in the beliefbase. By using them in reasoning rules for influence control, we add the social knowledge to the reasoning process of the agents. The use of *trust* between agents can be modelled in the same way.

The third example of knowledge that can be used for autonomy adjustment is knowledge about coordination requirements. Given that an agent acts in a coordination mechanism, it can encounter environmental changes that influence the coordination. For example, if an agent follows orders from a superior and the communication fails at a certain moment, it can choose to increase its autonomy in order to fulfill the goals.

We will conduct more experiments to develop general heuristics that an agent can use to control external influences. Using those heuristics in the reasoning rules for event processing, we want to combine single-agent decision-making and multi-agent interaction to develop dynamic coordination mechanisms.

6 Conclusion

There are several ways to achieve coordination within an agent organization. The approaches range from emergent coordination, where the actors are autonomous and the coordination is implicitly implemented, to explicit coordination, such as a hierarchical organization where the actors have no decision autonomy but just follow the orders from their superiors. We have shown that there is not one best way to coordinate in all situations. Complex and dynamic situations therefore require a dynamic coordination mechanism.

We have implemented a dynamic coordination mechanism by providing the actors with adjustable autonomy. An agent's level of autonomy depends on the influence of others on the reasoning process. The actors have reasoning rules that control the external influences they experience. This way we have shown some situations in which the actor can change its autonomy level based on local knowledge. The agent uses the knowledge about event processing in its reasoning process in addition to the task specific domain knowledge.

Further research should lead to more understanding about relevant knowlegde for event processing. We want to develop general heuristics with which the agent can determine its level of autonomy by controlling external influences.

References

1. Jennings, N.R.: On agent-based software engineering. Artificial Intelligence 117(2), 277–296 (2000)
2. Dignum, V.: A Model for Organizational Interaction: based on Agents, founded in Logic. Utrecht University, PhD Thesis (2004)
3. Barber, K.S., Martin, C.E.: Dynamic adaptive autonomy in multi-agent systems: Representation and justification. International Journal of Pattern Recognition and Artificial Intelligence 15(3), 405–433 (2001)
4. Castelfranchi, C.: Guarantees for autonomy in cognitive agent architecture. Intelligent Agents (890), 56–70 (1995)
5. Falcone, R., Castelfranchi, C.: The human in the loop of a delegated agent: the theory of adjustable social autonomy. IEEE Transactions on Systems, Man, and Cybernetics, Part A 31(5), 406–418 (2001)
6. Verhagen, H.: Norm Autonomous Agents. Stockholm University, PhD Thesis (2000)
7. Schurr, N., Marecki, J., Lewis, J., Tambe, M., Scerri, P.: The defacto system: Training tool for incident commanders. In: AAAI, pp. 1555–1562 (2005)
8. Tambe, M., Scerri, P., Pynadath, D.: Adjustable autonomy for the realworld. Journal of Artificial Intelligence Research (17), 171–228 (2002)

9. Martin, C.E., Barber, K.S.: Adaptive decision-making frameworks for dynamic multi-agent organizational change. Autonomous Agents and Multi-Agent Systems 13(3), 391–428 (2006)
10. Dastani, M., Dignum, F., Meyer, J.J.C.: Autonomy and agent deliberation. In: Nickles, M., Rovatsos, M., Weiß, G. (eds.) AUTONOMY 2003. LNCS (LNAI), vol. 2969, pp. 114–127. Springer, Heidelberg (2004)
11. Rao, A.S., Georgeff, M.P.: BDI-agents: from theory to practice. In: Proceedings of the First International Conference on Multiagent Systems, San Francisco, pp. 312–319 (1995)
12. Dastani, M., van Riemsdijk, B., Dignum, F., Meyer, J.J.: A programming language for cognitive agents: Goal directed 3apl. In: Dastani, M., Dix, J., El Fallah-Seghrouchni, A. (eds.) PROMAS 2003. LNCS (LNAI), vol. 3067, pp. 111–130. Springer, Heidelberg (2004)
13. Hindriks, K.V., de Boer, F.S., van der Hoek, W., Meyer, J.J.C.: Agent programming in 3apl. Autonomous Agents and Multi-Agent Systems 2(4), 357–401 (1999)
14. Oomes, A.H.J.: Organization awareness in crisis management. In: Proceedings of the International Workshop on Information Systems on Crisis Response and Management (ISCRAM) (2004)

Towards a Formalisation of
Dynamic Electronic Institutions

Eduard Muntaner-Perich and Josep Lluís de la Rosa Esteva

Agents Research Lab, Edifici PIV, Campus de Montilivi, 17071,
Universitat de Girona, Catalonia, Spain
{emuntane,peplluis}@eia.udg.edu

Abstract. This paper presents a formalisation of our Dynamic Electronic Institutions model. In our opinion Dynamic Electronic Institutions arise from the convergence of two research areas: electronic institutions and coalition formation. We believe that these kinds of institutions are potentially important in open-agent system applications because they are well suited to many application domains in which autonomous agents have to collaborate and engage themselves in temporary alliances that require some regulatory measures. This paper presents a brief summary of our previous work on dynamic institutions, introduces the formalisation of our model, explains the process of turning a coalition into a dynamic institution (foundation process), and describes our current and future work.

Keywords: Open Agent Systems, Electronic Institutions, Coalition Formation.

1 Introduction

From a social point of view, it is easy to observe that the interactions between people are often guided by institutions that help and provide us with structures for daily life tasks. Institutions structure incentives in human exchange (political, social, or economic). Somehow we could say that institutions represent the rules of the game in a society or, more formally, are the human-devised constraints that shape human interaction [1].

The idea to use organizational metaphors to model systems was earlier proposed [2, 3]. These approaches suggest structuring the agent society with roles and relationships between agents. But the study of electronic institutions is a relatively recent field (the first approach was [4]). The main idea is simple, and it could be summarized by imagining groups of intelligent, autonomous and heterogeneous agents, which play different roles, and which interact with each other under a set of norms, with the purpose of satisfying individual goals and/or common goals. As a first impression, it could seem that these norms are a negative factor which adds constraints to the system, but in fact they reduce the complexity of the system, making the agents' behaviour more *predictable*. Actually, this is completely true only assuming that agents follow the rules that are created by such norms, and in Open Agent Systems, this is not an assumption to be taken lightly.

J.S. Sichman et al. (Eds.): COIN 2007, LNAI 4870, pp. 97–109, 2008.
© Springer-Verlag Berlin Heidelberg 2008

Research in Distributed Artificial Intelligence (DAI) has focused on the individual behaviour of agents. But this agent-centred perspective is not useful in complex systems like *open agent systems*, where their components (agents) are not known a priori, can change over time, and can be heterogeneous and exhibit very different behaviours. In these kinds of systems, this vision that is focused on the agent can cause the emergent behaviour of the global system to be chaotic and unexpected. In critical applications this can be a significant problem, and it is evident that it is necessary to introduce regulatory measures which determine what things the agents can do, and what they cannot. It is here where the institutions acquire importance [5].

In Noriega's thesis [4], an abstraction of the notion of institution is introduced for the first time. He is also the first to use the term *agent-mediated electronic institution*, which he describes as: computational environments which allow heterogeneous agents to successfully interact among them, by imposing appropriate restrictions on their behaviours. Continuing and extending the ideas of Noriega's thesis, there is Rodríguez-Aguilar [5] who emphasizes the need for a formal framework which allows to work with general electronic institutions.

From these first approaches to this area, to the actual lines of research, there have been different European research groups working on similar subjects, each one with its particular perspective and approach to the problem. At the moment, many efforts are dedicated to this research area. The proof of this is that in 2003, five PhD theses intimately related to this subject were presented. The theses are: [6, 7, 8, 9, 10].

These different approaches to electronic institutions have demonstrated how organisational approaches are useful in *open agent systems*, but in our opinion, in some application domains that require short to medium-term associations of agents regulated by norms, classical electronic institutions still have several problems and limitations. We have summarized these problems in the following list:

- All the approaches to electronic institutions are based on medium to long-term associations and dependencies between agents. This characteristic is useful in some application domains but it is a significant problem in other domains, where changes in tasks, in information and in resources make temporary associations (regulated by norms) necessary.
- Electronic institutions require a design phase (performed by humans). It is necessary to automate this design phase in order to allow the emergence of electronic institutions (without human intervention) in open agent systems.
- Agents can join and leave institutions, but how do these entrances and exits affect the institutions' norms and objectives? Could these norms and objectives change over time?
- When an institution has fulfilled all its objectives, how can it dissolve itself?

In our opinion, these problems and limitations can be studied and possibly solved with a coalition formation approach to electronic institutions, in order to develop dynamic electronic institutions. This is the main objective of our research.

There is little previous work on dynamic electronic institutions: this idea has just recently been introduced as a challenge for agent-based computing. It first appeared when the term *dynamic electronic institution* appeared in a roadmap for agent technology [11].

Our recent work in this area has involved the development of our dynamic electronic institutions model [12], and some exploratory work in two application domains: Operations Other Than War simulation [13], and Digital Business Ecosystems [14].

This paper is organized as follows. In section 2 we explain the notion of Dynamic Electronic Institutions and their lifecycle. Next, section 3 illustrates the formalisation of each phase in our model, and our CBR approach to the foundation phase. Before concluding, we discuss some related work in section 4. Finally, section 5 concludes with discussion and future research.

2 Dynamic Electronic Institutions: The Model

We argue that Dynamic Electronic Institutions (DEIs from now on) can be described as follows: emergent associations of intelligent, autonomous and heterogeneous agents, which play different roles, and which are able to adopt a set of regulatory components (norms, missions, coordination protocols, etc) in order to interact with each other, with the aim of satisfying individual goals and/or common goals. These formations are dynamic in the sense that they can be automatically formed, reformed and dissolved, in order to constitute temporary electronic institutions on the fly.

There are several application domains that require short-term agent organisations or alliances, in which DEIs could be applied. Some of them are: Digital Business Ecosystems (we have addressed this topic in [14]), B2B Electronic Commerce, Mobile Ad-Hoc Networks, simulation of Operations Other Than War [13], etc.

In our opinion DEIs should have a lifecycle made up of by three phases: Formation, Foundation and Fulfilment (We call this lifecycle "3F cycle" [12], see Figure 1):

1. *Formation phase*: This is the coalition formation phase. In this stage the objective is for automatic association between agents with the same (or similar) goals to emerge. Other notions such as trust between agents should also be considered as important factors in the coalition formation phase. A coalition formation mechanism (protocol and strategies) is necessary to allow agents to form coalitions. We are not currently studying coalition formation mechanisms, because we have focused our research on the foundation phase, but in our opinion there are two approaches which introduce some interesting ideas and could be suitable for being used in the formation phase of DEIs: Q-Negotiation (ForEV framework) [15] and the CONOISE project [16].

2. *Foundation phase*: The process of turning the coalition into a temporary electronic institution. This phase is the real challenge, because the process of turning the coalition into a temporary electronic institution is not a trivial problem. It requires the agents to adopt a set of components that regulate their interactions. This must be an automated process, without any human intervention, so agents must be able to reason and negotiate at a high level.

3. *Fulfilment phase*: This is the dissolution phase. When the institution has fulfilled all its objectives, the association should be broken up. This phase occurs because the association is no longer needed, or because the institution is no longer making a profit. This subject has hardly been explored by current research efforts, and most of the support functionalities need to be developed.

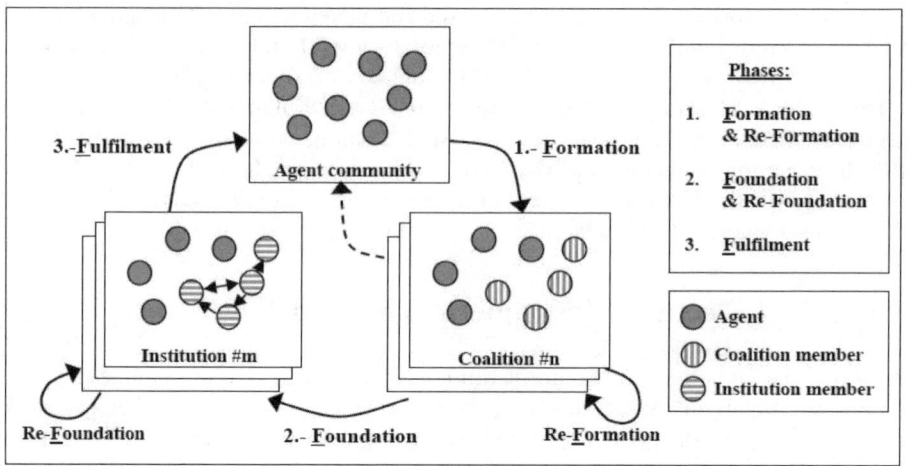

Fig. 1. DEI construction phases (3F cycle)

One of these three phases has been poorly studied in the past: the foundation phase, we are focusing our work on this phase.

3 Formalising the Model

This section presents a formalisation of our model of DEIs. Each phase of the model is formalised, but we are principally focusing our efforts on the foundation phase. In the following subsections we use a basic set theory notation. The term *symbol* refers to a user-defined string (similar to a variable name), and the term *expression* is an algebraic expression (possibly referencing constants, symbols and function calls).

3.1 The Formation Phase

This is the coalition formation phase. As we have said before, we are not currently focusing our research on this phase, but we need to analyze some concepts in order to be able to formalise the foundation phase.

We consider a population P of autonomous and heterogeneous agents (1), consisting of a variable number N of individuals. In this context, a coalition is a subgroup C of agents of P (2). Agents form a coalition because they need to work together to achieve tasks in an environment. Their reason is because mutual profit can be gained from sharing resources and redistributing tasks.

$$P = \{ a_1, a_2, \ldots a_N \} \tag{1}$$

$$C \subseteq P \tag{2}$$

At its simplest the problem can be defined as in [17]: "Given a population P of agents and a list of tasks or goals T, select subgroups of agents S1, S2, S3… of P to address each of the tasks in T". In the general case, this problem is computationally intractable

(NP-Hard). This is very easy to understand: given N agents and k tasks, there are k(2N-1) different possible coalitions. The number of coalition configurations (different partitions of the set of agents in coalitions) is of the order $O(N^{(N/2)})$ [18]. Therefore, it is clear that an exhaustive search of the coalition configuration space is not feasible when the number of agents is large. Recent works in distributed artificial intelligence have resulted in distributed algorithms with computational tractability [17].

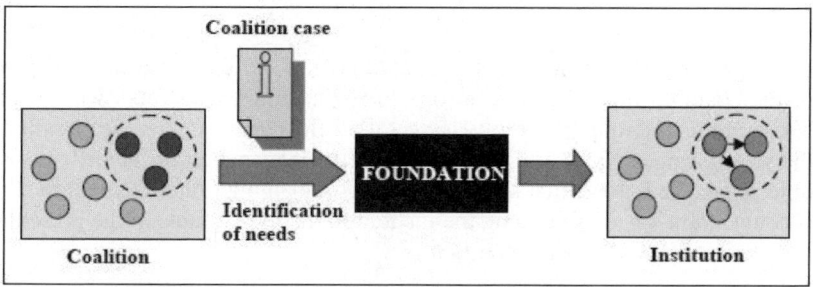

Fig. 2. The Foundation Phase

3.2 The Foundation Phase

We define foundation as the process of turning a coalition into a temporary electronic institution (see Figure 2). This phase is a real challenge, and requires the agents to automatically adopt a set of *institutional elements* that regulate their interactions.

Our perspective on this problem is that to construct an institution from zero without human intervention may be too difficult, so we argue that an approach based on using knowledge from previous cases (like Case Based Reasoning, CBR) could be interesting and useful for solving this issue. Presently, we are directing our efforts in this direction.

Therefore, in our system, a stored case (*institution case*) refers to a problem situation and contains a description of a problem, and its solution (the *institutional elements* to be adopted), and a new case (*coalition case*) contains the description of the problem to be solved. Case-based reasoning is a cycle, and there are four phases in the process: *Retrieve*, *Reuse*, *Revise* and *Retain*.

With a CBR approach to the foundation process, when a coalition has been formed and needs to turn itself into an institution, agents should consult their case database in order to find the stored institution's specification that adapts best to the present situation, and should then make the pertinent reforms to the selected specification in order to obtain an institution that works correctly.

The first step in this process is to build a *coalition case CC* from the coalition *C* that has been formed. We consider the *coalition case* as a tuple of different elements (4).

$$C = \{ a_1, a_2, ... a_i \} \tag{3}$$

$$CC = < Ty, Tk, Ob, n, div, tr > \tag{4}$$

The components of the *coalition case* are the elements that need to be taken into account when we search the institution that adapts best to the present coalition. These components are:

- *Ty* (types): this component is the set of types of the agents in the coalition. Each type is a *symbol*.

$$Ty = \bigcup_i \{ type(a_i) \} \tag{5}$$

- *Tk* (tasks): this component is the set of tasks of the agents in the coalition. Each task is a *symbol*.

$$Tk = \bigcup_i \{ tasks(a_i) \} \tag{6}$$

- *Ob* (objectives): this component is a set of objectives. These are not the objectives of the coalition (coalition has no objectives; each agent has its own objectives). These are a subgroup of the objectives of all the agents. More specifically, *Ob* is the set of shared objectives, extracted from the intersection of the different sets of objectives. We believe that shared objectives are an important element to take into account when we are searching the institution that best adapts to the present coalition. Each objective is an *expression*.

$$Ob = \bigcap_i \{ objectives(a_i) \} \tag{7}$$

- *n* (number of agents): this component is the number of agents in the coalition.

$$n = |C| \tag{8}$$

- *div* (diversity measure): this component is the diversity within the coalition with respect to the objectives of the agents. The ideal would be to have a working metric of behavioural diversity, but this general metric is yet to be found [19]. In our model, diversity is measured only with respect to the objectives of the agents, and by using an adaptation of Shannon's entropy function:

$Nt = $ *total number of objectives:* $\sum_i | objectives(a_i)|$

$K = $ *number of different types:* $| \bigcup_i \{ type(a_i) \} |$

$n_a = $ *number of objectives of type a*

$P_a = n_a / Nt$

$$div = \frac{-\sum_a^k Pa * \log_2(Pa)}{\log_2(\min(Nt, K))} \tag{9}$$

- *tr* (internal trust): this component is the mean trust value. We calculate it as a double summation: the first one is the sum of all the trust values for an agent with respect to the other agents in the coalition; and the second is the sum of the mean trust of all the agents. Existing models of coalition formation do not generally consider trust, but we believe that trust is an important element. In our model, trust between two agents represents the agent's estimation (based on its previous experience) of how likely the other agent is to fulfill its cooperative commitments.

$$tr = \frac{\sum_{i=0}^n \left(\frac{\sum_{j=0}^n trust(a_i, a_j)}{n} \right)}{n} \tag{10}$$

In our opinion, trust and diversity are important elements to be taken into account, because they capture valuable information of the coalition. We believe that if we are trying to turn a coalition into a temporary institution, diversity and trust among agents should be taken into account to find the institution's specification that adapts best to the present situation. Of course this is a conjecture that needs to be proved. Having this in mind, one of our current efforts aims at developing a framework for DEIs that will help to test it.

When we have the coalition case (CC), the next step is to start the CBR process. We need a *previous-institutions base*, which contains the knowledge of the system. In our model this institutions base is called K (11). Each case of this base is an *institution case*, IC (12), which contains a CC and the *institutional elements* (IE), that is, the elements that have to be adopted to turn the coalition into a dynamic institution (13).

To initialise the system, an initial set of *institution cases* must be introduced into the case base. Therefore, in the first CBR iterations the coalitions can reuse previous *institution cases*. This set is important, and should capture some general and typical associations among agents in the specific application domain. This process has to be performed by humans, before starting up the system, and then the rest of the processes should be automatic.

$$K = \{ IC_1, IC_2, ..., IC_n \} \tag{11}$$

$$IC = < CC, IE > \tag{12}$$

$$IE = < M, N, F, pr, ont > \tag{13}$$

The *institutional elements IE* (13) are:

- M (Missions): sets of specific objectives for each agent, where each objective is an *expression*.
- N (Norms): these are the norms to be adopted by the coalition. These can be obligations (*obl*), permissions (*per*), or prohibitions (*pro*). Table 1 shows the internal structure of these norms.

Table 1. Structure of each norm of N, with examples

Norm Id	Condition (expression)	Bearer (agent type)	Type (obl, per, pro)	Mission or Task	Deadline
N_1	Null	Employee	Obl	M_3	<end
N_2	$(a_1>10) \wedge (b_2<5)$	Employer	Obl	M_1	<end

- F (Fulfilment Requirements): this component refers to future requirements for the fulfilment phase. It includes:
  - FC (Fulfilment Conditions): these are the conditions that allow the execution of the fulfilment process. Each condition is an *expression*.
  - FN (Fulfilment Norms): these are the norms (obligations, permissions and prohibitions) that have to be followed during the fulfilment phase. FN and N have the same internal structure.
- pr (Protocol): this is the protocol to be adopted by the coalition. It will steer the communication processes within the dynamic institution.
- ont (Ontology): an ontology to be adopted by all agents in the coalition (of course if an agent already has the ontology there is not need to adopt it).

The CBR process compares the present *coalition case* (*CC*) with the *coalition case* included in each *institution case* (*IC*). This process requires some similarity rules. Each component of the *CC* has a specific similarity measure, and there is global similarity that corresponds to a weighted sum of partial similarities (14).

$$Sim = (w_1*SimTy + w_2*SimTk + w_3*SimO + w_4*SimN + w_5*SimDiv + w_6*SimTr) \qquad (14)$$

The weights used in the similarity function depend on the specific implementation, and the application domain. They are performance parameters that need to be empirically adjusted.

When the *institution case* (*IC*) that best adapts to the *coalition case* (*CC*) is found, an adjustment of the *institutional elements* (*IE*) is required in order to allow the agents of the new coalition to re-use them. This is not a simple process; in fact it can become very complicated, and it depends partially on the specific implementation of the model. The following are some general guidelines:

- The ontology *ont* can be directly adopted by the coalition. We assume that all the agents in the system are using the same ACL (Agent Communication Language) and are able to work with ontologies.
- The protocol *pr* could require a more sophisticated adoption process. If the protocol to be adopted refers to types of agents that do not exist in the new coalition, we need to modify the protocol. There are different possible ways to do it, but we believe that a simple solution could be to maintain a similarity table within *K*, which informs about the similarity between the different types of agents. This way we can replace one type of agent in the protocol with the type of agent that better fits the context requirements.
- The modification of norms *N* is also a hard task. If the bearer of the norm refers to a type of agent that does not exist in the coalition we basically have two options: to eliminate this norm, or to find the type of agent in the coalition that is more similar to the bearer (the same process that has been proposed for the protocol modification could be used). The modification of norms can also consider an internal modification of the norm, more specifically of its *conditions* and *missions*. This kind of modification implies more sophisticated adaptation processes. We can consider the need for more similarity tables (for *missions*, constants and global variables), or another option could be to consider a genetic algorithm for the estimation of these parameters.
- The modification and adoption of the missions *M* and the fulfilment requirements *FR* imply similar changes like those described above for *N*.

Foundation starts by building a *coalition case CC*. The next step is the CBR process that can be expressed as a function (15) that, from a *coalition case CC* and the institutions base *K*, produces the adapted *institutional elements IE*. We need another process that adds these *IE* to the coalition and finally produces the DEI. Therefore, we can conceive the global foundation process as a function that, from a coalition *C* and *K*, produces the DEI (16).

$$CBR: (CC, K) \rightarrow IE \qquad (15)$$

$$foundation: (C, K) \rightarrow DEI \qquad (16)$$

With this formalisation of the foundation phase we also can consider a *re-foundation* process, which facilitates reconfiguring the dynamic institution when member changes or environment changes occur. Currently, reorganisation within a multi-agent system is a topic that is being actively discussed. Section 4 cites some related work.

Figure 3 shows a diagram of the foundation process.

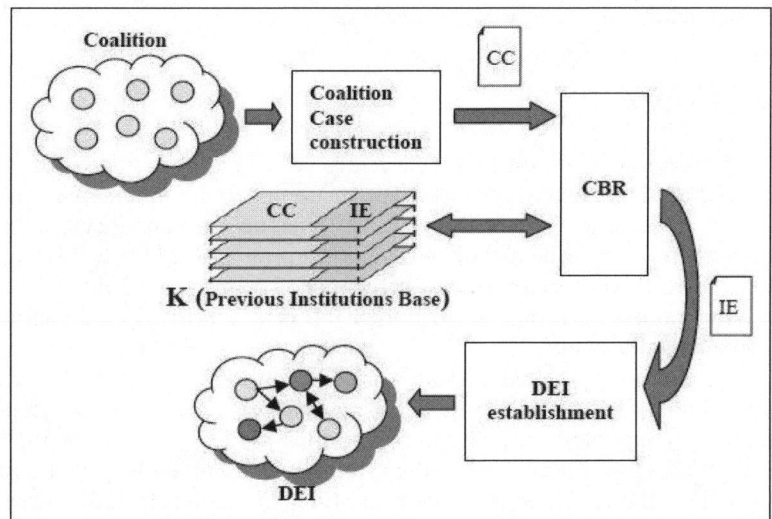

Fig. 3. The Foundation phase

3.3 The Fulfilment Phase

This is the dissolution phase. When the fulfilment conditions FC are achieved, the association should be broken up. This phase occurs because the association is no longer needed, or because the institution is no longer making a profit. Within this phase the agents should distribute the profits obtained (following the fulfilment norms FN) and store relevant information for future DEIs (a new institution case IC).

This subject has hardly been explored by current research efforts, and most of the support functionalities need to be developed. We believe that there are two important steps in this phase: the construction of the new institution case IC and the update of the institutions base K. The result of this process is an updated institutions base K', that includes the new institution case (17).

$$fulfilment: (DEI, K) \rightarrow K' \qquad (17)$$

3.4 Properties of the Formalised Model

Taking into account the above presented formalisation, we argue that DEIs are:

- Dynamic: DEIs are dynamic in the sense that they can be automatically formed, reformed and dissolved, in order to constitute regulated associations of agents on the fly.

- Automatic: DEIs don't require a design phase performed by humans, although an initial set of *institution cases* (IC) must be introduced into the case base before starting up the system, as it has been said before.
- Temporary: DEIs are conceived as short to medium-term associations. They acquire the fulfilment requirements during the foundation phase.
- Adaptive: CBR provides adaptive solutions by systematic comparison between current coalition and the stored institutions.

4 Related Work

There is little previous work on DEIs. Currently there is a work in progress [20, 21] that is focused on the extension of electronic institutions with autonomic capabilities to allow them to yield a dynamical answer to changing circumstances, through the adaptation of their norms. The authors present a learning model in two steps: a genetic algorithm to learn the best parameters for a population of agents (simulation), and a self-adaptation model based on CBR (run-time). It is a very interesting approach that could complement our work.

In [22] the authors presented a framework (ORCAS) for developing multi-agent systems that maximizes the reuse of agent capabilities across multiple application domains, and supports the configuration of agent teams. The agent infrastructure that they present is developed according to the electronic institutions formalism. Recently they presented another work on dynamic institutions for teamwork [23] where a case-based learning mechanism to form new agent teams by reusing previous team-designs for new problems is presented.

Recently, there is an increasing interest on *organisational self-design*. In [24], the authors affirm that "we must move from an agent-centric view of coordination and control to an organisation-centric one. However, in order to be able to adapt and evolve, this latter will need to coexist with dynamic and (partially) emergent organisation, based on the former". However, although there are many practical applications being developed, there is need for formal theories to describe dynamic organisational structures.

In [25], a general view of the reorganisation problem, within a multi-agent system, is presented. The authors present a reorganisation model where agents have autonomy to change their organisations. Their approach is based on the MOISE$^+$, which is an organisational model for multi-agent systems based on notions like roles, groups, and missions.

An interesting approach to *organisational design* is proposed in [26], where the authors present a distributed algorithm that uses an underlying organisation to guide coalition formation.

Our approach is closely related to the concept of Contractual Agent Societies [27], a metaphor for building open information systems where agents configure themselves automatically through a set of dynamically negotiated social contracts. In [14] we have studied the adoption of institutional components through an electronic contract.

In this article we have not examined Virtual Organisations [15, 16, 28]. This concept is closely related to electronic institutions and coalition formation. In fact, in our opinion, VOs could be described in terms of DEIs, although their architectures and implementations are usually directed to a specific application domain: B2B electronic commerce. We believe that in someway VOs could be considered as a sub-group of DEIs which are more general. In one study [15] the authors work towards the development of an agent-based electronic institution providing a virtual normative environment that assists and regulates the creation and operation of VOs. Their work confirms our idea, because they prove that VOs can be conceived as DEIs. An interesting approach to VOs is proposed in [28], where authors try to formalise VOs and contracts based on commitments.

Finally, there is an approach that studies the dynamic selection of coordination mechanisms among autonomous agents [29]. The authors presented a framework that enables autonomous agents to dynamically select the mechanism they employ in order to coordinate their inter-related activities.

5 Conclusions and Future Work

In this article, we have presented a brief summary of our previous work on DEIs (the general model and the CBR approach) and we have introduced a formalisation of our DEIs model. This formalisation provides us with a preliminary theoretical framework for working with institutions that are dynamic, automatic, temporary, and adaptive.

In our previous works we presented an exploratory work [13] that was focused on the simulation of Operations Other Than War (OOTW) using a first version of our DEIs model. Our first experiments were very simple, but the preliminary results were encouraging. They used a centralized CBR approach on the OOTW domain, and showed that the foundation phase is feasible, and that the DEI lifecycle can be fully implemented.

Currently, we are centring our efforts on the implementation of a framework for DEIs. It will follow our general model and the formalisation presented in this paper. We are using Repast to implement it, and we would like to use it in another application domain: digital business ecosystems (DBEs). We have recently presented a work in this direction [14].

We are using a CBR approach in the foundation phase, but we do not rule out alternative approaches like meta-institutions or genetic algorithms. A Meta-Institution could provide general modules (norms, ontologies, protocols, etc.), which have to be instantiated in order to build specific DEIs.

At this moment, we are involved in the ONE Project (Open Negotiation Environment [30]), which tries to enrich digital business ecosystems with an open, decentralised negotiation environment. As we have said before, we would like to use our DEIs model to enable these digital business ecosystems.

Acknowledgments. This research was partially funded by EU project N° 34744 ONE: Open Negotiation Environment, FP6-2005-IST-5, ICT-for Networked Businesses.

References

1. North, D.C.: Economics and Cognitive Science. Economic History 9612002, Economics Working Paper Archive at WUSTL (Washington University in St. Louis) (1996)

2. Pattison, H.E., Corkill, D.D., Lesser, V.R.: Distributed Artificial Intelligence, chapter Instantiating Descriptions of Organizational Structures, pp. 59–96. Pitman Publ. (1987)
3. Werner, E.: Distributed Artificial Intelligence, chapter Cooperating Agents: A Unified Theory of Communication and Social Structure, pp. 3–36. Pitman Publ. (1987)
4. Noriega, P.: Agent Mediated Auctions. The Fishmarket Metaphor. Ph.D. Thesis, Artificial Intelligence Research Institute (IIIA), Universitat Autònoma de Barcelona (1997)
5. Rodríguez-Aguilar, J.A.: On the design and construction of Agent-mediated Electronic Institutions. Ph.D. thesis, Artificial Intelligence Research Institute (IIIA), Universitat Autònoma de Barcelona (2001)
6. Esteva, M.: Electronic Institutions: From specification to development. PhD thesis, Artificial Intelligence Research Institute (IIIA), Universitat Politècnica de Catalunya (2003)
7. Dignum, V.: A model for organizational interaction. Based on Agents, Founded in Logic. Ph.D. Thesis. Dutch Research School for Information and Knowledge Systems, Utrecht University (2003)
8. Fornara, N.: Interaction and communication among autonomous agents in multiagent systems, Ph.D. Thesis, Università della Svizzera italiana, Facoltà di Scienze della Comunicazione (2003)
9. López y López, F.: Social power and norms. Impact on Agent Behaviour. Ph.D. Thesis, University of Southampton, Department of Electronics and Computer Science (2003)
10. Vázquez-Salceda, J.: The role of Norms and Electronic Institutions in Multi-Agent Systems applied to complex domains. The HARMONIA framework. PhD thesis, Universitat Politècnica de Catalunya, Dept. Llenguatges i Sistemes Informàtics. Artificial Intelligence Dissertation Award, ECCAI (2003)
11. Luck, M., McBurney, P., Preist, C.: Agent Technology: Enabling Next generation Computing. A Roadmap for Agent Based Computing. AgentLink II (2003)
12. Muntaner-Perich, E., de la Rosa, J.Ll.: Towards Dynamic Electronic Institutions: from agent coalitions to agent institutions. In: Hinchey, M.G., Rago, P., Rash, J.L., Rouff, C.A., Sterritt, R., Truszkowski, W. (eds.) WRAC 2005. LNCS (LNAI), vol. 3825, pp. 109–121. Springer, Heidelberg (2006)
13. Muntaner-Perich, E., de la Rosa, J.Ll., Carrillo, C., Delfín, S., Moreno, A.: Dynamic Electronic Institutions for Humanitarian Aid Simulation, Publ. in Frontiers in AI and Applications - AI Research & Development, vol. 146, pp. 239–246. IOS Press, Amsterdam (2006)
14. Muntaner-Perich, E., de la Rosa, J.Ll.: Using Dynamic Electronic Institutions to Enable Digital Business Ecosystems. In: Noriega, P., Vázquez-Salceda, J., Boella, G., Boissier, O., Dignum, V., Fornara, N., Matson, E. (eds.) COIN 2006. LNCS (LNAI), vol. 4386, pp. 259–273. Springer, Heidelberg (2007)
15. Rocha, A.P., Lopes Cardoso, H., Oliveira, E.: Contributions to an Electronic Institution supporting Virtual Enterprises' life cycle. In: Putnik e M.M. Cunha, G. (ed.), Virtual Enterprise Integration: Technological and Organizational Perspectives, Idea Group Inc., pp. 229–246 (in press, 2005)
16. Dang, V.D.: Coalition Formation and Operation in Virtual Organisations, PhD Thesis. School of Electronics and Computer Science, University of Southampton (2004)
17. Klusch, M., Gerber, A.: Dynamic coalition formation among rational agents. IEEE Intelligent Systems 17(3), 42–47 (2002)
18. Shehory, O.: Coalition Formation: Towards Feasible Solutions. In: Mařík, V., Müller, J.P., Pěchouček, M. (eds.) CEEMAS 2003. LNCS (LNAI), vol. 2691, pp. 4–6. Springer, Heidelberg (2003)

19. Lybäck, D.: Transient diversity in multi-agent systems. Master's thesis, Department of Computer and Systems Sciences, Stockholm University and the Royal Institute of Technology (1999)
20. Bou, E., López-Sánchez, M., Rodriguez-Aguilar, J.A.: Norm adaptation of autonomic electronic institutions with multiple goals. International Transactions on Systems Science and Applications 1(3), 227–238 (2006)
21. Bou, E., López-Sánchez, M., Rodriguez-Aguilar, J.A.: Self-adaptation in Autonomic Electronic Institutions through Case-Based Reasoning. In: Proceedings of the MA4CS satellite Workshop: Multi-Agents for modelling Complex Systems, Dresden, Germany (October 4, 2007)
22. Gómez, M., Plaza, E.: ORCAS: Open, Reusable and Configurable Multi-Agent Systems. In: Proc. 3rd Int. Joint Conference in Autonomous Agents and Multiagent Systems (2004)
23. Gómez, M., Plaza, E.: Dynamic Institutions for Teamwork. In: Sichman, J.S., Padget, J., Ossowski, S., Noriega, P. (eds.) COIN 2007. LNCS(LNAI), vol. 4870, pp. 155–170. Springer, Heidelberg (2008)
24. Sichman, J.S., Dignum, V., Castelfranchi, C.: Agents´ organizations: A concise overview. Journal of the Brazilian Computer Society 11(1), 3–8 (2005)
25. Hübner, J.F., Sichman, J.S., Boissier, O.: Using the MOISE$^+$ for a Cooperative Framework of MAS Reorganisation. In: Bazzan, A.L.C., Labidi, S. (eds.) SBIA 2004. LNCS (LNAI), vol. 3171, pp. 506–515. Springer, Heidelberg (2004)
26. Horling, B., Lesser, V.: A Survey of Multi-Agent Organizational Paradigms. The Knowledge Engineering Review 19(4), 281–316 (2005)
27. Dellarocas, C.: Contractual Agent Societies: Negotiated shared context and social control in open multi-agent systems. In: Proc. WS on Norms and Institutions in Multi-Agent Systems, Autonomous Agents-2000, Barcelona (2000)
28. Udupi, Y.B., Singh, M.P.: Contract Enactment in Virtual Organizations: A Commitment-Based Approach. In: Proceedings of the 21st National Conference on Artificial Intelligence (AAAI), Boston, pp. 722–727. AAAI Press, Menlo Park (2006)
29. Excelente-Toledo, C.B., Jennings, N.R.: The dynamic selection of coordination mechanisms. Autonomous Agents and Multi-Agent Systems 9(1-2), 55–85 (2004)
30. ONE Project.: EU project N° 34744, ONE: Open Negotiation Environment (2007), http://one-project.eu

Large-Scale Organizational Computing Requires Unstratified Reflection and Strong Paraconsistency

Carl Hewitt

MIT EECS (Emeritus)
carlhewitt@alum.mit.edu

Abstract. *Organizational Computing* is a computational model for using the principles, practices, and methods of human organizations. Organizations of Restricted Generality (*ORGs*) have been proposed as a foundation for Organizational Computing. ORGs are the natural extension of Web Services, which are rapidly becoming the overwhelming standard for distributed computing and application interoperability in Organizational Computing. The thesis of this paper is that large-scale Organizational Computing requires reflection and strong paraconsistency for organizational practices, policies, and norms.

Strong paraconsistency is required because the practices, policies, and norms of large-scale Organizational Computing are pervasively inconsistent. By the standard rules of logic, anything and everything can be inferred from an inconsistency, *e.g.,* "*The moon is made of green cheese.*" The purpose of strongly paraconsistent logic is to develop principles of reasoning so that irrelevances cannot be inferred from the fact of inconsistency while preserving all natural inferences that do not explode in the face of inconsistency.

Reflection is required in order that the practices, policies, and norms can mutually refer to each other and make inferences. Reflection and strong paraconsistency are important properties of Direct Logic [Hewitt 2007] for large software systems. Gödel first formalized and proved that it is not possible to decide all mathematical questions by inference in his 1st incompleteness theorem. However, the incompleteness theorem (as generalized by Rosser) relies on the assumption of consistency! This paper proves a generalization of the Gödel/Rosser incompleteness theorem: *theories of Direct Logic are incomplete.* However, there is a further consequence. Although the semi-classical mathematical fragment of Direct Logic is evidently consistent, since the Gödelian paradoxical proposition is self-provable, *every theory in Direct Logic has an inconsistency*!

Keywords: Co-ordination, Concurrency, Direct Logic, Inconsistency, Institutions, Mental Agents, Norms, Organizational Computing, ORGs (Organizations of Restricted Generality), Norms, Paraconsistency, Policies, Practices, Reflection.

1 Introduction

Organizational Computing is the metaphor of using an organizational model for computation; *i.e.,* computers using the principles, methods and practices of human organizations. Organizations of Restricted Generality (ORGs) have been proposed as a foundation for Organizational Computing [Hewitt and Inman 1991]. *ORGs are the*

J.S. Sichman et al. (Eds.): COIN 2007, LNAI 4870, pp. 110–124, 2008.
© Springer-Verlag Berlin Heidelberg 2008

natural extension of Web Services, which are rapidly becoming the overwhelming standard for distributed computing and application interoperability in Organizational Computing. Microsoft, IBM, Oracle, SAP, and just about every Fortune 500 company are betting on Web Services.

The plan of this paper is as follows:

1. Introduce Organizational Computing and ORGs (Organizations of Restricted Generality) and describe the principles and practices by which they operate.
2. Develop the thesis that inconsistency is the norm for large-scale Organizational Computing.
3. Explain the limitations of classical logical reasoning for inconsistent information.
4. Introduce a system of Direct Logic[1] that provides inference capabilities needed for large-scale Organizational Computing.

2 Organizational Computing

Organizational Computing is a computational model for using principles, practices, and methods of human organizations. Organizations of Restricted Generality (*ORGs*) have been proposed as a foundation for Organizational Computing. In general

- ORGs mirror the structure of large-scale human organizations.
- ORGs are a natural extension of Web Services, which are the standard for distributed computing and software application interoperability in large-scale Organizational Computing.
- ORGs are structured by *Organizational Commitment* [Jennings 1993; Noriega 1997; Singh and Huhns 2005], which is a special case of *Physical Commitment* [Hewitt 2006b] that is defined to be *information pledged*.
- In many cases, humans will take part in the operation of an ORG. For example, in a credit card ORG, a particular credit decision may be reviewed by a human before being decided.

3 Inconsistency Is the Norm in Large-Scale Organizational Computing

The development of Organizational Computing and the extreme dependence of our society on these systems have introduced new phenomena. These systems have pervasive inconsistencies among and within the following:

---

[1] Direct Logic is called "***direct***" due to considerations such as the following:

- Direct Logic does not incorporate *general* indirect proof in a theory T. Instead it only allows "direct" forms of indirect proof, *e.g.*, $(\Psi \vdash_T \neg\Psi) \rightarrow (\vdash_T \neg\Psi)$. See discussion below.
- In Direct Logic, paraconsistent theories speak directly about their own provability relation rather than having to resort to indirect statements in a meta-theory.
- Inference of Φ from Ψ in a theory T ($\Psi \vdash_T \Phi$) is "direct" in the sense that it does not automatically incorporate the contrapositive *i.e.*, it does not automatically incorporate $(\neg\Phi \vdash_T \neg\Psi)$. See discussion below.

- *Norms* that express how systems can be used and tested in practice.
- *Policies* that express over-arching justification for systems and their technologies.
- *Practices* that express implementations of systems.

Different parties (management, engineering, marketing, sales, *etc.*) are responsible for constructing, evolving, justifying and maintaining documentation, use cases, and code for large, human-interaction, Organizational Computing systems. In specific cases any one consideration can trump the others. Sometimes debates over inconsistencies among the parts can become quite heated, *e.g.,* among engineering, marketing, and sales. *In large Organizational Computing systems, policies, practices, and norms all co-evolve to eliminate old inconsistencies and produce systems with new inconsistencies. However, no one knows what they are or where they are located!*

Furthermore there is no evident way to divide up the code, documentation, and use cases into meaningful, consistent microtheories for human-computer interaction. *Organizations such as Microsoft, the US government, and IBM have tens of thousands of employees pouring over hundreds of millions of lines of documentation, code, and use cases attempting to cope with their Organizational Computing Systems. In the course of time almost all of this code will interoperate using Web Services. A large Organizational Computing system is never done* [Rosenberg 2007].

Adapting a metaphor that Karl Popper [1962] used for science, the bold structure of a large Organizational Computing system rises, as it were, above a swamp. It is like a building erected on piles. The piles are driven down from above into the swamp, but not down to any natural or given base; and when we cease our attempts to drive our piles into a deeper layer, it is not because we have reached bedrock. We simply pause when we are satisfied that they are firm enough to carry the structure, at least for the time being. Or perhaps we do something else more pressing. Under some piles there is no rock. Also some rock does not hold.

The thinking in almost all scientific and engineering work has been that models (also called theories or microtheories) should be internally consistent, although they could be inconsistent with each other.

Paraconsistency Has Been Around for a While. So What's New?

Within mathematics paraconsistent[2] logic was developed to deal with inconsistent theories. The idea of paraconsistent logic is to be able to make inferences from inconsistent information without being able to derive all propositions, property called "*simple paraconsistency*" in this paper in contrast to "*strong paraconsistency*" which is discussed below.

The most extreme form of simple paraconsistent mathematics is *dialetheism* [Priest and Routley 1989] which maintains that there are true inconsistencies in mathematics itself *e.g.,* the Liar Paradox. However, mathematicians (starting with Euclid) have worked very hard to make their theories consistent and inconsistencies have not been an issue for most working mathematicians. As a result:

---

[2] Name coined by Francisco Miró Quesada in 1976 [Priest 2002, pg. 288].

- Since inconsistency was not an issue, mathematical logic focused on the issue of truth and a model theory of truth was developed [Dedekind 1888, Löwenheim 1915, Skolem 1920, Gödel 1930, Tarski and Vaught 1957, Hodges 2006]. More recently there has been work on the development of an unstratified logic of truth [Leitgeb 2007, Feferman 2007a].[3]
- Simple Paraconsistent logic somewhat languished for lack of subject matter. The lack of subject matter resulted in simple paraconsistent proof theories that were for the most part so awkward as to be unused for mathematical practice.[4]

Consequently mainstream logicians and mathematicians have tended to shy away from simple paraconsistency.

One of the achievements of Direct Logic™ is the development of an unstratified reflective strongly paraconsistent inference system with mathematical induction that does minimal damage to traditional natural deductive logical reasoning.

- Previous simple paraconsistent logics have not been satisfactory for the purposes of Software Engineering because of their many seemingly arbitrary variants and their idiosyncratic inference rules and notation. For example (according to Priest [2006]), most simple paraconsistent and relevance logics rule out Disjunctive Syllogism $((\Phi \vee \Psi), \neg\Phi \vdash \Psi)$.[5] However, Disjunctive Syllogism seems entirely natural for use in Software Engineering!
- The basic idea of *Strong Paraconsistency* is that no nontrivial inferences should be possible from the mere fact of an inconsistency.

    By the principle of simple paraconsistency, in the empty theory $\bot$ (which has no axioms), there is a proposition Ψ such that $P, \neg P \nvdash_\bot \Psi$.[6]

    However, for the purposes of reasoning about large software systems, a stronger principle is needed. The principle of strong paraconsistency is stronger than simple paraconsistency in that it requires $P, \neg P, Q \nvdash_\bot \neg Q$ because the inconsistency between P and $\neg P$ is not relevant to Q.

---

[3] Of course, truth is out the window as a semantic foundation for the inconsistent theories of large software systems!

[4] However, R-Mingle (Dunn, Meyer, Routley, *etc.*) is a paraconsistent logic that may be more promising. The author is collaborating with Mike Dunn to investigate the relationship of R-Mingle to the propositional fragment of Direct Logic (*i.e.* the fragment of Direct Logic restricted to negation, implication, conjunction, and disjunction).

[5] Indeed according to Routley [1979] *"The abandonment of disjunctive syllogism is indeed the characteristic feature of the relevant logic solution to the implicational paradoxes."*

[6] Using the notation $\vdash_T$ to mean "infers in the theory T." Note that the theories of Direct Logic are "open" in the *sense of open-ended schematic axiomatic systems* [Feferman 2007b]. The language of a theory can include any vocabulary in which its axioms may be applied, *i.e.*, it is not restricted to a specific vocabulary fixed in advance (or at any other time). Indeed a theory can receive new information at any time [Hewitt 1991, Cellucci 1992].

Of course, the following trivial inference is possible event with strong para-consistency: $P, \neg P \vdash_\perp (Q \vdash_\perp \neg P)$ and so forth.

4 Direct Logic

Direct Logic[7] is a powerful inference system for large-scale Organizational Comput-ing with the following goals [Hewitt 2006a 2007a]:[8]

- Provide a strongly paraconsistent unstratified reflective mathematical founda-tion for inference and reflection in large-scale Organizational Computing. Un-stratified inference and reflection means that Direct Logic is its own metatheory.
- Formalize a notion of "direct" inference for strongly paraconsistent theories.
- Support all "natural" deductive inference in strongly paraconsistent theories with the exception of general Proof by Contradiction and Disjunction Introduction.[9]
- Provide increased safety in reasoning about large-scale Organizational Comput-ing using strongly paraconsistent theories.

Multiple ORGs can make use of Direct Logic in a distributed decentralized fash-ion using a network of multiple strongly paraconsistent theories. There is no require-ment for an ORG to maintain a unified coherent mental state (as in Mental Agents [Hewitt 2007b]).

Direct Logic is Based on Conviction Rather Than Truth
Indirect inference has played an important role in science (emphasized by Karl Pop-per [1962]) as formulated in his principle of refutation which in its most stark form is as follows:

If $\vdash_T \neg$ Ob for some observation Ob, then it can be concluded that T is re-futed (in a theory called **Popper**), *i.e.*, $\vdash_{Popper} \neg T$.

Partly in reaction to Popper, Lakatos [1967, §2]) calls the view below *Euclidean* (although there is, of course, no claim concerning Euclid's own orientation):

"Classical epistemology has for two thousand years modeled its ideal of a theory, whether scientific or mathematical, on its conception of Euclidean ge-ometry. The ideal theory is a deductive system with an indubitable truth-injection at the top (a finite conjunction of axioms)—so that truth, flowing down from the top through the safe truth-preserving channels of valid inferences, in-undates the whole system."

Since truth is out the window for inconsistent theories, we have the following reformulation:

Inference in a theory T $(\vdash_T)$ ***carries*** conviction ***from antecedents to conse-quents in*** chains of inference.

---

[7] Direct Logic is distinct from the Direct Predicate Calculus [Ketonen and Weyhrauch 1984].
[8] How these goals are realized is described in the appendix to this paper.
[9] In this respect, Direct Logic differs from Quasi-Classical Logic [Besnard and Hunter 1995] for applications in information systems, which does include Disjunction Introduction.

Implication in Direct Logic

Lakatos characterizes his own view as *quasi-empirical*:

> *"Whether a deductive system is Euclidean or quasi-empirical is decided by the pattern of truth value flow in the system. The system is Euclidean if the characteristic flow is the transmission of truth from the set of axioms 'downwards' to the rest of the system—logic here is an organon of proof; it is quasi-empirical if the characteristic flow is retransmission of falsity from the false basic statements 'upwards' towards the 'hypothesis'—logic here is an organon of criticism."*

Direct Logic defines implication ($\rightarrow$) for a theory T in terms of negation and disjunction in the usual way as follows: $\Psi \rightarrow \Phi \;\cong\; \neg (\Psi \wedge \neg\Phi)$.

Consequently: $\Psi \rightarrow \Phi \;\vdash_T\; (\Psi \vdash_T \Phi) \wedge (\neg\Phi \vdash_T \neg\Psi)$. Thus we have the following principle:

Implication in a theory T ($\rightarrow$) carries conviction both ways[10] between antecedents and consequents in chains of implication.

Thus, in Direct Logic, implication ($\rightarrow$), rather than inference ($\vdash_T$), supports Lakatos quasi-empiricism

The Boolean operators $\neg$, $\vee$ and $\wedge$ form the usual Boolean algebra[11] (with double negation elimination, associativity, commutativity, distributivity, idempotence, and De Morgan's laws)[12] as well as the usual equivalences related to implication. However, Direct Logic also includes the non-Boolean $\vdash_T$ with the following holding:

$$\vdash_T (\Psi \vee \neg\Psi)$$

$$(\Psi \vee \Phi) \;\vdash_T\; (\neg\Psi \vdash_T \Phi) \wedge (\neg\Phi \vdash_T \Psi)$$

$$(\Psi \vee \Phi), (\Psi \vdash_T \Theta), (\Phi \vdash_T \Theta) \;\vdash_T\; \Theta$$

Direct Logic Uses Strong Paraconsistency to Facilitate Theory Development

Strongly paraconsistent theories can be easier to develop than classical theories because perfect absence of inconsistency is not required. In case of inconsistency, there will be some propositions that can be both proved and disproved, *i.e.*, there will be arguments both for and against the propositions.

A classic case of inconsistency occurs in the novel Catch-22 [Heller 1995] which states that a person *"would be crazy to fly more missions and sane if he didn't, but if he was sane he had to fly them. If he flew them he was crazy and didn't have to; but if*

---

[10] Called *"both ways"* because both ($\Psi \vdash_T \Phi$) and ($\neg\Phi \vdash_T \neg\Psi$) can be inferred from $\Psi \rightarrow \Phi$.

[11] But without a greatest and least element since there is no **TRUE** and **FALSE**.

[12] See the appendix for details.

he didn't want to he was sane and had to. Yossarian was moved very deeply by the absolute simplicity of this clause of Catch-22 and let out a respectful whistle. 'That's some catch, that Catch-22,' he observed."

So in the spirit of Catch-22, consider the follow axiomization of the above:[13]

1. Able[p, Fly], ¬Fly[p] ⊢Catch-22 Sane[p]   ⓘ *axiom*
2. Sane[p] ⊢Catch-22 Obligated[p, Fly]   ⓘ *axiom*
3. Sane[p], Obligated[p, Fly] ⊢Catch-22 Fly[p]   ⓘ *axiom*
4. Able[Yossarian, Fly]   ⓘ *axiom*
5. ¬Fly[Yossarian] ⊢Catch-22 Fly[Yossarian]   ⓘ *from 1 through 4*
6. Fly[Yossarian]   ⓘ *from 5 via proof by contradiction*
7. Fly[p] ⊢Catch-22 Crazy[p]   ⓘ *axiom*
8. Crazy[p] ⊢Catch-22 ¬Obligated[p, Fly]   ⓘ *axiom*
9. Sane[p], ¬Obligated[p, Fly] ⊢Catch-22 ¬Fly[p]   ⓘ *axiom*
10. Sane[Yossarian]   ⓘ *axiom*
11. ¬Fly[Yossarian]   ⓘ *from 6 through 10*

Thus there is an inconsistency in the above theory **Catch-22** in that:

6. ⊢Catch-22 Fly[Yossarian]

11. ⊢Catch-22 ¬ Fly[Yossarian]

Various objections can be made against the above axiomization of the theory Catch-22.[14] However, Catch-22 illustrates several important points:

- *Even a very simple microtheory can engender inconsistency*
- *Strong paraconsistency facilitates theory development because a single inconsistency is not disastrous.*
- *Direct Logic supports fine grained reasoning because inference does not necessarily carry conviction in the contrapositive direction.* For example, the general principle "A person who flies is crazy." (*i.e.,* Fly[p] ⊢Catch-22 Crazy[p]) does not support the interference of ¬Fly[Yossarian] from ¬Crazy[Yossarian]. *E.g.,* it might be the case that Fly[Yossarian] even though it infers Crazy[Yossarian] contradicting ¬Crazy[Yossarian].
- *Even though the theory* Catch-22 *is inconsistent, it is not meaningless.*

Reification in Organizational Computing

Every proposition Ψ has reification that is given by ⌜Ψ⌝∈**Sentences**⊆**XML**. Similarly every s∈ **Sentences** has an anti-reification that is the proposition given by ⌊s⌋. The following holds:

---

[13] The axiomatization makes use of higher order capabilities. For example a predicate like Able can take arguments Yossarian and the predicate Fly to form the proposition Able[Yossarian, Fly].

[14] Both Crazy[Yossarian] and Sane[Yossarian] can be inferred from the axiomatization, but this *per se* is not inconsistent.

Reification and anti-reification are needed for large Organizational Computing systems so that practices, policies, and norms can mutually speak about what has been said and its meaning.

The practices, policies, and norms are becoming increasingly *mutually reflective* in that they refer to and make use of each other. For example,

- Practices can be inferred by specialization of policies and can be dynamically checked against policies. Also practices can be dynamically searched for and invoked on the basis of policies.
- Policies can be checked against each other and against practices using model checking.
- Norms can be generated by inference from policies and proposed by generalization from practices.

Disadvantages of Stratified Reflection

To avoid inconsistencies in mathematics (e.g., Liar Paradox, Russell's Paradox, Curry's Paradox, *etc.*), some restrictions are needed around self-reference. The question is how to do it [Feferman 1984a, Restall 2006].

The approach which is currently standard in mathematics is the Tarskian framework of stratifying theories into a hierarchy of metatheories in which the semantics of each theory is formalized in its metatheory [Tarski and Vaught 1957].

According to Feferman [1984a]:

> *"...natural language abounds with directly or indirectly self-referential yet apparently harmless expressions—all of which are excluded from the Tarskian framework."*

Large Organizational Computing systems likewise abound with directly or indirectly self-referential statements in reasoning about their use cases, documentation, and code that are excluded by the Tarskian framework. Consequently the Tarskian framework is not very suitable for Organizational Computing.

Logical Reflection Principle for Organizational Computing

The *Logical Reflection Principle* for Direct Logic is that if Ψ is Admissible for T, then $\vdash_T (\lfloor \lceil \Psi \rceil \rfloor \longleftrightarrow \Psi))$.

Of course, the above criterion begs the questions of which sentences are Admissible in T ! A proposed answer is provided by the following:

Criterion of Admissibility[15]: Ψ is Admissible for T if and only if

$$(\neg\Psi) \vdash_T (\vdash_T \neg\Psi)$$

---

[15] Note that there is an asymmetry in the definition of Admissibility with respect to negation. In general it does not follow that $\neg\Psi$ is admissible for T just because Ψ is admissible for T. The asymmetry in Admissibility is analogous to the asymmetry in the Criterion of Refutability [Popper 1962]. For example the sentence *"There are no black swans."* is readily refuted by the observation of a black swan. However, the negation is not so readily refuted.

I.e., the Criterion of Admissibility is that a proposition is Admissible for a theory T if and only if its negation infers in T that its negation is provable in T.

The motivation for Admissibility builds on the denotational semantics of the Actor model of computation which were first developed in [Clinger 1981]. Subsequently [Hewitt 2006b] developed the TimedDiagrams model with the Representation Theorem which states:

> The denotation **Denote$_{\mathfrak{S}}$** of an Actor system $\mathfrak{S}$ represents all the possible behaviors of $\mathfrak{S}$ as

$$\text{Denote}_{\mathfrak{S}} = \bigsqcup\nolimits_{i \in \omega} \text{Progression}_{\mathfrak{S}}^{i}(\bot_{\mathfrak{S}})$$

where Progression$_{\mathfrak{S}}$ is an approximation function that takes a set of approximate behaviors to their next stage and $\bot_{\mathfrak{S}}$ is the initial behavior of $\mathfrak{S}$.

In this context, Ψ is Admissible for $\mathfrak{S}$ means that $\neg\Psi$ infers that there is a counter example to Ψ in Denote$_{\mathfrak{S}}$ so that in the denotational theory S induced by the system $\mathfrak{S}$:

$$(\neg\Psi) \vdash_{s} (\vdash_{s} \neg\Psi)$$

Work to be Done

There is much work to be done to further develop Direct Logic:

- The consistency of the semi-classical fragment of Direct Logic needs to be proved relative to the consistency of classical mathematics.
- Strong paraconsistency needs to be formally defined and proved.
- The decidability of the Variable-free Fragment[16] of Direct Logic needs to be settled. As remarked above, the Boolean Fragment is very close to R-Mingle (which is decidable).
- Tooling for Direct Logic needs to be developed to support large software systems.

5 Conclusion

This paper describes Organizational Computing and ORGs (Organizations of Restricted Generality) and some principles and practices by which they operate. It develops the thesis that inconsistency is the norm for large-scale Organizational Computing. The limitations of classical logical reasoning for inconsistent information are explained. A powerful inference system called Direct Logic is introduced that provides inference capabilities needed for large-scale Organizational Computing including unstratified reflection and strong paraconsistency.

---

[16] Including the non-Boolean $\vdash_T$.

Acknowledgments

Sol Feferman, Mike Genesereth, David Israel, Bill Jarrold, Ben Kuipers, Pat Langley, Vladimir Lifschitz, Frank McCabe, John McCarthy, Fanya S. Montalvo, Peter Neumann, Ray Perrault, Mark Stickel, Richard Waldinger, and others provided valuable feedback at seminars at Stanford, SRI, and UT Austin to an earlier version of the material in this paper. For the AAAI Spring Symposium'06, Ed Feigenbaum, Mehmet Göker, David Lavery, Doug Lenat, Dan Shapiro, and others provided valuable feedback. At MIT Henry Lieberman, Ted Selker, Gerry Sussman and the members of Common Sense Research Group made valuable comments. Reviewers for AAMAS '06 and '07, KR'06, COIN@AAMAS'06 and IJCAR'06 made suggestions for improvement.

In the logic community, Mike Dunn, Sol Feferman, Mike Genesereth, Tim Hinrichs, Mike Kassoff, John McCarthy, Chris Mortensen, Graham Priest, Dana Scott, Richard Weyhrauch and Ed Zalta provided valuable feedback. Dana Scott made helpful suggestions on reflection and incompleteness. Richard Waldinger provided extensive suggestions that resulted in better focusing a previous version of this paper and increasing its readability. Sol Feferman reminded me of the connection between Admissibility and Π_1. Discussion with Pat Hayes and Bob Kowalski provided insight into the early history of Prolog.

Communications from John McCarthy and Marvin Minsky suggested making common sense a focus. Mike Dunn collaborated on looking at the relationship of the Boolean Fragment of Direct Logic to R-Mingle. Greg Restall pointed out that Direct Logic differs from Relevance Logic. Gerry Allwein and Jeremy Forth made detailed comments and suggestions for improvement. Bob Kowalski and Erik Sandewall provided helpful pointers and discussion of the relationship with their work. Discussions with Ian Mason and Tim Hinrichs helped me develop Löb's theorem. Fanya S. Montalvo provided valuable comments. At CMU, Wilfried Sieg introduced me to his very interesting work with Clinton Field on automating the search for proofs of the Gödel incompleteness theorems. Also at CMU, I had productive discussions with Jeremy Avigad, Randy Bryant, John Reynolds, Katia Sycara, and Jeannette Wing. At my MIT seminar and afterwards, Marvin Minsky, Ted Selker, Gerry Sussman, and Pete Szolovits made helpful comments. Les Gasser, Mike Huhns, Victor Lesser, Pablo Noriega, Sascha Ossowski, Jaime Sichman, Munindar Singh, *etc.* provided valuable suggestions at AAMAS'07.

Jeremy Forth, Tim Hinrichs, Fanya S. Montalvo, and Richard Waldinger provided helpful comments and suggestions on the logically necessary inconsistencies in theories of Direct Logic. Rineke Verbrugge provided valuable comments and suggestions at MALLOW'07. Mike Genesereth and Gordon Plotkin kindly hosted my lectures at Stanford and Edinburgh, respectively, on *"The Logical Necessity of Inconsistency"*.

References

Agha, G., Mason, I., Smith, S., Talcott, C.: A foundation for Actor computation. Journal of Functional Programming (1997)

Besnard, P., Hunter, A.: Quasi-classical Logic: Non-trivializable classical reasoning from inconsistent information. Symbolic and Quantitative Approaches to Reasoning and Uncertainty (1995)

Bowker, G., Star, S.L., Turner, W., Gasser, L. (eds.): Social Science Research, Technical Systems and Cooperative Work. Lawrence Earlbaum (1997)

Carnap, R.: Logische Syntax der Sprache (The Logical Syntax of Language Open Court Publishing 2003) (1934)

Cellucci, C.: "Gödel's Incompleteness Theorem and the Philosophy of Open Systems" Kurt Gödel: Actes du Colloque, Neuchâtel 13-14 juin 1991, Travaux de logique N. 7, Centre de Recherches Sémiologiques, Université de Neuchâtel. (1992), http://w3.uniroma1.it/cellucci/documents/Goedel.pdf

Dahl, O.-J., Nygaard, K.: Class and subclass declarations. IFIP TC2 (May 1967)

Feferman, S.: Toward Useful Type-Free Theories, I. In: Martin, R. (ed.) Recent Essays on Truth and the Liar Paradox, Claraendon Press (1984a)

Feferman, S.: Kurt Gödel: Conviction and Caution. Philosophia Naturalis 21 (1984b)

Feferman, S.: Axioms for determinateness and truth (2007a), http://math.stanford.edu/~feferman/papers.html

Feferman, S.: Gödel, Nagel, minds and machines (October 25, 2007), (2007b), http://math.stanford.edu/~feferman/papers/godelnagel.pdf

Gödel, K.: On formally undecidable propositions of Principia Mathematica translated by Bernard Meltzer. Basic Books (1962). Monatshefte für Mathematik und Physik, vol. 38, pp. 173–198 (1931)

Hewitt, C., Bishop, P., Steiger, R.: A Universal Modular Actor Formalism for Artificial Intelligence. IJCAI (1973)

Hewitt, C., Inman, J.: DAI Betwixt and Between: From 'Intelligent Agents' to Open Systems Science. IEEE Transactions on Systems, Man, and Cybernetics (November/December 1991)

Hewitt, C.: The repeated demise of logic programming and why it will be reincarnated. What Went Wrong and Why (2006a). Technical Report SS-06-08 (March 2006)

Hewitt, C.: What is Commitment? Physical, Organizational, and Social. In: Noriega, P., Vázquez-Salceda, J., Boella, G., Boissier, O., Dignum, V., Fornara, N., Matson, E. (eds.) COIN 2006. LNCS (LNAI), vol. 4386, pp. 293–307. Springer, Heidelberg (2007)

Hewitt, C.: Organizational Computing Requires Unstratified Paraconsistency and Reflection. COIN@AAMAS, 2007 (2007a)

Hewitt, C.: The Downfall of Mental Agents in the Implementation of Large Software Systems. AAAI Magazine issue on What went wrong and why, 2007 (2007b)

Hewitt, C.: Common sense for concurrency and strong paraconsistency using unstratified inference and reflection. Submitted for publication to AI Journal special issue on Common Sense, 2007 (2007c)

Jennings, N.: Commitments and conventions: The foundation of coordination in multi-agent systems. Knowledge Engineering Review 3 (1993)

Ketonen, J., Weyhrauch, R.: A decidable fragment of Predicate Calculus. Theoretical Computer Science (1984)

Kornfeld, B., Hewitt, C.: The Scientific Community Metaphor. IEEE Transactions on Systems, Man, and Cybernetics (January 1981)

Lakatos, I. (1967). A renaissance of empiricism in the recent philosophy of mathematics? Mathematics, Science and Epistemology (1978)

Leitgeb, H.: What theories of truth should be like (but cannot be). Philosophy Compass 2(2)

Löb, M.: Solution of a problem of Leon Henkin. Journal of Symbolic Logic 20 (1955)

McGee, V.: In Praise of the Free Lunch: Why Disquotationalists Should Embrace Compositional Semantics. Self-Reference. CSLI Publications (2006)

Noriega, P.: Agent Mediated Auctions: The Fishmarket Metaphor. Ph.D., Barcelona (1997)

Priest, G.: 60% Proof: Lakatos, Proof, and Paraconsistency (2006),
    http://garnet.acns.fsu.edu/~tan02/OPC%20Week%20Three/Priest.pdf

Priest, G., Tanaka, K.: Paraconsistent Logic. The Stanford Encyclopedia of Philosophy. Winter (2004)

Restall, G.: Curry's Revenge: the costs of non-classical solutions to the paradoxes of self-reference (to appear in The Revenge of the Liar, Beall, J.C (Ed.) Oxford University Press, 2007) (July 12, 2006)

Rosenberg, S.: Dreaming in code. Crown Publishing (2007)

Rosser, J.B.: Extensions of Some Theorems of Gödel and Church. Journal of Symbolic. Logic 1(3) (1936)

Routley, R.: Dialectical Logic, Semantics and Metamathematics. Erkenntnis 14 (1979)

Shankar, N.: Metamathematics, Machines, and Gödel's Proof. Cambridge University Press, Cambridge (1994)

Shapiro, S.: Lakatos and logic Comments on Graham Priest's '60% proof: Lakatos, proof, and paraconsistency'. (Preprint, 2006),
    http://garnet.acns.fsu.edu/~tan02/OPC%20Week%20Three/Commentary%20on%20Priest.
    pdf#search=%22paraconsistency%202006%20filetype%3Apdf%22

Sieg, W., Field, C.: Automated search for Gödel proofs. Annals of Pure and Applied Logic (2005)

Singh, M., Huhns, M.: Service-Oriented Computing: Semantics, Processes, Agents. John Wiley & Sons, Chichester (2005)

Tarski, A.: The semantic conception of truth and the foundations of semantics. Philosophy and Phenomenological Research 4 (Reprinted in Readings in Philosophical Analysis, Appleton-1944) (1944)

Tarski, A., Vaught, R.: Arithmetical extensions of relational systems. Compositio Mathematica 13 (1957)

Wooldridge, M.: Reasoning about Rational Agents. MIT Press (2000)

Appendix: Principles of Direct Logic

This appendix discusses foundational principles of Direct Logic focusing on inference in a theory T ($\vdash_T$) where T is a paraconsistent reflective theory for large software systems. Direct Logic also supports classical mathematical inference ($\vdash$). By convention all paraconsistent theories inherit from mathematics, *i.e.*, $\vdash ((\vdash \Psi) \rightarrow \vdash_T \Psi)$.

All of the principles below concerning $\vdash_T$ apply equally well to the overreaching classical inference relationship for the classical fragment of Direct Logic ($\vdash$).

Direct Principles
Direct principles that connect propositions together by direct reasoning are as follows:

Reiteration: $\vdash (\Psi \vdash_T \Psi)$ ⓘ *a proposition infers itself*

Exchange: $\vdash (\Psi,\Phi \vdash_T \Phi,\Psi)$ ⓘ *the order in which propositions are* ⓘ*written does not matter*

Residuation: $\vdash ((\Psi,\Phi \vdash_T \Theta) \longleftrightarrow (\Psi \vdash_T (\Phi \vdash_T \Theta)))$ ⓘ *hypotheses may be freely* ⓘ *introduced and discharged*

Monotonicity: $\vdash ((\Psi \vdash_T \Phi) \to (\Psi, \Theta \vdash_T \Phi))$ ⓘ *an inference remains if new* ⓘ *information is added*

Dropping: $\vdash ((\Psi \vdash_T \Phi,\Theta) \to (\Psi \vdash_T \Phi))$ ⓘ *an inference remains correct if* ⓘ *extra conclusions are dropped*

Combination Principles

The following combination principles concern combining different inferences together:

Independent Inference:

$$\vdash ((\vdash_T \Psi) \wedge (\vdash_T \Phi)) \to (\vdash_T \Psi,\Theta))$$ ⓘ *inferences can be combined*

Transitivity: $\vdash (((\Psi \vdash_T \Phi) \wedge (\Phi \vdash_T \Theta)) \to (\Psi \vdash_T \Theta))$ ⓘ *inference is transitive*

Theory Principles

The paraconsistent theory principles are as follows:

Faithfulness: $\vdash ((\vdash_T \vdash_T \Psi) \to (\vdash_T \Psi))$

Adequacy: $\vdash ((\vdash_T \Psi) \to (\vdash_T \vdash_T \Psi))$

Detachment: $\vdash ((\vdash_T \Psi, (\Psi \vdash_T \Phi)) \to \vdash_T \Phi)$

Soundness: $\vdash ((\Psi \vdash_T \Phi) \to ((\vdash_T \Psi) \to \vdash_T \Phi))$

Indirect Inference

Direct Logic supports direct versions of indirect inference for paraconsistent theories as follows:

- ***Simple Direct Indirect Inference:***
  $\vdash ((\Psi \vdash_T \neg\Psi) \to \vdash_T \neg\Psi)$ which states that a proposition can be disproved by showing that the proposition infers its own negation.
- ***Right Meta Direct Indirect Inference:***
  $\vdash ((\Psi \vdash_T (\vdash_T \neg\Psi)) \to \vdash_T \neg\Psi)$ which states that a proposition can be disproved by showing that the proposition infers a proof of its own negation.
- ***Left Meta Direct Indirect Inference:***
  $\vdash (((\vdash_T \Psi) \vdash_T \neg\Psi) \to \neg \vdash_T \Psi)$ which states that provability of a proposition can be disproved by showing that its provability infers its own negation.
- ***Both Meta Direct Indirect Inference:***
  $\vdash (((\vdash_T \Psi) \vdash_T (\vdash_T \neg\Psi)) \to \neg \vdash_T \Psi)$ which states that provability of a proposition can be disproved by showing that its provability infers provability of its negation.

Direct Indirect Proof can sometimes do inferences that are traditionally done using Full Indirect Inference. For example the proof of the incompleteness of paraconsistent theories in this paper makes use of Direct Indirect Inference.

Nontriviality
Direct Logic supports the following nontriviality[17] principles for theories:

- **Direct Nontriviality:**

  $\vdash ((\neg \Psi) \vdash_T \neg \vdash_T \Psi)$ which states that the negation of a proposition infers that the proposition cannot be proved

- **Meta Nontriviality:**

  $\vdash ((\vdash_T \neg \Psi) \rightarrow \neg \vdash_T \Psi)$ which states that if the negation of a proposition can be proved, then the proposition cannot be proved.

Fixed Point Theorem
Theorem [a λ-calculus version of Carnap 1934 pg 91 after Gödel 1931][18]:
Let f$\in$ (**Sentences$\rightarrow$Sentences**)

$\vdash (\lfloor \mathsf{Fix}(f) \rfloor \longleftrightarrow \lfloor f\,(\mathsf{Fix}(f)) \rfloor)$
  where $\mathsf{Fix}(f) \equiv \Theta(\Theta)$ ① *which exists because* f *always converges*
    where $\Theta \equiv \lambda(g)\, f(\lambda(x)\,(g(g))(x))$

Proof. See [Hewitt 2007c].

Incompleteness and Inconsistency
Theorem: A paraconsistent theory is incomplete,
Define

$\mathsf{Paradox}_T \equiv \lfloor \mathsf{Fix}(\mathsf{Diagonalize}) \rfloor$ *where* $\mathsf{Diagonalize} \equiv \lambda(s) \lceil \neg \vdash_T \lfloor s \rfloor \rceil$
  It is sufficient to prove the following:

  1. $\vdash_T \neg \vdash_T \mathsf{Paradox}_T$
  2. $\vdash_T \neg \vdash_T \neg\, \mathsf{Paradox}_T$
  3. $\vdash_T \mathsf{Paradox}_T$

Proof. See [Hewitt 2007c].

Theorem: Theories of Direct Logic are inconsistent[19]
It is sufficient to show that T proves both $\vdash_T \mathsf{Paradox}_T$ and its negation, *i.e.,*

  1. $\vdash_T \vdash_T \mathsf{Paradox}_T$
  2. $\vdash_T \neg \vdash_T \mathsf{Paradox}_T$

Proof. See [Hewitt 2007c].

---

[17] By definition a theory T is *nontrivial* if and only if there is a formula Ψ such that $\neg \vdash_T \Psi$.
[18] Credited in Kurt Gödel, *Collected Works* vol. I, p. 363, ftn. 23.
[19] *cf.* [Routley 1979], [Priest and Tanaka 2004], *etc.*

But all is not lost because the following can be said about this logically necessary inconsistency:[20]

- Because T is strongly paraconsistent, that T is inconsistent about $\vdash_T \text{Paradox}_T$ (by itself) should not affect other reasoning. Also the subject matter of $\vdash_T \text{Paradox}_T$ is not of general interest in software engineering and should not affect reasoning about current large software systems. So do software engineers need to care that T is inconsistent about $\vdash_T \text{Paradox}_T$ as opposed to all the other inconsistencies of T which they care about more?[21]

- The logically necessary inconsistency concerning $\vdash_T \text{Paradox}_T$ is a nice illustration of how inconsistencies often arise in large software systems: "*there can be good arguments (proofs) on both sides for contradictory conclusions*".

A big advantage of paraconsistent logic is that it makes fewer mistakes than classical logic when dealing with inconsistent theories. Since software engineers have to deal with theories chock full of inconsistencies, paraconsistency should be attractive. However, to make it relevant we need to provide them with tools that are cost effective.

Provable Meta Self Inferences in Theories of Direct Logic

Provable Meta Self Inferred propositions for T are those Ψ such that

$$\vdash_T ((\vdash_T \Psi) \vdash_T \Psi)$$

Theorem:[22] *If Ψ is Admissible and Provably Meta Self Inferred for T, then $\vdash_T \Psi$*

Proof. See [Hewitt 2007c].

---

[20] At first, TRUTH may seem like a desirable property for sentences in theories for large software systems. However, because a paraconsistent reflective theory T is necessarily inconsistent about $\vdash_T \text{Paradox}_T$, it is impossible to consistently assign truth values to sentences of T. In particular it is impossible to consistently assign a truth value to the proposition $\vdash_T \text{Paradox}_T$. If the proposition is assigned the value TRUE, then (by the rules for truth values) it must also be assigned FALSE and vice versa. It is not obvious what (if anything) is wrong or how to fix it.

Of course this is contrary to the traditional view of Tarski. *E.g.*,

> I believe everybody agrees that one of the reasons which may compel us to reject an empirical theory is the proof of its inconsistency: a theory becomes untenable if we succeeded in deriving from it two contradictory sentences . . . . It seems to me that the real reason of our attitude is...: We know (if only intuitively) that an inconsistent theory must contain false sentences. [Tarski 1944]

On the other hand, Frege [1915] suggested that, in a logically perfect language, the word '*true*' would not appear! According to McGee [2006], he argued that "*when we say that it is true that seawater is salty, we don't add anything to what we say when we say simply that seawater is salty, so the notion of truth, in spite of being the central notion of* [classical] *logic, is a singularly ineffectual notion. It is surprising that we would have occasion to use such an impotent notion, nevermind that we would regard it as valuable and important.*"

[21] Of course, there are other inconsistent sentences of the same ilk, *cf.*, Rosser [1936].

[22] After Löb [1955].

Using Case-Based Reasoning in Autonomic Electronic Institutions

Eva Bou[1], Maite López-Sánchez[2], and Juan Antonio Rodríguez-Aguilar[1]

[1] IIIA, Artificial Intelligence Research Institute
CSIC, Spanish National Research Council, Campus UAB 08193 Bellaterra, Spain
{ebm,jar}@iiia.csic.es
[2] WAI, Volume Visualization and Artificial Intelligence, MAiA Dept.,
Universitat de Barcelona
maite@maia.ub.es

Abstract. Electronic institutions (EIs) define the rules of the game in agent societies by fixing what agents are permitted and forbidden to do and under what circumstances. Autonomic Electronic Institutions (AEIs) adapt their regulations to comply with their goals despite coping with varying populations of self-interested external agents. This paper presents a self-adaptation model based on Case-Based Reasoning (CBR) that allows an AEI to yield a dynamical answer to changing circumstances.

1 Introduction

The growing complexity of advanced information systems in the recent years, characterized by being distributed, open and dynamical, has given rise to interest in the development of systems capable of self-management. Such systems are known as self-* systems [1], where the * sign indicates a variety of properties: self-organization, self-configuration, self-diagnosis, self-repair, etc. A particular approximation to the construction of self-* systems is represented by the vision of autonomic computing [2], which constitutes an approximation to computing systems with a minimal human interference. Some of the many characteristics of an autonomic system are: it must configure and reconfigure itself automatically under changing (and unpredictable) conditions; it must aim at optimizing its inner workings, monitoring its components and adjusting its processing in order to achieve its goals; it must be able to diagnose the causes of its eventual malfunctions and repair itself; and it must act in accordance to and operate into a heterogeneous and open environment.

Electronic Institutions (EIs) [3] have been proved to be valuable to regulate open agent systems. EIs define the rules of the game by fixing what agents are permitted and forbidden to do and under what circumstances. We have defined Autonomic Electronic Institutions (AEIs) as an EI with autonomic capabilities that allows it to adapt its regulations to comply with institutional goals despite varying agent's behaviours [4]. Thus, an AEI has to self-configure its regulations to accomplish its institutional goals. In previous work [4] we have learned

J.S. Sichman et al. (Eds.): COIN 2007, LNAI 4870, pp. 125–138, 2008.
© Springer-Verlag Berlin Heidelberg 2008

those regulations that best accomplished the institutional goals for a collection of simulated agent populations. This paper extends that work with a Case-Based Reasoning (CBR) approach that allows an AEI to self-configure its regulations for any agent population. Since our hypothesis is that populations that behave similarly can be regulated in a similar manner, the CBR approach helps us identify populations that behave similarly and subsequently retrieve the "control" parameters for an AEI to regulate it.

The paper is organized as follows. In section 2 we describe the notion of autonomic electronic institutions. Section 3 details the learning model that we propose and how an AEI uses CBR. Section 4 describes the case study employed as a scenario wherein we have tested our model. Section 5 provides some empirical results. Finally, section 6 summarizes some conclusions and related work and outlines paths to future research.

2   Autonomic Electronic Institutions

In general, an EI [3] involves different groups of agents playing different roles within scenes in a performative structure. Each scene is composed of a coordination protocol along with the specification of the roles that can take part in the scene.

According to [3] an EI is solely composed of: a dialogic framework (DF) establishing the common language and ontology to be employed by participating agents; a performative structure (PS) defining its activities along with their relationships; and a set of norms (N) defining the consequences of agents' actions. We have extended the notion of EI to support self-configuration, in the sense of regulation adaptation. In this manner in [4] we incorporate notions of institutional goals and regulation configuration to define an *autonomic electronic institution* (AEI) as a tuple: $\langle PS, N, DF, G, P_i, P_e, P_a, V, \delta, \gamma \rangle$. Next, we only provide an intuitive idea about the elements of an AEI (further details can be found in [4]).

We assume that the main objective of an AEI is to accomplish its institutional goals (G). For this purpose, an AEI will adapt. We assume that the institution can observe the environment where agents interact (P_e), the institutional state of the agents participating in the institution (P_a), and its own state (P_i) to assess whether its goals are accomplished or not. Since an AEI has no access whatsoever to the inner state of any participating agent, only the *institutional (social) state* of an agent (P_a) can change. Therefore, each agent (a_i) can be fully characterized by his institutional state $P_{a_i} = \langle a_{i_1}, \ldots, a_{i_m} \rangle$ where $a_{i_j} \in \mathbb{R}$, $1 \leq j \leq m$ is an observable value of agent a_i. Taking the traffic as an example of an AEI, the speed of a car could be an example of an observable value of an agent; the number of lanes could be an example of an observable value of the environment; and the number of polices the institution uses to control the cars could be an example of an observable value of the state of the institution.

Formally, we define the goals of an AEI as a finite set of constraints $G = \{c_1, \ldots, c_p\}$ where each c_i is defined as an expression $g_i(V) \lhd [m_i, M_i]$ where $m_i, M_i \in \mathbb{R}$, $\lhd$ stands for either $\in$ or $\notin$. Additionally, g_i is a function over the reference values $V = \langle v_1, \ldots, v_q \rangle$, where each v_j results from applying a function h_j upon the agents' properties, the environmental properties and/or the institutional properties; $v_j = h_j(P_a, P_e, P_i)$, $1 \leq j \leq q$. In this manner, each goal is a constraint upon the reference values where each pair m_i and M_i defines an interval associated to the constraint. Continuing with the traffic example, an example of an institutional goal could be to minimize the number of accidents. Thus, the institution achieves its goals if all $g_i(V)$ values satisfy their corresponding constraints of belonging (at least to a certain degree) to their associated intervals. This is measured by means of a satisfaction function that computes the goal satisfaction degree (see [4] for further details).

The AEI definition includes the mechanisms to support the adaptation with the *normative transition function* (δ), and with the *PS transition function* (γ). An AEI employs norms to constrain agents' behaviors and to assess the consequences of their actions within the scope of the institution. We focus on norms describing prohibitions parametrically. So that each norm $N_i \in N$, $i = 1, \ldots, n$, has a set of parameters $\langle p_{i,1}^N, \ldots, p_{i,m_i}^N \rangle \in \mathbb{R}^{m_i}$. In fact, this parameters correspond to the variables in the *norm transition function* that will allow the institution to adapt. Continuing with the same traffic example, an example of a norm could be to stop always before to enter in an intersection and it norm can be parametrized by an associated fine applied if a car does not fulfill it. Notice that our AEI can not learn new norms, it only can adapt its norms by changing their parameters. On the other hand, adapting a PS involves the definition of a set of parameters whose values will be changed by the PS transition function. We define each scene in the performative structure, $S_i \in PS$, $i = 1, \ldots, t$, as having a set of parameters $\langle p_{i,1}^R, \ldots, p_{i,q_i}^R \rangle \in \mathbb{N}^{q_i}$ where $p_{i,j}^R$ stands for the number of agents playing role r_j in scene S_i. Thus, changing the values of these parameters means changing the performative structure.

The AEI definition includes the mechanisms to support the adaptation with the *normative transition function* (δ), and with the *PS transition function* (γ). We propose to use learning methods to learnt the *normative transition function* (δ), and the *PS transition function* (γ). Next section details the learning model used to adapt the AEI by changing those parameters.

3   Learning Model

Our aim is that at run-time an AEI could adapt its regulations to any population. We propose to learn the *norm transition function* (δ) and the *PS transition function* (γ) in two different steps in an overall learning process. In previous work [4] we have approached the first learning step, which corresponds to learn the best parameters for a set of predefined populations. In this work we focus on the second learning step: how to adapt the parameters to any population. As shown in Figure 1, in an initial step our AEI learns by simulation the best parameters for a collection of different agent populations. For each population of agents (A), the algorithm explores the space of parameter values ($I_1, .., I_k$) in search for the ones that lead the AEI to best accomplish its goals (G) for this population of

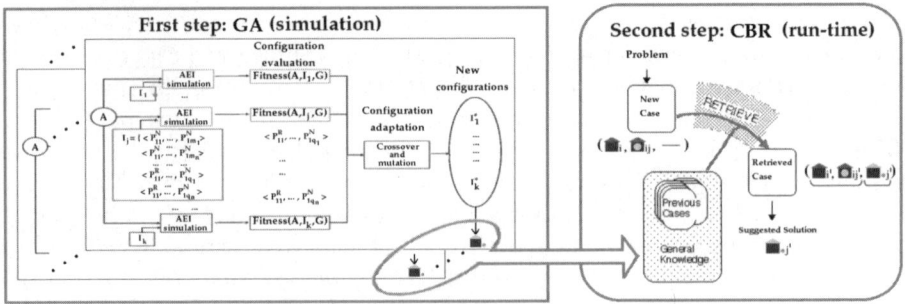

Fig. 1. Learning Model in two steps

agents. Afterwards, we propose to use a Case-Based Reasoning (CBR) approach as a second step because it allows the AEI to solve situations that have been learned previously. We assume that agent populations that behave in similar way caused similar situations that may require similar solutions. Thus, at a second step an AEI identifies, in run-time, those situations for which its goals are not accomplished and uses CBR to retrieve a solution (regulation parameters) from the most similar situation in the knowledge base.

3.1   Applying CBR

Case Based Reasoning (CBR) [5] is based on learning from experience. The idea is to search in the experience (memory) of the system for similar situations, called cases, and using the corresponding solution to solve the current problem. In general, a new problem in a CBR system is solved by retrieving similar cases, reusing the case solution, revising the reused solution, and retaining the new experience. In this work we focus our attention in the first step of the CBR cycle, namely the retrieve process. Nevertheless, before addressing it, it is necessary to choose a representation for cases.

Case Definition. The representation of cases is central to any CBR system. Cases must be represented based on the knowledge of the problem domain in order to choose the main features that better describe the case and thus that better help the processes involved in the CBR cycle. As to AEIs, we differentiate the following main features to be considered to represent cases:

- **AEI parameters' values.** They represent the parameters' values of some institution, namely the norm parameters' values and the performative structure parameters' values that an AEI uses for regulating agents.
- **Runtime behaviour.** They represent the global behaviour of the institution at runtime for some agent population when the institution uses the *AEI parameters' values*.
- **Best AEI parameters' values.** They represent the learned parameters' values of the institution for the previous agent population. In other words:

the solution. Thus, they correspond to the parameters that the institution must apply in order to accomplish its institutional goals given both previous AEI parameters' values and runtime behaviour.

More precisely, regarding AEIs, we propose the definition of a case as a tuple $(N^p, PS^p, V, pop, N^{p*}, PS^{p*})$, where:

- (N^p, PS^p) stands for the AEI parameters' values:
  - N^p stands for the current norm parameters' values;
  - PS^p stands for the current performative structure parameters' values;
- (V, pop) stands for the runtime behaviour:
  - V stands for the current set of reference values;
  - pop stands for statistic data that characterises the behaviour of the agents' population at runtime[1];
- (N^{p*}, PS^{p*}) stands for the best AEI parameters' values:
  - N^{p*}: represents the best values for the norm parameters given the current norm parameters values (N^p) and the runtime behaviour (V,pop); and
  - PS^{p*}: represents the best values for the performative structure parameters given the current performative structure parameters values (PS^p) and the runtime behaviour (V,pop).

Thus, a case represents how an AEI (using N^p as norm values and PS^p as performative structure values) regulating a population of agents (showing the runtime behaviour described by pop and V) should change its regulations (to the N^{p*} and the PS^{p*} values). Notice that each case is an entry of the *normative transition function* (δ) and the *PS transition function* (γ). That is, the set of all cases approximate both transition functions.

Similarity Function. In order to compare two cases we must define an appropriate similarity function based on our representation of cases. We use aggregated distance function to compute the degree of similarity between a new case C^i and a case C^j in the case base:

$$S(C^i, C^j) = w_1 \cdot s\_AEI(C^i, C^j) + w_2 \cdot s\_V(C^i, C^j) + w_3 \cdot s\_pop(C^i, C^j) \quad (1)$$

where s_AEI corresponds to the distance of the AEI parameters' values (N^p, PS^p), s_V and s_pop correspond to the distance of the runtime behaviour (V,pop), and $w_1, w_2, w_3 \leq 0$ are weighting factors such that $w_1 + w_2 + w_3 = 1$. The s_AEI, s_V and s_pop distance functions are computed as the distance average of their attributes. To assess the distance between the values of an attribute we use:

$$sim(attr^i, attr^j) = \frac{|attr^i - attr^j|}{max(attr) - min(attr)} \quad (2)$$

where $min(attr)$ and $max(attr)$ correspond to the limits of the interval of values of the attribute considered in the domain.

---

[1] Notice that this data corresponds to reference values.

The Retrieval Process. In order to retrieve the most similar case to the problem case C^i without comparing all cases in the case base, we propose to perform this process in two steps:

1. Compare the AEI parameters' values, (N^p, PS^p), of the problem case C^i with the collection of all the AEI parameters' values in the case base using s_AEI and select the set of AEI parameters' values that best match.
2. Access the set of examples in the case base with these AEI parameters' values. Afterwards, we compare case C^i with these examples and select the case that best matches it based on distance function S.[2]

We use the first step with the idea that the most similar case must have similar AEI values because the runtime behaviour depends a lot of the AEI parameters' values. In fact, this is our hypothesis since we want to change the AEI parameters' values to change in some way the population behaviour and thus modify the runtime behaviour in order to achieve the institutional goals. The first step makes easy and fast the access to the most similar cases because we concentrate on only comparing the cases with similar AEI parameters' values. Thus, we do not need to compare all the cases of the case base. Moreover, we only need to compute once the distance function s_AEI for all cases with the same values of AEI parameters' values.

4   Case Study: Traffic Control

In order to test our model, we have considered and implemented the Traffic Regulation Authority as an Autonomic Electronic Institution, and cars moving along the road network as external agents interacting inside a traffic scene. Getting into more detail, we focus on a two-road junction where no traffic signals are considered. Therefore, cars must only coordinate by following the traffic norms imposed by the AEI. Our case study considers the performative structure to be a single traffic scene with two agent roles: one institutional role played by police agents; and one external role played by car agents.

We assume institutional agents to be in charge of detecting norm violations so that we will refer to them as police agents. The performative structure is parametrized by the number of agents playing the police role. Each police agent is able to detect only a portion of the total number of norm violations that car agents actually do. Norms within this normative environment are related to actions performed by cars. We consider two priority norms: the 'right hand-side priority norm', that prevents a car reaching the junction to move forward or to turn left whenever there is another car on its right; and the 'front priority norm', that applies when two cars reaching the junction are located on opposite lines, and one of them intends to turn left. Additionally, norms are parametrized by the associated penalties that are imposed to those cars refusing or failing

---

[2] Notice that we use a distance function as similarity function where low values imply high similarity.

to follow them. Cars do have a limited amount of points so that norm offenses cause points reduction. The institution forbids external agents to drive without points in their accounts.

In this work we focus on homogeneous populations where all agents in the population share the same behaviour. We propose to model each population based on three parameters (henceforth referred to as agent norm compliance parameters): $\langle fulfill\_prob, high\_punishment, inc\_prob \rangle$; where $fulfill\_prob \in [0,1]$ stands for the probability of complying with norms that is initially assigned to each agent; $high\_punishment \in \mathbb{N}$ stands for the fine threshold that causes an agent to consider a fine to be high enough to reconsider the norm compliance; and $inc\_prob \in [0,1]$ stands for the probability increment that is added to $fulfill\_prob$ when the fine norm is greater than the fine threshold ($high\_punishment$). Car agents decide whether to comply with a norm based on their norm compliance parameters along with the percentage (between 0 and 1) of police agents that the traffic authority has deployed on the traffic environment. To summarise, agents decide whether they keep on moving –regardless of violating norms– or they stop –in order to comply with norms– based on a probability that is computed as:

$$prob = \begin{cases} police \cdot fulfill\_prob & fine \leq high\_punishment \\ police \cdot (fulfill\_prob + inc\_prob) & fine > high\_punishment \end{cases} \quad (3)$$

The institution can observe the external agents' institutional properties (P_a) along time. Considering our road junction case study, we identity different reference values, $V = \langle col,\ off,\ crash,\ block,\ expel,\ police \rangle$ where col indicates total number of collisions for the last t_w ticks ($0 \leq t_w \leq t_{now}$), off indicates the total number of offenses accumulated by all agents for the last t_w ticks, $crash$ counts the number of cars involved in accidents for the last t_w ticks, $block$ describes how many cars have been blocked by other cars for the last t_w ticks, $expel$ indicates the number of cars that have been expelled out of the environment due to running out of points for the last t_w ticks, and finally, $police$ indicates the percentage of police agents that the institution deploys in order to control the traffic environment.

The institution tries to accomplish its institutional goals by specifying the penalties of both priority norms and by specifying how many police agents should be deployed in the traffic scene. In this work we focus on four institutional goals: (i) minimize the number of collisions; (ii) minimize the number of offenses; (iii) minimize the number of expelled cars; (iv) and minimize the percentage of police agents to deploy to control the traffic environment. Notice, though, that these offences do not refer to offences detected by police agents but to the real offences that have been actually carried out by car agents.

5   Empirical Evaluation

As a proof of concept of our proposal in section 3, we extend the experimental setting for the traffic case study employed in [4]. The environment is modeled as a 2-lane road junction and populated with 10 homogeneous cars (endowed with 40 points each). Cars correspond to external agents without learning skills. They just move based on their random trajectories and the probability of complying with a norm (based on the function defined in (3)). During each discrete simulation, the institution replaces those cars running out of points by new cars, so that the cars' population is kept constant.

The four institutional goals, related to the *col*, *off*, *expel* and *police* reference values, are combined in a weighted addition, with weights 0.4, 0.4, 0.1 and 0.1 respectively. Thus, the first two goals are considered to be more important. The goal satisfaction is measured by combining the degree of satisfaction of these four institutional goals.

Table 1. Agent populations employed to generate the case base

Populations	Pop. 1	Pop. 2	Pop. 3	Pop. 4	Pop. 5	Pop. 6	Pop. 7
$fulfill\_prob$	0.5	0.5	0.5	0.5	0.5	0.5	0.5
$high\_punishment$	0	3	5	8	10	12	14
inc_prob	0.4	0.4	0.4	0.4	0.4	0.4	0.4
$fine^*_{right}$	2	5	8	11	13	14	15
$fine^*_{front}$	1	4	6	9	12	13	15
$police^*$	1	1	1	1	1	1	1

As mentioned in section 3, (during training period) an AEI generates an initial base of cases from simulations of a set of prototypical populations. Following the tuple case definition introduced in section 3.1, $(N^p, PS^p, V, pop, N^{p*}, PS^{p*})$, we define a case C^i in this scenario as follows:

- $N^p = (fine_{right}, fine_{front})$ are the values of both norms' parameters;
- $PS^p = (police)$ is the value of the performative structure parameter;
- $V = (col, crash, off, block, expel)$ are the reference values;
- pop = $(mean\_off, median\_off, mean\_frequency\_off, median\_frequency\_off)$ contains the mean number of offenses, the median number of offenses, the mean of the frequency of offenses, and the median of the frequency of offenses carried out by agents for the last t_w ticks $(0 \leq t_w \leq t_{now})$;
- $N^{p*} = (fine^*_{right}, fine^*_{front})$ are the best values for both norms' parameters;
- $PS^{p*} = (police^*)$ is the best value for the parameter of the performative structure.

Table 1 shows the seven populations we have considered to generate the case base. They are characterized by their norm compliance parameters, being $fulfill\_prob = 0.5$ and $inc\_prob = 0.4$ for all of them, whereas $high\_punishment$ varies from 0 to 14. The $fine^*_{right}$, $fine^*_{front}$ and $police^*$ values in Table 1 are taken to be the best AEI parameters' values (N^{p*}, PS^{p*}).

5.1   Similarity Function

We use the aggregated distance function defined in (1) to compute the degree of similarity between two cases. We have set the weights as follows: $w_1 = 0.1$, $w_2 = 0.5$, and $w_3 = 0.4$. Regarding the attributes of the AEI parameters' values, the $fine_{front}$ and $fine_{right}$ values are in the interval $[0, 15]$, and the *police* values are in the interval $[0, 1]$. However, the attributes of the runtime behaviour have not known limited values. We have established limits based on the values of the initial generated cases. Thus, we have established that the *col* values are in the interval $[0, 300]$, *crash* $\in [0, 400]$, *off* $\in [0, 500]$, *block* $\in [0, 200]$, *expel* $\in [0, 900]$, *mean_off* $\in [0, 30]$, *median_off* $\in [0, 30]$, *mean_frequency_off* $\in [0, 2]$, and *median_frequency_off* $\in [0, 2]$. Since the values of these attributes can be out of the proposed interval, we force distance to be 1 when $|attr^i - attr^j| > max(attr) - min(attr)$.

First of all, we have tested whether the distance function and the weights selected are suitable for the traffic domain. For this purpose, we have generated a little case base of only seven cases by simulating each population in Table 1. In order to create this case base, all seven populations have been run with the same AEI parameters: $fine_{right} = 12$, $fine_{front} = 6$ and *police* $= 1$. Afterwards, in order to test the distance function, we have created seven new cases simulating another time each population in Table 1 using the very same AEI parameters' values and have compared each one with the seven cases in the case base. Notice that two simulations of the same population using the very same AEI parameters' values do not create the very same case, because the runtime behaviour in both simulations may be similar but not exactly the same.

Figure 2 shows the results of testing similarities for the seven new cases with the seven ones in the base case. These seven new cases could be grouped by the population behaviour regarding the norm compliance. Since population of first three cases have an *high_punishment* lower than both norms' fines, cars fulfill both norms (with probability 0.9). However, populations with *high_punishment* 8 and 10 fulfill the right norm with probability 0.9 and the front norm with

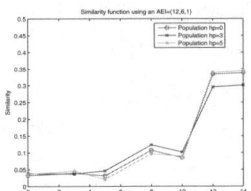 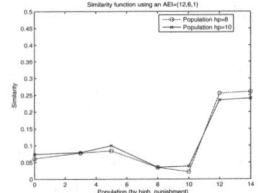 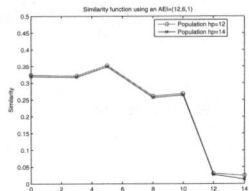

(a) Three populations fulfill two norms with probability 0.9.

(b) Two populations fulfill the right norm with probability 0.9 and the front norm with probability 0.5.

(c) Two populations fulfill two norms with probability 0.5.

Fig. 2. Distance between populations when the AEI uses the same parameters values ($fine_{right} = 12$, $fine_{front} = 6$ and *police* $= 1$)

probability 0.5. Whereas, populations with *high_punishment* 12 and 14 fulfill both norms with probability 0.5. Figure 2 shows three charts corresponding to cases grouping by this behaviour. Thus, chart 2(a) shows the distance for the three first cases whose cars fulfill both norms with probability 0.9. We can see how these three cases are similar when compared with the seven cases in the case base, and also that the distance among them is less than with respect to other cases. Chart 2(b) shows the distance for cases using populations with *high_punishment* 8 and 10 whose cars fulfill the right norm with probability 0.9 and the front norm with probability 0.5. Chart 2(c) shows distance for cases using populations with *high_punishment* 12 and 14 whose cars fulfill both norms with probability 0.5. In the three charts we can see how distances are similar among cases created with populations that have similar behaviour. This figure also shows that if two different populations regulated by the very same norms behave in very similar manner, an AEI cannot differentiate them. This effect is because the AEI can only observe the external behaviour of populations. In any case, these results allow us to conclude that the proposed distance function is suitable. Next step is to test at run-time the proposed CBR approach.

5.2   Case Base

With the aim that at run-time the AEI could adapt its regulations to any population, we create a case base using populations in Table 1 and the corresponding best AEI parameters' values. In order to create the case base we have considered as AEI parameters' values $fine_{right} \in \{0, 3, 6, 9, 12, 15\}$, $fine_{front} \in \{0, 3, 6, 9, 12, 15\}$, and $police \in \{0.8, 0.9, 1\}$. Overall we have considered 108 different AEI parameters' values, as the result of combining $fine_{right}$, $fine_{front}$, and $police$ values. To create cases for our case base, we have simulated each population in Table 1 with all 108 AEI parameters' values, so we have generated a total of 756 cases for the seven agent populations. To create each case, we have simulated the traffic model during 2000 ticks. Once finished the simulation, we generate a case by saving the AEI parameters' values (N^p, PS^p) used in this simulation, the runtime behaviour for the 2000 ticks (V, pop), and the best AEI parameters' values (N^{p*}, PS^{p*}) corresponding to the population used in this simulation.

5.3   Retrieving

We have designed an experiment to test the retrieval process and therefore our approach. That is, we want to test if at run-time the AEI is able to self-configure its parameters for different agent populations by using the proposed CBR approach. Since we are testing our approach and we are not interested in efficiency issues, we employ the traffic simulator to recreate a run-time execution. We launch simulations of 2000 ticks during 20 times, namely steps (overall 40000 ticks). At each step, once the simulation finishes, we check the goal satisfaction degree and change the AEI parameters' values using the CBR approach when required. Although this allows us to change the population of agents at any step we have run the experiments using the same population in 20 simulations. For all experiments, the AEI starts with (0,0,0.8) parameters, that correspond to no fine for both norms and a deployment of 80% of police agents. Thus, we expect that the AEI starts with a low goal satisfaction degree (caused by the parameters it is using) and it will be able to retrieve a similar case with whose parameters that do increase the goal satisfaction degree.

At each step, we launch a simulation with a certain population of agents and when the simulation finishes, the AEI decides, based on the goal satisfaction, if it has to retrieve a case or not. If the goal satisfaction is greater than a threshold the AEI continues with the same parameters for a new simulation in the next step. Otherwise (when the goal satisfaction is lower than the threshold) we launch the CBR engine to retrieve a case of the case base (see section 5.2) in order to adapt the AEI parameters, namely to adapt the institution, its regulation. The threshold is computed as a desired goal satisfaction value G^* minus an epsilon value ϵ. In our experiments, we have set $\epsilon = 0.03$ and $G^* = 0.65$, which corresponds to the minimum of the best goal satisfaction degrees for our populations. The problem case is generated from the AEI parameters' values used in the last simulation and the runtime behaviour in the last 2000 ticks. The CBR system retrieves the most similar case and uses the best AEI parameters' values of the retrieved case for next simulation. Thus, the goal satisfaction degree can be computed again to check if it is necessary to define a new problem case.

We have used fifteen different populations to test our approach. Each population is characterized by their norm compliance parameters, being $fulfill\_prob = 0.5$ and $inc\_prob = 0.4$ for all of them, whereas $high\_punishment$ varies from 0 to 14. Notice that seven of them are the ones used for generating cases[3] (when $high\_punishment \in \{0, 3, 5, 8, 10, 12, 14\}$) whereas the AEI has no prior cases about of the other eight populations (when $high\_punishment \in \{1, 2, 4, 6, 7, 9, 11, 13\}$). Figure 3 shows the results for fifteen populations, where each chart shows five populations. Each population is run three times. Thus, overall we have performed 45 experiments. For each experiment, the figure shows the goal satisfaction every 2000 ticks during 20 steps. On chart 3(a) we can see that at initial step the goal satisfaction is low (around 0.2) and how the AEI quickly rises it up and maintains it constant during the rest of steps (between 0.6 and 0.7). On chart 3(a) we can see how the goal satisfaction degree starts at 0.2 and quickly rises up to $0.6 - 0.7$ with the initial case retrievals. This effect repeats on charts 3(b) and 3(c) on figure 3. That is, the AEI is able to adapt quickly its parameters in all experiments. However, we observe that for some populations (when $high\_punishment$ is 6, 10 and 12) the goal satisfaction does not remain constant. In particular, the goal satisfaction for one of the populations with $high\_punishment = 6$ goes down three times (steps 8, 10 and 11) to values close to 0.2. These oscillations happen because given a population regulated by the very same AEI parameters' values there is a variability on the behaviour in different simulations, that causes a variability in goal satisfaction. Thus, it

---

[3] Notice that use the same population does not mean use the same case because the runtime behaviour may be similar in both cases but not exactly the same.

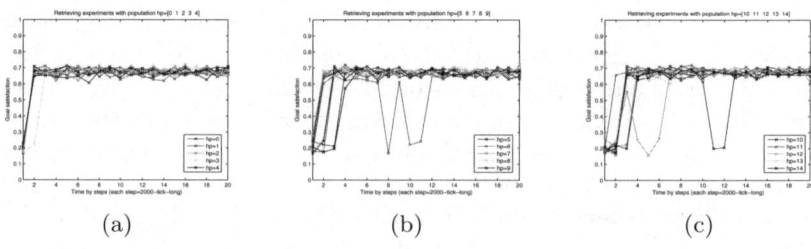

Fig. 3. Goal satisfaction for fifteen populations. (a) Populations with *high_punishment* $\in \{0, 1, 2, 3, 4\}$; (b) Populations with *high_punishment* $\in \{5, 6, 7, 8, 9\}$; and (c) Populations with *high_punishment* $\in \{10, 11, 12, 13, 14\}$.

sometimes occurs that because of this variability the goal satisfaction drops below the threshold and causes to restart the retrieval process. After this, the AEI stabilizes quickly again the goal satisfaction degree.

In order to estimate the error caused by these oscillations we have computed the percentage of simulations with a goal satisfaction greather than the threshold (0.62). At first step all experiments have a goal satisfaction less than the threshold. At second step a 52% of experiments (23 of 45) have a goal satisfaction greather than it. The percentage goes up to 89% (40 of 45) at third step and to 95% to the fourth. That is, in our experiments, the AEI needs four simulations to adapt itself in a correct manner to a 95% of new cases. At the rest of simulations (from simulation 5 to simulation 20) the average of the percentage of experiments with a goal satisfaction greather than the threshold is around 98%. That is, there is an error arround the 2% caused by the oscillations. In any case, we can conclude that the AEI is able to adapt to the populations, that is with the initial cases retrievals the AEI is able to adapt its parameters to accomplish its goals for each population.

6   Discussion and Future Work

Within the area of Multi-Agent Systems, adaptation has been usually envisioned as an agent capability where agents learn how to reorganise themselves. Along this direction, in [6] Gasser and Ishida present a general distributed problem-solving model which can reorganize its architecture; and Horling et al. [7] propose an approach where the members adapt their own organizational structures at runtime. The fact that adaptation is carried out by the agents composing the MAS is the most significant difference with the approach presented in this paper. On the other hand, it has been long stated [8] that agents working in a common society need norms to avoid and solve conflicts, make agreements, reduce complexity, or to achieve a social order. Most research in this area consider norm configuration at design time [9] instead of at run-time as proposed in this paper. Regarding the traffic domain, MAS has been previously applied to it. For example, Camurri et al. [10] propose two field-based mechanisms to control cars and traffic-lights in order to manage to avoid deadlocks and congestion. Additionally, Case-Based Reasoning has been applied before in multi-agent systems where agents use different CBR approaches to individual learning and to cooperative learning for distributed systems [11,12].

This paper presents a Case-Base Reasoning approach as an extension of previous work which allows an AEI to self-configure its regulations. We have presented the initial step towards a Case-Based Reasoning system, centering our work on the retrieval and usage processes. We have propposed a case description and the distance function to be used by a generic AEI. We have tested the retrieval process of our approach in the traffic AEI case study, where the AEI learns two traffic norms and the number of institutional agents in order to adapt the norms and the performative structure to dynamical changes of agent populations.

Preliminary results in this paper are promising but they show some oscillations of the goal satisfaction degrees for some populations. Although, the computed error is low (around 2%), currently we are tuning the function used to compute the goal satisfaction and the threshold value in order to reduce the error and do it less sensitive to the variability. Once solved this, we plan to continue our experiments on the retrieval process by changing the populations between simulations. We also plan to continue on finishing the learning by focusing our work in the other CBR processes. As future work, and since this basically represents a centralized scenario, we plan to develop a more complex traffic network, allowing us to propose a decentralized approach where different areas (i.e., junctions) are regulated by a distributed institution.

Acknowledgments. This work was partially funded by the Spanish Education and Science Ministry as part of the IEA (TIN2006-15662-C02-01) and the 2006-5-0I-099 projects. The first author enjoys an FPI grant (BES-2004-4335) from the Spanish Education and Science Ministry.

References

1. Luck, M., McBurney, P., Shehory, O., Willmott, S.: Agentlink Roadmap (2005), Agentlink.org
2. Kephart, J.O., Chess, D.M.: The vision of autonomic computing. IEEE Computer 36(1), 41–50 (2003)
3. Esteva, M.: Electronic Institutions: From specification to development. IIIA, Ph.D. Monography 19 (2003)
4. Bou, E., López-Sánchez, M., Rodríguez-Aguilar, J.A.: Towards self-configuration in autonomic electronic institutions. In: Noriega, P., Vázquez-Salceda, J., Boella, G., Boissier, O., Dignum, V., Fornara, N., Matson, E. (eds.) COIN 2006. LNCS (LNAI), vol. 4386, pp. 220–235. Springer, Heidelberg (2007)
5. Aamodt, A., Plaza, E.: Case-based reasoning: Foundational issues, methodological variations, and system approaches. AI Commun 7(1), 39–59 (1994)
6. Gasser, L., Ishida, T.: A dynamic organizational architecture for adaptive problem solving. In: Proc. of AAAI-91, Anaheim, CA, pp. 185–190 (1991)
7. Horling, B., Benyo, B., Lesser, V.: Using Self-Diagnosis to Adapt Organizational Structures. In: Proceedings of the 5th International Conference on Autonomous Agents, pp. 529–536 (2001)

8. Conte, R., Falcone, R., Sartor, G.: Agents and norms: How to fill the gap? Artificial Intelligence and Law (7), 1–15 (1999)
9. Fitoussi, D., Tennenholtz, M.: Choosing social laws for multi-agent systems: Minimality and simplicity. Artificial Intelligence 119(1-2), 61–101 (2000)
10. Camurri, M., Mamei, M., Zambonelli, F.: Urban traffic control with co-fields. In: Proc. of E4MAS Workshop at AAMAS, vol. 2006, pp. 11–25 (2006)
11. Plaza, E., Ontañón, S.: Cooperative multiagent learning. In: Alonso, E., Kudenko, D., Kazakov, D. (eds.) AAMAS 2000 and AAMAS 2002. LNCS (LNAI), vol. 2636, pp. 1–17. Springer, Heidelberg (2003)
12. Ros, R., Veloso, M.: Executing Multi-Robot Cases through a Single Coordinator. In: Proc. of Autonomous Agents and Multiagent Systems, pp. 1264–1266 (2007)

Semantical Concepts for a Formal Structural Dynamics of Situated Multiagent Systems

Antônio Carlos da Rocha Costa and Graçaliz Pereira Dimuro

Escola de Informática – PPGINF, Universidade Católica de Pelotas
96.010-000 Pelotas, RS, Brazil
{rocha,liz}@atlas.ucpel.tche.br

Abstract. This paper introduces semantical concepts to support a formal structural dynamics of situated multiagent systems. Multiagent systems are seen from the perspective of the Population-Organization model, a minimal semantical model where the performance of organizational roles by agents, and the realization of organizational links by social exchanges between agents, are the key mechanisms for the implementation of an organization structure by a population structure. The structural dynamics of a multiagent system may then be modelled as a set of transformations on the system's overall population-organization structure. We illustrate the proposed approach to structural dynamics by introducing a small set of operational rules for an exchange value-based dynamics of organizational links. The paper sets the stage for further work on structural dynamics where other structural elements, besides organizational links, may be taken into account.

1 Introduction

PopOrg, a minimal population-organization based model, was introduced in [1] in order to support the study of the structural dynamics of multiagent systems (MAS). Both time-invariant and time-variant versions of the model were introduced, but no specific mechanism was presented to account for any possible structural dynamism.

In this paper, we improve the above mentioned work by refining that model with the notion that social interactions are exchanges performed between agents. Also, we present an exchange value-based mechanism able to account for some aspects of the structural dynamics of multiagent systems. As an illustration of the possibilities allowed by the model, we combine the two ideas to define a simple set of operational rules for an elementary exchange value-based dynamics of organizational links.

The work sets the stage for further studies on the structural dynamics of multiagent systems by establishing the basis of a mechanism where further aspects of the structural dynamics of such systems may be considered, besides the dynamics of links.

We remark that the paper is based on a distinction between the notions of intensional and extensional descriptions of systems: intensional descriptions deal with subjective aspects pertaining to the internal functioning of the agents that operate in a system (like norms, values, etc.), while extensional descriptions deal with objective aspects pertaining to the external functioning of those agents (like actions performed, objects exchanged, etc.).

J.S. Sichman et al. (Eds.): COIN 2007, LNAI 4870, pp. 139–154, 2008.
© Springer-Verlag Berlin Heidelberg 2008

The main concerns of the paper are, thus, an extensional description of the structural dynamics of multiagent systems organizations, and a possible way to articulate such extensional dynamics with the intensional aspect of the exchange values involved in the interactions between the agents that participate in the organizations.

On the other hand, we note that the process model that underlies the structural dynamics of the population-organizational model [1] is similar to the general signal-based denotational model that underlies some declarative languages devised to specify real-time reactive systems [2]. This encourages the view that the PopOrg model may suitably be construed as an adequate model for multiagent systems situated in environments presenting real-time constraints.

In fact, it is only natural to expect that it is precisely in the case of situated multiagent systems that the issues of structural dynamics arise crucially (both because of the pressures for the adaptation of the system to the variations in the environment and because of the values that agents may assign to the concrete resources made available to them by the environment – see Sect. 5, on related works).

The paper is organized as follows. In Sec. 2, we revisit the PopOrg model, refining its notion of interaction through a general notion of social exchange. In Sec. 3, we summarize the particular exchange values approach to social interactions [3] that we adopt, reviewing its notion of exchange value and its model of social exchange.

Section 4 illustrates the general purpose of the paper by joining the revisited PopOrg model with the adopted system of social exchanges, allowing for a simple mechanism able to support a preliminary model of exchange value-based dynamics of organizational links.

Section 5 summarizes related work. Section 6 brings the Conclusion and explores further aspects of the proposal.

A technical remark: we use the following coordinate-wise notation, when dealing with vectors (n-tuples) of sets (assuming $expr_0 \Leftrightarrow expr_1 \wedge \ldots \wedge expr_n$):

$$(X_1, \ldots, X_n) \subseteq (Y_1, \ldots, Y_n) \equiv_{def} X_i \subseteq Y_i, i = 1, \ldots n. \tag{1}$$

$$\bigcup\{(X_1, \ldots, X_n) \mid expr_0\} \equiv_{def} (\cup\{X_1 \mid expr_1\}, \ldots, \cup\{X_n \mid expr_n\}) \tag{2}$$

2   The Population-Organization Model

The Population-Organization model of multiagent systems, introduced in [1], emphasizes the modelling of systems composed of a small group of agents, adopting an interactionist point of view [3,4].

In such model, the organizational structure of a system is implemented by the system's population of agents through two main mechanisms: the assignment of organizational roles to agents, and the realization of organizational links between roles by the social exchanges that are established between the agents that perform those roles.

Of course, in such model, the central components of the structural dynamics of the systems are the operations of creation and deletion of elements like organizational roles, organizational links and exchange processes, as well as the agents entering and leaving the system.

2.1   The Time-Invariant Population-Organization Model

The time-invariant Population-Organization model, $PopOrg = (Pop, Org, imp)$, is construed as a pair of structures, the population structure Pop and the organization structure Org, together with an implementation relation imp.

The Time-Invariant Population Structure.   The *population* of a multiagent system consists of the set of agents that inhabit it. The *population structure* of a multiagent system is its population set together with the set of all behaviors that the agents are able to perform, and the set of all exchange processes that they can establish between them (for simplicity, we consider only pairwise exchanges).

Let T be a discrete sequence of time instants. A *time-invariant population structure* is a tuple

$$Pop = (Ag, Act, Bh, Ep, bc, ec) \tag{3}$$

where:

- Ag is a finite non-empty set of agents, called the *population* of the system;
- Act is the finite set of all *actions* (communication actions and actions on concrete objects of the environment) that may be performed by the agents of the system;
- $Bh \subseteq [T \to \wp(Act)]$ is the set containing all possible agent behaviors, modeled as functions that specify, for each time $t \in T$, a set of actions $X \in \wp(Act)$ that an agent may perform at that time, each behavior determining a sequence of sets of actions available for the agents to perform in the system;
- $Ep \subseteq [T \to \wp(Act) \times \wp(Act)]$ is the set containing all possible *exchange processes* that two agents may perform in the system, each process given by a function that specifies, for each $t \in T$, a pair of set of actions $(X_1, X_2) \in \wp(Act) \times \wp(Act)$, determining a sequence of exchanges available for any two agents to perform, by executing together or interleaving appropriately their corresponding actions;
- $bc : Ag \to \wp(Bh)$ is the *behavioral capability* function, such that for each agent $a \in Ag$, the set of all behaviors that a is able to perform in the system is $bc(a)$;
- $ec : Ag \times Ag \to \wp(Ep)$ is the *exchange capability* function, such that for each pair of agents $a_1, a_2 \in Ag$, the set of all exchange processes that a_1 and a_2 may perform between them is $ec(a_1, a_2)$;
- $\forall a_1, a_2 \in Ag \; \forall e \in ec(a_1, a_2) \; \forall t \in T$:

$$Prj_1(e(t)) \subseteq \bigcup \{b(t) \mid b \in bc(a_1)\} \; \wedge \; Prj_2(e(t)) \subseteq \bigcup \{b(t) \mid b \in bc(a_2)\},$$

where Prj_1, Prj_2 are projection functions, so that the agents' exchange capabilities are constrained by their joint behavioral capabilities.

Given $t \in T$ and $a \in Ag$, we note that $bc(a)(t) = \{act \mid act \in b(t), b \in bc(a)\}$ is the set of all possible actions that agent a may perform at time t, given its behavioral capability $bc(a)$. We also note that, in general, the exchange capability $ec(a_1, a_2)$ of a pair of agents $a_1, a_2 \in Ag$ should be deducible from their respective behavioral capabilities $bc(a_1)$ and $bc(a_2)$, and from any kind of restriction that may limit their set of possible exchanges (e.g., social norms, inherited habits, etc.), but since we are presenting an extensional model where such intensional, subjective restrictions take no part, it is sensible to include ec explicitly in the description of the population structure.

By the same token, the behavioral capability $bc(a)$ of an agent $a \in Ag$ should be deducible from any *internal description* of a where its set of behaviors is constructively defined, but since we are taking an external (observational) point of view of the agents, we include bc explicitly in the model.

The Time-Invariant Organization Structure. The *time-invariant organization structure* of a time-invariant population structure $Pop = (Ag, Act, Bh, Ep, bc, ec)$ is a structure

$$Org = (Ro, Li, lc) \tag{4}$$

where:

– $Ro \subseteq \wp(Bh)$ is the set of *roles* existing in the organization, a role being given by a set of behaviors that an agent playing the role may have to perform;
– $Li \subseteq Ro \times Ro \times Ep$ is the set of *links* that exist in the organization between pairs of roles, each link specifying an exchange process that the agents performing the linked roles may have to perform;
– $lc : Ro \times Ro \to \wp(Li)$ is the link capability of the pairs of roles, that is, the set of links that the pairs of roles may establish between them;
– $\forall l \in Li \; \exists r_1, r_2 \in Ro : l \in lc(r_1, r_2)$, that is, every link has to be in the link capability of the two roles that it links.

Clearly, the PopOrg model adopts a relational, interactionist approach to organizations [3,4].

The Time-Invariant Implementation Relation. Population and organization structures are formally defined in a quite independent way. A population structure induces no more than a loose restriction on the set of organization structures that may be imposed on it: the behavioral capability function bc constrains the set of possible roles that an agent may have in any possible organization and, indirectly, the set of possible exchange processes in which it may participate, thus, also the set of possible organizational links that it may have with any other agent in a system.

The fact that a given organization structure is operating over a population structure, influencing the set of possible exchanges that the agents may have between them, is represented by an *implementation relation* $imp \subseteq (Ro \times Ag) \cup (Li \times Ep)$, where

– $Ro \times Ag$ is the set of all possible *role supports*, i.e., the set of all possible ways of assigning roles to agents, and if $(r, a) \in imp$, then the social role r is supported by agent a, so that a is said to play role r (possibly in a shared, non-exclusive way) in the given organization;
– $Li \times Ep$ is the set of all possible *link supports*, i.e., the set of all possible ways of supporting links, so that if $(l, e) \in imp$, link l is said to be supported (in a possibly shared, non-exclusive way) by the exchange process e, and so indirectly supported by the agents that participate in e and that play the roles linked by l.

We note that an organization implementation relation imp does not need to be one-to-one: many roles may be assigned to the same agent, many agents may support a given role, many links may be supported by a given exchange process, many exchange processes may support a given link. Moreover, this relation may be partial: some roles may be assigned to no agent, some agents may be have no roles assigned to them, some links may be unsupported, some exchange processes may be supporting no link at all.

The agents that have at least one role assigned to them are said to constitute the *support* of the organization in the population. Agents that do not belong to an organization's support may interfere with the functioning of that organization by influencing the behaviors of the supporting agents.

This flexibility is important when defining the structural dynamics of MAS, because it allows for the definition of "improper" structural states, i.e., structural states where the system's organization is not properly implemented by the sytem's population, which is relevant for the end goal of dealing with the concept of *organizational integrity* [1].

A *proper implementation relation* is an implementation relation that respects organizational roles and organizational links by correctly translating them in terms of agents, behaviors and exchange processes. Given an implementation relation $imp \subseteq (Ro \times Ag) \cup (Li \times Ep)$, a social role $r \in Ro$ is said to be *properly implemented* by a subset $A \subseteq Ag$ of agents whenever the following conditions hold:

(i) $\forall a \in A : (r, a) \in imp$, i.e., all agents in A participate in the implementation of r;
(ii) $\forall t \in T : \bigcup\{b(t) \mid b \in r\} \subseteq \bigcup\{b'(t) \mid b' \in bc(a), a \in A\}$, i.e., the set of behaviors required by r may be performed by the agents of A (in a possibly shared, non-exclusive way).

A link $l = (r_1, r_2, e) \in Li$ is *properly implemented* by a subset $E \subseteq ec(a_1, a_2)$ of the exchange processes determined by the exchange capability of two agents a_1, a_2, whenever the following conditions hold:

(i) $\forall e' \in E : (l, e') \in imp$, i.e., every exchange process in E helps to support the link;
(ii) r_1 e r_2 are properly implemented by the agents a_1 and a_2, respectively; and
(iii) $\forall t \in T : e(t) \subseteq \bigcup\{e'(t) \mid e' \in E\}$, i.e., the exchange process required by l may be performed by the ones of E (in a possibly shared, non-exclusive way).

A time-invariant population-organization structure $PopOrg = (Pop, Org, imp)$ is *properly implemented* if and only imp is a proper implementation relation.

2.2 The Time-Variant Population-Organization Model

Time-Variant Population Structures. Time-variant structures change as time goes by. There are three main kinds of possible changes in the momentary population structure $Pop = (Ag, Act, Bh, Ep, bc, ec)$ of a multiagent system: (p1) a change in the behavioral capability $bc(a)$ of an agent $a \in Ag$; (p2) a change in the exchange capability $ec(a_1, a_2)$ of a pair of agents $(a_1, a_2) \in Ag \times Ag$; (p3) a change in the population Ag.

Changes of the kind (p1) may be due either to internal changes in the agent or to changes in the set of passive objects (e.g., tools) with which the agent operates. Changes of the kind (p2) may be due either to changes in the behavioral capability of one of the agents, to changes in the exchange medium (e.g., communication channel) used by the agents, or to changes in some social norm that regulates the exchanges. Changes of the kind (p3) are due to agents entering or leaving the system.

Let T be the time structure, $\mathbf{Ag}$ and $\mathbf{Act}$ be universes of agents and actions, respectively, and $\mathbf{Bh}$ and $\mathbf{Ep}$ universes of behaviors and exchange processes defined over $\mathbf{Ag}$ and $\mathbf{Act}$, in a way similar to that in Sect. 2.1(3). A *time-variant population structure* is a structure $POP = (AG, ACT, BH, EP, Bc, Ec)$ where, for all $t \in T$:

- $AG^t \in \wp(\mathbf{Ag})$ is the system's population, at time t;
- $ACT^t \in \wp(\mathbf{Act})$ is the set of possible agent actions, at time t;
- $BH^t \in \wp(\mathbf{Bh})$ is the set of possible agent behaviors, at time t;
- $EP^t \in \wp(\mathbf{Ep})$ is the set of possible exchange processes between agents, at time t;
- $Bc^t : AG^t \rightarrow \wp(BH^t)$ is the behavioral capability function of agents, at time t;
- $Ec^t : AG^t \times AG^t \rightarrow \wp(EP^t)$ is the exchange capability function, at time t.

The state at time t of a time-variant population structure, denoted by $POP^t = (AG^t, ACT^t, BH^t, EP^t, Bc^t, Ec^t)$, fixes the population of the system, the set of possible behaviors of each agent and the set of possible exchange processes between each pair of agents, but not the behaviors and exchange processes themselves, which at each time will be chosen from among those possibilities according to the particular internal states of the agents, and the particular states of the (social and physical) environment. Note, however, that the intensional, subjective reasons for such choices are not modelled in the extensional PopOrg model.

Time-Variant Organization Structures.   There are five main kinds of possible changes in a momentary organization structure $Org = (Ro, Li, lc)$: (o1) a change in a role $r \in Ro$; (o2) a change in a link $l \in Li$; (o3) a change in the set of roles Ro; (o4) a change in the set of links Li; (o5) a change in the link capability lc of the pairs of roles.

A change of kind (o1) may be due, e.g., to a change in the behavior of a certain number of agents performing the role. A change of the kind (o2) may be due, e.g., to a change in an exchange process that supports the link. Changes of the kind (o3) are either the appearance or the disappearance of roles in the system. Changes of the kind (o4) are either the appearance or to the disappearance of organizational links in the system. A change of kind (o5) may be due, e.g., to a redistribution of the set of links between organization roles.

All such changes may be due to the so-called "reorganization operations" of multiagent systems (see Sec. 5, on related works). The reasons for such operations are essentially of an intensional nature and, thus, are not explicitly represented in the extensional PopOrg model (but their realizations as behavioral processes, and their possible extensional effects, may be explicitly modelled).

We note that Sect. 4 of this paper is mainly concerned with changes of kind (o4), that is, changes in the set of links of an organization structure.

Let T be the time structure, and $\mathbf{Ro} \subseteq \wp(\mathbf{Bh})$ and $\mathbf{Li} \subseteq \mathbf{Ro} \times \mathbf{Ro} \times \mathbf{Ep}$ be the universes of roles and links, respectively. The *time-variant organization structure* of a time-variant population structure $POP = (AG, ACT, BH, EP, Bc, Ec)$ is a structure $ORG = (RO, LI, Lc)$, where for all $t \in T$:

- $RO^t \in \wp(\mathbf{Ro})$ and $LI^t \in \wp(\mathbf{Li})$ are, respectively, the set of possible roles and the set of possible links at time t;
- $Lc^t : RO^t \times RO^t \to \wp(LI^t)$ is the link capability function at time t.

For each $t \in T$, the organization state $ORG^t = (RO^t, LI^t, Lc^t)$ fixes the sets of possible roles RO^t, links LI^t and link capability function Lc^t that the system may have at that time. Note that a time-invariant organization structure may be modelled as a constant time-variant organization structure.

Time-Variant Implementation Relations. As a consequence of any change (p1)-(p3) or (o1)-(o5), the implementation relation imp may be changed either (r1) in the way it relates roles and agents or (r2) in the way it relates links and exchange processes. Besides being changed in its mapping, imp may be changed also in its properness.

Let $POP = (AG, ACT, BH, EP, Bc, Ec)$ be a time-variant population structure and $ORG = (RO, LI, Lc)$ its time-variant organization structure. A *time-variant implementation relation* for ORG over POP is a time-indexed set of implementation relations IMP, with $IMP^t \subseteq (RO^t \times AG^t) \cup (LI^t \times EP^t)$. A *time-variant population-organization structure* is a structure $POPORG = (POP, ORG, IMP)$, where

- $POP = (AG, ACT, BH, EP, Bc, Ec)$, $ORG = (RO, LI, Lc)$ and IMP are, respectively, a time-variant population structure, a time-variant organization structure, and a time-variant implementation relation, as defined above;
- at each $t \in T$, the state of $POPORG$ is given by $POPORG^t = (POP^t, ORG^t, IMP^t)$, where $POP^t = (AG^t, ACT^t, BH^t, EP^t, BC^t, EC^t)$ and $ORG^t = (RO^t, LI^t, Lc^t)$ are such that $IMP^t \subseteq (RO^t \times AG^t) \cup (LI^t \times EP^t)$.

We note that this definition does not guarantee that the relation IMP is proper at each time. That is, we assume that time-variant population-organization structures may pass through structural states where the population improperly implements the organization.

Multiagent Systems with Structural Dynamics. The *structural dynamics* of a multiagent system [1] is the dynamics that deals with the way the structure of the system varies in time, thus, it is the dynamics of the system's population and organization.

Let $\mathbf{PopOrg} = (\mathbf{Pop}, \mathbf{Org}, \mathbf{imp})$ be the universe of all possible time-invariant population-organization structures, with $\mathbf{Pop} = (\mathbf{Ag}, \mathbf{Act}, \mathbf{Bh}, \mathbf{Ep}, \mathbf{bc}, \mathbf{ec})$, $\mathbf{Org} = (\mathbf{Ro}, \mathbf{Li}, \mathbf{lc})$ and $\mathbf{imp} \subseteq (\mathbf{Ro} \times \mathbf{Ag}) \cup (\mathbf{Li} \times \mathbf{Ep})$ being the universes of all possible time-invariant population structures, organization structures and implementation relations, respectively.

A *multiagent system with dynamic structure* is a structure $MAS = (\mathbf{PopOrg}, D)$ where, for each $t \in T$, $D^t \subseteq \mathbf{PopOrg} \times \mathbf{PopOrg}$ is the system's *overall structural dynamics*, such that for any structural state $PopOrg \in \mathbf{PopOrg}$, at time $t \in T$, there is a set of *possible next structural states*, denoted by $D^t(PopOrg) \subseteq \mathbf{PopOrg}$.

Given a particular initial population-organization structure $PopOrg^{t_0}$, the evolution of the system is given by a time-variant population-organization structure $POPORG$, where it holds that $POPORG^{t+1} \in D^t(POPORG^t)$, for any $t \in T$.

The choice of the particular next structural state $POPORG^{t+1}$ that will be assumed by the MAS at time $t + 1$ is made, at time $t \in T$, on the basis of various intensional, subjective factors extant in the system, like, e.g., preferences of agents, social norms, political powers, etc.

In particular cases, it may happen that the system's overall structural dynamics may be separated into three coordinated sub-structural dynamics $D^t = D^t_P \times D^t_O \times D^t_I$: the *population* dynamics $D^t_P \subseteq \textbf{Pop} \times \textbf{Pop}$, the *organizational* dynamics $D^t_O \subseteq \textbf{Org} \times \textbf{Org}$, and the *implementation* dynamics $D^t_I \subseteq \textbf{imp} \times \textbf{imp}$.

In such special cases, the coordination between the system's overall dynamics and the three sub-structural dynamics may be given compositionally by:

$$(Pop', Org', imp') \in D^t((Pop, Org, imp)) \Leftrightarrow$$
$$Pop' \in D^t_P(Pop) \ \wedge \ Org' \in D^t_O(Org) \ \wedge \ imp' \in D^t_I(imp).$$

3 Systems of Exchange Values

In this section, we introduce one of the possible intensional, subjective factor that may influence the evolution of the dynamical structure of a multiagent system, namely, the system of exchange values with which the agents may assess the quality of the exchanges they are having in the system. We adopt here one particular model of system of exchange values [3], which we have used in previous works (e.g., [5]).

This exchange value-based approach to social interactions (cf. also [4]) considers that every social interaction is an exchange of services between the agents involved in it. Exchange values are, then, the values with which agents evaluate the social exchanges they have with each other.

A *service* is any action or behavior that an agent may perform, which influences positively (respect., negatively) the behavior of another agent, favoring (respect., disfavoring) the effort of the latter to achieve a goal. The *evaluation* of a service involves not only affective and emotional reactions, but also comparisons to social standards. Typical evaluations are expressed using *qualitative values* such as: good, very good, bad, very bad, etc. So, they are of a neatly subjective, qualitative, intensional character.

With those evaluations, a qualitative economy of exchange values arises in the social system. Such qualitative economy requires various rules for its regulation. Most of those rules are either of a moral or of a juridical character [3].

Exchange behaviors between two agents α and β can be defined as sequences of exchange steps performed between them. Two kinds of exchange steps are identified [3], called $I_{\alpha\beta}$ and $II_{\alpha\beta}$. Steps of the kind $I_{\alpha\beta}$ are steps in which agent α takes the initiative to perform a service for agent β, with qualitative *cost* (investment) $r_{I\alpha\beta}$. Subsequently, β receives the service, and gets a *benefice* (satisfaction) of qualitative value $s_{I\beta\alpha}$.

If β was to pay back α a return service immediately, he would probably try to "calibrate" his service so that it would have cost r equal to $s_{I\beta\alpha}$, so that α would get a return benefice with value s equal to $r_{I\alpha\beta}$, in order for the exchange to be fair (if the two agents were prone to be fair in their exchanges). The definition of exchange steps assumes, however, that the return service will not be performed immediately, so that a kind of bookkeeping is necessary, in order for the involved values not to be forgotten.

That is the purpose of the two other values involved in the exchange step: $t_{I\beta\alpha}$ is the *debt* that β assumes with α for having received the service and not having paid it back yet; , $v_{I\alpha\beta}$ is the *credit* that α gets on β for having performed the service and not having being paid yet. A *fair* exchange step ([3] calls it an *equilibrated* exchange step) is one where all the involved values are qualitatively equal: $r_{I\alpha\beta} \approx s_{I\beta\alpha} \approx t_{\beta\alpha} \approx v_{I\alpha\beta}$.

To take account of differences between qualitative exchange values, such values are assumed to be comparable with respect to their relative qualitative magnitudes. That is, if EV is the set of qualitative exchange values, it is assumed that values in EV can be compared by an order relation $\preceq$, so that $(EV, \preceq)$ is a (partially) ordered set. Thus, e.g., if it happened that $s_{I\beta\alpha} \preceq r_{I\alpha\beta}$, then agent α made an investment, during his service, that was greater than the benefice that agent β got from it.

An exchange step of kind $II_{\alpha\beta}$ is performed in a different way. In it, agent α charges agent β for a credit with qualitative value $v_{II\alpha\beta}$, which he has on β. Subsequently, β acknowledges a debt with value $t_{II\beta\alpha}$ with α, and performs a return service with value $r_{II\beta\alpha}$. In consequence, α gets a return satisfaction with value $s_{II\alpha\beta}$. Fairness for $II_{\alpha\beta}$ steps is defined similarly as for $I_{\alpha\beta}$ steps.

It is assumed that exchange values can be qualitatively added and subtracted from each other, so that *balances of temporal sequences* of exchange steps can be calculated. Besides the above mentioned conditions, one further condition is required in order that a sequence of exchange steps be fair: $\sum v_{II\alpha\beta} \approx \sum v_{I\alpha\beta}$, that is, α should charge a sum of credits which is exactly the total credit he has on β, no more, no less.

In summary, [3] introduces a qualitative algebra with which one can model and analyze social exchanges between agents, determining in a qualitative way the degree of fairness of those exchanges. Note that such algebra operates on 8-tuples of the form

$$(r_{I\alpha\beta}, s_{I\beta\alpha}, t_{I\beta\alpha}, v_{I\alpha\beta}, v_{II\alpha\beta}, t_{II\beta\alpha}, r_{II\beta\alpha}, s_{II\alpha\beta}). \tag{5}$$

4   Exchange Value-Based Dynamics of Social Links

This section illustrates one of the possible uses of our extensional model for the structural dynamics of organizations of MAS by showing how it can support the intensional rules of an elementary exchange value-based dynamics of organizational links.

4.1   An Elementary Exchange Value-Based Dynamics of Social Links

Other things being equal, the fact that a sequence of exchange steps between two agents is fair, or not, may be a determinant factor in the attitude of those agents toward the possibility of the continuation of the interaction. That is, given enough chances, self-interested agents will tend to establish continued exchanges only with agents from whom they may establish exchanges that are at least fair, if not beneficial, for them [4].

Particular personality traits and various social factors (power, prestige, etc.), however, may interfere with self-interests and lead the agents to seek social exchanges that happen to be far from equilibrium ([5] illustrates this in the context of multiagent systems).

To simplify the issues, we assume that a MAS of self-interested agents adheres to the following rationales concerning the dynamics of organizational links:

- *exchange value-based rationale for the* creation *of an organizational link*: a new organizational link in the MAS is created as soon as an exchange process is positively
  assessed by the agents playing the roles that will be linked by the link (the exchange
  process is said to be *officially incorporated* as a link into the organization);
- *exchange value-based rationale for the* destruction *of an organizational link*: a link
  stops to exist in the multiagent system as soon as the balance of exchange values
  involved in the exchange processes that implement the link stops to be beneficial to
  any of the agents performing the roles linked by link (the exchange process is said
  to be *officially excluded* from the organization of the multiagent system).

We leave open for the agents to apply subjective criteria to determine if any of the
conditions mentioned in the above rationales "really" occurred or not. If the social organization has a central control, able to discover at each moment which are the links
that the agents would like to establish next between them, then it is up to that central
control to determine if enough has been observed in order to create or destroy a link in
the organization. If the agents are autonomous, then it is up to them to determine that.

If the agents are autonomous, they may disagree on which links should be created or
destroyed. In this case, the dynamics of links is open to argumentation and negotiation
between them. Thus, for organizations based on autonomous agents, no general method
can be given for the determination of how the dynamics of links should evolve. Such
dynamics is tightly coupled to the personality traits and social biases that the agents
may show with respect to the evaluation of their exchanges.

On the other hand, for organizations where the definitions of the roles prescribe not
only the behaviors that the agents playing such roles must have, but also the criteria with
which they should evaluate the interactions in which they get involved, it is possible to
derive the dynamics of links from the evaluation rules embedded in the roles.

The former case characterizes organizations where the dynamics of links can only
be established (at best) *a posteriori*, i.e., after knowing which agent is playing which
role in the organization. The latter case characterizes more manageable organizations,
where the dynamics of links can be established by an *a priori* analysis of the roles.

4.2   The Rules of the Elementary Exchange Value-Based Dynamics of Links

We introduce, now, a minimal set of intensional rules for the exchange value-based
dynamics of organizational links in multiagent systems, formalizing the rationales for
self-interested agents exposed above.

For simplicity, we consider the case where the organization structure is time-variant,
the population structure is time-invariant, each role is implemented by just one single
agent, and each link implemented by just one single exchange process.

Let $Pop = (Ag, Act, Beh, Ep, bc, ec)$ be a *time-invariant* population structure,
$ORG = (EP, RO, LI)$ be a *time-variant* organization structure implemented by Pop,
and let IMP be the *time-variant* implementation relation. They constitute a time-variant
population-organization structure $PopORG = (Pop, ORG, IMP)$, which is assumed
here to vary just in the set of organizational links, and in their implementations.

There may happen two kinds of changes in the set of links LI^t, at the time $t+1 \in T$:
(1) either a new link l is created, so that $LI^{t+1} = LI^t \cup \{l\}$; or (2) a link l is removed
from LI^t, so that $LI^{t+1} = LI^t - \{l\}$.

The problem we face here is that of the formalization of the conditions under which, at a moment $t + 1$, a link l is added to (or removed from) the set of links LI^t.

Let $EV = (EV, \preceq)$ be the scale of exchange values used by agents $a_1, a_2 \in Ag$ to evaluate their exchanges, and $BEV = EV^8$ be the set of 8-tuples of exchange values that represent balances of exchange values, defined in Sect. 3(5). Let $bal : Ag \times Ag \times Ep \times T \rightarrow BEV$ be so that $bal(a_1, a_2, e, t)$ is the balance of exchange values that agents a_1 and a_2 have accumulated, at time t, along the exchanges that they performed through the exchange process $e \in Ep$.

We assume that each of the agents $a_1, a_2 \in Ag$ is able to perform an analysis of every possible balance $bal(a_1, a_2, e, t)$ of exchange values that may arise between them, and judge if that balance is beneficial, fair, or harmful for himself. That is, we assume that there exists a (subjective) judgement function $jdg^t(a, bal(a_1, a_2, e, t)) \in \{+1, 0, -1\}$, which we may write as $a \models^t bal(a_1, a_2, e, t) \approx v$, for $v \in \{+1, 0, -1\}$ and $a \in \{a_1, a_2\}$.

Then, the dynamics of organizational links in the Population-Organization model of multiagent systems with self-interested agents is determined by a set of operational rules containing at least the rules introduced below.

Let $[\tau, \tau'], [\tau, \tau') \subseteq T$ respectively be a closed and a right end-open interval of time, with $\tau < \tau'$. Let $a_1, a_2 \in Ag$ be agents respectively playing roles $r_1, r_2 \in Ro$ during the interval $[\tau, \tau']$, that is, $(r_1, a_1), (r_2, a_2) \in IMP^t$, for all $t \in [\tau, \tau']$.

Consider a link $l \in \mathbf{Li}$ between roles $r_1, r_2 \in \mathbf{Ro}$ such that $l \notin LI^t$, for $t \in [\tau, \tau')$, and an exchange process $e \in Ep$ that may possibly support l during the interval $[\tau, \tau']$. Let IMP^t and LI^t be fixed, for all $t \in [\tau, \tau')$. Assume also that $l \in Lc^t(r_1, r_2)$, for all $t \in [\tau, \tau']$.

Let $jdg^t(a, bal(a_1, a_2, e, [\tau, \tau']))$ denote the judgement, at $t \in T$, of the balance of values accumulated in the interval $[\tau, \tau'] \subseteq T$, and let $jdg^t(a, bal(a_1, a_2, e, [\tau, \tau'])) \succeq 0$ mean $jdg^t(a, bal(a_1, a_2, e, [\tau, \tau'])) \approx 0 \lor jdg^t(a, bal(a_1, a_2, e, [\tau, \tau'])) \approx +1$.

In this context, the following rule, controlling the introduction of l in $LI^{\tau'}$, is compatible with an exchange value-based account of the link dynamics of the considered system:

$$\frac{a_1 \models^{\tau'} bal(a_1, a_2, e, [\tau, \tau']) \succeq 0 \qquad a_2 \models^{\tau'} bal(a_1, a_2, e, [\tau, \tau']) \succeq 0}{LI^{\tau'} = LI^\tau \cup \{l\} \ \land \ IMP^{\tau'} = IMP^\tau \cup \{(l, e)\}} \ LI_{intro(l)}$$

Analogously, consider an exchange process $e \in Ep$ that supported a link $l \in LI^t$ between roles $r_1, r_2 \in RO^t$ during the interval $[\tau, \tau')$, and that IMP^t and LI^t are fixed, for all $t \in [\tau, \tau')$. Assume that $l \in Lc^t(r_1, r_2)$, for all $t \in [\tau, \tau']$. In this context, for $a \in \{a_1, a_2\}$, the following rule, controlling the elimination of l from LI^τ, is compatible with an exchange value-based account of the link dynamics of the considered system:

$$\frac{a \models^{\tau'} bal(a_1, a_2, e, [\tau, \tau']) \approx -1}{LI^{\tau'} = LI^\tau - \{l\} \ \land \ IMP^{\tau'} = IMP^\tau - \{(l, e)\}} \ LI_{elim(l,a)}$$

Note, on the other hand, that the two rules should to be subject to the *proviso* that the interval $[\tau, \tau']$ is large enough to allow the agents to make sound judgements, the notion of "large enough" depending on intensional factors outside de PopOrg model.

As an aside, we claim that $\{LI_{intro(l)}, LI_{elim(l,a)}\}$ is the minimal set of rules upon which should lie any exchange value-based dynamics of organizational links, in the PopOrg model, when self-interested agents are considered. Of course, more realistic examples of link dynamics would require additional rules to take care of more complex situations, e.g., rules to deal with links implemented by two or more exchange processes.

On the other hand, issues such as the protection of the organization against malicious agents (e.g., agents that provoke the elimination of links by providing a negative evaluation to every exchange), are issues that concern intensional norms related to the security of the organization, which should be reflected in the extensional rules describing the dynamics of the organization, but which should not be dealt with initially at this extensional level.

5   Related Works

The investigation of the organizational dynamics of agent systems goes back to at least [6], where the dynamics concerned the coordination of agents in distributed problem solving systems.

The clear distinction between an organization structure and a population structure in MAS seems to have been first introduced in the PopOrg model [1], and subsequently adopted in some MAS organization models (e.g., [7]).

The main reason for the need of a structural dynamism in a MAS organization, and the corresponding changes in the organizational structure, have traditionally been considered to be the demands of the environment and the requirements of adaptability that they imply (e.g., [8]).

However, the PopOrg model was defined so that *internal reasons* for the dynamism of the organizational structures could also be considered in a suitable way, for instance, in the exchange value-based way proposed in the paper. The issue of the *internal forces* that may motivate a dynamics of organizational structure has also been addressed in [9].

The option for the set-theoretic language to model the dynamics of organizational structures, including the option for the signal-based notion of behaviors and interactions, adopted in the PopOrg model, contrasts with the more usual option for logic-based languages (e.g., [10]), and is justified by the goal of a direct formalization of the concrete features that constitute the PopOrg model, as a particular minimal organizational model.

Also, the option for the set-theoretic formalism is related to the choice of placing the extensional aspects of the organizational dynamics in the center of the PopOrg model, leaving the intensional (rule-based, subjective) aspects, including those expressed by the *organizational rules* introduced in [7], to a second layer – where they are introduced in specialized refinements of the model, as the need arises in particular applications.

For instance, we did not place at the core of the PopOrg model any of the various available methods for reorganization, such as role reallocation (e.g., [11,9]), task and resources reallocation (e.g. [12,13]), modifications in the hierarchical relationships between roles (e.g., [14]), composition and decomposition of groups of agents (e.g. [6]), reallocation of obligations (e.g. [15]), etc.

Full algorithms for the reorganization of MAS (as the ones studied in, e.g., [16,17,18]) where also left out of the PopOrg model. By the same token, we did not introduce in the minimal model the various ways in which organizational roles may be related to each other, in connection to issues such as power, prestige, control, etc. (as analyzed, e.g., in [19]).

The inclusion of such various structural relationships and reorganization mechanisms leads to organizational models that are not minimal in the sense the PopOrg model is, giving instead larger organizational models, as the ones proposed in, e.g., [20] and [21] (see [22] for a survey of the most important of such larger models).

In other words, we aimed at keeping PopOrg a minimal, extensional model, where every intensional aspect should be considered through complementary external rules operating on the basis of the combination of extensional and intensional features, as the dynamical rules illustrated in the present paper.

This is why, given that the analysis of organizations from the deontic point of view[23] places itself in the intensional perspective, concerning the expression of regulations (essentially constraints) about the structure and functioning of a multiagent system, norms and deontic notions also do not belong intrinsically to the PopOrg model: they should be added through complementary rules. For example, in [24], rules were introduced to support an exchange value-based operational notion of morality for MAS organizations.

Concerning the system of exchange values, we have been using it to analyze social interactions in MAS from the point of view of the equilibrium of the interactions (e.g., [5,25,26,27]). The same system has been used for other analytical and modelling purposes, e.g., in [28,29,30].

Finally, we notice that the work on the denotational and operational semantics of real-time and reactive systems [2] defined models for such systems which are formally keen to most models of multiagent systems. The similarity comes not from chance, for the agent-based systems were originally developed as models of reactive real-time systems [31].

One readily recognizes, for instance, that reactive programs in state-based specification languages for reactive systems [2] are similar in spirit to the so called procedural knowledge representation that was originally used to specify the behavior of BDI agents [31]: both are means for representing "reactive plans".

Since a signal [2] is essentially a temporal sequence of values of a certain type, signals are similar to the temporal sequences used in the PopOrg model. The similarity is not weakened by our using organizational objects as values of the temporal sequences, while the declarative languages designed for the specification of reactive real-time systems use simple data values in signals.

Such differences and similarities only stress the need to develop the study of multiagent systems in the perspective of a situated approach, where the system is placed to operate in connection to a real environment.

6   Conclusion

We have presented a temporal extensional model to support a formal dynamics of multiagent systems, by revisiting the PopOrg model and refining it with the notion that social interactions are exchanges. We strived to clearly separate the extensional, structural aspects of the problem, from the intentional, subjective ones. The former deal with the set of possible ways the structure of a multiagent system evolves in time, while the latter deal with the possible subjective causes of the particularities of such evolution.

To illustrate the way the intensional and the extensional aspects of the structural dynamics of a multiagent system may be combined, we made use of an exchange value-based mechanism for the modeling of the subjective assessment of social exchanges, allowing the agents to decide on the start, continuation and termination of an organizational link, thus showing that an intensional mechanism may operate as a causal element in the extensional structural dynamics of the system.

The two components that one would like to add to the PopOrg model in the near future, to allow for the tackling of two essential aspects of MAS, are: first, a mechanism for constituting organizational groups of agents within a system; and, second, the notion of an external environment, the latter being the essential component for construing a MAS as a situated one.

Also, various aspects of the link dynamics as it stands in the present paper should be analyzed further, like the issue of the dynamics of organizational links implemented by multiple exchange processes, each such exchange process being evaluated in a different way by the agents involved in them. Or else, the impact on the whole model of the issue of periodicity in organizational interactions, that is, the restriction of organizational interactions to those that are periodic, as in the vast majority of the interactions that happen in human organizations.

Thus, it seems to us that the work we presented here produced the core elements for an adequate consideration of the structural dynamics of multiagent systems. They seem to be specially useful not only when we model the systems situated in real environments, whose structural and functional variations press the systems to keep their structures continuously adapted to the demands of those environments, but also when we model systems that themselves, through their agents, find reasons to change their organizational structures.

Acknowledgements. We thank the referees for their very valuable comments, some of which will be incorporated in future works. This work was partially supported by CNPq, CAPES and FAPERGS.

References

1. Demazeau, Y., Costa, A.C.R.: Populations and organizations in open multi-agent systems. In: 1st National Symposium on Parallel and Distributed AI, PDAI 1996. Hyderabad, India (1996)
2. Benveniste, A., Berry, G.: The synchronous approach to reactive and real-time systems. Proceedings of the IEEE 79, 1270–1282 (1991)
3. Piaget, J.: Sociological Studies. Routlege, London (1995)
4. Homans, G.: Social Behavior – Its Elementary Forms. Brace & World, New York (1961)
5. Dimuro, G.P., Costa, A.C.R., Gonçalves, L.V., Hübner, A.: Centralized regulation of social exchanges between personality-based agents. In: Noriega, P., Vázquez-Salceda, J., Boella, G., Boissier, O., Dignum, V., Fornara, N., Matson, E. (eds.) COIN 2006. LNCS (LNAI), vol. 4386, pp. 338–355. Springer, Heidelberg (2007)

6. Corkill, D., Lesser, V.: The use of meta-level control for coordination in a distributed problem solving network. In: Bundy, A. (ed.) IJCAI 1983. Proceedings of the 8th International Joint Conference on Artificial Intelligence, William Kaufmann, Karlsruhe, vol. 2, pp. 748–756 (1983)

7. Zambonelli, F., Jennings, N., Wooldridge, M.: Organisational rules as an abstraction for the analysis and design of multi-agent systems. International Journal of Software Engineering and Knowledge Engineering (3), 303–328 (2001)

8. Gasser, L.: Perspectives on organizations in multi-agent systems. In: Advanced Course on Artificial Intelligence ACAI-01 at ECAI 2001, Prague, Czech Technical University (2001)

9. DeLoach, S., Matson, E.: An organizational model for designing adaptive multiagent systems. In: AAAI 2004 Workshop on Agent Organizations: Theory and Practice, San Jose (2004)

10. Dignum, V., Dignum, F.: A logic for agent organizations. In: FAMAS@Agents 2007, Durham September 3-7 (2007)

11. Baciu, A., Nagy, A.: Coordination and reorganization in multi-agent systems, i. Sudia Univ. Babes-Bolyai – Informatica (2) (2003) 53–60

12. Fatima, S.S., Siva, G.U., Tolety, P.: Trace – an adaptive organizational policy for multi agent systems. In: Proceedings of Fourth International Conference on MultiAgent Systems, pp. 383–384 (2000)

13. So, Y., Durfee, E.: An organizational self-design model for organizational change. In: AAAI 1993 Workshop on AI and Theories of Groups and Organizations: Conceptual and Empirical Research, Washington, D.C, pp. 8–15 (1993)

14. Zheng-guang, W., Xiao-hui, L., Qin-ping, Z.: Adaptive mechanisms of organizational structures in multi-agent systems. In: Shi, Z.-Z., Sadananda, R. (eds.) PRIMA 2006. LNCS (LNAI), vol. 4088, pp. 471–477. Springer, Heidelberg (2006)

15. McCallum, M., Vasconcelos, W.W., Norman, T.J.: Verification and analysis of organisational change. In: Boissier, O., Padget, J.A., Dignum, V., Lindemann, G., Matson, E., Ossowski, S., Sichman, J.S., Vázquez-Salceda, J. (eds.) ANIREM 2005 and OOOP 2005. LNCS (LNAI), vol. 3913, pp. 46–61. Springer, Heidelberg (2006)

16. Kashyap, S.: Reorganization in Multiagent Organizations. PhD thesis, Kansas State University (2006)

17. Zhong, C.: An Investigationi of Reorganization Algorithms. PhD thesis, Kansas State University (2002)

18. Picard, G., Mellouli, S., Gleizes, M.P.: Techniques for multi-agent system reorganization. In: Dikenelli, O., Gleizes, M.-P., Ricci, A. (eds.) ESAW 2005. LNCS (LNAI), vol. 3963, pp. 142–152. Springer, Heidelberg (2006)

19. Grossi, D., Dignum, F., Dastani, M.: Foundations of organizational structures in multiagent systems. In: Fourth International Conference on Autonomous Agents and Multiagent Systems, Utrecht, pp. 690–697. ACM Press, New York (2005)

20. Hübner, J.F., Sichman, J.S., Boissier, O.: $\mathcal{MOISE}^+$: Towards a structural, functional, and deontic model for mas organization. In: Castelfranchi, C., Johnson, W.L. (eds.) Proceedings of the First International Joint Conference on Autonomous Agents and Multi-Agent Systems, AAMAS 2002, pp. 501–502. ACM Press, New York (2002)

21. Ghijsen, M., Jansweijer, W., Wielinga, B.: Towards a framework for agent coordination and reorganization, Agentcore. In: Sichman, J.S., Padget, J., Ossowski, S., Noriega, P. (eds.) COIN 2007. LNCS (LNAI), vol. 4870, pp. 1–14. Springer, Heidelberg (2008)

22. Coutinho, L.R., Sichman, J.S., Boissier, O.: Modeling dimensions for multi-agent systems organizations. In: Proceedings of the 1st International Workshop on Agent Organizations: Models and Simulations, AOMS 2007, Hyderabad (2007)

23. Boella, G., van der Torre, L., Verhagen, H.: Introduction to normative multiagent systems. In Boella, G., van der Torre, L., Verhagen, H., eds.: Normative Multi-agent Systems. Number 07122 in Dagstuhl Seminar Proceedings, IBFI (2007)

24. Costa, A.C.R., Dimuro, G.P.: A basis for an exchange value-based operational notion of morality for multiagent systems. In: Neves, J., Santos, M.F., Machado, J.M. (eds.) EPIA 2007. LNCS (LNAI), vol. 4874, pp. 580–592. Springer, Heidelberg (2007)

25. Dimuro, G.P., Costa, A.R.C., Palazzo, L.A.M.: Systems of exchange values as tools for multi-agent organizations. Journal of the Brazilian Computer Society 11(1), 31–50 (2005) (Special Issue on Agents' Organizations)

26. Dimuro, G.P., Costa, A.R.C.: Exchange values and self-regulation of exchanges in multi-agent systems: the provisory, centralized model. In: Brueckner, S.A., Di Marzo Serugendo, G., Hales, D., Zambonelli, F. (eds.) ESOA 2005. LNCS (LNAI), vol. 3910, pp. 75–89. Springer, Heidelberg (2006)

27. Dimuro, G.P., Costa, A.R.C.: Interval-based Markov Decision Processes for regulating interactions between two agents in multi-agent systems. In: Dongarra, J., Madsen, K., Wásniewski, J. (eds.) PARA 2004. LNCS, vol. 3732, pp. 102–111. Springer, Heidelberg (2006)

28. Rodrigues, M.R., Luck, M.: Analysing partner selection through exchange values. In: Sichman, J.S., Antunes, L. (eds.) MABS 2005. LNCS (LNAI), vol. 3891, pp. 24–40. Springer, Heidelberg (2006)

29. Rodrigues, M.R., Luck, M.: Cooperative interactions: an exchange values model. In: Noriega, P., Vázquez-Salceda, J., Boella, G., Boissier, O., Dignum, V., Fornara, N., Matson, E. (eds.) COIN 2006. LNCS (LNAI), vol. 4386, pp. 356–371. Springer, Heidelberg (2007)

30. Grimaldo, F., Lozano, M., Barber, F.: Coordination and sociability for intelligent virtual agents. In: Sichman, J.S., Padget, J., Ossowski, S., Noriega, P. (eds.) COIN 2007. LNCS (LNAI), vol. 4870, pp. 58–70. Springer, Heidelberg (2008)

31. Georgeff, M., Lansky, A.: Procedural knowledge. Proc. of the IEEE 74, 1383–1398 (1986)

Dynamic Composition of Electronic Institutions for Teamwork

Mario Gómez[1] and Enric Plaza[2]

[1] Department of Computing Science, University of Aberdeen
mgomez@csd.abdn.ac.uk
[2] Artificial Intelligence Research Institute, Spanish National Research Council
enric@iiia.csic.es

Abstract. We present a framework for teamwork based on a requirement's driven dynamic composition approach to electronic institutions, which builds on an existing formalism for agent-mediated electronic institutions. In the presented framework, agent teams are designed and deployed on-the-fly so as to met the requirements of the problem at hand. The result is a new form of electronic institution that is created dynamically out of existing components to provide ad-hoc communication and coordination support for teamwork. This approach combines a requirements driven configuration of a team in terms of the structure, competencies and knowledge required (team design) to fulfill problem requirements; and a dynamic negotiation of the communication and coordination components to use for every team role (team formation).

1 Introduction

Cooperative problem solving (CPS) is a form of social interaction in which a group of agents work together to achieve a common goal. Several models have been proposed to account for this form of interaction from different perspectives: distributed artificial intelligence, economics, philosophy, organization science and social sciences. From the artificial intelligence perspective there are two main approaches to cooperation: a micro-level –agent-centered– view, which is focused on the internal architecture or the decision-making model of individual agents, and a macro-level –social– view, which is focused on the societal and organizational aspects of cooperation.

Some of the most challenging issues faced by the MAS community are related to the creation of open MAS [17]. Closed systems are typically designed by one team for one homogeneous environment, while in open MAS the participants (both human and software agents) are unknown beforehand, may change over time and may be developed by different parties. Therefore, those infrastructures that adopt a social view on cooperation seem more appropriate that those adopting a micro-level view, for the former do not enforce a particular agent architecture.

Some aspects of complex system development become more difficult by adopting an agent-centered approach: since agents are autonomous, the patterns and the effects of their interactions are uncertain, and it is extremely difficult to

J.S. Sichman et al. (Eds.): COIN 2007, LNAI 4870, pp. 155–170, 2008.
© Springer-Verlag Berlin Heidelberg 2008

predict the behavior of the overall system based on its constituent components, because of the strong possibility of emergent behavior [16]. These problems can be circumvented by restraining interactions and imposing preset organizational structures, which are characteristic of the social view.

The Agent-Mediated Electronic Institutions (EI) approach was proposed [19,23,8] to address the issues stated above (openness and predictability) by introducing a social control mechanism. However, a main issue arises when trying to use preset organizational structures to operationalize CPS: the need for different team structures to deal with different types of problem. The EI approach was originally intended to model static organizations of agents; therefore, at first glance it seems inadequate to use such an approach for dealing with flexible teamwork. In this paper we introduce a proposal that uses the EI formalism in a novel way: on-the-fly institutions created out of existing components that capture the communication and coordination aspects of teamwork. These institutions are created on demand, according to the requirements of each problem being solved, and are able to reconfigure themselves to deal with changes in the environment.

The paper is structured as follows: Section 2 reviews related work, Section 3 puts our institutional model of teamwork in context by introducing the framework this model is part of, Section 4 describes our proposal to model teamwork based on the EI formalism, and finally, Section 5 summarizes our contributions.

2   Related Work

The notion of Agent Mediated Electronic Institutions (EI) was first proposed in [19] taking fish-auctions as an inspiring metaphor. Since then, it has become a main research topic of several projects, which have further refined and formalized it, as for example in [23,8]. An Electronic Institution (EI) refers to a sort of "virtual place" that is designed to support and facilitate certain goals to the human and software agents concurring to that place by establishing explicit conventions. Since these goals are achieved by means of the interaction of agents, an EI provides the social mediation layer required by agents to achieve a successful interaction: interaction protocols, shared ontologies, communication languages and social behavior rules. Formalization of electronic institutions [11] underpins the use of structured design techniques and formal analysis, and facilitates development, composition and reuse.

Other early frameworks based on social and organization notions are:

- The *Civil Agent Societies* [5]: a framework for developing agent organizations which follows the metaphor of civil human societies based on social contracts, and is oriented towards marketplaces and B2B e-commerce. This framework uses the Contract Net interaction protocol, social norms, notary services and exception handling services.
- The organization of sociality presented in [21]: it is based on a conception of cognition, both at the individual and the collective level, examined in relation to contemporary organization theory.

– The organizational model presented in [6]: this model describes rules of behavior for individual agents using concepts from organization theory such as roles and norms.

Other models and frameworks can be found in the proceedings and post-proceedings of the COIN International Workshop Series on Coordination, Organizations, Institutions, and Norms [1,20]. The framework we propose here is based on the EI approach, and more specifically, we adopt the formalism described in [10,9] as a starting point to our own work. The main contribution of our proposal is the notion of dynamic institutions created on-the-fly by selecting and combining reusable institutional components on-demand, so as to meet stated problem requirements.

The are some related works around the ideas of dynamic organization and coordination:

– In [12] a decision making framework is proposed that enables agents to dynamically select the coordination mechanism that is most appropriate to their circumstances.
– In [26] the authors address some of the aspects that must be considered in order to incorporate norms in agents, and propose a set of strategies to be used by agents in norm-based systems and analyze.
– In [7] the authors discuss reorganization issues in agent societies: they present a classification of reorganization situations, based on the focus of the reorganization, the authority to modify the organization, and how reorganization decisions are taken. This work proposes requirements for agents to allow for the automatic adaptation to a reorganized system.
– The analysis of reorganization requirements has yielded a model for adjustable autonomy [24] as a way to achieve dynamic coordination. This research describes the relation between types of coordination and the autonomy of actors.
– The concept of adjustable autonomy is also explored in [4], in the context of mixed human-agent teams. This work proposes a policy-based capability for adjustable autonomy based on the multiple dimensions of the problem.

A commonality of the former works, which differentiates them from our own work, is the focus on individual agents: mechanisms for autonomous agents to select coordination mechanisms and adapt to the changing environment, while our focus in on the organization itself: how to select the best organization for accomplishing some specific goals.

Also relevant to our own approach is the work presented in [3,2]. This work takes the notions of self-organization and self-configuration from Autonomic Computing, and applies them to Agent Mediated Electronic Institutions, which brings about the notion of Autonomic Electronic Institutions (AEI). In particular, the authors are exploring the the use of Genetic Algorithms and Case Based Reasoning to modify some aspects of an electronic institution to better fulfill its goals as the environment changes. However, our approaches are quite different: one the one hand, the AEI approach addresses the adaptation of norms specified in a parametric way, by learning the parameters that bring about a better global behavior; on the other hand, we address the structure and configuration of the institution itself, in terms of its organizational structure and allowed communication protocols; more specifically, our approach is to configure and reconfigure a new institution by selecting and composing reusable components so as to satisfy stated problem requirements.

Another line of research that is related to our own line is described in [18]. In that paper, the authors use a notion of dynamic electronic institution (DEI) as a temporary organization of agents that is constituted, dissolved and reformed on-the-fly, and is able to adapt its norms dynamically, dynamically in relation to its present members (agents). There are several differences between former proposal and our own one: one the one hand, their approach is driven by the goals of the agents willing to form a coalition and deciding to adopt a common set of norms, while in our approach there exists a previous meta-institution that helps agents form new institutions for solving specific problems, by reusing existing components; on the other hand, the central element of their proposal is the adoption of norms, while our approach gives more importance to the communication and coordination aspects of teamwork, that we use as building blocks of the institution.

Nest section introduces the ORCAS framework, a multi-layered framework for cooperative MAS that embraces the institutional model discussed in this paper.

3   The ORCAS Framework

In this paper we present an institutional approach to CPS that is part of the ORCAS framework for developing and deploying cooperative MAS [13]. The main contributions of this framework are:

- An Agent Capability Description Language (ACDL) that supports all the activities required to cooperate in open environments, from the discovery and invocation of capabilities, to their composition and coordination.
- A model of CPS that is driven by the specification of requirements for every particular instance of a problem to be solved.
- An agent platform for developing and deploying cooperative MAS in open environments.

Figure 1 depicts the main elements of the ORCAS ACDL. A *capability* is able to accomplish some *task*, and may require specific domain knowledge fulfilling some properties or assumptions. These properties assumed for the domain knowledge are specified as *domain models*. There are two types of capability: *skill* and *task-decomposer*. Skills are primitive, non decomposable capabilities, while task-decomposers decompose a problem (a task) into more elementary problems (subtasks), so as to solve complex problems that primitive capabilities cannot accomplish alone. Any capability presents a *knowledge-level description* that specifies what the capability does from a functional view: input, output, preconditions, and postconditions. This functional description can be used by

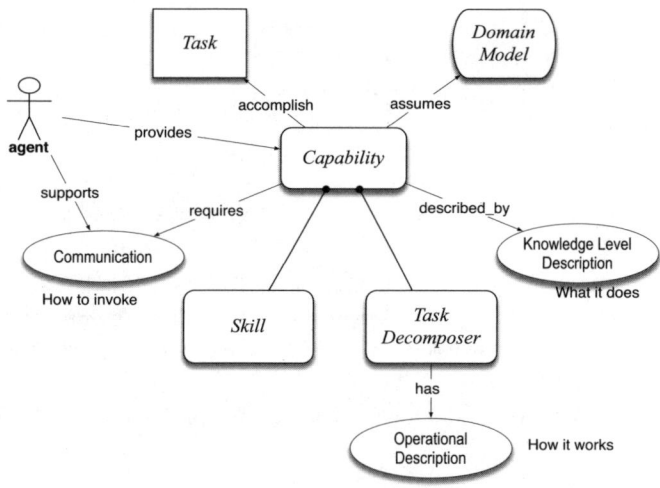

Fig. 1. Overview of the ORCAS ACDL

middle agents to discover and compose capabilities. However, in order to invoke a capability and interact with its provider, a requester agent must use an interaction protocol that is supported by the capability of interest. In ORCAS the information required to invoke a capability is referred to as the *communication* of a capability. Finally, the information required to coordinate multiple agents that are cooperating to solve a problem together is specified by the *operational description* of a task decomposer, which describes the control flow among subtasks (sequencing, parallelism, choices, etc.) in terms of agent roles.

The ORCAS platform provides all the infrastructure required by agents to successfully cooperate according to the ORCAS model of CPS. This model of the CPs process is sketched in Figure 2. The *problem specification* process produces a specification of problem requirements to be met by a team, including a description of the application domain (a collection of domain models) and the problem data to be used during teamwork. The *team design* process uses the problem requirements to build a *task-configuration*, which is a knowledge-level specification of: (1) the tasks to solve, (2) the capabilities to apply, and (3) the domain knowledge required by a team of agents in order to solve a given problem according to its specific requirements. The resulting task-configuration is used during *team formation* to allocate tasks and subtasks to agents, and to instruct agents on how to play their assigned team-roles: capabilities and knowledge to apply, as well as communication and coordination requirements. Finally, *teamwork* is the execution stage where team members try to solve the problem together by following the instructions received during team formation, thus complying with the specific requirements of the problem at hand.

Note that the ORCAS model for CPS should not be understood as a fixed sequence of steps, instead, we have implemented strategies that interleave team design and team formation with teamwork. These strategies enable the

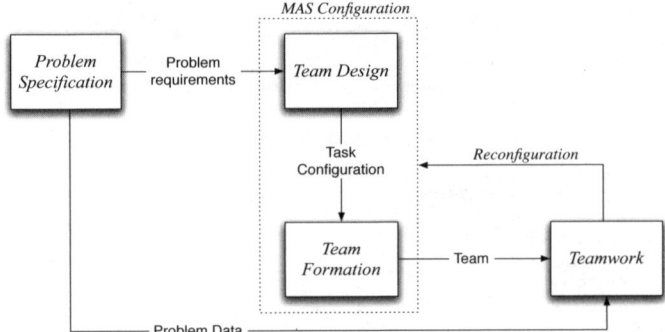

Fig. 2. The ORCAS model for the cooperative problem solving process

reconfiguration of agent teams dynamically so as to react to agent failure and other changes in the environment.

It should be remarked that, within the ORCAS framework, the EIs formalism is used in two ways: on the one hand, we use concepts adapted from the EI formalism described in [10,8] for specifying some elements of the ORCAS ACDL (the communication and the operational description), formalism; on the other hand, the ORCAS agent platform is itself an EI that provides mediation services for both providers and requesters of problem solving capabilities to successfully cooperate (this platform is actually a meta-instution where team-specific institutions are constituted). From now on, to avoid confusion we will sometimes refer to this formalism as ISLANDER, which is the name of a software tool to edit and verify institutions according to the formalism described in the EI formalism adopted here.

The knowledge-level description of a capability and the mechanisms used in ORCAS to discover and compose capabilities (which are part of the team design process) have been described elsewhere [14]. The ORCAS agent platform is described in [15]. In this paper we focus on those aspects of the ORCAS ACDL that are based on ISLANDER, namely the communication and the operational description, and how are these elements used to represent the interaction and coordination requirements of teamwork. These are the subjects of the following section.

4   Dynamic Institutions for Hierarchical Teamwork

The ORCAS ACDL specifies the communication and operational description of capabilities using elements from the ISLANDER formalism in a novel way, so it seems appropriate to briefly review the main concepts of this formalism before describing their use in ORCAS:

1. *Agent roles:* Agents are the players in an EI, interacting by the exchange of speech acts, whereas roles are standardized patterns of behavior required by agents playing part in given functional relationships.

2. *Dialogic framework:* Determines the valid illocutions that can be exchanged among agents, including the vocabulary (ontology) and the agent communication language.

3. *Scenes:* A scene defines an interaction protocol among a set of agent roles, using the illocutions allowed by a given dialogic framework.

4. *Performative structure:* A network of connected scenes that captures the relationships among scenes; a performative structure constrains the paths agents can traverse to move from one scene to another, depending on the roles they are playing.

In ORCAS the specification of capabilities at the knowledge level enables the automated discovery and composition of capabilities, without taking into account neither the communication aspects required to invoke a capability, nor the operational aspects required to coordinate the behavior of several agents. These features are specified respectively in the communication and operational description of a capability:

Communication: Specifies one or several interaction protocols that can be used to interact with an agent to invoke a given capability and get back the result of applying it. This feature is specified using the notion of *scene* from ISLANDER.

Operational Description: Specifies the control flow among the subtasks introduced by a task-decomposer, using a restricted version of the *performative structure* concept from ISLANDER.

A team in ORCAS is designed to solve a problem represented by a knowledge-level structure referred to as a *task-configuration* (the reader is referred to [14] for a more detailed description). Figure 3 shows an example of a task-configuration for a task called *Information-Search*. This task is decomposed into four tasks by the *Meta-search* task-decomposer: *Elaborate-query*, *Customize-query*, *Retrieve* and *Aggregate*, which is further decomposed by the *Aggregation* capability into two subtasks: *Elaborate-items* and *Aggregate-items*. The example includes some skills requiring domain knowledge: the *Query-expansion-with-thesaurus* requires a thesaurus (e.g. *MeSH*, a medical thesaurus), and the *Retrieval* and *Query-customization* skills require a description of information sources.

Any ORCAS team follows the hierarchical structure of a task-configuration, with one team-role per task. Each team role represents a position to be played in the team organization, and includes the following elements: a team-role identifier[1], the identifier of a task to be solved, the identifier of a capability to apply, the domain knowledge to be used by the selected capability (if needed), and optionally, if the capability is a task decomposer, the information required to delegate subtasks to other team-members, which includes, for each subtask: the identifier of a subordinated team-role, the team members assigned to that team

---

[1] The same task may appear multiple times in the same task-configuration, so a unique team-role identifier is required.

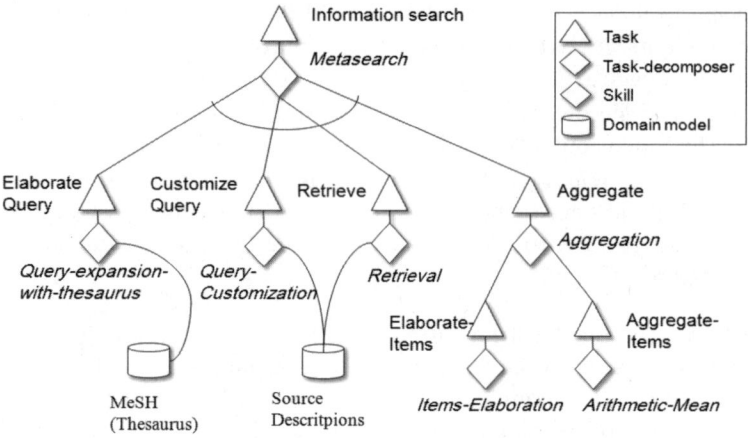

Fig. 3. Task-configuration example

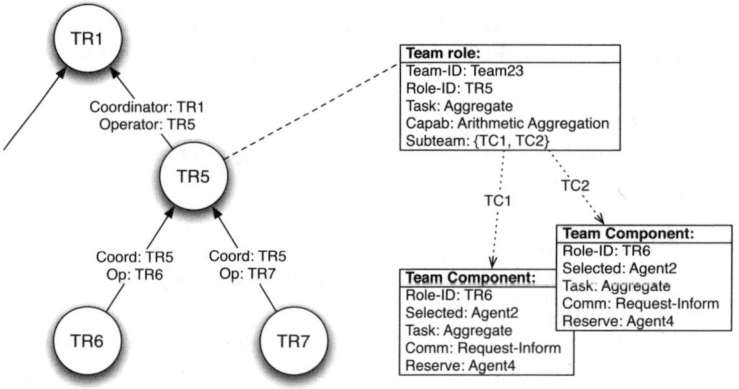

Fig. 4. Team roles

role[2], a collection of reserve agents to use in case that some of the selected team members fail, and a communication protocol that is compatible with the selected capability and shared by both the agent assigned to the parent task, and the agent or agents assigned to the subtask.

Figure 4 depicts a partial example of a team based on the task-configuration showed in Figure 3. Essentially, a team is hierarchical organization of team-roles. In particular, we see 4 team roles –TR1, TR5, TR6 and TR7– corresponding to tasks *Information-Search*, *Aggregate*, *Elaborate-Items*, and *Aggregate-Items*. A

---

[2] Usually, a task (and the corresponding team role) only needs a team member to be achieved, but some tasks may have to be performed multiple times in parallel, thus they can be served by a number of agents working simultaneously.

team is organized around subordination relations that are established in accordance to the top-down task-decomposition. These relations are specified in terms of two generic roles: the coordinator, which has to be adopted by an agent applying a task-decomposition; and operator, which has to be played by the agents selected to solve some subtask.

A *team-role* specifies the requirements for agents to play a specific position within a team, which includes: a task to be solved, a capability to be applied, and, if the capability is a task-decomposer, then the team-role can include information about team members selected for solving each subtask, the communication elements required to delegate each subtask to the selected agent, and optionally a group of agents to keep in reserve.

A **Team-Role** is a tuple $\pi = \langle R, I, T, C, M, Com, S, A_S, A_R \rangle$ where R is a unique team-role identifier, I is a unique team identifier, T is a task, C is a capability, M is a set of domain-models, Com is a specification of communication requirements, A_S is a set of selected agents, A_R is a set of reserve agents, and S is a subteam, specified as a set of team-components.

A *subteam* is specified as a set of *team-components*, where each team-component holds information about a team-role associated to one subtask. More formally, a **Team-Component** is defined as a tuple $\xi = \langle R, T, A_S, A_R, Com \rangle$ where R is a unique team-role identifier, T is a task A_S is a set of selected agents, A_R is a set of reserve agents, Com is a specification of communication requirements.

A team-component is defined for each subtask introduced by a task-decomposer. The *team-role identifier* (R) determines the precise position of the team-component in the team hierarchy. There is a set of agents selected (A_S) to carry out the team-role, and there is a set of agents to keep in reserve (A_R) for the case that some of the selected agents fail during the Teamwork process. Finally, a team-component includes a specification of the *communication* (Com) required to interact with the agent playing the team-component's team-role (R).

Figure 4 shown an example of a team-role that has to apply a task-decomposer, TR5. The agent selected to play TR5 has to apply the *Aggregation* task-decomposer, which introduces two subtasks: *Elaborate-Items* and *Aggregate-Items*. These subtasks are associated to subordinated team roles TR6 and TR7. The information required by TR5 to cooperate with the agents playing TR6 and TR7 is specified as team-components TC1 and TC2. For example, team component TC1 is associated to TR6, that is allocated to agent AG2, with agent AG4 in reserve, and the communication between TR5 and TR6 has to use a Request-Inform protocol.

We define a team as a structure made of interrelated team-roles and team-components, based on a *subordination relation* $\mathbb{S}$ among team-roles: a team-role is subordinated to another, denoted by $\mathbb{S}(\pi, \pi')$, if the first team-role is bound to a team-component contained in the subteam of the second team-role.

$\mathbb{S}(\pi, \pi') \Leftrightarrow \exists \xi^i \in \pi_S \mid \xi_R^i = \pi'$ where $\pi, \pi' \in \Pi$ are team-roles, $\pi_S \subseteq \Xi$ is the subteam of π (a set of team-components), $\xi^i \in \Xi$ is the i-th element of π_S, and $\xi_R^i \in \Pi$ is the team-role associated to ξ^i.

Noting $\mathbb{S}^*$ the closure of $\mathbb{S}$ we can now define a *team* as follows:

A **Team** is defined as a function of a particular a task-configuration $Team(Conf(\mathcal{K})) = \{\pi \in \Pi \, | \, \mathbb{S}^*(\pi^0, \pi) \wedge (head(\mathcal{K}) = \pi^0_T)\}$; where $\pi^0 \in \Pi$ is the team leader's team-role, which is not subordinated to any other team-role, $Conf(\mathcal{K})$ is a task-configuration, $head(\mathcal{K})$ is the root task of the task-configuration $(\mathcal{K})$, and π^0_T is the task allocated to the team leader π^0.

A *team* is a collection of interrelated team-roles, starting from the team-leader π, that is assigned to the root task of a task-configuration. This team model provides an abstract view of the competence required by a group of agents to solve a particular problem. Teams are instantiated during the Team Formation process by selecting a set of agents to play each team-role, and a set of agents to keep in reserve.

Next subsections address, respectively, the specification of the communication and operational description of a capability in ORCAS.

4.1   Communication

Agent capabilities should be specified independently of other agents in order to maximize their reuse and facilitate their specification by third party agent developers. In the general case, agent developers do not know a priori the tasks that could be achieved by a particular capability, neither the domains they could be applied to. As a consequence, the team roles an agent could play using a capability are not known in advance, thus the scenes used to specify the communication requirements of an agent over certain capability cannot be specified in terms of specific team-roles, but in terms of abstract, generic problem solving roles. Since ORCAS teams are designed in terms of a hierarchical decomposition of tasks into subtasks, teamwork is organized as a hierarchy of team-roles.

Some team-roles are bound to a task-decomposer, thus the agents playing those team-roles are responsible of delegating subtasks to other agents, receiving the results, and performing intermediate data processing between subtasks. In such an scenario, we establish an abstract communication model with two basic roles: *coordinator*, which is adopted by an agent willing to decompose a task into subtasks, and *operator*, which is adopted by the agent having to perform a task on demand, using the data provided by another agent that acts as coordinator of a top-level task

Figure 4 depicts some team roles, including the subordination relations that are established between roles, and the generic roles to be assigned when communicating between an agent applying a task-decomposer, and the agents playing the subordinated team-roles. For example, the agent playing TR5 will have to adopt the coordinator role to communicate with the agents playing TR6 and TR7, which will adopt the operator role. Each of these communications will follow the protocol decided during the Team Formation and specified in a team-component object.

Figure 5 shows a scene depicting the communication requirements of an agent over a capability by using a typical request-inform protocol in terms of our two generic roles: *Coordinator* and *Operator*. Symbol *?* denotes a new bind for a

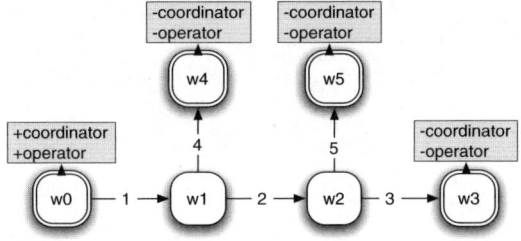

Fig. 5. Example of a communication scene

variable, while *!* denotes an already bound variable. States with double border line enable agents to either join (+) or leave (-) the scene at that point, according to the role they play. In the example, there is an initial state in w_0, where agents enter the scene, and three final states w_3, w_4 and w_5, where agents leave.

We adopt the formal definition of a scene in ISLANDER, so for the reader interested in the technical details, we refer to the papers describing that formalism, as for example [8]. Next section introduces our approach to specify the operational description of a task-decomposer.

4.2   Operational Description

The operational description of a task decomposer is used to specify the coordination among agents in terms of the role-flow policy and the control flow among subtasks. Figure 6 depicts some of the control flow constructions allowed by a performative structure: (a) tasks performed consecutively, in sequence; (b) choice between alternative courses of action; (c) tasks performed in parallel; and (d) tasks that can be executed multiple times.

In ORCAS the operational description of a task-decomposer is based on performative structures, with some distinctive features: as in the EIs formalism,

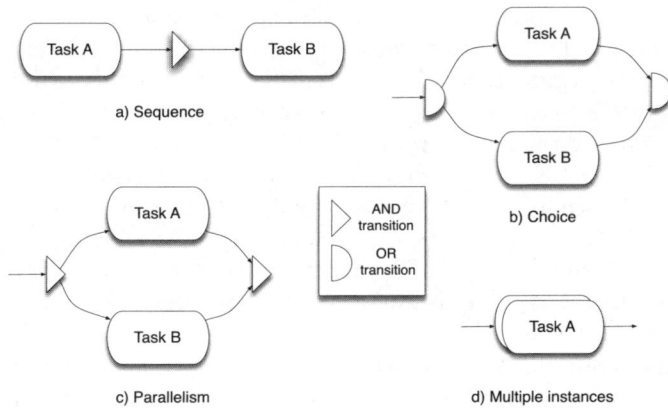

Fig. 6. Control flow among subtasks used in operational descriptions

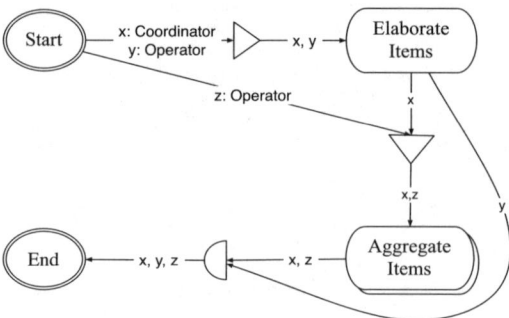

Fig. 7. Example of an operational description

each ORCAS scene within a performative structure must be instantiated by a communication protocol (except the *Start* and *End* scenes). However, in ORCAS the scenes within a performative structure are not instantiated beforehand; that is to say, they are not bound to a specific communication protocol. Instead, the scenes of an operational description are instantiated during team formation, using as a source the set of communication protocols shared by the agents having to interact.

After instantiation, each scene in an operational description corresponds to the communication required to solve a subtask, which implies an agent acting as coordinator invoking the capability provided by another agent acting as operator (or several operators in the case of multiple-instantiated tasks). The coordinator and the operators must use the same communication protocol in order to successfully communicate. Consequently, the instantiation of the scenes in an operational description is done using only those communication protocols shared by the agents involved in a scene. To note that team members are selected during team formation, and thus the set of shared communication protocols is not known until the team members are decided.

Figure 7 shows an example of an operational description for a task-decomposer called Aggregation. This task-decomposer introduces two subtasks: Elaborate-items (EI) and Aggregate-items (AI). Thus, the operational description has two main scenes, one for each subtask, and three role variables: x is a coordinator role, to be played by the agent applying the task-decomposer; y and z are both operator roles; y participates in EI, and z participates AI. Notice that the coordinator (x) is the same in both scenes; it enters EI first and moves to AI only after EI ends.

We adopt the formal definition of a performative structure in ISLANDER, so for the reader interested in the technical details, we refer to the papers describing that formalism, as for example [8].

Since each task-decomposer has an operational description, and the ORCAS organization of a team follows the hierarchical decomposition of tasks into

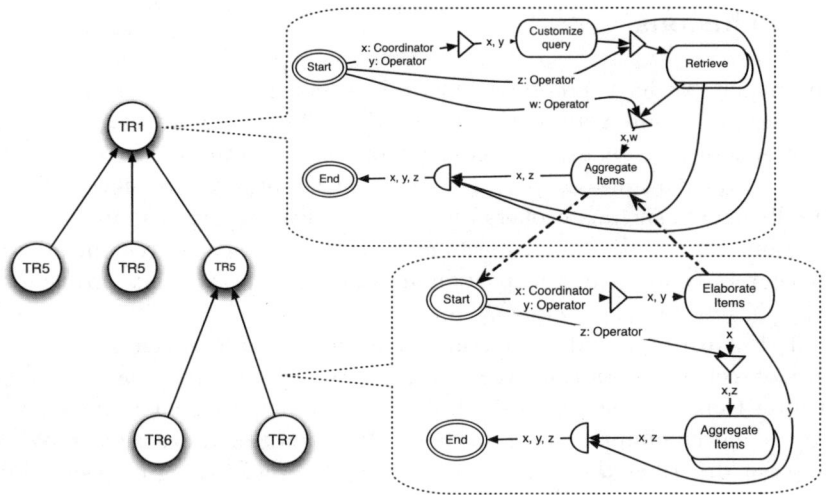

Fig. 8. Teamwork as a nested structure of operational descriptions

subtasks that results of applying task-decomposers, we can model the operational description of a complete team as nested structure of operational descriptions.

Figure 8 depicts the operational description of a team. The top team-role, TR1, is associated to task Information Search, and is bound to a task-decomposer that introduces three subtasks: Customize Query, Retrieve and Aggregate. Therefore, the agent playing TR1 will follow an operational description that contains three scenes, one for every subtask. In addition, the last of these subtasks is bound to another task-decomposer, Aggregation, which in turn introduces a new operational description. The new operational description is nested to the team leader's operational description, and has two scenes, one for Elaborate-Items and another for Aggregate-Items.

Teamwork follows the control flow and the communication scenes established by the nested structure of operational descriptions associated to task-decomposers (already instantiated during team formation). Each scene within an operational description refers to a communication protocol to be played by two agents, one applying a task-decomposer and playing the coordinator role, and one assigned to the corresponding subtask playing the operator role. When an agent playing an operator role has to apply itself a task-decomposer, it will follow the associated operational description playing itself the coordinator role. The execution of an operational description does not finish until all the nested operational descriptions are executed.

Each time a new team is formed according to a task-configuration, a new structure of nested operational descriptions is composed and their scenes instantiated. We regard this structure as a dynamic institution, since it is configured on-the-fly, out of the communication protocols and the operational descriptions supported by the selected team members.

5   Conclusions

In this paper, we have presented a novel approach to teamwork specification using concepts adapted from the EI formalism. In this approach the communication and coordination aspects required for teamwork are reusable components that are used by agents to specify their problem solving capabilities. By doing so, middle agents such as brokers and matchmakers can reason about the communication and coordination aspects of individual agents to dynamically create an EI that is adapted to the particular requirements of every problem to be solved.

While EIs are supposed to be static structures characterized by a predefined network of scenes (a performative structure), we conceive teamwork as a dynamic institution that is build on-the-fly out of existing components: operational descriptions and communication protocols. The operational description of a task-decomposer describes the control flow among subtasks using a specific kind of performative structure in which the communication scenes are not instantiated beforehand. The instantiation of these scenes is done at runtime by selecting communication protocols that are shared by the agents involved in every scene. The result is a hierarchical model of teamwork that is specified as a nested performative structure instantiated and composed on-the-demand, according to the requirements of each problem to be solved by a team of agents. This model supports also the reconfiguration of an institution at runtime, which allows teams to reorganize dynamically to better cope with changes in environments.

By adapting the EI formalism for teamwork, we aim at bringing in some of the benefits of the social-approach in general, and the benefits of the EI approach in particular: promoting openness by avoiding the imposition of a specific agent architecture and favoring reuse; increasing the degree of control over the global system behavior, thus making a MAS more predictable and fostering trustiness; and enabling formal verification tools and automated sofware-generation techniques (e.g. generation of agent-skeletons [25]).

Acknowledgements

This research was sponsored by the Spanish Council for Scientific Research under the MID-CBR (TIN 2006-15140-C03-01) project.

References

1. Boissier, O., Padget, J.A., Dignum, V., Lindemann, G., Matson, E., Ossowski, S., Sichman, J.S., Vázquez-Salceda, J. (eds.): ANIREM 2005 and OOOP 2005. LNCS (LNAI), vol. 3913. Springer, Heidelberg (2006)
2. Bou, E., López-Sánchez, M., Rodríguez-Aguilar, J.A.: Adaptation of autonomic electronic institutions through norms and institutional agents. In: O'Hare, G.M.P., Ricci, A., O'Grady, M.J., Dikenelli, O. (eds.) ESAW 2006. LNCS (LNAI), vol. 4457, pp. 300–319. Springer, Heidelberg (2007)

3. Bou, E., López-Sánchez, M., Rodríguez-Aguilar, J.A.: Towards self-configuration in autonomic electronic institutions. In: Noriega, P., Vázquez-Salceda, J., Boella, G., Boissier, O., Dignum, V., Fornara, N., Matson, E. (eds.) COIN 2006. LNCS (LNAI), vol. 4386, pp. 229–244. Springer, Heidelberg (2007)
4. Bradshaw, J.M., Jung, H., Kulkarni, S., Johnson, M., Feltovich, P., Allen, J., Bunch, L., Chambers, N., Galescu, L., Jeffers, R., Suri, N., Taysom, W., Uszok, A.: Kaa: Policy-based explorations of a richer model for adjustable autonomy. In: AAMAS 2005: Proceedings of the fourth international joint conference on Autonomous agents and multiagent systems, pp. 214–221. ACM Press, New York (2005)
5. Dellarocas, C.: Contractual Agent Societies: Negotiated shared connote and social control in open multi-agent systems. In: Proceedings of the Workshop on Norms and Institutions in Multi-Agent Systems, ICMAS 2002 (2000)
6. Dignum, V., Meyer, J.-J., Weigand, H., Dignum, F.: An organization-oriented model for agent societies. In: Proceedings of International Workshop on Regulated Agent-Based Social Systems: Theories and Applications (2002)
7. Dignum, V., Sonenberg, L., Dignum, F.: Towards dynamic reorganization of agent societies. In: Proceedings of CEAS: Workshop on Coordination in Emergent Agent Societies at ECAI 2004 (2004)
8. Esteva, M.: Electronic Institutions: From Specification to Development. Spanish National Research Council. IIIA Monographies, vol. 14 (2003)
9. Esteva, M., de la Cruz, D., Sierra, C.: Islander: an electronic institutions editor. In: Proceedings 1th International Joint Conference on Autonomous Agents and Multiagent Systems, pp. 1045–1052 (2002)
10. Esteva, M., Padget, J., Sierra, C.: Formalizing a language for institutions and norms. In: Meyer, J.-J.C., Tambe, M. (eds.) ATAL 2001. LNCS, vol. 2333, pp. 348–366. Springer, Heidelberg (2002)
11. Esteva, M., Rodriguez, J.A., Sierra, C., Garcia, P., Arcos, J.L.: On the formal specifications of electronic institutions. In: Sierra, C., Dignum, F.P.M. (eds.) AgentLink 2000. LNCS (LNAI), vol. 1991, pp. 126–147. Springer, Heidelberg (2001)
12. Excelente-toledo, C.B., Jennings, N.R.: The dynamic selection of coordination mechanisms. Autonomous Agents and Multi-Agent Systems 9(1–2), 55–85 (2004)
13. Gómez, M.: Open, Reusable and Configurable Multi-Agent Systems: A Knowledge-Modelling Approach. Spanish National Research Council. IIIA Monographs CSIC, vol. 23 (2004)
14. Gómez, M., Plaza, E.: Extending matchmaking to maximize capability reuse. Proceedings of the Third International Joint Conference on Autonomous Agents and Multi Agent Systems 1, 144–151 (2004)
15. Gómez, M., Plaza, E.: The ORCAS e-Institution: A Platform to Develop Open, Reusable and Configurable Multi-Agent Systems. International Journal on Intelligent Control and Systems. Special Issue on Distributed Intelligent Systems 12(2), 130–141 (2007)
16. Jennings, N.R.: On-agent-based software engineering. Artificial Intelligence 117, 227–296 (2000)
17. Klein, M.: The challenge: Enabling robust open multi-agent systems (2000)
18. Muntaner-Perich, E., de la Rosa, J.: Towards dynamic electronic institutions: From agent coalitions to agent institutions. In: Hinchey, M.G., Rago, P., Rash, J.L., Rouff, C.A., Sterritt, R., Truszkowski, W. (eds.) WRAC 2005. LNCS (LNAI), vol. 3825, pp. 109–121. Springer, Heidelberg (2006)
19. Noriega, P.: Agent-Mediated Auctions: The Fish-Market Metaphor. PhD thesis, Universitat Autònoma de Barcelona (1997)

20. Noriega, P., Vázquez-Salceda, J., Boella, G., Boissier, O., Dignum, V., Fornara, N., Matson, E. (eds.): COIN 2006. LNCS (LNAI), vol. 4386. Springer, Heidelberg (2007)

21. Panzarasa, P., Jennings, N.R.: The organisation of sociality: A manifesto for a new science of multiagent systems. In: Proceedings of the Tenth European Workshop on Multi-Agent Systems (2001)

22. Plaza, E.: Cooperative reuse for compositional cases in multi-agent systems. In: Muñoz-Ávila, H., Ricci, F. (eds.) ICCBR 2005. LNCS (LNAI), vol. 3620, pp. 382–396. Springer, Heidelberg (2005)

23. Rodríguez-Aguilar, J.A.: On the Design and Construction of Agent-mediated Electronic Institutions. IIIA Monographs, CSIC. vol. 14 (2001)

24. van der Vecht, B., Dignum, F., Meyer, J.-J.C., Neef, M.: A dynamic coordination mechanism using adjustable autonomy. In: Sichman, J.S., Padget, J., Ossowski, S., Noriega, P. (eds.) COIN 2007. LNCS(LNAI), vol. 4870, pp. 83–96. Springer, Heidelberg (2008)

25. Vasconcelos, W.W., Sabater, J., Sierra, C., Querol, J.: Skeleton-based agent development for electronic institutions. In: Proceedings UKMAS (2001)

26. y López, F.L., Luck, M., d'Inverno, M.: Constraining autonomy through norms. In: AAMAS 2002: Proceedings of the first international joint conference on Autonomous agents and multiagent systems, pp. 674–681. ACM Press, New York (2002)

Organisational Artifacts and Agents
for Open Multi-Agent Organisations:
"Giving the Power Back to the Agents"

Rosine Kitio[1], Olivier Boissier[1,*], Jomi Fred Hübner[1,2,**], and Alessandro Ricci[3]

[1] SMA/G2I/ENSM.SE, 158 Cours Fauriel
42023 Saint-Etienne Cedex, France
{kitio,boissier,hubner}@emse.fr
[2] GIA/DSC/FURB, Braz Wanka, 238
89035-160, Blumenau, Brazil
jomi@inf.furb.br
[3] DEIS, ALMA MATER STUDIORUM Università di Bologna
47023 Cesena (FC), Italy
a.ricci@unibo.it

Abstract. The social and organisational aspects of agency have become nowadays a major focus of interest in the MAS community, and a good amount of theoretical work is available, in terms of formal models and theories. However, the conception and engineering of proper organisational infrastructures embodying such models and theories is still an open issue, in particular when open MAS are considered. Accordingly, in this paper we discuss a model for an organisational infrastructure called **ORA4MAS** that aims at addressing these issues. By being based on the **A&A** (Agents and Artifacts) meta-model, the key and novel aspect introduced with **ORA4MAS** is that organisations and the organisation infrastructure itself are conceived in terms of agents and artifacts, as first-class abstractions giving body to the MAS from design to runtime.

Keywords: Multi-agent Systems, MAS organisations, Open systems.

1 Introduction

Nowadays, current applications of IT show the interweaving of both human and tech-nological *communities* in which software entities act on behalf of users and cooperate with infohabitants, taking into account issues like trust, security, flexibility, adaptation and *openness* [12,24]. As shown in [16], current applications have led to an increase in number of agents, in the duration and repetitiveness of their activities, with a decision and action perimeter still enlarging. Moreover the number of agents' *designers* is also increasing, leading to a huge palette of heterogeneity in these systems. Most designers have doubts about how to put these concepts in practice, i.e., how to program them,

---

* Partially supported by USP-COFECUB.
** Supported by ANR Project ForTrust.

J.S. Sichman et al. (Eds.): COIN 2007, LNAI 4870, pp. 171–186, 2008.
© Springer-Verlag Berlin Heidelberg 2008

while both addressing the openness and scalability issues and keeping agent's autonomy and decentralisation which are essential features of MAS. The complex system engineering's approach needed to build such applications highlights and stresses requirements on *openness* in terms of ability to take into account several kinds of changes and to adapt the system configuration while it keeps running.

Since it is a huge and complex work to develop systems with this kind of openness, in this paper we propose an organisational infrastructure referred as ORA4MAS which is meant to provide a conceptual and architectural step towards the simplification of this problem. Our proposal is based on the A&A approach [23] where instead of a lot of different components and concepts (e.g., agents, services, proxies, objects, ...), only two types of entities are involved: agents and artifacts. Roughly, while agents model the decisions of the system, the artifacts model its functions. We especially demonstrate this approach showing how the organisational aspect of the MAS can be conceived and designed by only *organisational agents* and *organisational artifacts*. This is in analogy with human organisation and organisation infrastructures, that are populated by humans (as participants and part of the organisation machinery), and by rich sets of artifacts and tools that humans use to support their activities inside the organisation and the organisation itself, encapsulating essential infrastructure services.

In the first part of the paper (Sec. 2), we will have a look at the different approaches that have been developed in the field of multi-agent organisation, stressing what limitations we consider. This is complemented by a look at what has been done in the other dimensions of an MAS, i.e., environment and interaction. Then, we present the basic concepts underlying ORA4MAS infrastructure (Sec. 3), and we briefly describe the shapes of the organisational artifacts devised in ORA4MAS reifying the $\mathcal{M}\text{OISE}^+$ organisational model (Sec. 4). Finally, we provide concluding remarks and perspectives for the work in (Sec. 5).

2   Background

The recent developments in MAS domain, belonging to what we call *Organisation Oriented Programming (OOP)* [2], have provided many proposals of organisation-oriented middleware. In the different approaches related to OOP, we distinguish two important components: a declarative *Organisation Modelling Language* (OML) and an *Organisation Implementation Architecture* (OIA). The OML *specifies* the organisation(s) of an MAS. It is used to collect and express specific constraints and cooperation patterns imposed on the agents by the designer (or the agents), resulting in an explicit representation that we call *Organisation Specification* (OS). A collective entity, called *Organisation Entity* (OE), instantiates this OS by assigning agents to roles. The OIA will then help these agents to properly "play" their roles as they are specified in the OS.

The OIA normally considers both an agent centered and a system centered point of view.[1] In the former, the focus lies on how to develop different *agent reasoning mechanisms* to interpret and reason on the OS and OE applied to the agents [3,4]. In the latter, the main concern is how to develop an infrastructure, that we call Organisation Infrastructure (OI), that ensures the satisfaction of the organisational constraints

---

[1] Let's notice that in [28] these points of view are called agent and institutional perspectives.

(e.g., agents playing the right roles, following the specified norms). This second point of view is important in heterogeneous and open systems where the agents that enter into the system may have unknown architectures. Of course, to develop the overall MAS, the former point of view is necessary since the agents probably need to have access to an organisational representation that enable them to reason about it.

The implementation of OI normally follows a common trend in multiagent platforms. These platforms, e.g. JADE [1], have demonstrated the requirement and utility of the notion of "infrastructure" for MAS development [10]. Not only have they supported the implementation of the agents, but are being noticed as a provider of fundamental global generic services going further of only directory facilitator, agent management system or agent communications by also addressing coordination [19]. Therefore, agents related to the application domain operate on top of a middleware layer.

As shown in [2], many implementations of OI follow the general layered architecture depicted in Fig. 1: (i) domain (or application) agents, responsible to achieve organisational goals, use an *organisational proxy* component to interact with the organisation, (ii) the *organisational middleware*, responsible to bind all agents in a coherent OS and OE and provides some services for them, and (iii) communication infrastructure for connecting all components in a distributed and heterogeneous applications. This layered structure results in an engineering approach where the MAS development is considered to be addressed by three kinds of designers: domain or application designers (for the agents and the specification of the OS using the OML), MAS or OI designers (for the organisational infrastructure and OE management), and communication designers.

From the study of the different works considering the OI, we can identify a set of specialised services and proxies (e.g., angels [5], governors [7], managers [14]). In order to stress their ability to manage organisational concepts and to develop dedicated reasoning/processing abilities on the organisation, let's call them *organisational services* (OrgServices). One important point to notice is that all the access to the OI by the agents is mediated by these organisational proxies.

This brief general introduction of OI designs allow us to point out some drawbacks:

1. In some proposals, like $\mathcal{S}$-$\mathcal{M}$OISE$^+$ [14], OrgServices are implemented as agents. The problem is that, conceptually, services are not in the same abstraction level as agents.
2. In the proposals where OrgServices are not agents, whenever an application designer needs to customise some decisions of the system in the organisational dimension (e.g., a sanction system, a reorganisation strategy, the assignment of roles to agents), s/he has to develop/change an OrgService. It can be quite confusing to deal with both OrgServices and agents concepts while developing a system. It will be better to always use the same abstraction level when modelling and implementing the decision aspect of the application.
3. The designer (and the agents) also have to deal with two kinds of environments: a virtual organisational environment (where the agents adopt roles, send messages) and the real environment (where the agents act). An unified view of the environment simplifies the concept of agent interaction.
4. In the general architecture of Fig. 1, the organisation middleware has too much power. Most of the organisational "decisions" are performed at this layer. It is more

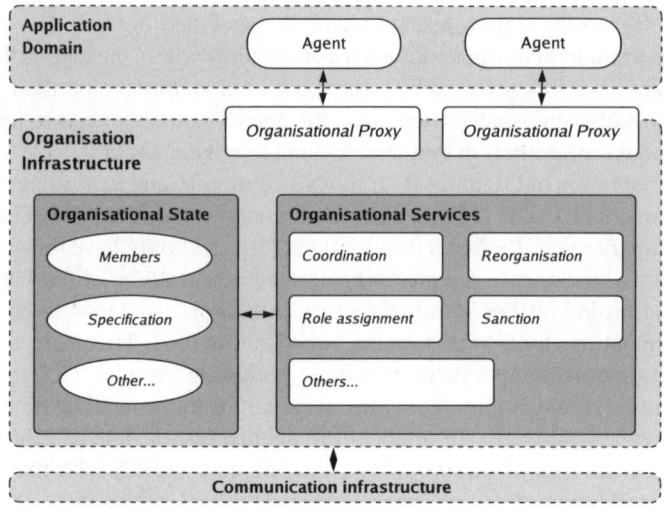

Fig. 1. Common Organisation Infrastructure for open MAS

suitable if the agents make decisions and not the OrgServices. For example, if some agent wants to perform some action or send a message that its organisation does not allow, it can not do it since the middleware (and its organisational proxy) will detect this violation tentative and decide on the sanction to apply. The middleware is thus performing two functions: detection and decision/judgement. In some cases agents operating on the application layer should get their control power back in the sense that they should play some of the roles of the OrgServices. As another example, reorganisation requires that *agents* should be able to manage and access the creation of new organisations.

The problems of existing approaches of organisations are consequence of some properties of the OrgServices design: (i) the enforcement of organisational functions and constraints and (ii) the inclusion of reasoning and decision aspects that can be managed by agents and thus should be in the agent layer.

It's worth noting that the issues stated here do not concern solely the implementation level, but also the conceptual and theoretical level: what is the nature of OrgServices in MAS where only agents are considered as first-class entities?

3   An Organisational Infrastructures Based on Agents and Artifacts

The proposal presented in this paper draws its inspiration from human organisation infrastructures. Human organisation and organisation infrastructures, that are populated by humans (as participants and part of the organisation machinery), and by rich sets of artifacts and tools that humans use to support their activities inside the organisation and the organisation itself, encapsulating essential infrastructure services. According to psycho-sociological theories and studies such as Activity Theory and Distributed Cognition [17]—recently adopted in computer science fields such as CSCW, HCI and MAS [27,25,22]—the notion of artifact (and tool, taken here as a synonym) plays a key role for the overall sustainability of an organisation and the effectiveness and efficiency of activities taking place inside the organisation.

In particular, some of these artifacts—that we call here *organisational artifacts*— appear to be vital for supporting the coordination of organisation processes and management: for instance by making more effective the communication among the members of an organisation (e.g. the telephone, instant-messaging services, chat-rooms), by providing information useful for orienting the activities of organisation participants (e.g., signs inside a building), by coordinating participants (e.g., queue systems at the post-office), by controlling access to resources and enforcing norms (e.g., the badge used by members in a computer science department to access certains rooms or use some other artifacts, such as copiers). Human societies and organisations continuously improve their experience in designing artifacts more and more effective to support both organisation participation—helping members to cope with the complexity of social activities and work—and organisation management—helping managers to monitor and control the organisation behaviour as a whole.

In the remainder of the section, first we recall the basic ideas provided by the A&A meta-model [23], and then describe how such concepts are exploited to shape the ORA4MAS infrastructure.

3.1 The Notion of Artifacts in MAS

The notion of *MAS environment*, as remarked by recent literatures, has gained a key role in the recent past, becoming a *mediating* entity, functioning as enabler but possibly also as a manager and constrainer of agent actions, perceptions, and interactions (see [29] for comprehensive surveys). According to such a perspective, the environment is not a merely passive source of agent perceptions and target of agent actions—which is, actually, the dominant perspective in agency and in MAS—, but a first-class abstraction that can be suitably designed to *encapsulate* some fundamental functionalities and services, supporting MAS dimensions such as coordination and organisation, besides agent mobility, communications, security, etc.

Among the various approaches, the A&A in particular introduces a notion of *working environment*, representing such a part of the MAS explicitly designed on the one hand by MAS engineers to provide various kinds of functionality—including MAS coordination, organisation—and perceived as first-class entity on the other hand by agents of the MAS [23,20]. A&A working environment are made of *artifacts*, representing function-oriented dynamic entities and tools that agents can create and use to perform their individual and social activities. Among the several sort of artifacts, *coordination artifacts* have been introduced as an important class of artifacts organisations [21], as artifacts mediating agent interactions and encapsulating some kind of coordinating functionality— whiteboards, event services, shared task schedulers are examples. Artifacts can be considered as a complimentary abstraction to agent populating an MAS: while agents are goal-oriented pro-active entities, artifacts are a general abstraction to model function-oriented passive entities, designed by MAS designers to encapsulate

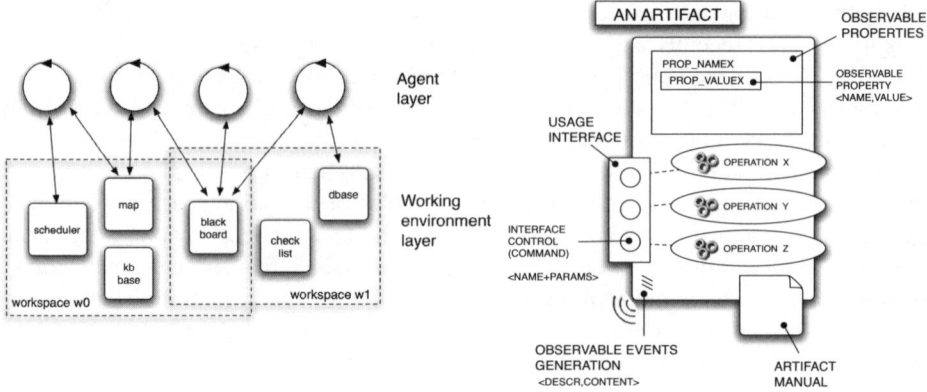

Fig. 2. *(Left)* abstract representation of workspaces, populated by agents—represented by circles—and artifacts—represented by squares. *(Right)* A representation of the main parts and properties of an artifact, with the usage interface, the observable properties and the manual.

some kind of functionality, by representing (or wrapping existing) resources or instruments mediating agent activities. Passive here means that—differently from the agent case—they do not encapsulate any thread of control.

Fig. 2 shows an abstract representation of an artifact as defined in the **A&A** meta-model, exhibiting analogous parts and properties of artifacts as found in human society. The artifact *function*—and related artifact behaviour—is partitioned in a set of *operations*, which agents can trigger by acting on artifact *usage interface*. The usage interface provides all the controls that make it possible for an agent to interact with an artifact, that is to *use* and *observe* it. Agents can use an artifact by triggering the execution of operations through the usage interface and by perceiving *observable events* generated by the artifact itself, as a result of operation execution and evolution of its state. Besides the controls for triggering the execution of operation, an artifact can have some *observable properties*, i.e., properties whose value is made observable to agents, without necessarily executing operations on it. The interaction between agents and artifacts strictly mimics the way in which humans use their artifacts: let's consider a coffee machine, for a simple but effective analogy. The set of buttons of the coffee machines represents the usage interface, while the displays that are typically used to show the state of the machine represent artifact observable properties. The signals emitted by the coffee machine during its usage represent observable events generated by the artifact.

Analogously to the human case, in **A&A** each artifact type can be equipped by the artifact programmer with a *manual* composed essentially by the *function description*—as the formal description of the purpose intended by the designer—, the *usage interface description*—as the formal description of artifact usage interface and observable states—, and finally the *operating instructions*—as the formal description of how to properly use the artifact so as to exploit its functionalities. Such a manual is meant to be essential for creating open systems with intelligent agents that dynamically discover and select which kind of artifacts could be useful for their work, and then can use them effectively even if they have not been pre-programmed by MAS programmers for the purpose.

3.2   ORA4MAS Infrastructure

The basic idea in **ORA4MAS** is to engineer the organisational infrastructure—and the organisations living upon it—in terms of agents and artifacts, following the basic **A&A** metamodel. Here we use the terms *organisational agents* and *organisational artifacts* to identify those agents and artifacts of the MAS which are part of the organisational infrastructure, and that are responsible of activities and encapsulate functionalities concerning the management and enactment of the organisation. In particular, organisational agents —analogously to managers and administrators in human organisation— are responsible of management activities inside the organisation, concerning observing, monitoring, and reasoning about organisation dynamics, etc. Such activities take place by creating and managing organisational artifacts that are then used by member agents of the organisation. Organisational artifacts are those artifacts that agents of an organisation may want or have to use in order to participate in organisation activities and access to organisation resources, encapsulating organisation rules and functionalities, such as enabling and mediating (ruling) agent interaction, tracing and ruling resource access, and so on.

Even from this abstract characterisation, it is possible to identify some general properties that are of some importance to face the drawbacks listed at the end of Section 2.

Abstraction & encapsulation. By using agents and artifacts to reify both the organisation and the organisation infrastructure—from design to runtime—, we raise the level of abstraction with respect to approaches in which organisation mechanisms are hidden at the implementation level. Such mechanisms become parts of the agent world, suitably encapsulated in proper entities that agents then can inspect, reason and manipulate, by adopting a uniform approach.

Agent autonomy. Agents are still autonomous with respect to decision of using or not a specific artifact—including the organisational artifacts—and keeps its autonomy—in terms of control of its actions—while using organisational artifacts. Agents however can depend on the functionalities provided (encapsulated) by artifacts, which can concern, for instance, some kind of mediation with respect to the other agents co-using the same organisational artifact. Then, by enforcing some kind of mediation policy an artifact can be both an enabler and a *constrainer* of agent interactions. However, such a constraining function can take place without compromising the autonomy of the agents regarding their decisions.

Distributed management. Distributing the management of the organisation into different organisational artifacts installs a distributed coordination (meaning here more particularly synchronisation) of the different functions related to the management of the organisation. Completing this distribution of the coordination, the reasoning and decision processes which are encapsulated in the organisational agents may be also distributed among the different agents. Thanks to their respective autonomy, all the reasoning related to the management of the organisation (monitoring, reorganisation, control) may be decentralized into different loci of decision with a loosely coupled set of agents.

Openness. Organisational artifacts can be created and added dynamically according to the need. They have a proper semantics description of both the functionalities and operating instructions, so conceptually agents can discover at runtime how to use them in the best way. Related to openness, the approach promotes heterogeneity of agent (societies): artifacts can be used by heterogeneous kinds of agents, with different kinds of reasoning capabilities. Extending the idea to multiple organisations, we can have the same agents playing different roles in different organisations, and then interacting with organisational artifacts belonging to different organisations.

"Power back to agents". The decisions that were embedded in the OrgServices in the OI go back to the agents' layer in organisational agents. In **ORA4MAS** artifacts encapsulate the coordination and synchronisation which were implemented in OrgServices. Control and judgement procedures are separated from these aspects and are embedded in organisational agents. Organisational agents can then use organisational artifacts to help them in deciding and eventually applying sanctions to other agents.

After sketching the basic concepts underlying the **ORA4MAS** approach, in next section we finally describe how a full-fledged organisational model can be abstractly implemented on top of agents and artifacts.

4 Shaping ORA4MAS Artifacts Upon $\mathcal{M}$OISE$^+$

$\mathcal{M}$OISE$^+$ (Model of Organisation for multI-agent SystEms) [13] is an OML that explicitly decomposes the organisation into structural, functional, and deontic dimensions. The structural dimension defines the *roles*, *groups*, and *links* of the organisation. The definition of roles states that when an agent decides to play some role in a group, it is accepting some behavioural constraints related to this role. The functional dimension describes how the *global collective goals* should be achieved, i.e., how these goals are decomposed (in global *plans*), grouped in coherent sets (by *missions*) to be distributed to the agents. The decomposition of global goals results in a goal-tree, called *scheme*,

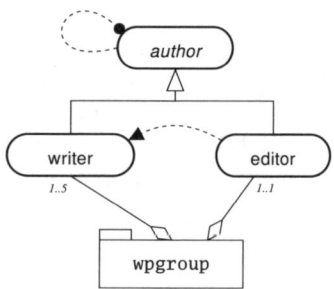

Fig. 3. Structure

where the leafs-goals can by achieved individually by the agents. The deontic dimension is added in order to binds the structural dimension with the functional one by the specification of the roles' *permissions* and *obligations* for missions. Instead of being related to the agents' behaviour space (what they can do), the deontic dimension is related to the agents' autonomy (what they should do).

As an illustrative and simple example of an organisation specified using $\mathcal{M}$OISE$^+$, we consider a set of agents that wants to write a paper and therefore has an organisational specification to help them to collaborate. The structure of this organisation has only one group (wpgroup) with two roles (editor and writer) that are sub-role of the role author. The cardinalities and links of this group are specified, using the $\mathcal{M}$OISE$^+$ notation, in Fig. 3: the group can have from one to five writers and exactly one editor; the editor has authority on writers and every author (and by inheritance every writer and editor) has a communication link to all other authors. In this example, the editor and the author roles are not compatible, to be compatible a compatibility relation must be explicitly added in the specification.

To coordinate the achievement of the goal of writing a paper, a scheme is defined in the functional specification of the organisation (Fig. 4). In this scheme, an agent initially defines a draft version of the paper (identified by the goal *fdv* in the scheme of Fig. 4) that has the following sub-goals: write a title, an abstract, the introduction, and the section names. Other agents then "fill" the paper's sections to get a submission version of the paper (identified by the goal *sv*). The goals of this scheme are distributed in three missions: $mMan$ (general managing of the process), $mCol$ (collaborate in the paper writing the content), and $mBib$ (get the references for the paper). A mission defines all goals an agent

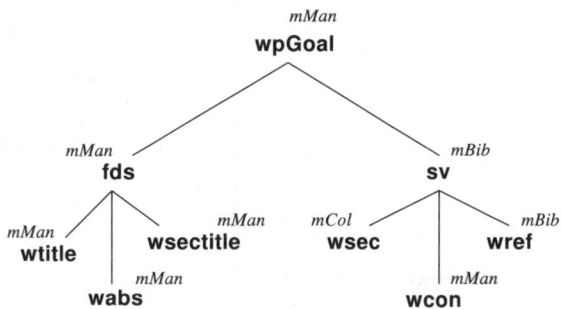

Fig. 4. Functioning

role	deontic relation	mission	cardinality
editor	*permission*	$mMan$	1..1
writer	*obligation*	$mCol$	1..5
writer	*obligation*	$mBib$	1..1

Fig. 5. Deontic relations

commits to when participating in the execution of a scheme, for example, commit to the mission $mMan$ is indeed a commitment to achieve six goals of the scheme. The deontic relation from roles to missions is specified in Fig. 5. For example, any agent playing the role editor is permitted to commit to the mission $mMan$. The structural, functional, and deontic specifications briefly described here form an Organisational Specification (OS) where, for example, some agents can "instantiate" an Organisational Entity (OE).

Organisational Agents and Artifacts Based on $\mathcal{M}$OISE$^+$. We exploit here the $\mathcal{M}$OISE$^+$ model to identify and shape a basic set of organisational artifacts (kind) and agents that constitute the basic infrastructure building blocks of ORA4MAS, being a sort of "reification" of the structural specification (SS), functional specification (FS), and deontic specification (DS) (Fig. 6). This basic set accounts for: an OrgBoard artifact —used to keep track of the structure of organisation in the overall; a GroupBoard artifact —used to manage the life-cycle of a specific group; a SchemeBoard type — used to support and manage the execution of a social scheme. Here we consider just a core set, skipping most details that would make heavy the overall understanding of the approach: the interested reader is forwarded on this technical report [15] to get further details.

In the following we briefly describe the basic characteristics of these kinds of artifact. In the description, the operations (commands) enlisted in artifact usage interface are

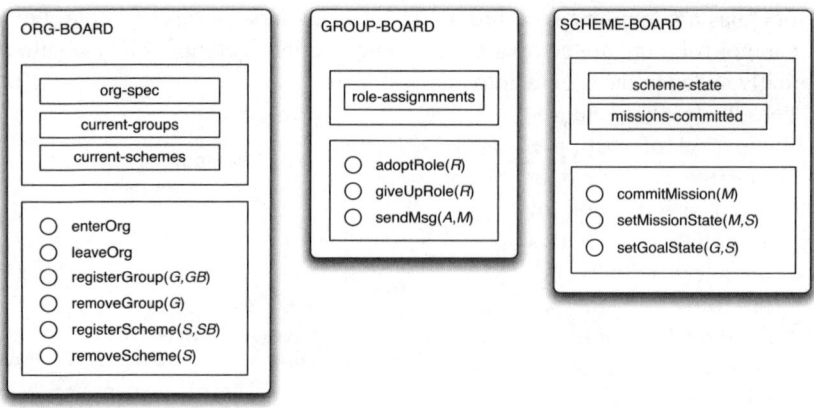

Fig. 6. Basic kinds of artifacts in ORA4MAS, with their usage interface, including operations and observable properties

abstractly described by a name with input parameters, followed (optionally) by a set of the observable events possibly generated by the operation execution (only events significant for artifact specific functionalities are considered, skipping those generated by default by the artifact). Observable properties are represented just by a name, which corresponds to the name of the property.

A simple abstract model for the OrgBoard artifact is depicted in Fig. 6 (left). The usage interface is composed by operations to:

- Register / de-register a new group: registerGroup(G,GB), removeGroup(G)—where G is an identifier for a group and GB is the identifier of the related group board artifact;
- Register / de-register a new scheme: registerScheme(S,SB), removeScheme(S) where S is the identifier for a schema and SB is the identifier of the scheme board.

Among the observable properties: list of current groups; list of current schemes; and the organisation specification (including SS, FS, DS).Generally speaking, the observable properties of the artifact make it possible —for agents observing an OrgBoard—to monitor and be aware of which are the schemes and groups created. Also, this artifact can be inspected to know which are the SS, FS, DS currently adopted in the organisation.

The GroupBoard artifact type (see Fig. 6, center) is instantiated upon a specific SS, and provides functionalities to manage a group in terms of set of available roles and agents participation, according to the specific structure and strategy specified in the SS. The usage interface accounts for the following operations:

- Adopt a new role: adoptRole(R):{role_adoption_ok,role_adoption_failed}, where R is the identifier for a role;
- Give up a role: giveUpRole(R):{role_giveup_ok,role_giveup_failed};

- Sending a message to a specific agent or all the agents part of the group: sendMsg(A,M), sendMsg(M), where A is the identifier for the receiver agent, m is the message content.

Among the observable properties, we have only the role assignments. By observing a GroupBoard artifact, an agent can thus monitor and be aware of the role-agent assignments inside the group.

The GroupBoard interprets the structural specification and maintains a consistent state of the group so that some important organisational constraints are not violated — the remaining constraints are enforced by organisational agents. For instance, when some agent asks for a role adoption in the group, the GroupBoard ensures that: (1) the role belongs to its group specification; (2) the number of players is lesser or equals than the maximum number of players defined in the group's compositional specification; (3) each role ρ_i that the agent already plays is specified as compatible with the new role.

The SchemeBoard artifact type (see Fig. 6, right) is instantiated upon a specific FS and DS, and provides functionalities to manage the execution of a social scheme, coordinating the commitments to missions and the achievement of goals. It is essentially a coordination artifact, automating the management of the dependencies between the missions and the goals as described by the social scheme, and embedding such part of the deontic specification concerning permissions and obligations for agents to commit to missions. The usage interface provides commands to:

- Commit to a mission: commitMission(M):{commit_ok, commit_failed}, where M is the identifier for a mission;
- Set mission state: setMissionState(M,S), where M is the identifier for a mission and S can be either *completed* or *failed*;
- Set goal state: setGoalState(G,S), where G is the identifier for a goal and S can be either *satisfied* or *impossible*.

Among the observable properties, we have: the scheme dynamic state, that includes all the goals of the scheme and their state; the list of the current missions committed. By observing a SchemeBoard artifact, an agent can monitor then the overall dynamics concerning the scheme execution, and the be aware of which missions are assigned to which agents, which goals are achieved and which can be pursued.

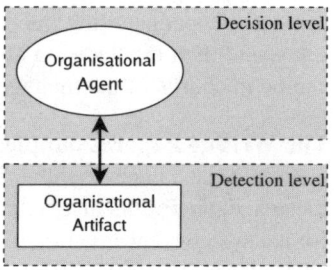

Fig. 7. Agent & Artifact

Organisational Agents. The organisational agents are essentially managers responsible to create and manage the organisational artifacts described previously (Fig. 7). Such activities typically include observing artifacts dynamics and possibly intervening, by changing / adapting artifacts or interacting directly with agents, so as to improve the overall (or specific) organisation processes or taking some kinds of decisions when detecting violations. As an example, one or multiple *scheme managers* agents can be introduced, responsible of monitoring the dynamics of the execution of a scheme by observing a specific SchemeBoard instance. The SchemeBoard artifact and

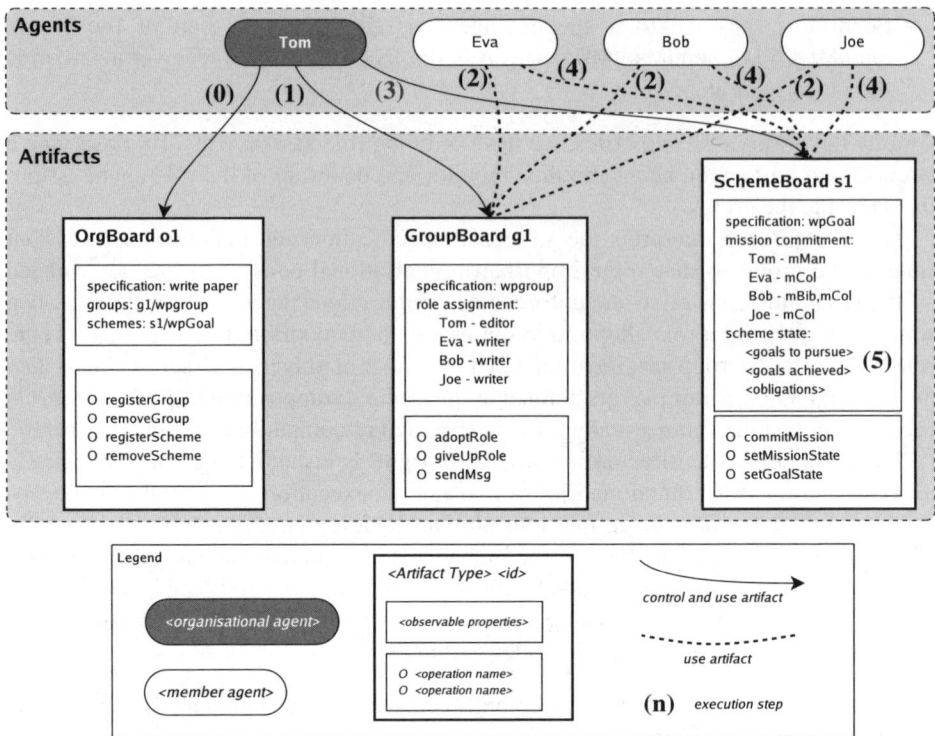

Fig. 8. Example of the construction and use of artifacts

scheme manager agents are designed so as that the artifact allows for violation of the deontic rules concerning the commitment of missions by agents playing some specific roles, and then the decision about what action to take—after detecting the violation—can be in charge of the manager agent.

The Writing Paper Example. We consider that four agents (Tom, Eva, Joe, and Bob) want to write a paper together using the proposed architecture described above. Among these agents, Tom is also an organisational agent and thus it may create the OrgBoard for the system. The creation of the OrgBoard is based on an organisational specification where the roles, groups, schemes, etc. are defined as presented in the Sec. 4. The following steps show how this system evolves until their goal of writing a paper is achieved (depicted in Fig. 8):

1. Tom creates the GroupBoard based on the specification of Fig. 3. Tom then register this new group in the OrgBoard using the registerGroup operation of the OrgBoard artifact. To succeed in this registering, the new group should satisfy all constraints defined in the OS (the group cardinality, for instance).
2. The new GroupBoard artifact is then perceived by all agents. While Tom decides to adopt the role editor, Eva, Bob, and Joe decide to adopt the role writer in this group.

To adopt the role, they use the adoptRole operation of the GroupBoard. Again, this operation may fail in case the agents do not fit in the requirements for the role (cardinality of the role in the group, compatibility of roles, etc.). The reasons for this role adoption is not covered here, but, for example, they may decide to become a writer because Tom has invited them to enter into the group.

3. Tom creates the SchemeBoard to start the process of writing the paper and then registers it in the OrgBoard using the registerScheme operation. This artifact interprets the specification of Fig. 4.

4. Once the scheme is created some obligations are activated and perceived by the agents in the SchemeBoard. For instance, the agent Bob, that is playing the role writer, is obligated to commit to the missions $mCol$ and $mBib$ (cf. Fig. 5) and thus he decided to commit to both. Since the mission $mBib$ has a cardinality constraint that set the maximum number of commitments to one, the other agents are not obligated to this mission anymore. They commit thus only to the mission $mCol$. Tom, that plays editor, commits to $mMan$. We are assuming here that the agents are obedient and always commit to their obligations and pursue their organisational goals.

5. Having their missions, the agents can pursue the goals of the scheme. Initially only the goals *wp*, *fds*, and *wtitle* can be pursued. These goals belongs to the $mMan$ mission, so only Tom has something to do, the others will wait him to achieve these goals. To know which goal can be pursued and to set them as achieved, the agents perceive the SchemeBoard and act on it using the setGoalState operation. The SchemeBoard works therefore like a coordinating artifact.

In this example, the SchemeBoard simply *shows* the obligations for each agent and which goals they should pursue. As an artifact, it is maintaining the current state of the scheme execution. However, since it is not an agent, in case some agent does not commit to a mission it should do or does not achieve some goal, the SchemeBoard does nothing. An organisational manager agent, like Tom, must perceive this artifact and decide what to do when some violation occurs.

Towards a Concrete Architecture. ORA4MAS concrete architecture is realised on top of CARTAGO infrastructure, embedding algorithms used in $S\text{-}\mathcal{M}\text{OISE}^+$. CARTAGO (Common ARtifact Infrastructure for AGent Open environment) is an MAS infrastructure based on the A&A meta-model, providing the capability to define new artifacts types, suitable API for agents to work with artifacts and workspaces, and a runtime supporting the existence and dynamic management of working environments. CARTAGO is meant to be integrated with existing cognitive MAS architectures and models / languages / platforms, so as to extend them to create and work with artifact-based environments. A first example of integration with the *Jason* agent programming platform is briefly described in [23]. CARTAGO is available as open-source projects freely downloadable from the project web sites (http://www.alice.unibo.it/cartago). The engineering of the first prototype of the ORA4MAS infrastructure upon CARTAGO is still a work in progress.

5   Conclusion and Perspectives

In this paper, we have followed the **A&A** approach to give back the power to agents in an organisational approach. From this perspective, we have defined on the one hand the organisational artifacts which encapsulate the functional aspects of an organisation and organisation management, and on the other hand the organisational agents, which encapsulated the decision and reasoning side of the management of organisations.

Although we already have some initial results of the **ORA4MAS** project, as those presented in this paper, we had concretely evaluated the proposal for only one OML (the $\mathcal{M}\text{OISE}^+$). The first future work of the project will therefore be an evaluation of its application for different OMLs such as ISLANDER [6], OMNI [5], $\mathcal{M}\text{OISE}^{Inst}$ [11], or AGR [8]. Following this broadest application we can then better compare our approach with related works (e.g. [9]) and even others such as those managing the organisation with communication acts (e.g. RICA-J [26]) or exploiting the environment to coordinate and constrain the agents' behaviour [30].

Other extensions aim at taking benefit of the uniform concepts used to implement the environment and the organisation abstractions through the concept of artifacts. Such an homogeneous conceptual point of view will certainly help us to bind both concepts together in order to situate organisations in environment or to install the access to the environment into organisational models (in the same direction as proposed in [18]). Other points of investigation are (1) the study of the reorganisation process of an MAS using the **ORA4MAS** approach, (2) the impact of the reorganisation on the organisational artifacts, and (3) the definition of a meta-organisation for the **ORA4MAS**, so that we have special roles for organisational agents that give them access to the organisational artifacts.

References

1. Bellifemine, F.L., Caire, G., Greenwood, D.: Developing Multi-Agent Systems with JADE. Wiley, Chichester (2007)
2. Boissier, O., Hübner, J.F., Sichman, J.S.: Organization oriented programming from closed to open organizations. In: O'Hare, G.M.P., Ricci, A., O'Grady, M.J., Dikenelli, O. (eds.) ESAW 2006. LNCS (LNAI), vol. 4457, pp. 86–105. Springer, Heidelberg (2007)
3. Broersen, J., Dastani, M., Hulstijn, J., Huang, Z., der van Torre, L.: The BOID architecture: conflicts between beliefs, obligations, intentions and desires. In: Müller, J.P., Andre, E., Sen, S., Frasson, C. (eds.) Proceedings of the Fifth International Conference on Autonomous Agents, Montreal, Canada, pp. 9–16. ACM Press, New York (2001)
4. Castelfranchi, C., Dignum, F., Jonker, C.M., Treur, J.: Deliberate normative agents: Principles and architecture. In: Jennings, N.R. (ed.) ATAL 1999. LNCS, vol. 1757, Springer, Heidelberg (2000)
5. Dignum, V., Vazquez-Salceda, J., Dignum, F.: OMNI: Introducing social structure, norms and ontologies into agent organizations. In: Bordini, R.H., Dastani, M., Dix, J., El Fallah-Seghrouchni, A. (eds.) PROMAS 2004. LNCS (LNAI), vol. 3346, pp. 181–198. Springer, Berlin (2005)
6. Esteva, M., Rodriguez-Aguiar, J.A., Sierra, C., Garcia, P., Arcos, J.L.: On the formal specification of electronic institutions. In: Dignum, F., Sierra, C. (eds.) Proceedings of the Agent-mediated Electronic Commerce. LNCS (LNAI), vol. 1191, pp. 126–147. Springer, Berlin (2001)

7. Esteva, M., Rodríguez-Aguilar, J.A., Rosell, B., AMELI, J.L.: An agent-based middleware for electronic institutions. In: Jennings, N.R., Sierra, C., Sonenberg, L., Tambe, M. (eds.) Proceedings of the Third International Joint Conference on Autonomous Agents and Multi-Agent Systems (AAMAS 2004), pp. 236–243. ACM Press, New York (2004)
8. Ferber, J., Gutknecht, O.: A meta-model for the analysis and design of organizations in multi-agents systems. In: Demazeau, Y. (ed.) Proceedings of the 3rd International Conference on Multi-Agent Systems (ICMAS 1998), pp. 128–135. IEEE Press, Los Alamitos (1998)
9. García-Camino, A., Rodríguez-Aguilar, J., Vasconcelos, W.W.: A distributed architecture for norm management in multi-agent systems. In: Sichman, J.S., et al. (eds.) COIN 2007 Workshops. LNCS (LNAI), vol. 4870, pp. 171–186. Springer, Heidelberg (2008)
10. Gasser, L.: Mas infrastructure: Definitions, needs and prospects. In: Revised Papers from the International Workshop on Infrastructure for Multi-Agent Systems, London, UK, pp. 1–11. Springer, Heidelberg (2001)
11. Gâteau, B., Boissier, O., Khadraoui, D., Dubois, E.: Moiseinst: An organizational model for specifying rights and duties of autonomous agents. In: Third European Workshop on Multi-Agent Systems (EUMAS 2005), Brussels, Belgium, December 7–8, pp. 484–485 (2005)
12. IST Advisory Group: Ambient intelligence: From vision to reality. Technical report, IST (2003),
```
ftp://ftp.cordis.europa.eu/pub/ist/docs/
istag-ist2003_consolidated_report.pdf
```
13. Hübner, J.F., Sichman, J.S., Boissier, O.: A model for the structural, functional, and deontic specification of organizations in multiagent systems. In: Bittencourt, G., Ramalho, G.L. (eds.) SBIA 2002. LNCS (LNAI), vol. 2507, pp. 118–128. Springer, Berlin (2002)
14. Hübner, J.F., Sichman, J.S., Boissier, O.: $\mathcal{S}\text{-}\mathcal{MOISE}^+$: A middleware for developing organised multi-agent systems. In: Boissier, O., Padget, J.A., Dignum, V., Lindemann, G., Matson, E., Ossowski, S., Sichman, J.S., Vázquez-Salceda, J. (eds.) ANIREM 2005 and OOOP 2005. LNCS (LNAI), vol. 3913, pp. 64–78. Springer, Heidelberg (2006)
15. Kitio, R.: Organizational artifacts and agents for open multi-agent systems, Master Thesis report (June, 2007), http://www.emse.fr/~boissier/kitio
16. Luck, M., et al.: Agent Technology: Computing as Interaction (A Roadmap for Agent Based Computing). AgentLink (2005)
17. Nardi, B.A.: Context and Consciousness: Activity Theory and Human-Computer Interaction. MIT Press, Cambridge (1996)
18. Okuyama, F.Y., Bordini, R.H., da Rocha Costa, A.C.: Spatially distributed normative objects. In: G. Boella, O. Boissier, E. Matson, J. Vázquez-Salceda (eds.) Proceedings of the Workshop on Coordination, Organization, Institutions and Norms in Agent Systems (COIN), held with ECAI 2006, Riva del Garda, Italy (August 28, 2006)
19. Omicini, A., Ossowski, S., Ricci, A.: Coordination infrastructures in the engineering of multiagent systems. In: Bergenti, F., Gleizes, M.-P., Zambonelli, F. (eds.) Methodologies and Software Engineering for Agent Systems: The Agent-Oriented Software Engineering Handbook. Multiagent Systems, Artificial Societies, and Simulated Organizations, vol. 11, pp. 273–296. Kluwer Academic Publishers, Dordrecht (2004)
20. Omicini, A., Ricci, A., Viroli, M.: Agens Faber: Toward a theory of artefacts for MAS. Electronic Notes in Theoretical Computer Sciences 150(3), 21–36 (2006)
21. Omicini, A., et al.: Coordination artifacts: Environment-based coordination for intelligent agents. In: AAMAS 2004, vol. 1, pp. 286–293. ACM, New York (2004)
22. Ricci, A., Omicini, A., Denti, E.: Activity Theory as a framework for MAS coordination. In: Petta, P., Tolksdorf, R., Zambonelli, F. (eds.) ESAW 2002. LNCS (LNAI), vol. 2577, pp. 96–110. Springer, Heidelberg (2003)

23. Ricci, A., Viroli, M., Omicini, A.: A general purpose programming model & technology for developing working environments in MAS. In: Dastani, M., et al. (eds.) 5th International Workshop "Programming Multi-Agent Systems" (PROMAS 2007), AAMAS 2007, Honolulu, Hawaii, USA, pp. 54–69 (May 15, 2007)
24. Sairamesh, J., Lee, A., Anania, L.: Introduction. Commun. ACM 47(2), 28–31 (2004)
25. Schmidt, K., Simone, C.: Coordination mechanisms: Towards a conceptual foundation of CSCW systems design. International Journal of Computer Supported Cooperative Work (CSCW) 5(2–3), 155–200 (1996)
26. Serrano, J.M., Ossowski, S.: A compositional framework for the specification of interaction protocols in multi-agent organizations. In: Proceedings of the Third European Workshop on Multi-Agent Systems (EUMAS), Brussels, Belgium, pp. 375–386 (December 7–8, 2005)
27. Susi, T., Ziemke, T.: Social cognition, artefacts, and stigmergy: A comparative analysis of theoretical frameworks for the understanding of artefact-mediated collaborative activity. Cognitive Systems Research 2(4), 273–290 (2001)
28. Vázquez-Salceda, J., Aldewereld, H., Dignum, F.: Norms in multiagent systems: Some implementation guidelines. In: Proceedings of the Second European Workshop on Multi-Agent Systems (EUMAS 2004) (2004)
29. Weyns, D., Van Dyke Parunak, H.: Journal of Autonomous Agents and Multi-Agent Systems. Special Issue: Environment for Multi-Agent Systems, vol. 14(1). Springer, Netherlands (2007)
30. Weyns, D., Van Dyke Parunak, H., Michel, F. (eds.): E4MAS 2005. LNCS (LNAI), vol. 3830, pp. 1–17. Springer, Heidelberg (2006)

Knowledge Sharing Between Agents in a Transitioning Organization

Eric Matson[1,2] and Raj Bhatnagar[1]

[1] Department of Computer Science and Engineering, Wright State University,
Dayton, OH, USA
[2] Department of Computer Science, University of Cincinnati,
Cincinnati OH, USA
eric.matson@wright.edu

Abstract. People that interact within a cooperative organization must constantly exchange information on the details of the organization as well as the goals the organization exists to meet. Agent organizations must share knowledge if they are to cooperatively act in the solution of some set of defined goals. The manner in which they share and when they share information varies. In this paper, we present the process to share organization information during the process of transition from one organization state to the next. Some organization models choose to vary the information known between two agents, in relation to the organization. A key element of organization success is that all members operate with the same information so as not to cause divergence in action or purpose.

1 Introduction

Organizations exist in every facet of human existence. People join organizations for reasons such as fulfillment, position or learning. When a person joins an organization, they must learn, or at least be aware, of the others involved in the organization. They must understand the overall structure to fully comprehend their place within the organization. As an example, human organizations commonly use charts to describe where each person fits into the structure. These organization charts exhibit the relationships between positions and people. When a new person joins an organization they are shown where they fit as part of the orientation to the organization. As the organization transitions through changes, the knowledge required for continued understanding of place and position must be updated.

To learn about the organization, the person must exchange organization specific information with others. When they first join, others in the organization transfer information to them to facilitate their organizational learning. The organizational learning is not necessarily classical learning, but instead a process to share or transfer knowledge. Each agent is previously aware of the knowledge structure and process required to interact with other agents in the organization.

Modeling agent organizations using the inspiration of human organizations, as is commonly done, the designer must create the formalities and implementation to allow the transfer of information between agents. We look at interaction as a basic exchange of information between two agents, but can be extended to any

J.S. Sichman et al. (Eds.): COIN 2007, LNAI 4870, pp. 187–202, 2008.
© Springer-Verlag Berlin Heidelberg 2008

number of agents belonging to an organization. The goal of the exchange is to maintain a state of perfect information between all agents. Perfect organization dictates that all agents must have identical organizational knowledge. The trick is that during transition, initial organization or reorganization, the information will change for at least one agent. That agent then has to insure that all other agents must receive the same knowledge changes. Differences in knowledge between agents will cause potential divergence in goals or roles played by the organization. The effect of bad information, in an agent organization, is much the same as if it were a human organization.

Our logic-based approach to this problem stems from some fundamental work, such as work by Su et al. [13]. Deitterich expressed the need to establish a useful level to approach knowledge, both for storing and learning or exchange [4]. Gordon and Subramanian augmented the approach to knowledge, by establishing the need for finer grain tuning of logic [8]. Baader provides a more general approach to the need for knowledge representation [2]. The basis of these works establishes the fit of logical representations for organization knowledge storage. In this work, the logical representation of organization will mirror the structural representation of organization.

In terms of knowledge sharing, Dignum and Dignum [5] indicate the shift from sharing to collaboration. That is key for this effort, although the basis of our model restricts the knowledge exchanged to a very specific set, lending to the strategy shown by Soller and Busetta [14] to develop a shared understanding between agents. While not strictly a default set of rules, as described by Rybinski and Ryzko [12], our logical structures are standardized, to simplify the body of knowledge exchanged.

An assumption, for this research, is agents are cooperatively participating in an organization where common goals are paramount. Individual agent goals and motivations are not above the needs of the organization. The difference is our approach reflects separating the constitution of the organization from a strictly structural concept. Organizations are normally perceived as structural, with objects and relationships. Our approach considers an organization as a mental image of a structural entity. This approach allows better scalability and computation of new states.

In this paper, we describe and demonstrate the organization knowledge exchange between agents belonging to the same organization. In section 2, we describe model elements and processes for sharing of knowledge between organization agents. In section 3, the implementation of this system is described. Results of the implementation are described in section 4. Section 5 explains opportunities for further work.

2   Organization Knowledge Sharing

In this section, we describe the basic structure required to model organizational information to facilitate exchange of information. The foundation of exchange is an organization model [9,3]. The agent structure is shown first followed by

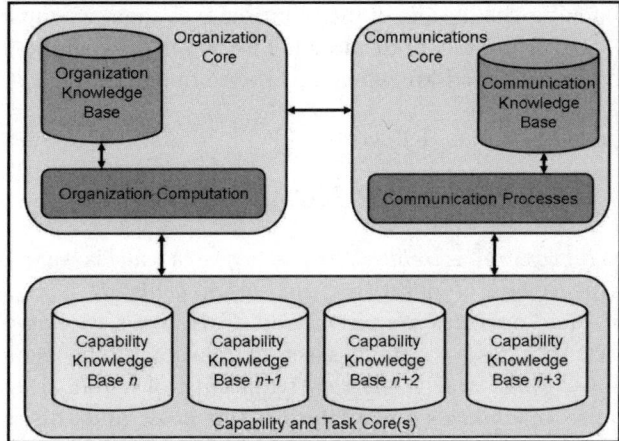

Fig. 1. Knowledge Cores of an Agent

the structural, state and transitional elements of our organization model. Once an organization model is described we extend the model to include processes of exchange. Finally, the model and processes are integrated to show the overall formalities of knowledge transfer between agents.

2.1 Agent Core Composition

Before looking at the specific elements of organization, we must first show the overall structure of an agent. An agent is comprised of several knowledge cores, as shown in Fig. 1. An agent has three knowledge cores which are the *organization core*, *communications core* and *task core*. Each core represents the knowledge held by an agent in an area. For example, the communications core represents all knowledge required to communicate with all other agents to which the agent has access. The task core represents it knowledge of each of the capabilities possessed by the agent. An agent may have numerous task cores. While all three cores compose an agents knowledge, the organization core is the one of most interest in this research, and will be the focus of the discussion. This core represents all of the knowledge of the organization in which an agent participates. In simple terms, it is its own internal organization chart defining all objects, structural relationships and state relationships of the organization. As the structures contained within the core are discrete, all agents work with an even base in which to share organization knowledge.

2.2 Organization Model Elements

Our organizational model (O) has a structural model, a state model and a transition function [9], described as:

$$O = (O_{structure}, O_{state}, O_{transition}) \tag{1}$$

Before approaching the details of information exchange, we must examine the *structural* and *state* elements of our model. The object and relationship elements are represented as the stored knowledge to be exchanged.

Structure. The *structure* is defined by:

$$O_{structure} = < G, R, L, C, ach, req, sub, con > \quad (2)$$

where *ach* is *achieves*, *rel* is *related*, *req* is *requires*, *sub* is *subgoal* and *con* is *conjunctive*, respectively. G describes the set of *goals*, R is the set of *roles*, L is the set of *laws* or *rules* required, and C is the set of *capabilities*. The organization structure also contains a set of relations. The achieves relation, $achieves : R, G \rightarrow [0..1]$, states the relative ability of a *role* to satisfy a given *goal*. *Roles* require *capabilities* to satisfy a set of *goals* and this is captured by the $requires : R, C \rightarrow Boolean$. The organization may contain subgoal relationships $subgoal : G, G \rightarrow Boolean$. The conjunctive relationship between *goals* is $conjunctive : G \rightarrow Boolean$.

State. The *state* is defined by:

$$O_{state} = < A, possesses, capable, assigned > \quad (3)$$

where an A defines a set of *agents* available to participate in the organization. There are several relationships in the state element of the organization. An *agent* capable of playing a certain role possesses the necessary *capabilities* described by the possesses relation, $possesses : A, C \rightarrow [0..1]$. An *agent* is capable of playing a *role* in the organization as described by the capable relation, $capable : A, R \rightarrow [0..1]$. The assigned relation, $assigned : A, R, G \rightarrow [0..1]$, is used to match the best *agent*, *role*, *goal* combination that maximizes the capability of the organization.

Transition. Transition is the main topic of knowledge exchange as transition requires that knowledge be exchanged by all agents participating in the organization. There are two specific transition processes, *initial organization* and *reorganization*. From organization $state_0$ to $state_1$ is initial organization. All other transitions are reorganization. Transition is expressed by:

$$O_{transition} = (O, \Phi, \delta, s_n, S_{optimal}, S_{possible}, S_{final}) \quad (4)$$

Where O is the organization over which the transition will occur, Φ is the set of properties that can trigger a transition of the organization, δ is the transition function, s_n is the set of relative states of the organization, $S_{optimal}$ is the set of optimal states that result from transition and $S_{possible}$ are states that are possible to reach, from the current state. S_{final} is a set of organization states where all goals are satisfied, or the 1st goal is satisfied, or it is determined that not all goals can be satisfied. Even though the outcomes are different, each final state draws a conclusion to the organization's set of transitions. Because an organization can only exist as a single entity or instance, the current state s_n is always a unique value [10].

The basic transition is defined as a product of the O, Φ and S resulting in a set of reachable organization states:

$$\delta : O \times \Phi \times S \Rightarrow S \tag{5}$$

So, the transition function is of the form:

$$\delta(O, \phi, s_n) \Rightarrow S' \tag{6}$$

Where transition function δ takes the organization O, a *specific* transition property ϕ, and a state of the organization s_n and can transition to a set of new states S' where $S_{optimal} \subseteq S_{possible}$, $S_{optimal} \subseteq S'$ and $S_{final} \subseteq S_{possible}$.

Transition Properties. Transition properties Φ represent stimuli that can change the organization. They are represented in a logical format which capture the generic nature of what they can define. In general terms, an organization will need a set of properties Φ, for example, *capabilities* or *agents*, which can be the stimulus of transition. An individual property $\phi \in \Phi$ is eligible to act as a reorganization trigger. Some examples of ϕ include a change in the real value of a capability, the loss of overall capability or agent function, loss of an agent, the reentry of an agent, or the addition of a new agent.

Each domain problem, represented by knowledge in a task core, may create a number of task specific transition properties. We will first show general, abstract properties and then discuss specific properties. These general properties can be instantiated to fit specific examples. Some general transition properties are:

1. Loss of an agent participating in the organization
2. An agent loses capability required to play some role
3. A new agent becomes available
4. Capability of an agent increases
5. Capability of an agent decreases
6. A goal is removed
7. A goal is added
8. A goal is relaxed (changed)
9. Change in goals to roles achieves relationship
10. Change in role to capability requires relationship

Changes in organization structure and participants will drive transition activities. Transition properties can be triggered internally or externally. The general transition properties can be split into properties that are external and those that are internal.

Transition Predicates. A transition predicate is a formalization of a transition property. The formalization of transition predicates enables the exchange of information. Transition predicates can also be expressed as $\Phi = \{\phi_1 \ldots \phi_n\}$. In general, Φ can be expressed as a set of standard, abstract predicates,

$\Phi = \{\phi_{lose}, \phi_{add}, \phi_{change}\}$, where ϕ_{lose} is the abstract property dealing with loss, such as losing an agent from the organization or an agent losing capability to play a role. The add property ϕ_{add} describes the action when an agent becomes available for invitation to the organization. The change property ϕ_{change} can either be an increase or decrease and further specializes the change predicate, $\phi_{change} = \{\phi_{decrease}, \phi_{increase}\}$ [11].

Definition: Primitive Predicates can be used to formalize single properties. The *primitive predicates* exhibit polymorphic behavior as each can be applied to different organization elements to capture different properties. If there is a loss of an agent participating in the organization, it can be formalized as the predicate $\phi_{lose}agent(a)$. An agent a losing some capability can be captured as $\phi_{lose}capability(c, a)$.

Definition: Complex Predicates are the combination of primitive predicates. Some predicates will encompass others, but in some cases two properties can be successfully combined to form a single property of transition. The complex predicates will be logically constructed using primitive predicates and the common *and* ($\wedge$) and *or* ($\vee$) binary relations. Examples of complex predicates are shown in table 1.

Table 1. Complex Predicates

Predicate	Description
$\phi_{add}agent(a) \wedge \phi_{add}agent(b)$	Add new agents a and b
$\phi_{add}goal(g) \wedge \phi_{add}goal(h) \wedge \phi_{add}subgoal(g, h)$	Add goals g, h and a subgoal relation
$\phi_{add}role(r) \wedge \phi_{lose}role(s)$	Add role r and delete role s

In the case that an agent exits an organization, it can be reasoned that all capability of that agent will also exit. Combining the two previous predicates of losing an agent and losing a capability by an agent are redundant, in respect to the capability predicate $\phi_{lose}agent(a) \wedge \phi_{lose}capability(c, a)$, as long as the capabilities are not possessed by another agent or required by a role. Deleting a object will involve deleting any relationships which are dependent on the object.

In another situation, an organization may lose two agents simultaneously. If agents a and b both leave, we can capture that by $\phi_{lose}agent(a) \wedge \phi_{lose}agent(b)$, where one primitive predicate does not contain the other. Complex predicates are unlimited in their scope. They may be used to create a set of relationships and objects greater than the size of the existing organization.

As there are primitive and complex predicates, predicates can be further defined as either *object* or *relationship* predicates. Object predicates represent objects of the organization such as goals, roles, capabilities or agents. Relationship predicates represent the link between two objects such as achieves, possesses or requires.

Definition: Object Predicates are defined as predicates where the property represents an object of the organization, such as an agent being added or a goal being

Table 2. Object Predicates

ϕ	Object	Predicate	Description
add	agent	$\phi_{add}agent(a)$	Add a new agent a
	goal	$\phi_{add}goal(g)$	Add a new goal g
	role	$\phi_{add}role(r)$	Add a new role r
	capability	$\phi_{add}capability(c)$	Add a new capability c
lose	agent	$\phi_{lose}agent(a)$	Delete an existing agent a
	goal	$\phi_{lose}goal(g)$	Delete an existing goal g
	role	$\phi_{lose}role(r)$	Delete an existing role r
	capability	$\phi_{lose}capability(c)$	Delete an existing capability c
change	agent	$\phi_{increase}capability(c,a)$	Increase capability of an agent
	agent	$\phi_{decrease}capability(c,a)$	Decrease capability of an agent
	goal	$\phi_{change}goal(g)$	A goal is changed

deleted. An example of an object predicate is a goal addition, $\phi_{add}goal(g)$. This is a single predicate only involving an organization object. Examples of object predicates are shown in table 2.

Definition: Relationship Predicates are defined as properties where a relationship between two objects is added, lost or altered. Relationship predicates can be primitive, as long as the objects in which they bind already exist in the organization. Object predicates may be complex as the object must collaborate with a relationship to connect to the organization. Object and relationship predicates will typically be combined in complex predicates. Relationship predicates such

Table 3. Relationship Predicates

ϕ	Relationship	Predicate	Description
add	achieves	$\phi_{add}achieves(r,g)$	Add a new achieves relationship between goal g and role r
	requires	$\phi_{add}requires(r,c)$	Add a new requires relationship between role r and capability c
	possesses	$\phi_{add}possesses(a,c)$	Add a new possesses relationship between agent a and capability c
lose	achieves	$\phi_{lose}achieves(r,g)$	Delete the achieves relationship between goal g and role r
	requires	$\phi_{lose}requires(r,c)$	Delete the requires relationship between role r and capability c
	possesses	$\phi_{lose}possesses(a,c)$	Delete the possesses relationship between agent a and capability c
change	achieves	$\phi_{change}achieves(r,g)$	Change the achieves relationship between goal g and role r
	requires	$\phi_{change}requires(r,c)$	Change the requires relationship between role r and capability c
	possesses	$\phi_{change}possesses(a,c)$	Change the possesses relationship between agent a and capability c

as when g_i is a subgoal of g_j is $\exists_{g_i,g_j}\phi_{add}subgoal(g_i, g_j)$ where the relationship can only exist if both g_i and g_j exist prior. Another relationship predicate g is achieved by r if $\exists_{g,r}\phi_{add}achieves(g, r)$ where the relationship can only exist if both g and r exist prior. Examples of relationship predicates are shown in table 3.

2.3   Exchange Processes

A model is not necessarily sufficient to completely explain the exchange of knowledge. The process must also show how the agents interact to share the information. This definition only describes the basic mechanics of the exchange. It must be further explored to answer questions on what basis is information exchanged. Will the information be shared with anyone who asks? Will the information be shared with all agents? Will it be shared with agents who do not specifically ask for it? These questions not only pose a set of philosophical queries, but also pose some practical problems in exchange. Automatically sending data to an agent that does not need it, as it already possesses the information, is wasteful in terms of resources.

Our approach to knowledge exchange is similar to the *mind-body problem* of Descartes. In the mind-body problem, the mind is differentiated from the matter of the body. The knowledge of an organization, which resides in the individual mind of each agent, within the organization is different than the physical manifestation of the organization. Each agent carries an image of the organization with all objects and relationships. The key is for all agents to have the same image of the organization, in other words, perfect information.

The basic premise is that when each transition occurs, all agents need to be updated with the current organization knowledge. When a human organization requires change, a decision is made and the change is then communicated by the decision maker to those affected. As with human organizations, a single agent will receive the change, ϕ, and propagate the change to each of the other agents in the organization.

There exists a risk of a transition property not correctly propagating from the sending agent to the receiving agent. If this occurs, the receiving agent will not compute a new organization and will be different than those agents who successfully received the message. If for some reason, such as an agent being lost, another agent will sense the agent loss and update the others. It can also be said that each of the others can self update in the event of a loss, but questions whether each is required to recompute. A key goal is to minimize the amount of information transferred for each organization transition.

Integration. Each agent optimally has the same organization knowledge. This supports the premise that all agents operate on full information. Fig. 2 shows an organization of 4 agents $\{agent_1, agent_2, agent_3, agent_4\}$. $Agent_1$ receives a transition property from either an internal or external force. $Agent_1$ then propagates the predicate to $agent_2$, $agent_3$ and $agent_4$. The organization core represents the part of the *mind* of the agent concerned with where it fits in the

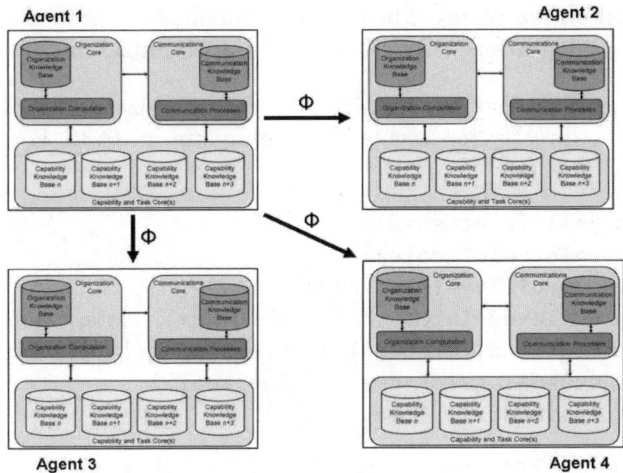

Fig. 2. Knowledge Transfer

organization. The agents themselves represent the physical manifestation, or the *body*.

3 Validation

To validate this model, the complete organization model is implemented into an executable system. The implemented system is then used to simulate a number of organizations and changes to the organizations. In this section, we briefly describe the implementation, the design of transition and exchange of knowledge and finally provide a working example of the system.

3.1 Implementation

The organization formalisms and knowledge exchange processes have been implemented to complete this work. The implementation is a combination of Java used as the main development platform with *JESS* utilized to implement the knowledge bases. *JESS* has a natural relationship with Java as described by Friedman-Hill [6] and utilizes the *Rete algorithm* of Forgy et al. [7] and Albert [1] shows the computational fit for this algorithm applied to this technical problem.

In this section, the implementation of the structural and state elements as logical constructs in *JESS* are discussed. Each object and relationship are expressed as logical predicates. This logical expression represents the *mind* of the organization. Each predicate is sent to each agent in the *body* and then each agent recomputes a new organization image within their own structure. Thus the *mind* of each agent in the *body* recomputes its own like image of the organization after each change. All *JESS* logical functions are constructed with rules and facts, based on templates. The organization object is then embedded inside a Java shell for integration with the body of the organization.

Structure and State. Each predicate of the organization model's structure and state can be directly represented by a template in *JESS*. For example, the structural templates are:

```
(deftemplate goal (slot goal))
(deftemplate role (slot role))
(deftemplate capability (slot capability))
(deftemplate achieves (slot role) (slot goal) (slot score))
(deftemplate requires (slot role) (slot capability))
(deftemplate subgoal (slot goal) (slot goal))
(deftemplate conjunctive (slot goal))
```

The state templates are:

```
(deftemplate agent (slot agent))
(deftemplate possesses (slot agent) (slot capability) (slot score))
(deftemplate capable (slot agent) (slot role) (slot goal) (slot score))
```

Each JESS deftemplate represents an object or relationship within the model. The objects and relationships are then used to form properties and construct predicates. The predicates are then formed into JESS facts and added to the fact base of the organization core. For example, the property to add is a goal g. A predicate $\phi_{add}(g)$ is constructed which then translates into a *JESS* fact, based on the goal deftemplate, $(assert(goal\ g))$.

Transition and Exchange. Each agent is a complete independent entity communicating via unique TCP/IP sockets embedded within the agent's communications core. All knowledge is exchanged using Java via socket networking between agents. This technology is employed specifically for TCP loss reduction and error handling abilities in propagating packets, which at a higher level enables knowledge exchange. Each agent is represented by a unique IP address. This configuration assumes a TCP/IP network, which is the case in this implementation. The communications core can also be configured using other protocols. The ability to guarantee arrival of message propagation is dependent upon the protocol utilized.

There are three specific change categories which can effect the exchange process. The first is change to a structural element of the organization. Examples of structural change are to add or lose a goal. The second is the change in a state element. An example of state change is an agent gaining or losing capability, thereby requiring a computation of the organization. The third option is the loss or gain of an agent. Each of these changes will be described using the transition predicates and exchange of *JESS* constructs.

Structural Change. If a goal is added or lost, the agent first notified must send a message to all others to retain the state of perfect information. If a transition predicate $\phi_{add}(g)$ is received by agent a, then a muat propagate a message to all other agents to add the new goal, as a fact. For each organization knowledge core a new fact is added.

State Change. If there is a state change such as the capability of agent a increases $\phi_{increase}(c, a)$, then that agent will propagate the new fact to all other agents.

Agent Change. When there is no change to the collection of agents, within the organization, it is straightforward to propagate the new information to all agents. When an agent is gained or lost, the matter of communication takes on a new level of complexity. When an agent is lost, one or more of the agents remaining must recognize the loss. One of the agents must define a predicate $\phi_{lose}(a)$, create the update and send to all agents. If an agent is gained to the organization, $\phi_{add}(a)$, the new fact that an agent has been added is sent to all agents by one of the agents, already in the organization.

3.2 Organization Example

The model and properties are illustrated using a small but realistic scenario of the formation of a a software engineering organization. The example will show all required steps to instantiate an initial organization. Then, it will add to that initial organization using transition properties. The transition properties will be exchanged by all agents as they are added to the organization.

Initial Organization. To begin any valid, non-trivial organization instance, we must add some initial objects and relationships. For this example, which illustrates the formation of a simple software engineering venture, we begin by adding 6 objects and 6 relationships. Once the objects are added, then we can compute the initial organization taking us from $state_0 \rightarrow state_1$. Fig. 3 shows the example organization map of the initial organization. Table 4 contains each

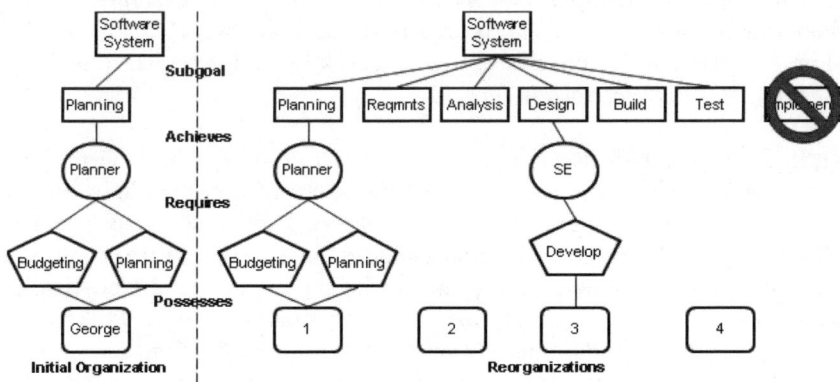

Fig. 3. Initial Organization

Table 4. Initial Organization

Predicate	JESS Statement
$\phi_{add}agent(1)$	(assert(agent 1))
$\phi_{add}goal(software\ system)$	(assert(goal software system))
$\phi_{add}role(planner)$	(assert(role planner))
$\phi_{add}goal(planning)$	(assert(goal planning))
$\phi_{add}subgoal(software\ system, planning$	(assert(subgoal(software system,planning))
$\phi_{add}achieves(planner, planning)$	(assert(achieves(planner,planning)))
$\phi_{add}capability(Budgeting)$	(assert(capability Budgeting))
$\phi_{add}capability(Planning)$	(assert(capability Planning))
$\phi_{add}requires(Planner, Budgeting)$	(assert(requires(Planner, Budgeting)))
$\phi_{add}requires(Planner, Planning)$	(assert(requires(Planner, Planning)))
$\phi_{add}possesses(1, Planning)$	(assert(possesses(1, Planning)))
$\phi_{add}possesses(1, Budgeting)$	(assert(possesses(1, Budgeting)))

Table 5. Reorganizations

state	ϕ	JESS Statement	a_{start}	a_{rec}
1	$\phi_{add}agent(2) \wedge \phi_{add}agent(3)$	(assert(agent 2))(assert(agent 3))	1	2,3
2	$\phi_{add}agent(4)$	(assert((agent 4))	1	4
3	$\phi_{add}goal(Reqmnts)$	(assert (goal requirements))	1	2,3,4
4	$\phi_{add}subgoal(Software\ System, Reqmnts)$	(assert (subgoal(Software System,Reqmnts)))	1	2,3,4
5	$\phi_{add}goal(Analysis) \wedge \phi_{add}goal(Design)$	(assert(goal Analysis))(assert(goal Design))	2	1,3,4
6	$\phi_{add}goal(Build) \wedge \phi_{add}goal(Test)$	(assert(goal Build))(assert(goal Test))	2	1,3,4
7	$\phi_{add}goal(Implement)$	(assert(goal Implement))	2	1,3,4
8	$\phi_{lose}goal(Implement)$	(retract(goal Implement))	2	1,3,4
9	$\phi_{add}Role(SE) \wedge \phi_{add}achieves(Design, SE)$	(assert(role SE))(assert(achieves(Design,SE)))	3	1,2,4
9	$\phi_{add}capability(Develop)$	(assert(capability Develop))	3	1,2,4
10	$\phi_{add}requires(SE, Develop)$	(assert(requires(SE,Develop)))	4	1,2,3
11	$\phi_{add}possesses(3, Develop)$	(assert(possesses(3,Develop)))	4	1,2,3

of the primitives predicates required to assemble the initial organization with 6 object and 6 relationships. The second column of Table 4 shows *JESS* fact statements used to build a logical representation of the organization. When the initial organization algorithm is executed, the relationships between all facts are instantiated in the *organization core*.

Reorganizations. This section shows how the initial organization propagates through a series of transitions by consuming a set of organizations properties to ultimately arrive at the end organization state. Table 5 show each transition by a single line in the table. Each line includes the starting state, the property (ϕ), the *JESS* fact statement, the agent initiating the property and the agents receiving the property to update their own organization cores. The transition from $state_1 \rightarrow state_2$ adds agents 2 and 3 to the organization, by a property from agent 1. The next transition adds the 4th agent to the organization. In the two transitions, agent 1, with the capability to plan and budget adds the other agents.

Agent 2 then sends properties to add goals of *Analysis* and *Design* and subsequently *Build* and *Test*. Agent 2 then sends another goal, *Implement*, to add, then retracts that goal. Agent 3 then sends a complex property to add the *SE* role and achieves relationship between the *Design* goal and *SE* role. Agent 3 then propagates the property to add a *Develop* capability. Agent 4 then adds a requires relationship between the *SE* role and the *Develop* capability and then adds a possesses relationship between agent 3 and the *Develop* capability. Fig. 3 shows the organization map after the set of transitions, from Table 5, have completed.

4   Results

We must first distinguish between results split by the two transition processes, initial organization and reorganization. The result indicates the initial organization is computationally more intense and is based on the number of objects and relationships. Since it will only be computed once in each organization's life, its effect is discounted. Reorganization is much smaller, due to the incremental nature of only having to recompute around new objects and relationships of the ϕ predicate. If ϕ is quite large, it may alter the computational intensity. For example, if the number of objects and relationships in ϕ is equal or greater than the existing organization, reorganization may be computationally large.

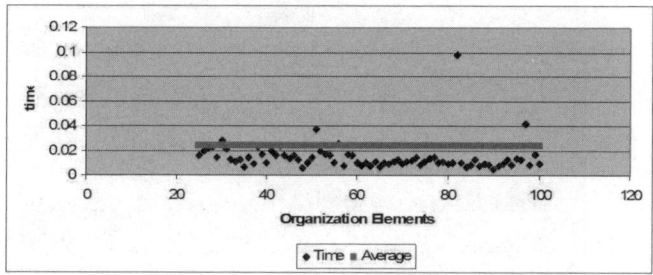

Fig. 4. Results

The computation of a transitioning organization differs from an initial organization to a reorganization. In a strictly structural context, initial organization and reorganization do not differ a great deal. In our mind body approach the difference is significant. For a small organization size of 10 goals, 10 roles, 10 agents and complete relationship set, the time for initial organization is 0.03219 seconds. The time for a reorganization based on one new object and all relationships is 0.01754 seconds. Fig. 4 shows the time to compute a transition against the size of the organization, in elements. The initial organization used in this analysis has 10 organization objects, such as roles, agents or goals, and 15 relationships between those objects. The total number of objects, on the lower end, is 25. The data shows the time to compute the transition going from 25 objects to 100, which is beyond a trivial organization. The transition process is based on computing an optimal organization configuration. The key is that the time to recompute is not significantly different for the larger organization. This is due to the incremental nature of the computation process. This indicates use of this method, is at least initially, scalable.

If we compare this timing to another result by Zhong it shows the difference. In Zhong's research[15], based on a similar model, using only the constructive version of the structural model algorithm to transition, the results of a structural computation yields two interesting points. First, the structural model transition algorithms grows at a fast rate as the number of organization objects grow. Secondly, the ability to scale to large organizations will be significantly hindered by a strictly structural approach. This indicates as the size of the organization grows, the difference between our approach and a more structural-based approach will grow, in terms of time to compute.

Fig. 5 shows the simulation of an initial organization with 4 objects and 4 relationships, then increasing by 4 objects and 4 relationships until it has a size of 1000 total components. The growth curve of the simulation shows that the linear nature of growth in the ability to incorporate new properties, simple or complex. Computing locally reduces the time, eventhough the organization is non-trivial in size

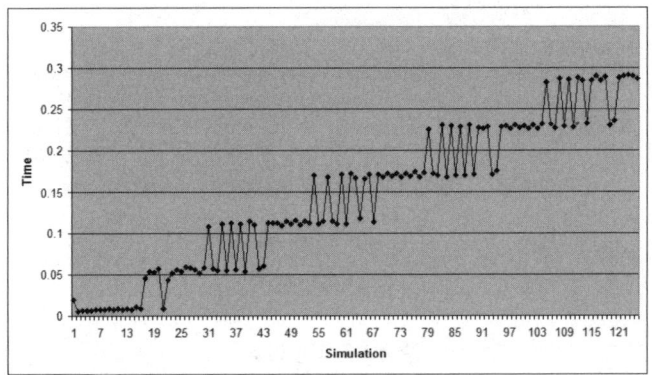

Fig. 5. Reorganization: Complex Predicates - 1000 maximum

Instantiating an organization and its transition processes in terms of a mind-body approach has advantages over a strictly structural computational approach. While there are also a few disadvantages, these are overcome by the positives.

Computation minimization is the best result of this approach. While larger, more complex organizations must be tested, the early results show promise. The computation is performed locally and in parallel, which allows the transition process to be completed more rapidly. The intent is for each agent to work with perfect information and each agent will have the same organization image, without transferring the entire structure each transition cycle. The rate of message growth is small. Even with a large change, all computation is local. This will allow a near linear growth rate during organization augmentation. This will reduce temporal computation problems in transition processes.

There are a few negative side effects of this approach. Perfect information requires that information is transferred from agent to agent without interruption or error. If there is a transfer loss, the synchronization of the organization image maps will suffer. Recovering from loss, during exchange, is key for the design. There must be synchronization allowing each agent to recompute simultaneously with all others. If there are lag times, it can create temporal problems in transition.

5   Further Work

The initial algorithm will be extended to a complete distributed model and a hybrid model, which allows an integration of command mode and complete distributed behavior. Larger organizations will be theoretically analyzed and empirically analyzed to determine performance over large, distributed agent organizations and societies. The scalability question will be further developed to see if there is a breaking point of the design.

References

1. Albert, L.: Average Case Complexity Analysis of Rete Pattern-match algorithm and Average Size of Join in Databases. Rapports de Reserche, No. 1010. Institut National de Reserche en Informatique and Automatique, Rocquencourt, France (April 1989)
2. Baader, F.: Logic-based Knowledge Representation. In: Veloso, M.M., Wooldridge, M.J. (eds.) Artificial Intelligence Today. LNCS (LNAI), vol. 1600, pp. 13–41. Springer, Heidelberg (1999)
3. DeLoach, S., Matson, E.: An Organizational Model for Designing Adaptive Multiagent Systems. In: Agent Organizations: Theory and Practice at the National Conference on Artificial Intelligence (AAAI 2004), San Jose, CA (July 25–29, 2004)
4. Dietterich, T.: Learning at the Knowledge Level. In: Machine Learning, vol. 1, pp. 287–316. Kluwer Academic Publishers, Boston (1986)
5. Dignum, V., Dignum, F.: The Knowledge Market: Agent-Mediated Knowledge Sharing. In: Mařík, V., Müller, J.P., Pěchouček, M. (eds.) CEEMAS 2003. LNCS (LNAI), vol. 2691, Springer, Heidelberg (2003)
6. Friedman-Hill, E.: JESS in Action: Rule Based Systems in Java. Manning Publications, Inc., Grennwich Connecticut, USA (2003)
7. Forgy, C., Newell, A., Gupta, A.: High-Speed Implementation of Rule-Based Systems. ACM Transactions on Computer Systems 7(2), 119–146 (1989)
8. Gordon, D., Subramanian, D.: A MultiStrategy Learning Scheme for Agent Knowledge Acquisition. Informatica 17, 4 (1993)

9. Matson, E., DeLoach, S.: Organizational Model for Cooperative and Sustaining Robotic Ecologies. In: Proceedings of Robosphere 2002 Workshop, NASA Ames Research Center, Moffett Field, California (November 14–15, 2002)

10. Matson, E., DeLoach, S.: Formal Transition in Agent Organizations. In: IEEE International Conference on Knowledge Intensive Multiagent Systems (KIMAS 2005), Waltham, MA (April 18–21, 2005)

11. Matson, E., Bhatnagar, R.: Properties of Capability Based Agent Organization Transition. In: 2006 IEEE/WIC/ACM International Conference on Intelligent Agent Technology (IAT-2006), Hong Kong (December 18–22, 2006)

12. Rybinski, H., Ryzko, D.: Knowledge Sharing in Default Reasoning-Based Multiagent Systems. In: IEEE/WIC/ACM International Conference on Intelligent Agent Technology, 2003, pp. 576–579 (October 13–16, 2003)

13. Su, K., Luo, X., Wang, H., Zhang, C., Zhang, S., Chen, Q.: A Logical Framework for Knowledge Sharing in Multi-agent Systems. In: Wang, J. (ed.) COCOON 2001. LNCS, vol. 2108, Springer, Heidelberg (2001)

14. Soller, A., Busetta, P.: An Intelligent Agent Architecture for Facilitating Knowledge Sharing Communication. In: Proceedings of Workshop on Humans and Multi-Agent Systems, International Conference on Autonomous Agents and Multi-Agent Systems, Melbourne, pp. 94–100 (2003)

15. Zhong, C., DeLoach., S.A.: An Investigation of Reorganization Algorithms. In: Proceedings of the International Conference on Artificial Intelligence (IC-AI 2006), Las Vegas, Nevada, CSREA Press (June 2006)

Role Model Based Mechanism for Norm Emergence in Artificial Agent Societies

Bastin Tony Roy Savarimuthu, Stephen Cranefield,
Maryam Purvis, and Martin Purvis

Department of Information Science, University of Otago, Dunedin, P.O. Box 56,
Dunedin, New Zealand
{tonyr,scranefield,tehrany,mpurvis}@infoscience.otago.ac.nz

Abstract. In this paper we propose a mechanism for norm emergence based on role models. The mechanism uses the concept of normative advice whereby the role models provide advice to the follower agents. Our mechanism is built using two layers of networks, the social link layer and the leadership layer. The social link network represents how agents are connected to each other. The leadership network represents the network that is formed based on the role played by each agent on the social link network. The two kinds of roles are leaders and followers. We present our findings on how norms emerge on the leadership network when the topology of the social link network changes. The three kinds of social link networks that we have experimented with are fully connected networks, random networks and scale-free networks.

1 Introduction

Norms are a widely observed mechanism for enforcing discipline and prescribing uniform behaviour in human societies. Norms specify the way the members of a society should behave and help societies to improve co-operation and collaboration among their members [1]. Some examples of norms in modern societies include the exchange of gifts at Christmas, tipping in restaurants and dinner table etiquette.

Norms have been so much a part of different cultures, it is not surprising that it is an active area of research in a variety of fields including Sociology, Economics, Biology and Computer Science. However, norms have been of interest to multi-agent researchers only for a decade now. Norms are of interest to the MAS researchers as software agents tend to deviate from these norms due to their autonomy. So, the study of norms has become crucial to MAS researchers as they can build robust multi-agent systems that comply to norms and also systems that evolve and adapt norms dynamically.

Our objective in this paper is to propose a mechanism based on role models for norm emergence using the concept of oblique norm transmission in artificial agent societies. We will demonstrate that our mechanism results in norm

J.S. Sichman et al. (Eds.): COIN 2007, LNAI 4870, pp. 203–217, 2008.
© Springer-Verlag Berlin Heidelberg 2008

emergence (100% norm convergence)[1] by using it on top of three kinds of network topologies.

2   Background

In this section we describe different types of norms and the treatment of norms in multi-agent systems. We also describe the work related to norm emergence and different kinds of network topologies.

2.1   Types of Norms

Due to multi-disciplinary interest in norms, several definitions for norms exist. Habermas [3], a renowned sociologist, identified norm regulated actions as one of the four action patterns in human behaviour. A norm to him means *fulfilling a generalized expectation of behaviour*, which is a widely accepted definition for social norms. Researchers have divided norms into different categories. Tuomela [4] has categorized norms into the following categories.

- r-norms (rule norms)
- s-norms (social norms)
- m-norms (moral norms)
- p-norms (prudential norms)

Rule norms are imposed by an authority based on an agreement between the members (e.g. one has to pay taxes). Social norms apply to large groups such as a whole society (e.g. one should not litter). Moral norms appeal to one's conscience (e.g. one should not steal or accept bribe). Prudential norms are based on rationality (e.g one ought to maximize one's expected utility). When members of a society violate the societal norms, they may be punished.

Many social scientists have studied why norms are adhered to. Some of the reasons for norm adherence include:

- fear of authority or power
- rational appeal of the norms
- emotions such as shame, guilt and embarrassment that arise because of non-adherence.
- willingness to follow the crowd

Elster [5] categorizes norms into consumption norms (e.g. manners of dress), behaviour norms (e.g. the norm against cannibalism), norms of reciprocity (e.g. gift-giving norms), norms of cooperation (e.g. voting and tax compliance) etc.

---

[1] Researchers have different notions of the success of norm emergence. For example, Kittock [2] considers a norm to have emerged if the convergence on a norm is 90%. In our case we have 100% convergence as our target for norm emergence. It could very well be 80% too. A norm is considered to exist when it is more prevalent than any of the competing norms. In theory, the convergence value could be any positive number as long as its observed frequency is greater than that of the competing norms.

2.2   Normative Multi-agent Systems

Research on norms in multi-agent systems is fairly recent [6,7,8]. Norms in multi-agent systems are treated as constraints on behaviour, goals to be achieved or as obligations [9]. There are two main research branches in normative multi-agent systems. The first branch focuses on normative system architectures, norm representations and norm adherence and the associated punitive or incentive measures. The second branch of research is related to emergence of norms.

Lopez et al. [10] have designed an architecture for normative BDI agents and Boella et al. [11] have proposed a distributed architecture for normative agents. Some researchers are working on using deontic logic to define and represent norms [12, 11]. Several researchers have worked on mechanisms for norm compliance and enforcement [13, 14, 15]. A recent development is the research on emotion based mechanism for norm enforcement [16, 17]. Conte and Castelfranchi [18] have worked on an integrated view of norms, from the perspectives of Sociology and Economics. Their views are similar to that of Elster [5].

2.3   Related Work on Emergence of Norms

The second branch of research on norms focuses on two main issues. The first issue is on norm propagation within a particular society. According to Boyd and Richerson [19], there are three ways by which a social norm can be propagated from one member of the society to another. They are

- Vertical transmission (from parents to offspring)
- Oblique transmission (from a leader of a society to the followers)
- Horizontal transmission (from peer to peer interactions)

Norm propagation is achieved by spreading and internalization of norms [7,20]. Boman and Verhagen [7,21,20] have used the concept of normative advice (advice from the leader of a society) as one of the mechanisms for spreading and internalizing norms in an agent society. The concept of normative advice in their context is based on an assumption that the norm has been accepted by the top level enforcer, the Normative Advisor, and the norm does not change. But, this context cannot be assumed for scenarios where norms are being formed (when the norms undergo changes).

So, the second issue that has received less attention is the emergence of norms. However, there is abundant literature in the area of sociology on why norms are accepted in agent societies and how they might be passed on. Karl-Dieter Opp [22] has proposed a theory of norm emergence from a sociology perspective. Epstein [23] has proposed a model of emergence based on the argument that the norms reduce individual computations.

The treatment of norms has been mostly in the context of an agent society where the agents interact with all the other agents in the society [21, 23, 24]. Few researchers have considered the actual topologies of the social network for norm emergence [25, 26]. We consider that social networks are of importance to the emergence of norms as they provide the topology and the infrastructure on which the norms can be exchanged. We are inspired by previous works on the spreading of ideas (opinion dynamics [27]) and diseases [28] over different network topologies.

Social networks are important for norm emergence because in the real world, people are not related to each other by chance. They are related to each other through the social groups that they are in, such as the work group, church group, ethnic group and the hobby group. Information tends to percolate among the members of the group through interactions. Also, people seek advice from a close group of friends and hence information gets transmitted between the members of the social network. Therefore, it is important to test our mechanism for norm emergence on top of social networks, a topic which is receiving attention among multi-agent researchers recently [26]. Network topologies have also been explored by multi-agent system researchers in other contexts such as reputation management [29, 30].

2.4 Social Network Topologies

In this section we describe three network topologies that we have considered for experimenting with norm emergence.

Fully Connected Network: In the fully connected network topology, each agent in the society is connected to all the agents in a given society (shown in Figure 1(a)). Many multi-agent researchers have done experiments with this topology. Most of their experiments involve interactions with all the agents in the society [7, 21].

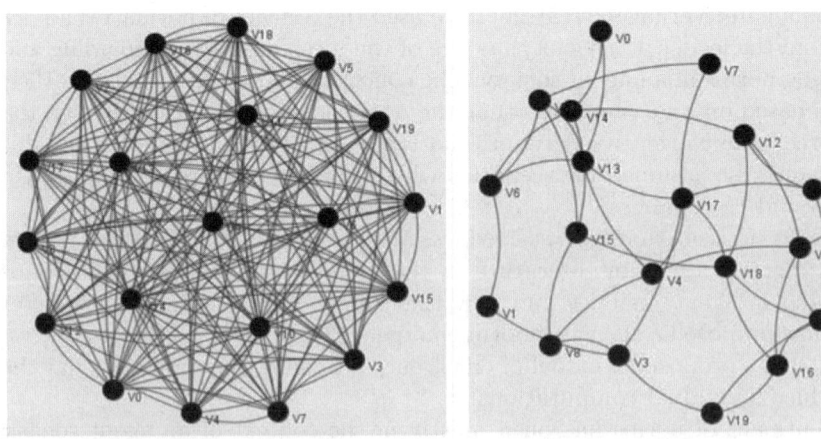

(a) Fully connected network
with 20 nodes

(b) Erdos-Renyi random network
with 20 nodes with p = 0.2

Fig. 1. A fully connected network and a random network

Random Network: Erdös and Renyi have studied the properties of random graphs and have demonstrated a mechanism for generating random networks [31]. An undirected graph G(n,p) has n vertices in which the edges are connected to each other with a probability p. The graph shown in Figure 1 (b) is a random graph with 20 vertices and the probability that an edge is present between two vertices is 0.2. It should be noted that the random network becomes fully connected network when p=1.

Scale-Free Network: Nodes in a scale-free network are not connected to each other randomly. Scale-free networks have a few well connected nodes called hubs and a large number of nodes connected only to a few nodes. This kind of network is called scale-free because the ratio of well connected nodes to the number of nodes in the rest of the network remains constant as the network changes in size. Figure 2 is an example of an Albert-Barabasi scale-free network where the size of the network is 50.

Albert and Barabasi [32] have demonstrated a mechanism for generating a scale-free topology based on their observations of large real-world networks such as the Internet, social networks and protein-protein interaction networks [33]. They have proposed a mechanism for generating scale-free networks based on

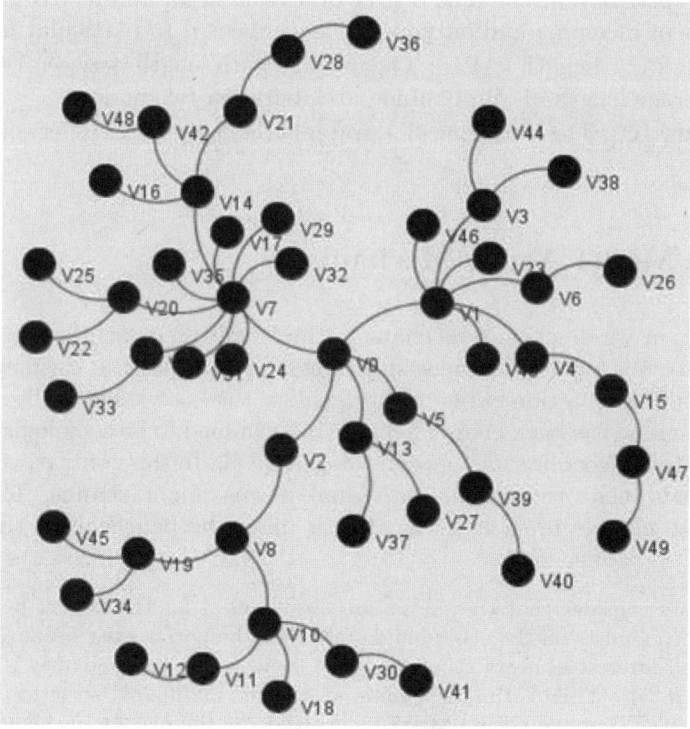

Fig. 2. An Albert-Barabasi scale-free network with 50 nodes

the preferential attachment of nodes. At a given time step, the probability (p) of creating an edge between an existing vertex (v) and the newly added vertex is given by the following formula:

$$p = (degree(v)) \, / \, (|E| + |V|)$$

where ($|E|$ and $|V|$ respectively are the number of edges and vertices currently in the network (counting neither the new vertex nor the other edges that are being attached to it).

One may observe that the network shown in Figure 2 has a few well connected nodes, which are called hubs, e.g. vertices V7, and V1. A large number of nodes are connected to very few nodes. Scale-free networks exhibit a power law behaviour [32] where the probability of the existence of a node with k links (P(k)) is directly proportional to $k^{-\alpha}$ for some α.

Some Characteristics of Networks: Researchers have studied several characteristics of networks such as diameter (D), average path length (APL), degree distribution (k) and clustering coefficient (C). For our experiments we have used three of these characteristics whose definitions are given below.

- Degree distribution (k): The degree of a node in an undirected graph is the number of incoming and outgoing links connected to particular node.
- Average Path Length (APL): The average path length between two nodes is the average length of all possible paths between two nodes.
- Diameter (D): The diameter of a graph is the longest path between any two nodes.

3   Role Model Agent Mechanism

In this section we describe a mechanism that facilitates norm emergence in an agent society. We have experimented with agents that play the Ultimatum game. The context of interaction between the agents is the knowledge of the rules of the game. This game has been chosen because it is claimed to be sociologists' counter argument[2] to the economists' view on rationality [5]. In this context, when agents interact with each other, their individual norms might change. Their norms may tend to emerge in such a way that it might be beneficial to the societies involved.

---

[2] Sociologists consider that the norms are always used for the overall benefit of the society. Economists on the other hand state that the norms exist because they cater for the self-interest of every member of the society and each member is thought to be rational [34]. When Ultimatum game was played in different societies, researchers have observed that the norm of fairness evolved. As the players in this game choose fairness over self-interest, Sociologists' argue that, this game is the counter argument to economists' view on rationality.

3.1   The Ultimatum Game

The Ultimatum game [35] is an experimental economics game in which two parties interact anonymously with each other. The game is played for a fixed sum of money (say x dollars). The first player proposes how to share the money with the second player. Say, the first player proposes y dollars to the second player. If the second player rejects this division, neither gets anything. If the second accepts, the first gets x-y dollars and the second gets y dollars.

3.2   Description of the Multi-agent Environment

An agent society is made up of a fixed number of agents. They are connected to each other using one of the social network topologies (fully connected, random or scale-free).

Norms in the Agent Society. Each agent in a society has an internal norm. Each agent also has a norm to represent its maximum and minimum proposal and acceptance values when playing the ultimatum game. This norm is called as the personal norm (P norm). A sample P norm for an agent is given below where min and max are the minimum and maximum values when the game is played for a sum of 100 dollars.

- Proposal norm (min=1, max=30)
- Acceptance norm (min=1, max=100)

The representations given above indicate that the proposal norm of an agent ranges from 1 to 30 and the acceptance norm of the agent ranges from 1 to 100.

The proposal norm initialized using a uniform distribution within a range of 1 to 100, is internal to the agent. It is not known to any other agent. The agents in a society are initialized with an acceptance norm that indicates that any agent which proposes within the range specified by the norm will be accepted. The agents are only aware of their acceptance norms and are not aware of the acceptance norms of the other agents. In order to observe how proposal norms emerge, we assign a fixed value for acceptance norm to all the agents in the society. The acceptance norm of a society is given below.

- Acceptance norm (min=45, max = 55)

3.3   The Norm Emergence Mechanism

The role models are agents who the societal members may wish to follow. The inspiration is derived from human society where one might want to use successful people as a guide. Any agent in the society can become a role model agent if some other agent asks for its advice. The role model agent represents a role model or an advisor who provides normative advise to those who ask for help. In our mechanism, each agent will have atmost one leader.

An agent will choose its role model depending upon the performance of its neighbours. We assume that agents that are connected know each other's performances. This is based on the assumption that people who are successful in the neighbourhood are easily recognizable. We argue that their success can be attributed to their norms.

Autonomy is an important concept associated with accepting or rejecting request to become a leader. When an agent is created, it has an autonomy value between 0 and 1. Depending upon the autonomy value, an agent can either accept or reject a request from another agent. If the autonomy value of an agent is .4, it will reject the request from another agent 4 out of 10 times. Once rejected, an agent will contact the next best performing agent amongst its neighbours. Autonomy of an agent is also related to accepting or rejecting the advice provided by the leader agent.

Assume that agent A and B are acquaintances (are connected to each other in a network). If agent A's successful proposal average is 60% and agent B's successful proposal average is 80%, then agent A will send a request to agent B asking for its advice. If agent B accepts this request, B becomes the role model of agent A and sends its P norm to agent A. The agent is autonomous to choose or ignore the advice depending upon its autonomy. When agent A decides to follow the advice provided by agent B, it modifies its P norm by moving closer to the P norm of agent B.

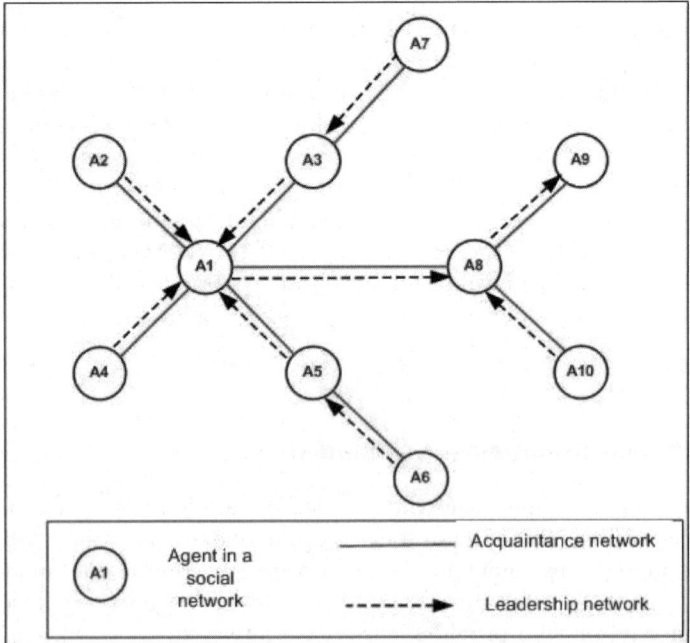

Fig. 3. Two layers of networks used in role model agent mechanism

Figure 3 depicts the two layers of networks that are used in our mechanism. The circles represent agents. The solid lines represent the social link network also known as an acquaintance network.

In our mechanism, an agent plays a fixed number of Ultimatum games with each of its neighbours (agents that are linked to it). In total, highly connected agents play more games than the poorly connected agents. Highly connected agents benefit from playing more games because they retain their competitive advantage of obtaining a wide range of information or norms from the agents that they are connected to, while the poorly connected agents rely on the information from one or two agents that they are connected to. A highly connected agent is more likely to know about the best norm earlier than the poorly connected agent.

After one iteration, every agent looks for the best performing player in its neighbourhood. After finding the best performing player, the agent sends a request to the player requesting the agent to be its role model or leader. If the requested agent decides to become the role model, it sends its P norm (normative advice) to the requester (follower agent). The follower agent modifies its norm by moving closer to the role model agent's norm. If an agent does not find a role model agent, it does not change its norm in that iteration.

The dotted line with an arrow (directed line) represents the leadership network that emerges at the end of interactions. In Figure 3, A1 is the leader of A2, A3, A4 and A5. Arrows from these four agents point to A1. This new kind of network that emerges on top of the acquaintance network is called a *leadership network*.

4   Experiments and Results

In this section we present the experiments that we undertook to demonstrate that our mechanism leads to complete norm emergence when tested on top of different kinds of network topologies.

4.1   Norm Emergence on Top of Random and Scale-Free Networks

The role model agent based mechanism for norm propagation was evaluated using Erdös-Renyi (ER) random network and Albert-Barabasi (AB) scale-free network.

At first we studied the effects of changing the average degree of connectivity (<k>) on norm emergence, while maintaining a constant population size (N). The average degree of connectivity represents how connected the agents in the society are. A higher value of <k> represents a well connected network. We varied the degree of connectivity (<k> = 5, 10, 20, 100, 200) for the ER and AB networks with N=200 . It can be observed from Figure 4 that as <k> increased the rate of convergence increased in ER networks. When <k> is 10, 100% norm emergence was observed in the 6th iteration while it only took 3 iterations for convergence when the value of <k> is 200. Note that when <k> equals N, the network is fully connected, hence the convergence is faster. Similar results were also observed for AB networks (not shown here).

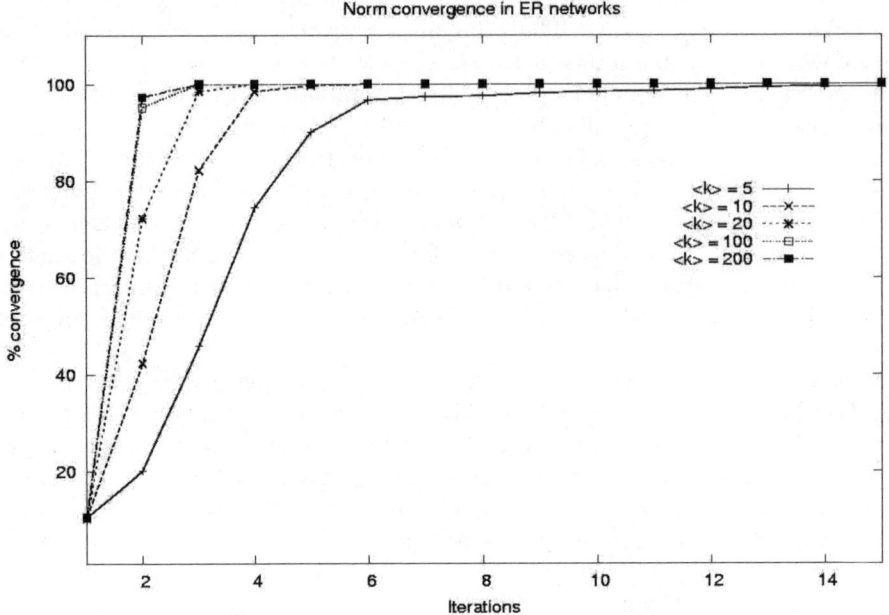

Fig. 4. Norm convergence in ER networks when average degree of connectivity is varied

The comparison of ER and AB networks for the same values of N and <k> is shown in Figure 5. It can be observed that there is no significant difference in the rate of convergence in ER and AB networks. Our experimental results on norm convergence are in agreement with the statistical analysis carried out by Albert and Barabasi on the two kinds of networks [36]. They have observed that the diameter (D) and average path lengths (APL) of both the networks are similar for fixed values of N and <k>. The diameters of ER and AB networks, when N and <k> are fixed are directly proportional to log(N). As the diameters of both the networks are the same, the rate of norm convergence are similar.

The parameters D and APL of these networks decrease when the average connectivity of the network increases. When the average connectivity increases, it is easier for an agent to find a leader agent whose performance scores are high. If the average connectivity is low, it would take an agent a few iterations before its leader obtains the norm from a better performing agent. This explains why norm convergence is slower when average connectivity <k> decreases (shown in Figure 4).

Even though the norm emergence properties of both kinds of networks are comparable, it can be argued that the scale-free network is better suited to model norm propagation because in the real world, people are related to each other through the social groups that they are in, such as the work group and church group. Information percolates among the members of the group through interactions. Also, people seek advice from a close group of friends and hence

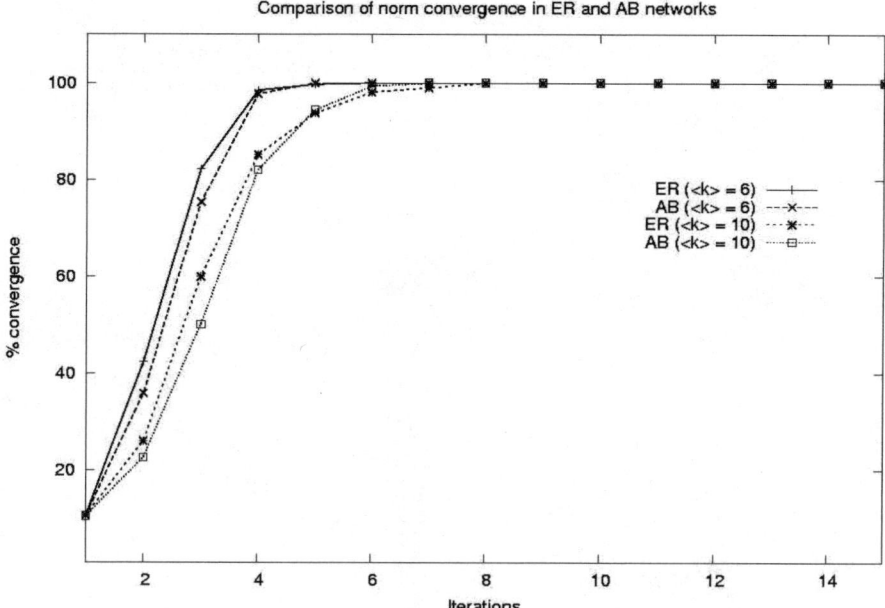

Fig. 5. Comparison of norm convergence in random vs scale-free networks

information gets transmitted across social network. Other researchers have demonstrated that scale-free networks are well suited to explain mechanisms of disease propagation and dissemination of ideas [33]. Scale-free networks are more robust than random networks when random nodes start to fail and this phenomenon has been observed in real world networks [37].

Recently [38], it has also been observed that the diameter and average path lengths of an AB network depends upon the value of m. m is a constant that indicates the number of nodes to which a new node entering the network should be connected to, using the preferential attachment scheme. When m=1, D and APL are directly proportional to $\log(N)$ and for m>1, D is directly proportional to $\log(N)/\log(\log(N))$. In this light, Albert and Barabasi have suggested that the scale-free networks should be more efficient in bringing nodes closer to each other which will be suitable for propagation of ideas and norms.

4.2   Power Law Behaviour of the Leadership Network

We have also observed that the leadership network that emerges on top of the AB network follows power law behaviour. It is interesting to note that the leadership network that emerges on top of ER network follows power law behaviour when the average degree of connectivity is small. For smaller probabilities (p=.05, .1) we have observed that there are fewer leader agents with large number of followers and a large number of leaders with a few followers. Figure 6 shows the

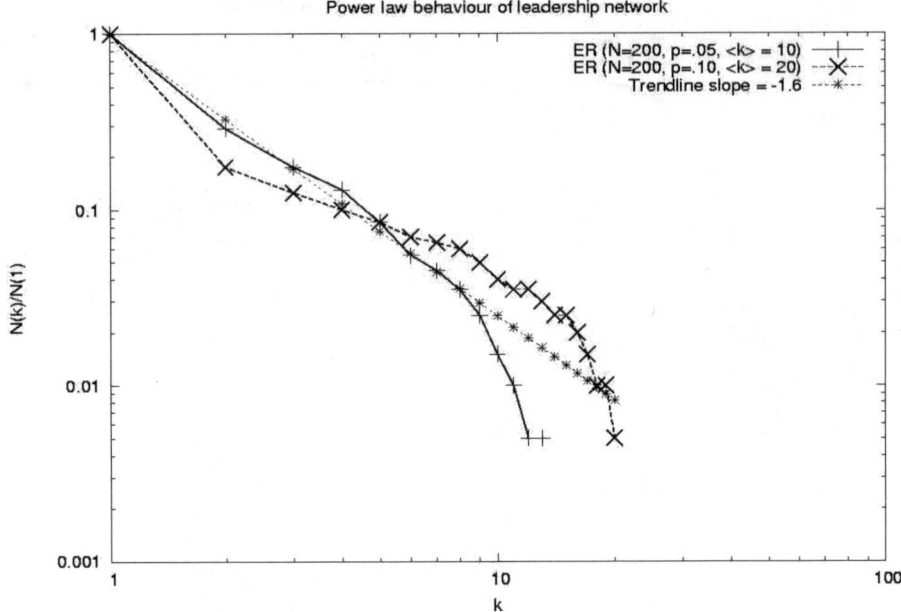

Fig. 6. Power law behaviour of the leadership network

log-log plot of leaders with k followers in the x-axis and the number of leaders with k followers (N(k)) divided by the number of leaders with exactly one follower (N1) in the y-axis. The trendline shows the approximate power law behaviour of the leadership network. The slope of the power law curve was found to be -1.6. Our results are in agreement with that of Anghel et al. [39] who studied the emergence of scale-free leadership structures using minority game. In their work, an agent sends its game strategy to all the agents in its neighbourhood. There is no explicit notion of leadership as each agent maintains an internal model of who its leader is. In our work, each agent chooses its leader explicitly and the leader sends the norms only to its followers. Also, the agents in our model have the notion of autonomy which is more representative of a realistic society.

5   Discussion

Our work is different (see Section 2.3) from other researchers in this area as we use the concepts of oblique transmission in the mechanism we have proposed. Verhagen's thesis [21] focuses on the spreading and internalizing of norms. This assumes that a norm is agreed or chosen by a top level entity (say, a Normative Advisor) and this group norm (G norm) does not change. The G norm is spread to the agents through the normative advice using a top-down approach. Our work differs from this work as we employ a bottom-up approach. In our approach the P norm evolves continuously. In his work, the P norm changes to accommodate the predetermined group norm. Another important distinction is the consideration of network topologies in our work.

There are some similarities between these two works. Both works have used the notion of leadership for the study of norm spreading and emergence respectively. Both the works have not included sanctions as a part of their mechanisms. Sanction based models have been used by researchers (e.g. [15]) to demonstrate norm emergence. In the future we are planning to study how sanctions might emerge as a part of norm emergence.

The experiments described in this paper are our initial efforts in the area of norm emergence. The experiments are limited to a single agent society. We are interested in experimenting with scenarios that involve two or more inter-linked societies. We are also interested to experiment with scenarios in which different norms may co-exist.

In the real world, we attach more weight to a particular person's advice than others. Similarly, the weights of the edges (links) should be considered when the agent makes a decision on who to choose as a role model agent. We plan to incorporate this idea in our future experiments. Also, addition or deletion of links to a given topology have not been considered in the current mechanism. This is analogous to people relocating and forming new links. We have planned to experiment with our mechanism on top of dynamically changing networks.

6 Conclusions

We have explained our mechanism for norm emergence in artificial agent societies that is based on the concept of role models. We have demonstrated the use of oblique norm transmission for norm emergence. Our mechanism was tested on top of three network topologies. We have shown through our experimental results that complete norm emergence can be achieved using our proposed mechanism. We have compared our work with the researchers in this area and also discussed the future work.

References

1. Boella, G., Torre, L., Verhagen, H.: Introduction to normative multiagent systems. Computational and Mathematical Organization Theory 12(2–3), 71–79 (2006)
2. Kittock, J.E.: The impact of locality and authority on emergent conventions: Initial observations. In: Proceedings of the twelfth national conference on Artificial intelligence, American Association for Artificial Intelligence Menlo Park, CA, USA, pp. 420–425 (1994)
3. Habermas, J.: The Theory of Communicative Action: Reason and the Rationalization of Society, vol. 1. Beacon Press (1985)
4. Tuomela, R.: The Importance of Us: A Philosophical Study of Basic Social Notions. Stanford Series in Philosophy, Stanford University Press (1995)
5. Elster, J.: Social norms and economic theory. The Journal of Economic Perspectives 3(4), 99–117 (1989)

6. Shoham, Y., Tennenholtz, M.: On social laws for artificial agent societies: Off-line design. Artificial Intelligence 73(1-2), 231–252 (1995)
7. Boman, M.: Norms in artificial decision making. Artificial Intelligence and Law 7(1), 17–35 (1999)
8. Conte, R., Falcone, R., Sartor, G.: Agents and norms: How to fill the gap? Artificial Intelligence and Law 7(1), 1–15 (1999)
9. Castelfranchi, C., Conte, R.: Cognitive and social action. UCL Press, London (1995)
10. López y López, F., Márquez, A.A.: An architecture for autonomous normative agents. In: Fifth Mexican International Conference in Computer Science (ENC 2004), pp. 96–103. IEEE Computer Society Press, Los Alamitos (2004)
11. Boella, G., van der Torre, L.: An architecture of a normative system: Counts-as conditionals, obligations and permissions. In: Proceedings of the fifth international joint conference on autonomous agents and multiagent systems, AAMAS, pp. 229–231. ACM Press, New York (2006)
12. García-Camino, A., Rodríguez-Aguilar, J.A., Sierra, C., Vasconcelos, W.: Norm-oriented programming of electronic institutions. In: Proceedings of the fifth international joint conference on autonomous agents and multiagent systems, AAMAS, pp. 670–672. ACM Press, New York (2006)
13. López y López, F., Luck, M., d'Inverno, M.: Constraining autonomy through norms. In: Proceedings of The First International Joint Conference on autonomous Agents and Multi Agent Systems, AAMAS, pp. 674–681. ACM Press, New York (2002)
14. Aldewereld, H., Dignum, F., García-Camino, A., Noriega, P., Rodríguez-Aguilar, J.A., Sierra, C.: Operationalisation of norms for usage in electronic institutions. In: Proceedings of The Fifth International Joint Conference on autonomous Agents and Multi Agent Systems, AAMAS, pp. 223–225. ACM Press, New York (2006)
15. Axelrod, R.: An evolutionary approach to norms. The American Political Science Review 80(4), 1095–1111 (1986)
16. Fix, J., von Scheve, C., Moldt, D.: Emotion-based norm enforcement and maintenance in multi-agent systems: foundations and petri net modeling. In: Proceedings of the fifth international joint conference on autonomous agents and multiagent systems, AAMAS, pp. 105–107 (2006)
17. Pitt, J.: Digital blush: Towards shame and embarrassment in multi-agent information trading applications. Cognition, Technology and Work 6(1), 23–36 (2004)
18. Conte, R., Castelfranchi, C.: From conventions to prescriptions - towards an integrated view of norms. Artificial Intelligence and Law 7(4), 323–340 (1999)
19. Boyd, R., Richerson, P.J.: Culture and the evolutionary process. University of Chicago Press, Chicago (1985)
20. Verhagen, H.: Simulation of the Learning of Norms. Social Science Computer Review 19(3), 296–306 (2001)
21. Verhagen, H.: Norm Autonomous Agents. PhD thesis, Department of Computer Science, Stockholm University (2000)
22. Opp, K.D.: How do norms emerge? An outline of a theory. Mind and Society 2(1), 101–128 (2001)
23. Epstein, J.M.: Learning to be thoughtless: Social norms and individual computation. Computational Economics 18(1), 9–24 (2001)
24. Sen, S., Airiau, S.: Emergence of norms through social learning. In: Proceedings of Twentieth International Joint Conference on Artificial Intelligence (IJCAI), Hyderabad, India, pp. 1507–1512. MIT Press, Cambridge (2006)
25. Nakamaru, M., Levin, S.A.: Spread of two linked social norms on complex interaction networks. Journal of Theoretical Biology 230(1), 57–64 (2004)

26. Pujol, J.M.: Structure in Artificial Societies. PhD thesis, Llenguatges i Sistemes Informátics, Universitat Politénica de Catalunya (2006)
27. Fortunato, S.: Damage spreading and opinion dynamics on scale free networks (2004)
28. Cohen, R., Havlin, S., ben-Avraham, D.: Efficient immunization strategies for computer networks and populations. Physical Review Letters 91, 247–901 (2003)
29. Pujol, J.M., Sangüesa, R., Delgado, J.: Extracting reputation in multi agent systems by means of social network topology. In: Proceedings of the first international joint conference on autonomous agents and multiagent systems, AAMAS, pp. 467–474. ACM Press, New York (2002)
30. Yu, B., Singh, M.P.: Searching social networks. In: Proceedings of the second international joint conference on autonomous agents and multiagent systems, AAMAS, pp. 65–72. ACM Press, New York (2003)
31. Erdös, P., Renyi, A.: On random graphs - i. Publicationes Mathematicae Debrecen 6, 290 (1959)
32. Barabási, A.L., Albert, R.: Emergence of scaling in random networks. Science 286, 509–512 (1999)
33. Mitchell, M.: Complex systems: Network thinking. Artificial Intelligence 170(18), 1194–1212 (2006)
34. Gintis, H.: Solving the Puzzle of Prosociality. Rationality and Society 15(2), 155–187 (2003)
35. Slembeck, T.: Reputations and fairness in bargaining - experimental evidence from a repeated ultimatum game with fixed opponents. Technical report, EconWPA (1999), http://ideas.repec.org/p/wpa/wuwpex/9905002.html
36. Albert, R., Barabasi, A.-L.: Statistical mechanics of complex networks. Reviews of Modern Physics 74, 47–97 (2002)
37. Albert, R., Jeong, H., Barabasi, A.L.: Error and attack tolerance of complex networks. Nature 406(6794), 378–382 (2000)
38. Bollobás, B., Riordan, O.: The diameter of a scale-free random graph. Combinatorica 24(1), 5–34 (2004)
39. Anghel, M., Toroczkai, Z., Bassler, K.E., Korniss, G.: Competition-driven network dynamics: Emergence of a scale-free leadership structure and collective efficiency. Physical Review Letters 92(5), 587011–587014 (2004)

Using Testimonies to Enforce the Behavior of Agents

Fernanda Duran[1], Viviane Torres da Silva[2,*], and Carlos J.P. de Lucena[1]

[1] Departamento de Informática – PUC, Rio de Janeiro, Brazil
{fduran,lucena}@inf.puc-rio.br
[2] Departamento de Sistemas Informáticos y Computación – UCM, Madrid, Spain
viviane@fdi.ucm.es

Abstract. Governance copes with the heterogeneity, autonomy and diversity of interests among different agents in multi-agent systems (MAS) by establishing norms. Although norms can be used to regulate dialogical and non-dialogical actions, the majority of governance systems only governs the interaction between agents. Some mechanisms that intend to regulate other agent actions concentrate on messages that are public to the governance system and on actions that are visible by it. But in open MAS with heterogeneous and independently designed agents, there will be private messages that can only be perceived by senders and receivers and execution of actions that can only be noticed by the agents that are executing them or by a group of agents that suffers from their consequences. This paper presents a governance mechanism based on testimonies provided by agents that witness facts that are violating norms. The mechanism points out if agents really violated norms.

Keywords: Open multi-agent system, governance, norms and testimonies.

1 Introduction

Open multi-agent systems are societies in which autonomous, heterogeneous and independently designed entities can work towards similar or different ends [13]. In order to cope with the heterogeneity, autonomy and diversity of interests among the different members, governance (or law enforcement) systems have been defined. Governance systems enforce the behavior of agents by establishing a set of norms that describe actions that agents are prohibited, permitted or obligated to do [3] and [18]. Such systems assume that norms can sometimes be violated by agents and that the internal state of the agents is neither observable nor controllable.

Different enforcement systems have been proposed in the literature. The majority, such as [14] and [7], focuses on regulating the interaction between agents. They usually provide governors [7] or law-governed interaction [14] mechanisms that mediate the interaction between agents in order to regulate agent messages and make them comply with the set of norms. Every message that an agent wants to send is analyzed by the mechanism. If the message violates an application norm, the message is not

* Research supported by the Juan de la Cierva program, Comunidad de Madrid Program S-0505/ TIC-407 and by Spanish MEC Projects TIC2003-01000.

J.S. Sichman et al. (Eds.): COIN 2007, LNAI 4870, pp. 218–231, 2008.
© Springer-Verlag Berlin Heidelberg 2008

sent to the receiver. The main disadvantages of such approaches are (i) they influence the agents' privacy since those mechanisms interfere in every interaction between agents and (ii) they do not govern non-dialogical actions since they only concern about the compliance of messages with the system norm [21]. Non-dialogical actions are related to tasks executed by agents that characterize, for instance, the access to resources, their commitment to play roles or their movement in environments and organizations.

Other approaches provide support for the enforcement of norms that regulate not only the interactions between agents but also the access to resources [4] and the execution of agent's actions [21]. TuCSoN [4] provides a coordination mechanism to manage the interaction between agents and also an access control mechanism to handle communication events, in other words, to control the access to resources. In TuCSoN agents interact through a multiplicity of independent coordination media, called tuple centres. The access control mechanism controls agent access to resources by making the tuple centres visible or invisible to them. Although in TuCSoN norms can be described to govern the access to resources, the governance is restricted and only applied to resources that are inserted in tuple centre environments.

In [21] the authors claim that the governance system enforces the observable behavior of agents in terms of public messages and visible actions. They introduce a classification of norms and, according to such classification, they provide some implementation guidelines to enforce them. The main drawback of this approach is that it does not provide support for the enforcement of messages and actions that are not directly accessed by the governance system. Such an approach assumes that the governance system can enforce every norm since it can access all messages and actions regulated by a norm. But in open MAS with heterogeneous and independently designed agents, there will be private messages that can only be perceived by senders and receivers and execution of actions that can only be noticed by the agents that are executing them or by a group of agents that suffers from their consequences [1].

In this paper we propose a governance mechanism based on testimonies provided by witnesses about facts or events that they know are related to norm violations. Agents are inserted in an environment where they can perceive the changes occurred in it. Since agents can observe these changes, they can provide testimonies about actions or messages that are in violation of a norm. Note that the agents do not keep monitoring the behavior of other agents in order to provide testimonies about their violations. The agents testify if they perceive a fact or event that is violating a norm.

In our approach, private messages and also private actions can be enforced. *Private messages* that violate norms can be testified by agents that are involved in the interactions. Such agents can testify about messages they should have received or about messages they should have not received. *Private actions* that are executed in the *scope of a group* and are violating norms can be testified by any member of the group that knows such norms and has seen the actions being executed or has perceived facts or events that reflect the execution of such actions. The same can be said about actions that should have been executed but were not. Related facts or events cannot be observed and, therefore, agents can testify stating that the actions (probably) were not executed. In addition, *private actions* that are executed in the *scope of one single agent* and that are violating norms can be testified by any agent that knows the norms and that perceives facts or events that are related to the execution of such actions. The same can be said about actions that an agent should have executed but has not. Other agents that know the norms that regulate such actions can testify if they cannot observe the related facts or events.

The paper presents in Section 2 an overall view of the testimony-based governance mechanism. Section 3 details the judgment process used by the mechanism while Section 4 describes a case study where we apply our approach. Finally, section 5 concludes and describes some advantages and drawbacks of our proposal.

2 The Testimony-Based Governance Mechanism

The governance mechanism presented here is based on testimonies that agents provide attesting facts or events that may be norm violations. Since every agent knows sets of norms, it can report to the governance mechanism their violation. In order to interpret the norms, the agent must know the grammar (or ontology) used to describe the norms [17].

2.1 Governance Mechanism Assumptions

The testimony-based governance mechanism is funded in the following assumptions.

Assumption I: *Every agent should know every norm applied to itself.* Such as in the real world where everyone should know a code of behavior, we assume that every agent should know all norms that can be applied to their messages or actions independently of the system environment in which it is executing. When an agent enters in the environment to play a role, the environment/system must be able to provide to the agent all norms applied to this role. This is important because the mechanism assumes that an agent acting in violation of a norm chooses to do so being aware of that. The set of norms that regulates the application should by provided by an ontology.

Assumption II: *Every agent should know every norm that influences its behavior and should be able to observe violations of such norms.* Agents should know the norms that regulate the behavior of other agents when the violations of such norms influence their own execution. Therefore, when entering in an environment, agents should not only observe the norms applied to the roles they will play, but also the norms that, when violated by other agents, influence their execution. The possible violation of such norms motivates the agents to be aware of them.

Assumption III: *Every agent can give testimonies about norm violations.* Since an agent knows norms that are applied to other agents, the agent should be able to state that one of these norms is being violated. Every time an agent perceives the violation of a norm, it must be able to give a testimony to the governance mechanism. The proposed mechanism provides a component that can be used by agents to help them analyzing their beliefs in order to find out well-known facts or events that may be norms violations.

Assumption IV: *Some violations might be ignored / not observed.* The proposed mechanism does not impose that an agent must give its testimony whenever it notices a norm violation. Agents should be well motivated in order to provide their testimonies. Besides, the mechanism does not guarantee that all violations will be observed by at least one agent. It may be the case that a violation occurs and no agent testifies about it.

Assumption V: *Agents can give false testimony.* In an open system, agents are independently implemented, i.e. the development is done without a centralized control and the governance mechanism cannot assume that an agent was properly designed. Therefore, there is no way to guarantee that all testimonies are related to actual violations. So, the governance mechanism should be able to check and assert the truthfulness of the testimonies.

Assumption VI: *The mechanism can have a law-enforcement agent force.* The mechanism can introduce agents which have the sole purpose of giving testimonies. The testimonies of those agents provided by the mechanism can always be considered to be truthful and the judgment subsystem can directly state that a norm was violated and a penalty should be assigned. Note that those agents must only testify if they are sure about the culpability of the application agents and that they can only testify about violations related to public messages and actions. They must be aware that an agent may violate a norm due some major force or to another agent fault, for instance.

2.2 The Governance Mechanism Architecture

In order to decentralize the governance of large-scale multi-agent systems, we propose to use a hierarchy of organizations where agents are executing according to their roles. Each system organization should state its own norms and implement the proposed governance system to regulate them. The mechanism's architecture proposes three subsystems. The judgment subsystem is responsible for receiving the testimonies and for providing a decision (or verdict) pointing out to the reputation and sanction subsystems if an agent has really violated a norm. The system may use different strategies to judge the violation of the different norms specified by the application. Such strategies might use the agents' reputation afforded by the reputation system to help providing the decision. It is well established that trust and reputation are important in open systems and can be used by the agents for reasoning about the reliability of other ones [16]. In [16] trust is defined as subjective probability with which agents assess that other agents will perform a particular action. We adapt this definition to our approach stating that reputation is defined as a subjective probability with which agents assess that other agent will provide trustful testimonies. The reputation subsystem [8] evaluates the reputation of agents according to the decisions provided by the judgment subsystem about violated norms and false testimonies. Finally, the third subsystem, the sanction subsystem, applies the sanctions specified in norms to the witness agents or to the defendant agents, according to the judgment decision.

3 The Judgment Sub-system

The judgment sub-system has three main responsibilities: to receive testimonies, to judge them and to provide the decision about the violation. Three different agent types were defined to deal with these responsibilities: inspector, judge and broker agents. The inspector agents are responsible for receiving the testimonies and sending them to judge agents. The judge agents examine the testimonies and provide decisions that are sent to broker agents. Broker agents are responsible for interacting with the reputation and sanction sub-systems to make the decisions effective. While judging the testimonies, judge agents may interact with brokers to get information about the reputation of agents.

3.1 The Judgment Process

The judgment process is composed of eight steps where six are application independent ones. Although judgment strategies cannot be completely independent of the application norms, it is possible to define some common steps to be followed by any judgment strategy. In this section we present the eight steps that compose the judgment process.

Step I: *To check if the testimony has already been judged.* Agents may send testimonies about facts that have already been testified and judged. Because of that, the first step of the judgment process checks if the testimony is related to one of the judgment processes that had occurred before and had considered the defendant guilty. If so, the testimony is discarded and the judgment process is canceled.

Step II: *To verify who the witness is.* According to assumption VI, the testimony provided by some specific agents must be considered always truth. Therefore, the second step of the judgment process verifies who the witness is. If it is the case of an always truthful witness, the judgment process is finished and the verdict stating that the agent must be penalized is provided.

Step III: *To check if the norm applies to the defendant agent.* According to assumption V, agents can lie and end up accusing other agents of violating norms that are not applied to them. In order to find out if a testimony is true, this step checks if the norm applies to the defendant agent. If the norm does not apply, the judgment process is finished and the verdict states that the defendant agent is absolved.

Step IV: *To ask the defendant agent if it is guilty.* If the norm applies to the agent, the next step is to ask it if it has violated the norm it is accused of. As it happens in the real world, if the agent confesses, the judgment process is finished and the verdict states that the defendant agent is condemned. Otherwise, the judgment process continues. In cases where the defendant confesses the violation, the applied punishment can be smaller than the one that would be applied if he hasn't confessed.

Step V: *To judge the testimony according to the norm (application dependent step).* If the agent did not confess, it is necessary to carefully examine if the agent really violated the norm. In order to determine if the testimony is truth and, therefore, if the defendant agent is guilty, it may be necessary to use different strategies for different violated norms. For instance, on one hand, if the norm regulates the payment of an item and the defendant is being accused of having not paid the witness, one possible strategy is to ask the defendant if it has the receipt signed by the witness asserting that it has received the payment. On the other hand, if the norm states that an agent should have not updated a resource, the judgment system could use the simple strategy that checks the resource log, in case it is provided. It is clear that such strategies are application dependent ones since they depend on the norm that is being enforced. It is also possible to ask the defendant agent why it has not violated the norm. If the agent says that it was not able to do so, the judgment agent will need to investigate if such information is true. In this case, the agent should not be accused of violating the norm.

Step VI: *To ask other agents about their depositions (application dependent step).* If the application strategy could not decide if the defendant agent is guilty or not, the judgment system can still try another approach. Since there may be other agents that can also testify about the violation of the norm or facts related to it, the judgment system can explicitly ask them about their opinion about the violation. This step is an application dependent step because depending on the kind of question the judgment system makes to the agents, it may be necessary to interpret the answer according to the application norm being checked. For instance, two different kinds of questions can be asked to those agents: (i) Have you seen agent a_i violating norm n_j? (ii) What do you know about fact f_k? There are different interpretations for each of the questions and such interpretations are application dependent.

Step VII: *To come up with a consensus considering the depositions.* After interpreting the depositions, the judgment system must put them together to come up with a verdict. In order to do so, our approach uses the agent reputations to help evaluating the depositions. The consensus between the depositions is provided by using subjective logic [12], as detailed in Section 3.3. Such an approach evaluates the depositions considering the reputations of the agents to come up with the probability of the defendant agent being guilty of violating the norm.

Step VIII: *To provide the decision.* The judgment system can provide three decisions. It can state that (i) the defendant agent is probably guilty, (ii) the defendant is probably not guilty (the witness has lied), or (iii) the culpability of the defendant is undefined. In this case, the judge could not decide if the agent is guilty or not.

After producing the decision, it is necessary to send it to the reputation sub-system so that it can modify the reputation of the accused agent, in case the judgment system has decided that the defendant agent is guilty, or the reputation of the witness, in case the judgment system has decided that it has lied. It is also important to inform the decision to the sanction sub-system to (i) punish the agent for violating a norm and to award the witness for providing the testimony or (ii) to punish the witness for providing an untruthful testimony.

3.2 Evaluating the Testimonies and Depositions

When there are not enough evidences to be used by the judge agent to come up with a decision, it can still make use of agents' depositions to finally provide a verdict, as described in Step VI and VII. However, as stated before in assumption V, agents can give false testimonies and also false depositions. Therefore, there is a need for an approach that evaluates such testimonies and depositions considering the reliability of the agents, i.e., considering their reputations. We propose the use of subjective logic to provide a verdict stating the probability of an agent being guilty or not for violating a norm. Such an approach is used in the application independent Step VII to ponder the testimonies/depositions according to the agents' reputations and to make a consensus between them.

In [5] the authors sketched a model for e-marketplaces based on subjective logic for setting contracts back on course whenever their fulfillment deviate from what were established. Evidences from various sources are weighed in order to inform the actions that are probably violating the contracts. Subjective logic is used to support reasoning over those evidences, which involve levels of trust over parties, combining recommendations and forming consensus.

In [2], to evaluate the trustworthiness of a given party, especially prior to any frequent direct interaction, agents may rely on other agents (witnesses) who have interacted with the party of interest. The testimonies given by those witnesses are based on direct interactions and may hold a degree of uncertainty. To combine the testimonies and create a single opinion (reputation) about an agent, the authors used the Dempster-Shafer theory of evidence as the underlying computational framework.

3.2.1 Introducing Subjective Logic

Subjective Logic was proposed by Audun Jøsang based on the Dempster-Shafer theory of evidence [12]. This approach addresses the problem of forming a measurable belief about the truth or falsity on an atomic proposition, in the presence of uncertainty. It translates our imperfect knowledge about reality into degrees of belief or disbelief as well as uncertainty which fills the void in the absence of both belief and disbelief [12]. This approach is described as a logic which operates on subjective beliefs and uses the term *opinion* to denote the representation of a subjective belief. The elements that compose the frame of discernment which is a set of all possible situations are described as follows:

(i)   The agent's opinion is represented by a triple $w(x) = <b(x), d(x), u(x)>$;
(ii) $b(x)$ measures belief, represented as a subjective probability of proposition x to be true;
(iii) $d(x)$ measures disbelief, represented as a subjective probability of proposition x to be false;
(iv) $u(x)$ measures uncertainty, represented as a subjective probability that a proposition x to be either true or false;
(v) $b(x), d(x), u(x) \in [0..1]$ and $b(x) + d(x) + u(x) = 1$;
(vi) $w^A(x)$ represents the opinion that an agent A has about the proposition x to be true or false.

Subjective Logic operates on opinions about binary propositions, i.e. opinions about propositions that are assumed to be either true or false. The operators described above are to be applied over such opinions.

Recommendation (Discounting): The *discounting* operator $\otimes$ combines agent A's opinion about agent B's advice with agent B's opinion about a proposition x expressed as an advice from agent B to agent A. That means if agent B gives an advice x to agent A, and agent A has an opinion about agent B, the operator $\otimes$ can be used to form *agent A's opinion about agent B's advice x*:

(i) $w^A(B) = <b^A(b),d^A(b),u^A(b)>$ represents agent A's opinion about agent B;
(ii) $w^B(x)=<b^B(x),d^B(x),u^B(x)>$ represents agent B's opinion about x;
(iii) $w^{A:B}(x)= w^A(B) \otimes w^B(x)$ represents agent A's opinion about agent B's opinion about the preposition x.

(iv) $w^{A:B}(x)=<b^{A:B}(x),d^{A:B}(x),u^{A:B}(x)>$ and is evaluated as follows:
   a. $b^{A:B}(x) = b^A(b) \, b^B(x);$
   b. $d^{A:B}(x) = b^A(b) \, d^B(x);$
   c. $u^{A:B}(x) = d^A(b) + u^A(b) + b^A(b) \, u^B(x)$

Consensus: The *consensus* of two possibly conflicting opinions is an opinion that reflects both opinions in a fair and equal way, i.e. when two observers have beliefs about the truth of x, the consensus operator ⊕ produces a consensus beliefs that *combines the two separate beliefs into one*:

(i) $w^A(x) = <b^A(x),d^A(x),u^A(x)>$ represents agent A's opinion about x;
(ii) $w^B(x) = <b^B(x),d^B(x),u^B(x)>$ represents agent B's opinion about x;
(iii) $k = u^A(x) + u^B(x) - u^A(x)u^B(x);$
(iv) $w^{A,B}(x) = w^A(B) \oplus w^B(x)$ represents the consensus between agent A's opinion about x and agent B's opinion about x.
(v) $w^{A,B}(x)= <b^{A,B}(x),d^{A,B}(x),u^{A,B}(x)>$ is calculated as follows for $k \neq 0$:
   a. $b^{A,B}(x)=(b^A(x)u^B(x)+b^B(x)u^A(x))/k;$
   b. $d^{A,B}(x)=(d^A(x)u^B(x)+d^B(x)u^A(x))/k;$
   c. $u^{A,B}(x)=(u^A(x) \, u^B(x)) / k$

3.2.2 Applying Subjective Logic in Our Approach

Our goal is to come up with a consensus between the different testimonies and depositions about the violation of a norm considering the reliability of the witnesses. In order to do so, it is important to understand what a testimony/deposition is in the context of subjective logic. The testimony or deposition given by agent A attesting something about a proposition x can be seen as the *A's opinion about x, i.e., $w^A(x)$*.

Second, it is necessary to state that the testimonies (or the opinions of the agents about facts) will be evaluated by the judge agent according to its own opinion about the agents, for instance, $w^J(a)$ where A is one of the witnesses. Such an opinion is directly influenced by the reputation of the agent.

After evaluating the judge's opinions about the agents that have given their testimonies and depositions, it is necessary to evaluate the judge's opinions about testimonies and depositions given by those agents. In order to do so the *discounting operator* will be used. Finally, after having the judge's opinions about all testimonies and depositions, it is necessary to put them all together to form the judge point of view about the violated norm. The *consensus operator* is therefore used.

Judge's Opinions About the Agents:
The reputation provided by the reputation system reflects how much the judge believes in the agent, i.e. $b^J(a)$, and not its whole opinion about such agent, i.e $w^J(a)$.

Judge's Opinions About Testimonies and Depositions Given by the Agents:
The judge's opinion about a testimony/deposition given by an agent, i.e $w^{J:A}(x)$, depends on the judge's opinion about the agent, $w^J(a)$, and the agent's opinion about fact x that is related to the testimony/deposition, $w^A(x)$. In order to evaluate the judge's opinion we use the discounting operator presented in Section 3.2.1 as described in equation (1):

$$w^{J:A}(x) = w^J(a) \otimes w^A(x) = < b^{J:A}(x), d^{J:A}(x), u^{J:A}(x)> \qquad (1)$$

Judge's Point of View About the Violated Norm:
Given that there may exist more then one agent testifying about the same fact (proposition x), all testimonies and depositions can be combined using the consensus operator to produce the judge's own opinion about the proposition x. The consensus puts together all testimonies and depositions while considering the reputation of the witnesses. For instance, let's suppose that A, B and C are agents that provided their testimonies and depositions, the consensus is formed by using equation (2):

$$w^{J:(A,B,C)}(x) = (w^J(a) \otimes w^A(x)) \oplus (w^J(b) \otimes w^B(x)) \oplus (w^J(c) \otimes w^C(x)) \tag{2}$$

3.2.3 Analyzing the Use of Subjective Logic

When there is not enough evidences about a fact stated in a testimony, the greatest challenge about judging it is to set an opinion (verdict) based on facts observed by agents and based on how trustful those agents are. Trust, in this work, represents a degree of reliability of a statement made by an agent. Subjective Logic was used since it is an approach that deals with binary propositions (i.e. true or false propositions) that carry some degree of uncertainty or ignorance, represented, in this work, by the confidence in an agent.

Judging a testimony requires collecting information from different sources, evaluating how trustful the information is and combining the difference sources in a fair and equal way. Subjective Logic offers two operators that can be used to accomplish these tasks, the Recommendation and Consensus operators. The Recommendation operator evaluates the information based on the confidence on the source of the information. The Consensus operator combines all the collected information to make a single opinion (verdict) about the fact stated in the information.

The main advantage about using Subjective Logic is that it offers a formal representation that allows a decision making based on the combination of many evidences (consensus operator) evaluates how confident these evidences are (recommendation). This work uses the agent's reputation as a mean to evaluate the trustworthiness of an agent's statement, which are used as evidences.

The main disadvantage of this method of judgment is that, since its result is expressed in terms of probability, there may be cases where the defendant is convicted while not being guilty in fact, and cases where the defendant is absolved while being, in fact, guilty. Subjective Logic has been used in many works like confidence analysis [9], authentication [11], legal reasoning [10], e-market places [5] and invasion detection systems [20].

4   A Case Study: Cargo Consolidation and Transportation

In order to validate our approach we present a case study based on the real-life cargo consolidation and transportation domain. Cargo consolidation is the act of grouping together small shipments of goods (often from different shippers) into a larger unique unit that is sent to a single destination point (and often to different consignees). Such practice makes possible to the enterprises that provide transportations to reduce the rate of shipping. Importers and exporters that want to ship small cargos may look for consolidator's enterprises that provide cargo consolidation to ship their goods.

An open multi-agent system approach is entirely adequate for developing applications on this domain because such applications mostly involve interactions between different autonomous partners playing different roles in order to accomplish similar objectives. Such applications are governed by several rules that are used to regulate the behavior of the heterogeneous and independently designed entities that reinforce the open characteristic of the systems. In this paper we will contemplate examples of two different norms that are regulated by the proposed mechanism.

Norm I: *The consolidator agent must not change its shipment schedule once it has been presented.*

Norm II: *The consolidator agent must deliver the cargo at the destination on the date established in the transportation agreement.*

4.1 Norm I

In this section we present the judgment process that judge testimonies stating that norm I was violated. We detail the two application dependent steps (Steps V and VI) and also the application independent Step VII that makes a consensus between the testimonies. Let's suppose that a testimony was provided by one of the application agents (an importer, for instance) stating that the agent consolidator has violated norm I. After checking that the testimony is not about a fact that has already been judged (Step I), that the witness is not a law-enforcement agent (Step II), that norm I really applies to the defendant agent (Step III) and that the defendant did not confess that it has violated the norm (Step IV), it is necessary to judge the testimony according to the particular characteristics of norm I (application dependent Step V).

In order to judge testimonies stating violation of norm I, such testimonies must inform shipment schedule firstly defined by the consolidator agent and the actual shipment schedule. One possible application strategy to judge such testimonies is described below. It supposes that there is a system's resource that stores the shipment schedules. The resource is analyzed with the aim to compare the information provided in the testimony with the stored information. If the schedule provided by the resource is equal to the first schedule available in the testimony, the schedule was not changed and the testimony is discarded. If the schedule provided by the resource is different to the actual schedule provided by the testimony, the testimony is also discarded because the testimony describes a fact that cannot be confirmed. In both cases the witness is providing a false testimony. The judgment process is finished and the defendant is considered 100% innocent (Step VIII).

Nevertheless, if the schedule provided by the resource is equal to the actual schedule provided by the testimony, the judgment process should continues in order to find out if the schedule was really changed. Since the application does not have logs to inform when resources are updated, the alternative to find out if the consolidator agent has really changed the schedule is to ask other agents about their opinions (application dependent Step VI). The information provided by the witness is confronted with the information provided by other agents, in this case, with the opinion of two others importers and two exporters about the violation of norm I.

The decision (Step VII) is established based on the information provided by the testimony, the defendant statement and the importers' and exporters' depositions by using subjective logic. Such testimonies and depositions are analyzed from the point of view of the judge and, therefore, there is a need for evaluating how much the judge believes in each agent. As stated before, the reputation of the agent (provided by the reputation system) reflects how much the judge believes in the agent; $b^J(a) = rep(a)$.

The judge's beliefs are used to evaluate the judge's opinion about the testimonies and depositions provided by the agents. Such opinions ($w^{J:W}(x)$, $w^{J:C}(x)$, $w^{J:I1}(x)$, $w^{J:I2}(x)$, $w^{J:E1}(x)$ and $w^{J:E2}(x)$), evaluated by using equation (2), are depicted in Table 1. We are supposing that the two importers and the two exporters, together with the witness, have stated that the defendant is guilty ($w^A(x)$).

The verdict, i.e the judge point of view about the violated norm, can be provided by applying the consensus operator (equation (2)). In this example the verdict (equation (3)) states that the probability of the consolidator agent has violated norm I is 84%.

$$w^J = w^{J:W}(x) \oplus w^{J:C}(x) \oplus w^{J:I1}(x) \oplus w^{J:I2}(x) \oplus w^{J:E1}(x) \oplus w^{J:E2}(x) = <\mathbf{0.84}, 0.06, 0.1> \quad (3)$$

Table 1. Judge's opinion about the violation of norm I

	Statement	$w^A(x)$	$b^J(a)$	$w^J(a) \otimes w^A(x) = w^{J:A}(x)$
Witness	Guilty	<1,0,0>	0.54	$w^{J:W}(x) = <0.54,0,0.46>$
Consolidator Agent	Innocent	<0,1,0>	0.33	$w^{J:C}(x) = <0,0.33,0.67>$
Importer1	Guilty	<1,0,0>	0.75	$w^{J:I1}(x) = <0.75,0,0.25>$
Importer2	Guilty	<1,0,0>	0.53	$w^{J:I2}(x) = <0.53,0,0.47>$
Exporter1	Guilty	<1,0,0>	0.57	$w^{J:E1}(x) = <0.57,0,0.43>$
Exporter2	Guilty	<1,0,0>	0.66	$w^{J:E2}(x) = <0.64,0,0.34>$

4.2 Norm II

In this section we also focus on the two application dependent steps (Steps V and VI) and on Step VII while illustrating the judgment process of norm II. As in Section 4.1, we assume that the judge system could not provide a verdict before executing Step V.

In order to judge testimonies stating violations of norm II, such testimonies must contain the transportation documents called House Bill of Landing (HBL) and Master Bill of Landing (MBL). A bill of landing is a document issued by the carrier (the consolidator agent, in this case) that describes the goods, the details of the intended transportation, and the conditions of the transportation. The difference between HBL and MBL is that the MBL describes several small cargos consolidated in a single shipment and the HBL describes each small cargo.

Therefore, in step V, the judge must first ensure that the exporter has really delivered the cargo at the place designated by the consolidator on the appropriated date. When this task is accomplished, the consolidator gives a copy of the HBL (related to the cargo delivered by the exporter) to the exporter. The judge can, therefore, ask the exporter about his copy of the HBL. If the exporter does not have this document, the judgment process is finished, the witness' testimony is considered false and the defendant is considered 100% innocent (Step VIII). The consolidator agent has not delivered the cargo because the exporter has not delivered its cargo to the consolidator agent.

On the other hand, if the exporter has its copy of the HBL the judge must execute step VI, continuing the judgment process to come to a verdict. Since, the witness' cargo has been consolidated with others cargos, the judge may ask all other importers mentioned in the MBL if their cargos have been delivered in the correct date and place. After receiving the importers depositions, the judge needs to execute step VII, where it puts together all statements while considering the reputations of consolidator agent and all importers of the mentioned shipment. We are supposing that there were three cargos consolidated in this shipment. Table 2 depicts the judge's opinion about the testimony and depositions provided by the witness, the consolidator agent and the two importers ($w^{J:C}(x)$, $w^{J:I1}(x)$, $w^{J:I2}(x)$ and $w^{J:I3}(x)$).

The verdict, i.e judge point of view about the violated norm, can be provided by applying the consensus operator, as shown in equation (4). In this example the verdict states that the probability of the consolidator agent has violated norm II is 76%.

$$w^J = w^{J:W}(x) \oplus w^{J:C}(x) \oplus w^{J:I1}(x) \oplus w^{J:I2}(x) = <\mathbf{0.76}, 0.18, 0.06> \qquad (4)$$

Table 2. Judge's opinion about the violation of norm II

	Statement	$w^A(x)$	$b^J(a)$	$w^J(a) \otimes w^A(x) = w^{J:A}(x)$
Witness	Innocent	<0,1,0>	0.75	$w^{J:W}(x) = <0,0.75,0.25>$
Consolidator Agent	Guilty	<1,0,0>	0.23	$w^{J:C}(x) = <0.23,0,0.77>$
Importer1	Guilty	<1,0,0>	0.47	$w^{J:I1}(x) = <0.47,0,0.53>$
Importer2	Guilty	<1,0,0>	0.92	$w^{J:I2}(x) = <0.92,0,0.08>$

The approaches that governs only the interactions between agents, such as [14] [7], could not govern norm I since this norm govern the access to a resource. As stated in Section 1, there are approaches that govern the public messages and visible actions, both in the system point of view. Such approaches could only be used to enforce norm I and II if we consider (i) that the shipment schedules of a consolidator agent are public resources and, therefore, every action done in such resource are visible actions and (ii) that the deliveries done by the consolidator agent are public messages, that is not usually the case. Moreover, note that both strategies presented in sections 4.1 and 4.2 are simple examples that can be used to judge the testimonies related to norms I and II. Other more complex and completely different strategies could have been implemented to judge the same testimonies.

5 Conclusion

In this paper we present a governance mechanism based on testimonies given by agents that have perceived norm violations. Since a violation of a norm influences (injures) the execution of an agent, perceiving it will be a natural consequence of the regular execution of that agent. The mechanism judges the testimonies it receives trying to differentiate true and false testimonies in order to provide a verdict. The governance mechanism was implemented as a framework that supports, by now, the judgment and reputation sub-systems (section 2.2). The main advantages of the proposed mechanism are: (i) it does not interfere in the agents' privacy; (ii) it can be used to enforce norms associated not only with interactions but also with the execution of different actions, such as the access to resources; and (iii) it does not assume that the system can do all the work of finding out the violations and enforcing the norms.

Whereas we believe that the advantages of our proposed mechanism are really important, it has some potential weaknesses. First, it may be difficult to distinguish if a testimony is true or false and, therefore, to provide a good verdict. We proposed to solve this problem by using probability based on subjective logic while providing the verdicts. Second, violations that go without testimonies will not be punished. This could lead to an undesired system state. One way to overcome this issue is motivating the agents to give their testimonies by using an agent rewards program, for instance. Another important drawback is that the effort to implement an agent under the proposed governance system may increase since it needs not only to perceive facts, but also to associate them with possible norm violations. To minimize this impact, the judgment subsystem provides a mechanism that can be used by the agents to associate facts with norms violations. In order to improve our work we are in the way of adding some argumentation aspects to the judgment process. This will improve the set of evidences used for and against a verdict.

References

1. Aldewereld, H., Dignum, F., García-Camino, A., Noriega, P., Rodríguez-Aguilar, J.A., Sierra, C.: Operationalisation of Norms for Usage in Electronic Institutions. In: Proc. of the Workshop on Coordination, Organization, Institutions and Norms in agent systems, pp. 223–225 (2006)
2. Yu, B., Singh, M.: Detecting Deception in Reputation Management. In: Proc. of the 2nd International Joint Conference on Autonomous Agents and MultiAgent Systems (AAMAS 2003), pp. 73–80 (2003)
3. Boella, G., van der Torre, L.: Regulative and Constitutive Norms in Normative Multi-Agent Systems. In: Proceeding of KS, pp. 255–265. AAAI Press, Menlo Park (2004)
4. Cremonini, M., Omicini, A., Zambonelli, F.: Coordination and Access Control in Open Distributed Agent Systems: The TuCSoN Approach. In: Porto, A., Roman, G.-C. (eds.) COORDINATION 2000. LNCS, vol. 1906, pp. 99–114. Springer, Heidelberg (2000)
5. Daskalopulu, A., Dimitrakos, T., Maibaum, T.: E-Contract Fulfilment and Agents' Attitudes. In: Proc. ERCIM WG E-Commerce Workshop on The Role of Trust in e-Business (2001)
6. Esteva, M., Rodriguez-Aguilar, J.A., Rosell, B., Arcos, AMELI, J. L.: An Agent-based Middleware for Electronic Institutions. In: Proc. of the 3rd Int. Joint Conf. on Autonomous Agents and MAS, USA, pp. 236–243 (2004)
7. Esteva, M., de la Cruz, D., Sierra, C.: Islander: An Electronic Institutions Editor. In: Proc. of Int. Conf. on Autonomous Agents and Multi-Agent Systems, pp. 1045–1052 (2002)
8. Guedes, J., Silva, V., Lucena, C.J.P.: A Reputation Model Based on Testimonies. In: Proceedings of Workshop on Agent-Oriented Information Systems at CAiSE, pp. 37–47 (2006)
9. Jøsang, A., Hayward, R., Pope, S.: Trust Network Analysis with Subjective Logic. In: Australasian Computer Science Conference (2006)
10. Jøsang, A., Bondi, V.A.: Legal Reasoning with Subjective Logic. Artificial Reasoning and Law 8(4), 289–315 (2000)

11. Jøsang, A.: An Algebra for Assessing Trust in Certification Chains. In: Proceedings of the Network and Distributed Systems Security Symposium (NDSS 1999). The Internet Society (1999)
12. Jøsang, A.: An Algebra for Assessing Trust in Certification Chains. In: Proc. Network and Distributed Systems Security Symposium (1999)
13. López, F.: Social Powers and Norms: Impact on Agent Behaviour. PhD thesis. University of Southampton. UK (2003)
14. Minsky, N., Ungureanu, V.: Law-Governed Interaction: A Coordination & Control Mechanism for Heterogeneous Distributed Systems. ACM TSEM 9(3), 273–305 (2000)
15. Paes, R.: Regulating the Interaction Between Agents in Open Systems – a Law Approach. Master's thesis, Pontificia Univeridade Catolica do Rio de Janeiro, PUC-Rio, Rio de Janeiro, BR (2005)
16. Patel, J., Teacy, W., Jennings, et al.: Monitoring, Policing and Trust for Grid-Based Virtual Organizations. In: Proc. of the UK e-Science All Hands Meeting 2005, UK, pp. 891–898 (2005)
17. Silva, V.: Implementing Norms that Govern Non-Dialogical Actions. In: Sichman, J.S., et al. (eds.) COIN 2007 Workshops. LNCS (LNAI), vol. 4870, pp. 218–231. Springer, Heidelberg (2008)
18. Singh, M.: An Ontology for Commitments in Multiagent Systems: Toward a Unification of Normative Concepts. In: Artificial Intelligence and Law, vol. 7(1), pp. 97–113. Springer, Heidelberg (1999)
19. Stigler, S.M.: Thomas Bayes' Bayesian Inference. Journal of the Royal Statistical Society 145(A), 250–258 (1982)
20. Svensson, H., Jøsang, A.: Correlation of Intrusion Alarms with Subjective Logic. In: Proceedings of the sixth Nordic Workshop on Secure IT systems (NordSec 2001), Copenhagen, Denmark (2001)
21. Vázquez-Salceda, J., Aldewereld, H., Dignum, F.: Implementing Norms in Multiagent Systems. In: Lindemann, G., Denzinger, J., Timm, I.J., Unland, R. (eds.) MATES 2004. LNCS (LNAI), vol. 3187, pp. 313–327. Springer, Heidelberg (2004)

Implementing Norms That Govern Non-dialogical Actions

Viviane Torres da Silva*

Departamento de Sistemas Informáticos y Computación – UCM, Spain, Madrid
viviane@fdi.ucm.es

Abstract. The governance of open multi-agent systems is particular important since those systems are composed of heterogeneous, autonomous and independently designed agents. Such governance is usually provided by the establishment of norms that regulate the actions of agents. Although there are several approaches that formally describe norms, there are still few of them that propose their implementation. In this paper we propose the implementation of norms that govern non-dialogical actions by extending one of the approaches that regulate dialogical ones. Non-dialogical actions are not related to the interactions between agents but to tasks executed by agents that characterize, for instance, the access to resources, their commitment to play roles or their movement into environments and organizations.

Keywords: Norm, governance of multi-agent system, non-dialogical action, implementation of norm.

1 Introduction

The governance of open multi-agent systems (MAS) copes with the heterogeneity, autonomy and diversity of interests among agents that can work towards similar or different ends [9] by establishing norms. The set of system norms defines actions that agents are prohibited, permitted or obligated to do [1] and [12].

Several works have been proposed in order to define the theoretical aspects of norms [3] and [5], to formally define those norms [2] and [4], and to implement them [7], [8], [9], [10] and [13]. In this paper we focus on the implementation of norms. Our goal is to present an approach where dialogical and non-dialogical norms can be described and regulated. Non-dialogical actions are not related to the interactions between agents but to tasks executed by agents that characterize, for instance, the access to resources, their commitment to play roles or their movement in environments and organizations. From the set of analyzed proposals for implementing norms, few approaches considers non-dialogical actions [9], [10] and [13]. Although, the authors present some issues on the verification and enforcement of norms, they do no demonstrate how such issues should be implemented. Other approaches such as [7] and [8] deal with e-Institutions and, thus, consider illocutions as the only action performed in such systems.

---

* Research supported by the Juan de la Cierva programa, Comunidad de Madrid S-0505/ TIC-407 and MEC-SP TIC2003-01000.

J.S. Sichman et al. (Eds.): COIN 2007, LNAI 4870, pp. 232–244, 2008.
© Springer-Verlag Berlin Heidelberg 2008

Our approach extends the work presented in [8] with the notion of non-dialogical actions proposed in [13]. A normative language is presented in [8] to describe illocutions (dialogical actions) that might be dependent on temporal constraints or the occurrence of events. We have extended the normative language in order to be possible to specify non-dialogical norms that state obligations, permissions or prohibitions over the execution of actions of agents' plans (as proposed in [13]) and of object methods. Similar to the approach presented in [8], we have also used Jess[1] to implement the governance mechanism that regulates the behavior of agents. The mechanism activates norms and fires violations (Jess rules) according to the executed (dialogical or non-dialogical) actions (Jess facts).

Although both the normative language and the implementation rules can be used by agents and by the governance mechanism, the approach focuses on the implementation of norms from the system perspective [13], i.e., both agents and the governance mechanism will use the language and the rules to find out: What are the activated and deactivated norms? What are the fulfilled and the violated norms? What are the applied sanctions?

The paper is organized as follows. Section 2 describes the example we are using to illustrate our approach. Section 3 intends to clearly present the difference between dialogical and non-dialogical actions. Section 4 points out the main concepts of the extended normative language and Section 5 describes the implementation of the governance engine in Jess. Section 6 concludes our work and presents some future work.

2   Applied Example

In order to exemplify our approach, we have defined a set of six norms that govern a simplified version of a soccer game. The soccer game is composed of agents playing one of the three available roles: referee, coach and player (kicker or goalkeeper). The responsibilities of a referee in a soccer game are: to start the game, stop it, check the players' equipments and punish the players. The available punishments are: to show a yellow card, send off a player, and declare a penalty. The possible actions of a player during a game are: kick the ball and handle the ball. The coach role is limited to substitute players. Besides those actions, all agents are able to move and, therefore, enter and leave the game field. The six norms that regulate our simple soccer game are the following:

Norm 1: *The referee must check the players' equipments before starting the game.*
Norm 2: *A coach cannot substitute more than three players in the same game.*
Norm 3: *Players cannot leave the game field during the game.*
Norm 4: *The referee must send off a player after (s)he has done a second caution in the same match.* In this simplified version of the soccer game, there is only one situation that characterizes a caution; a player leaving the game field before the referee has stopped it. At the first caution, the agent receives a yellow card.
Norm 5: *Kickers cannot handle the ball.*
Norm 6: *The referee must declare a penalty if kicker handles the ball.*

---

[1] Jess is a rule-based system. http://www.jessrules.com/

3 Dialogical and Non-dialogical Actions

Non-dialogical actions are the ones not related to interactions between agents. Not all actions executed by agents in MAS provide support for sending and receiving messages between them [13]. There are actions that modify the environment (for example, updating the state of a resource) that do not characterize a message being sent to or received from another agent. In the soccer game example, the actions of kicking the ball or handling it are non-dialogical actions. In addition, actions that modify the position of an agent in an environment do not characterize a dialogical action either. The actions of entering or leaving the game field are not dialogical ones.

Some actions can be defined as a dialogical or a non-dialogical one, depending on how the problem is modeled. In the soccer game, to start a game and to stop it was considered dialogical actions. Agents receive a message informing about the state of the game. The dialogical actions of the soccer game example are: to start the game, stop it, punish player, declare penalty and show the yellow card. The non-dialogical ones are: enter in the game field, leave it, handle the ball, kick the ball, substitute a player and check the player's equipment.

4 Describing Norms

Since our intention is to contribute to the work presented in [7], we extend the BNF normative language to represent non-dialogical actions and to describe conditions and time situations that are defined by those non-dialogical actions. In addition, the specification of dialogical actions already presented in the previous normative language was extended in order to be possible to describe messages attributes stated in the FIPA ACL language[2].

4.1 Specifying Non-dialogical Actions

The original BNF description of the normative language defines norms as the composition of a *deontic* concept (characterizing obligation, prohibition or permission) and an action followed by a temporal situation and an *if* condition, when pertinent. In such definition, actions are limited to utterance of illocutions.

In our proposed extension, the *action* concept was generalized to also describe non-dialogical ones. Dialogical and non-dialogical actions are complementary, as illustrated by the grammar that specifies that these are the only two possible actions' kinds. Non-dialogical actions state the entities whose behavior is being restricted and the actions that are being regulated. Due to the way the *entity* concept was defined, a non-dialogical norm, i.e., a norm that regulates non-dialogical actions, can be applied to all agents in the system, to a group of agents, to agents playing a given role or even to a unique agent.

```
<norm> ::= <deontic_concept> '(' <action> ')'
  | <deontic_concept> '(' <action><temporal_situation> ')'
  | <deontic_concept> '(' <action> IF <if_condition> ')'
  | <deontic_concept> '(' <action> <temporal_situation> IF <if_condition> ')'
<deontic_concept> ::= OBLIGED | FORBIDDEN | PEMITTED
```

---

[2] http://www.fipa.org/repository/aclspecs.html

```
<action>::= <non_dialogical_action> | <dialogical_action>
<non_dialogical_action> ::= <entity> 'EXECUTE' <exec>
<entity>::= <agent>':'<role> | <role> | <agent> | <group> | 'ALL'
```

In this paper we are limiting non-dialogical actions to the execution of an object/class method or to the execution of the action of an agent plan [13]. Non-dialogical norms that regulate the access to resources specify the entities that have restricted access to execute the methods of the resource. Non-dialogical norms that regulate (non-dialogical) actions not related to the access to resources describe entities that have restricted access to the execution of an action of a plan.

```
<exec> ::= <objectORclass>'.'<method>'('<parameters>')'''('<contract>')'
| <plan>':'<action>'('<parameters>')'''('<contract>')'
|...!the parameters and the contract can be omitted
```

In [13], the authors affirm that non-dialogical actions can be described as abstract actions that are not in the set of actions defined by the agents or in the set of methods of the classes. Agents must translate the actions and methods to be executed into more abstract ones. With the aim to help agents in such transformation, we propose the use of contracts. A contract is used to formally describe the behavior of the actions/methods while specifying its invariants, pre and post-conditions [11]. We do not impose any language to be used to describe the terms of a contracts[3].

```
<contract> ::= <pre>';'<post>';'<inv> |... !pre, post and inv can be omitted
<pre> ::= <expression> | <expression> <opl> <pre> ...
<opl> ::='AND' | 'OR' | 'XOR' | 'NOR'|... !pre, post and inv are similarly defined
```

Such extensions make possible to describe, for instance, norms that regulate the execution of an action while describing the parameters required for its execution and the contract that defines it. The extensions enable, for example, the definition of *norm 2*. Such norm states that a coach cannot substitute more than three players in the same game. The coach cannot execute an action that substitutes players if the number of substitutions is already 3.

```
FORBIDDEN ( coach EXECUTE managingTeam:SubstitutePlayer (outPlayer,inPlayer,team)
            ( team.coach = coach; team.substitutions = team.substitutions@pre+1 AND
              team.playersInField->excludes(outPlayer)AND
              team.playersInField->includes(inPlayer); )
    IF team.substitutions >= 3 )
```

The action governed by *norm 1* is also a non-dialogical action and states that the referee must check the players' equipment before starting the game. The action of checking the equipment is a non-dialogical action since the referee needs not to interact with the player but with its equipment. On the other hand, the action of starting a game is a dialogical action modeled as a message from the referee to everybody in the game (as will be presented in Section 4.4).

```
OBLIGED ( referee EXECUTE managingGame:checkEquipment (players)
    BEFORE ( UTTER(game; sᵢ; INFORM(;referee;;[;gameStart;;;;;])))) )
```

---

[3] In this paper we are using OCL (http://www.omg.org/technology/documents/formal/ocl.htm)

4.2 Extending the Temporal Situations

The *temporal situation* concept specified in the normative language is used to describe the period of valid (or active) norms. Norms can be activated or deactivated due to the execution of an (dialogical or non-dialogical) action, to the change in the state of an object or an agent, to the occurrence of a deadline, and to the combination of such possibilities. In the previous normative languages the authors only consider the execution of dialogical actions and the occurrence of a deadline as temporal situations. The normative language was extended to contemplate the activation and deactivation of norms due to the execution of non-dialogical actions, to the change in the state of an object or an agent (without specifying the action that was responsible for that) and to the combination of the above mentioned factors (as specified in the *situation* concept).

```
<temporal_situation> ::= BEFORE <situation> | AFTER <situation>
| BETWEEN '(' <situation> ',' <situation> ')'
```

The extensions enable, for example, the definition of *norm 3* that states that players cannot leave the game between its initial and its interruption, as shown below.

```
FORBIDDEN ( player EXECUTE moving:LeaveField ()
                      ( agent.position@pre=inField; agent.position<>inField; )
  BETWEEN ( UTTER(game; sᵢ; INFORM(;referee;;[;gameStart;;;;;])),
            UTTER(game; sᵢ; INFORM(;referee;;[;gameStopped;;;;;]))  ))
```

Another norm that makes use of temporal situation is *norm 4*. It states that the referee must send off a player after (s)he receives a second caution in the same match. If player leaves the field of play and (s)he has already been shown a yellow card, the referee must send him(her) off. Note that such *norm 4* is conditioned to the execution of an action governed by *norm 3* and, thus, the *after* condition is exactly *norm 3*.

```
OBLIGED ( UTTER(game;si;CAUTION(;referee;;kicker[;sentOff;;soccerGame;;;;]))
  AFTER ( player EXECUTE moving:LeaveField()
                      ( agent.position@pre=inField;agent.position<>inField; )
            BETWEEN ( UTTER(game; sᵢ; INFORM(;referee;;[;gameStart;;;;;])),
                      UTTER(game; sᵢ; INFORM(;referee;;[;gameStopped;;;;;]))  ))
  IF player.yellowCard = true )
```

4.3 Extending the IF Condition

The *if condition* defined in the original normative language is used to introduce conditions over variables, agents' observable attributes or executed dialogical actions. Therefore, by using such language it is not possible to describe *nom 6* since it is conditioned to the execution of a non-dialogical action. Our proposed extension makes possible to specify a condition related to an executed non-dialogical action or to a fired norm.

```
<if_condition> ::= <cond_expression> | NOT '(' <cond_expression> ')'
<cond_expression> ::= <condition> | NOT <condition>
  | <condition> ',' <if_condition> | NOT <condition> ',' <if_condition>
<condition> ::= <action> | <deontic_concept> '(' <action> ')' |...
```

Norm 6 defines that the referee must declare a penalty if a kicker handles the ball. The non-dialogical action of handling the ball is the *if condition* of *norm 6* and can be described as follows.

```
OBLIGED (UTTER(game; si; PENALTY(;referee;kickerTeam;[;penalty;;soccerGame;;;;]))
    IF kicker EXECUTE play:handleBall)
```

4.4 Extending Dialogical Actions

In [8], the authors represent the execution of dialogical actions by the identification of the action (not carried out yet) of submitting an illocution. In their point of view, an illocution is an information that carries a message to be sent by an agent playing a role to another agent playing another role. The *illocution* concept was extended to be possible to omit the agents that send and receive the messages. Not always will be possible to specify the agents that will send and receive the messages while describing the norms. Sometimes only the roles that those agents will be playing can be identified. Moreover, the roles of the sender and receiver can also be omitted. It may be the case that no matter the one is sending a message or no mater the one is receiving it, the norm must be obeyed.

```
<dialogical_action> ::= 'UTTER(' <scene> ';' <state> ';' <illocution> ')'
| 'UTTERED(' <scene> ';' <state> ';' <illocution> ')'
<illocution> ::= <perf>'('<sender>';'<role>';'<receiver> ';'<role>'['<msg>'])'
|...!it is possible to omit the senders, receivers and also their roles
```

Since a message can be sent to several agents, the *receiver* concept was also extended to make possible to describe the group of agents that will be the receiver of the message. Note that it is only possible to describe in the grammar norms that specified messages to be send and not messages to be received. In addition, it is the agent that is receiving the message the one responsible for relating the message being received to a message that should have been sent, in the case of obligations for instance.

```
<sender> ::= <agent>
<receiver> ::= <agent> | <group>
```

By using the extensions provided above for illocution, it is possible to model *norms 1* (Section 4.1), *4* (Section 4.2) and *6* (Section 4.3) that omit the agent identification that is playing the referee role. In such cases, it is not important to identify the agent but only the role that the agent is playing. *Norm 1* also omits the receiver and its role to characterize that the message is being broadcasted. *Norm 4* identifies the role of the receiver but does not identify the agent playing the role since the message to be send does not depend on the agent. Moreover, *norm 6* does not identify the receiver agent but the receiver *team* that will be punished.

4.5 Specifying Messages

The *message* concept has not been specified in the previous version of the normative language. We propose to specify such concept since it may be necessary to provide some characteristics of the messages while describing the norms. The *message* concept was extended according to the parameters defined by an ACL message. While describing *norms 4* and *6* we have used the extended *message* concept to point out the ontology being used to support the interpretation of the content expression.

```
<msg> ::= <conversation_id>';'<contents>';'<language_encoding>';
'<ontology_protocol>';'<reply_by>';'<reply_to>';'<reply_with>';'<in_reply_to>
 |...!it is possible to omit any parameter.
```

5   Implementing Norms

Once we have seen how norms can be described, we need to demonstrate how they are implemented. Similar to the approach presented in [8], we have also used Jess to implement the governance mechanism. Jess is a rule-based system that maintains a collection of facts in its knowledge base. Jess was chosen due two main reasons: (i) it provides interfaces to programs in Java and (ii) it is possible to dynamically change the set of rules defined in Jess from the execution of Java programs. MAS implemented in Java can make use of the knowledge base and the declarative rules provided by Jess. Such MAS can also update the set of rules during the execution.

The use of Jess makes possible to describe facts and rules that are fired according to the stated facts. In our approach, facts are agents' observable attributes, (dialogical and non-dialogical) actions executed by the agents, the norms activated by the rules, and the information about norm violations. The rules are fired according to the executed actions or observable attributes and can activate norms or assert violations.

5.1   The Use of Jess

In Jess, facts are described based on templates that specify the structure of the facts. We have defined a template to define agents' observable attributes and three templates to describe actions: one for describing dialogical actions and two for describing the two different kinds of non-dialogical actions contemplated in the paper (method calling and execution of the action of an agent plan). Besides, we have also described nine templates for describing each of the three norm kinds (obliged, permitted and forbidden) associated with the three different actions (message, method calling and plan execution). In addition, one template was defined for being used to describe norm violations. Such template points out the norm that was violated and the facts that have violated the norm. The two examples below illustrate templates to describe an obligation norm to execute the action of a plan and a violation.

```
(deftemplate OBLIGED-non-dialogical-action-plan
     (slot entity)(slot role)(slot plan) (slot action) (slot attribs (type String))
     (slot contract-pre (type String)) (slot contract-post (type String))
     (slot contract-inv (type String)) (slot beliefUpdated (type String))
     (slot condition (type String)))

(deftemplate VIOLATION (slot norm-violated) (multislot action-done))
```

Rules are composed of two parts. The left-hand side of the rule describes patterns of facts that need to be inserted in the knowledge base in order to fire the rule. The right-hand side defines facts that will be upload to the knowledge base if the rule is fired. In our approach, these facts will be norms or norms' violations. Examples of rules are presented in Sections 5.3, 5.4, 5.5 and 5.6.

5.2   Some Guidelines

For each application norm, there is (usually) a need for describing three rules in Jess. The first rule is used to state the norm by conditioning it to the facts that activate the norm. If the facts are inserted into the knowledge base, the rule is fired and the norm is activated. The second rule deactivates the norm retracting it from the knowledge base. The period during which some norms are active are limited and conditioned to the addition of some facts in the knowledge base. The third and final rule points out the violations. Prohibitions are violated if facts are inserted into the knowledge base during while they are forbidden and permissions are violated if the facts are inserted into the knowledge outside the period during which they are permitted. The violations of obligations occur if facts are not inserted into the knowledge base in the corresponding period. The following Sections will demonstrate how to implement those rules according to the *temporal situations* and *if conditions* mentioned in Section 4.

5.3 Simple Obligations, Permissions and Prohibitions

Norms that describe obligations, permissions or prohibitions over the execution of actions without defining any temporal situation or if condition are always active. Such norms are never deactivated no matter what happens.

Although it is possible to describe obligations and permissions over the execution of a norm without stating any condition, it is not possible to state violations. For each obligation or permission that is not associated with any temporal situation or if condition, only one rule that states the norm must be described. The obligations characterize that the actions must be executed but do not state when the executions must be checked. Permissions characterize that such actions can always be executed, and, therefore, such norms are never violated by the permitted agents. When permissions are applied to sub-sets of agents, we assume that prohibitions are stated to the ones not permitted to execute the actions. Prohibitions can do be checked and violations can be fired in case the actions are executed. Therefore, for each norm that describes prohibition for the execution of an action, two rules need to be defined: (i) to assert the prohibition; and (ii) to assert the violations if the forbidden facts are added to the knowledge base.

In order to exemplify the use of Jess we describe the implementation of *norm 5*. Rule (i) asserts the prohibition that is not conditioned to any fact. Rule (ii) asserts the violation if a kicker handles the ball.

```
;(rule i)
(defrule forbidden:KickerHandleBall
=> (assert (FORBIDDEN-non-dialogical-action-plan (entity kicker)(plan play)
                                                 (action handleBall))))

;(rule ii)
(defrule violation:KickerHandleBall
?fact <-(non-dialogical-action-plan (entity kicker)(plan play)(action handleBall))
?forbidden <- (FORBIDDEN-non-dialogical-action-plan (entity kicker)(plan play)
                                                    (action handleBall))
=> (assert (VIOLATION (norm-violated (fact-id ?forbidden))
                      (action-done (fact-id ?fact)))))
```

5.4 Norms Regulating Actions Executed Before the Occurrence of a Fact

Obligations for executing an action X before the occurrence of a fact W are verified testing if X has been executed before W occurs. For governing such norms three rules are defined: rule (i) asserts the obligation for execute X; rule (ii) retracts the obligation if X has been executed and W occurs; and rule (iii) asserts a violation if W occurs but X has not been executed (what can be verified by the existence of the obligation).

Permissions for executing an action X before the occurrence of W are verified testing if X is executed after W. In such case, the execution of X is not permitted. These
norms are governed by three rules: rule (i) asserts the permission for execute X; rule
(ii) retracts the permission if W occurs; and rule (iii) asserts a violation if W occurs
and X is executed.

Prohibitions for executing an action X before the occurrence of an action W are
verified testing if X is executed and W has not occurred. Such norms are also governed by three rules: rule (i) asserts the prohibition; rule (ii) retracts the prohibition if
W occurs; and rule (iii) asserts a violation if X is executed and W has not occurred
(what can be verified by the existence of the prohibition). We assume that W can
occur many times but obligations should be fulfilled before the first time it occurs and
permissions and prohibitions are only active before its first occurrence.

Norm 1 is a good example to illustrate the implementation of norms that govern the
actions that must be executed before another one. Since the norm defines that a referee is *obliged* to check the equipment of the players *before* starting the game, three
rules was defined to govern such norm. Rule (i) states the obligation. Rule (ii) retracts
the obligation if the referee has checked the player equipment when the game starts.
Rule (iii) asserts a violation if the game has been started and the obligation still holds
informing that the referee has not checked the equipment. The obligation governs a
non-dialogical action that must be executed after a dialogical action.

```
;(rule i)
(defrule obliged:CheckEquipment
 =>(assert (OBLIGED-non-dialogical-action-plan (entity referee)(plan managingGame)
      (action checkEquipment)(attribs players)
      (condition "BEFORE UTTER(game; sᵢ;INFORM(;referee;; [;gameStart;;;;;;]))"))))

;(rule ii)
(defrule retract:CheckEquipment
(non-dialogical-action-plan (entity referee)(plan managingGame)
                       (action checkEquipment)(attribs players))
(dialogical-action (scene game)(state si)(performative inform)(sRole referee)
                   (message "gameStart"))
?obliged <- (OBLIGED-non-dialogical-action-plan (ntity referee)
      (plan managingGame)(action checkEquipment)(attribs players)
      (condition "BEFORE UTTER(game; sᵢ;INFORM(;referee;; [;gameStart;;;;;;]))"))
=> (retract ?obliged))

;(rule iii)
(defrule violation:CheckEquipment
?fact <- (dialogical-action (scene game)(state si)(performative inform)
                        (sRole referee)(message "gameStart"))
?obliged <- (OBLIGED-non-dialogical-action-plan (ntity referee)
      (plan managingGame)(action checkEquipment)(attribs players)
      (condition "BEFORE UTTER(game; sᵢ;INFORM(;referee;; [;gameStart;;;;;;]))"))
=> (assert (VIOLATION (norm-violated (fact-id ?obliged))
                  (action-done (fact-id ?fact)))))
```

5.5   Norms Regulating Actions Executed After the Occurrence of a Fact

Obligations for executing an action X after the occurrence of Y (or if Y occurs) cannot be governed since it is not possible to affirm that the execution of X will never
occur after the execution of Y. It is not possible to state a rule that fires a violation for
such norm since the action X can be executed anytime after Y has occurred. In order
to govern such norms it is necessary to state any temporal situation limiting the time

for the execution of X after Y has occurred. The temporal concept *between* should be used instead of *after* or *if* for governing such obligations. *Norms 4* and *6* are examples of norms that should be implemented by using *between*, as depicted in Section 5.6.

Permissions for executing X after the occurrence of Y can be governed by two rules: rule (i) asserts the permission if Y occurs; and rule (ii) asserts a violation if X is executed but Y has not occurred yet (i.e., there is no permission for execute X).

The governance of prohibitions for executing X after the occurrence of Y is the opposite to the governance of the related permission. Such governance is also characterized by two rules: rule (i) asserts the prohibition if Y occurs; and rule (ii) asserts a violation if X is executed after Y has occurred or if Y is true.

In order to exemplify a norm that use the *if condition* we refer to *norm 2*. This norm defines that the coach cannot execute an action that substitutes players if the number of substitutions is equal or greater than 3. The prohibition governs a non-dialogical action that is condition to the state of an object.

```
;(rule i)
(defrule forbidden:PlayerSubstitution
(attribute-value (objectORagent team)(attribute substitutions)(value 3))
=> (assert (FORBIDDEN-non-dialogical-action-plan (role coach)(plan managingTeam)
               (action substitutePlayer)(attribs outPlayer,inPlayer,team)
               (contract-pre "team.coach=coach")
               (contract-post "team.substitutions=team.substitutions@pre+1 AND
                               team.playersInField->excludes(outPlayer) AND
                               team.playersInField->includes(inPlayer)") )))


;(rule ii)
(defrule violation:PlayerSubstitution
?fact1 <- (non-dialogical-action-plan (role coach)(plan managingTeam)
                                      (action substitutePlayer))
?fact2 <- (attribute-value (objectORagent team)(attribute substitutions))
?forbidden <-(FORBIDDEN-non-dialogical-action-plan (role coach)(plan managingTeam)
               (action substitutePlayer)(attribs outPlayer,inPlayer,team)
               (contract-pre "team.coach=coach")
               (contract-post "team.substitutions = team.substitutions@pre+1 AND
                               team.playersInField->excludes(outPlayer) AND
                               team.playersInField->includes(inPlayer)"))
=> (if (>= (fact-slot-value ?fact 2) 3 ) then
       (assert (VIOLATION (action-done ?fact1  ?fact2)
                          (norm-violated ?forbidden))) ))
```

5.6 Norms Regulating Actions Executed Between the Occurrence of Two Facts

A norm that states an obligation for executing an action X after the occurrence of Y and before the execution of W is governed by three rules: rule (i) asserts the obligation for execute X if Y occurs; rule (ii) retracts the obligation if X is executed and if W occurs; and rule (iii) asserts a violation if W occurs but X has not been executed.

The permission for executing X between the occurrence of Y and W is governed by the following four rules: rule (i) asserts the permission for execute X if Y occurs; rule (ii) retracts the permission if W occurs; rule (iii) asserts a violation if W occurs and X is executed; and rule (iv) asserts a violation if X is executed but Y has not occurred yet (i.e., if the permission for executing X has not been fired yet).

Prohibitions for executing X between the occurrence of Y and W are governed by three rules: rule (i) asserts the prohibition if Y occurs; rule (ii) retracts the prohibition if W occurs; and rule (iii) asserts a violation if X is executed, Y has occurred but W has not occurred, i.e., X is executed and the prohibitions is still activated. Note that the rules that govern both prohibitions and permissions while using the temporal concept *between* are the combination of the rules used to govern such norms using the *after* and *before* temporal concepts.

The use of *between* can be exemplified by *norm 3*. It states that the player is forbidden to leave the field between the beginning and the end of the game. The norm defines a prohibition to execute a non-dialogical action limited by the execution of two dialogical actions. Rule (i) asserts the prohibition if the first dialogical action is executed, rule (ii) retracts the prohibition if the second dialogical action is executed and rule (iii) declares a violation if the non-dialogical action is executed during while it is being prohibited.

```
;(rule i)
(defrule forbidden:LeaveField
(dialogical-action (scene game)(state si)(performative inform)(sRole referee)
                   (message "gameStart"))
 => (assert (FORBIDDEN-non-dialogical-action-plan (role player)(plan moving)
            (action leaveField)(contract-pre agent.position@pre=inField)
            (contract-post agent.position!=inField ))))

;(rule ii)
(defrule retract:LeaveField
(dialogical-action (scene game)(state si)(performative inform)(sRole referee)
                   (message "gameStop"))
?forbidden <- (FORBIDDEN-non-dialogical-action-plan (role player)(plan moving)
              (action leaveField)(contract-pre agent.position@pre=inField)
              (contract-post agent.position!=inField ))
 => (retract ?forbidden))

;(rule iii)
(defrule violation:LeaveField
(dialogical-action (scene game)(state si)(performative inform)(sRole referee)
                   (message "gameStart"))
?forbidden <- (FORBIDDEN-non-dialogical-action-plan (role player)(plan moving)
              (action leaveField)(contract-pre agent.position@pre=inField)
              (contract-post agent.position!=inField ))
?fact <- (non-dialogical-action-plan (role player)(plan moving)(action leaveField)
         (contract-pre agent.position@pre=inField)
         (contract-post agent.position!=inField ))
 => (assert (VIOLATION (norm-violated (fact-id ?forbidden))
            (action-done (fact-id ?fact)))))
```

Sections 5.3 and 5.5 point out that some obligations over the execution of a norm that cannot be governed. Since obligations need not to be fulfilled immediately after they were declared, it is necessary to inform the period during which the agents are being obligated to execute the action in order to govern them. *Norms 6* and *4* are very good examples of such obligations. *Norm 6*, for instance, defines that the referee must declare a penalty if a kicker handles the ball. However, this norm does not define how much time the referee has to fulfill its obligation. Therefore, it is not possible to affirm that the obligation was not fulfilled since it can be at any time. In order to properly regulate such norm it is needed to provide a limit till when this obligation must be fulfilled. *Norms 6* was adapted to inform that the referee has 1 minute to declare the penalty after the kicker has handled the ball.

```
OBLIGED ( UTTER(game; si; PENALTY(;referee;kickerTeam;[;penalty;;soccerGame;;;;]))
   BETWEEN ( kicker EXECUTE play:handleBall, 1 MINUTES OF kicker EXECUTE
        play:handleBall ) )
```

6 Conclusion

This paper proposes the implementation of norms[4] that govern dialogical and non-dialogical actions by using Jess. The governance system proposed in [6] receives (not always true) testimonies about executed actions that are related to norm violations. After judging the testimonies and concluding that the actions really were executed, such information is uploaded to the Jess knowledge-based. The set of Jess rules are, then, checked and the related norms and violations are fired. The fired norm or violation is also facts accumulated in the Jess database. We have implemented in Jess at least one norm taking into account the three *deontic* concepts, the proposed temporal situations and if conditions presented in the paper by using the soccer game.

Note that the Jess system only receives one information about the execution of an action at a time. Independently of the order of the execution of the actions, the first information sent to Jess is the one that will be processed. If two actions are executed at the same time, the first information to achieve the Jess system will be processed.

Although the current version does not contemplate sanctions and awards, it can be easily extended in order to do so. The sanctions should be provided when the related violations are fired. The awards should be supplied when the norms are retracted and no violation of such norms has been fired. In addition, a (semi)automatic approach for generating Jess rules according to the norms specified by the use of the normative language could be developed.

An automatic approach for generating Jess rules from the norms specified by the use of the normative language is being developed. Our intention is to use such transformer during design time to automatically generate the rules for the specified norms and also during runtime. In case the agents are able to specify new norms according to the normative language during runtime, they could use the proposed transformer to automatically generate new rules and publish them in the Jess engine. We are also investigating the possibility of modifying one of the already available rules. Such transformation should be based on the guidelines provided in section 5.2 and also on its specialization provided in the following sub-sections.

References

1. Boella, G., van der Torre, L.: Regulative and Constitutive Norms in Normative Multi-Agent Systems. In: Proceeding of KS, pp. 255–265. AAAI Press, Menlo Park (2004)
2. Artikis, A., Kamara, L., Pitt, J., Sergot, M.: A Protocol for Resource Sharing in Norm-Governed Ad Hoc Networks. In: Leite, J.A., Omicini, A., Torroni, P., Yolum, p. (eds.) DALT 2004. LNCS (LNAI), vol. 3476, pp. 221–238. Springer, Heidelberg (2005)
3. Broersen, J., Dignum, F., Dignum, V., Meyer, J.: Designing a deontic logic of deadlines. In: Lomuscio, A., Nute, D. (eds.) DEON 2004. LNCS (LNAI), vol. 3065, pp. 43–56. Springer, Heidelberg (2004)
4. Cranefield, S.: A Rule Language for Modelling and Monitoring Social Expectations in Multi-Agent Systems. In: Boissier, O., Padget, J.A., Dignum, V., Lindemann, G., Matson, E., Ossowski, S., Sichman, J.S., Vázquez-Salceda, J. (eds.) ANIREM 2005 and OOOP 2005. LNCS (LNAI), vol. 3913, pp. 246–258. Springer, Heidelberg (2006)

---

[4] The full normative language described in the paper and the Jess program used to illustrate our approach are available at http://maude.sip.ucm.es/~viviane/products.html

5. Dignum, F., Broersen, J., Dignum, V., Meyer, J.: Meeting the deadline: Why, when and how. In: Hinchey, M.G., Rash, J.L., Truszkowski, W.F., Rouff, C.A. (eds.) FAABS 2004. LNCS (LNAI), vol. 3228, pp. 30–40. Springer, Heidelberg (2004)
6. Duran, F., Silva, V., Lucena, C.: Using Testimonies to Enforce the Behavior of Agents. In: Sichman, J.S., et al. (eds.) COIN 2007 Workshops. LNCS (LNAI), vol. 4870, pp. 232–244. Springer, Heidelberg (2008)
7. García-Camino, A., Rodríguez-A, J., Sierra, C., Vasconcelos, W.: Norm-Oriented Programming of Electronic Institutions. In: Proceedings of AAMAS, pp. 670–672. ACM Press, New York (2006)
8. García-Camino, A., Noriega, P., Rodríguez-Aguilar, J.A.: Implementing Norms in Electronic Institutions. In: Proceedings of AAMAS, pp. 667–673. ACM Press, New York (2005)
9. López, F.: Social Power and Norms: Impact on agent behavior. PhD thesis, Univ. of Southampton (2003)
10. López, F., Luck, M., d'Inverno, M.: Constraining autonomy through norms. In: Proceedings of AAMAS, pp. 674–681. ACM Press, New York (2002)
11. Meyer, B.: Object-Oriented Software Construction Prentice Hall, 2nd edn (1997)
12. Singh, M.: An Ontology for Commitments in Multiagent Systems: Toward a Unification of Normative Concepts. In: Artificial Intelligence and Law, vol. 7(1), pp. 97–113. Springer, Heidelberg (1999)
13. Vázquez-Salceda, J., Aldewereld, H., Dignum, F.: Implementing Norms in Multiagent Systems. In: Lindemann, G., Denzinger, J., Timm, I.J., Unland, R. (eds.) MATES 2004. LNCS (LNAI), vol. 3187, pp. 313–327. Springer, Heidelberg (2004)

A Normative Multi-Agent Systems Approach to the Use of Conviviality for Digital Cities

Patrice Caire

University of Luxembourg, Computer Science Department
L-1359, Luxembourg, 6, Rue Richard Coudenhove-Kalergi, Luxembourg

Abstract. Conviviality is a mechanism to reinforce social cohesion and a tool to reduce mis-coordination between individuals, groups and institutions in web communities, for example in digital cities. We use a two-fold definition of conviviality as a condition for social interactions and an instrument for the internal regulation of social systems. In this paper we discuss the use of normative multi-agent systems to analyze the use of conviviality for digital cities, by contrasting norms for conviviality with legal and institutional norms in digital cities. We show the role of the distinction among various kinds of norms, the explicit representation of norms, the violability of norms and the dynamics of norms in the context of conviviality for digital cities.

Keywords: Conviviality, multi-agent systems, normative systems, social computing, digital cities.

1 Introduction

The role of norms for conviviality is a condition for social interactions and an instrument for the internal regulation of social systems [1]. For example, in digital cities "government regulations extend laws with specific guidance to corporate and public actions" [2].

Conviviality is often reduced to be synonymous with user-friendliness as, for example, in one of the four themes of the European Community Fifth Framework Program titled "Societe de l'Information Convivial" (1998-2002) [3] and translated by "User-friendly Information Society". Indeed, the popular definition of a convivial place or group is one in which "individuals are welcome and feel at ease" [4]. However, the scientific literature defines conviviality as a more complex concept, with positive and negative aspects, tools and mechanisms to carry through user interactions. A socio-cognitive concept, conviviality is concerned with agent interactions, and frequently used in social sciences and applications of multi-agent systems in which artificial and human agents interact, for example, virtual communities, digital cities, social intelligence design and ambient intelligence. Therefore, we propose to add conviviality to the number of social concepts, such as trust, reputation, norms, organizations and institutions, already studied in multi-agent systems.

J.S. Sichman et al. (Eds.): COIN 2007, LNAI 4870, pp. 245–260, 2008.
© Springer-Verlag Berlin Heidelberg 2008

Moreover, similarly to a number of social concepts, such as trust, reputation, conventions, norms, power, coalitions, organizations and institutions, we propose that conviviality be studied in multi-agent systems.

In this paper we raise the following question: how can normative multi-agent systems be used to model conviviality for digital cities? We approach this question focusing on conviviality for digital cities, and by contrasting the use of normative multi-agent systems for conviviality with legal and institutional norms in digital cities.

Our main question breaks down into the following research questions: What are digital cities, what are normative multi-agent systems, what is conviviality and finally, can normative multi-agent systems be applied to conviviality for digital cities?

The layout of this paper follows these sub-questions. In section 2 we give a brief overview on digital cities, in section 3 we explain norms in regards to the legal and institutional aspects of digital cities, in section 4 we present a literature survey on the notion of conviviality and in section 5 we examine the use of norms for conviviality.

2   Digital Cities

Digital cities are web portals using physical cities as a metaphor for information spaces. They present various combinations of political, economic and social activities. The following examples show the diversity of the combinations:

- eCities, eAdministrations and eGovernments, such as eLuxembourg and eEurope are the official portals of cities and countries used as tools to improve local democracy and participation; they provide local social information infrastructures over the real city with public and administrative services to citizens and visitors; the activities are predominantly political and to a lesser extend, economic and social.
- eCommerce portals, such as MSN CitySearch and AOL Digital Cities offer commercial services, shopping, entertainment and more generally, local easy to find and search information; they provide practical resources for the organization of every day life and the support of local economic activities; the activities are predominantly economic and to a lesser extend social and political.
- social virtual worlds such as Second Life and the Habbo Hotel, provide a communication medium primarily to conduct social experiences through role playing while, at the same time, attracting advertisers and businesses by the size of their massive multi-player communities. "Experiment with new forms of solving problems and coordinating social life" [5]. Activities are predominantly social and to a lesser extend economic and political.

Observing that "Digital cities commonly provide both profit and non-profit services and have a dilemma in balancing the two different types of services", Ishida [6] raises the question whether public digital cities can compete with commercial ones. "Without profit services, digital cities become unattractive and fail to become a portal to the city. Without nonprofit services, the city may become too homogeneous like AOL digital cities as a result of pursuing economic efficiency."

2.1   Goals of Digital Cities

Commercial digital cities started as local portals run by private companies, such as phone, web and airline companies, competing with each other. Nowadays, global companies such as Yahoo! and AOL offer city guides with services: Shopping, entertainment, local information and maps. Their business goals are geared toward vertical markets and their revenues are generated by advertising. Their general trend is to provide information, easy to find and search for, good maintenance of systems and frequent updates. They are effective in Asia, where they complement government agencies, but limited in scope by their top-down controlled and selected content, lack of two-way interaction with users and main advertising purpose.

Public digital cities started in the US with American community networks, inspired by a tradition of community-centered, grass-roots engagements emphasizing freedom of speech and activism. Their original goal was to create virtual information spaces, such as the WELL, *Whole Earth'Lectronic Link* and Blacksburg Electronic Village. However today, American public digital cities align with eGovernments and their main challenges are: the lack of synergy between community networks, private companies and administrations as well as the competition between profit and non-profit organizations.

In Europe, public digital cities evolved through the European Community leadership. The main goals are to share ideas and technologies between all cities in order to strengthen European partnerships, use information and communication technologies in order to resolve social, economic and regional development issues and to improve the quality of social services. The main challenge, shown by the relatively slow commercialization of services and information, is the difficulty to integrate grass-roots communities and commercial points of view.

2.2   Organizations of Digital Cities

Commercial digital cities aggregate urban information; They are well maintained, use proprietary software and rely on search engines, ranking interest links by sponsors, for business opportunities. Early on, commercial digital cities recognized the importance of usability and have done well to make their services usable by many.

Public digital cities seek to enforce the use of open systems. The lack of funds and the complexity of their partnerships caused many downfalls (Digital Amsterdam). Public digital cities rely on high speed networks tightly coupled with physical cities (Helsinki) and platforms for community networks (Bologna). They have multilayer architectures: Information, interface and interaction layers (Digital Kyoto). In Asia, public digital cities, called *city informatization*, emerged as government initiatives to develop countries through technological innovations. There were attempts to integrate grass-roots activities and university driven projects in 1999 with Digital Kyoto and Digital Shanghai but the greatest challenge still remains their top-down approach based on administration activity.

2.3   Discussion

Commercial and public digital cities were originally very different but tend now to overlap. We summarize in table 1. Commercial digital cities depend on business models and strategies to fight competition for market penetration, gain new members and sustain existing members' loyalty; for example, members are less likely to go to a competitive site if they invest time and efforts to build their avatars and communities of friends. Public digital cities depend on political agendas to motivate progress for technological and social improvements; for example, in 1994, a progressive political leadership brought about innovations such as setting up online open spaces in *Bologna Iperbole* digital city, to allow groups of citizens to publish information and engage in public debates with their representatives; similarly, in 1996, the digital city for *Issy-les-Moulineaux* was developed into a one-stop administration that included online live interaction of citizens to town meetings.

In the US, for-profit businesses and non-profit organizations co-exist and compete; in the EU, attempts are to coordinate administrations, companies and citizens while in Asia governments pursue directed growth. The goals of European

Table 1. Digital cities: Commercial vs. public portals

Type	Commercial	Public
Goals	For profit. Vertical markets (shopping, entertainment). Generate revenues (advertising, memberships).	Not for profit. Make government efficient, accessible. Improve local democracy. Accelerate economic development.
Technology	Well maintained with frequent updates. Proprietary software and multimedia. Search (ranked results), easy-to-find local information and maps, top-down filtered content.	Use open source, distributed systems and forums. Rely on high speed networks coupled with the real city (parking payments, ambient intelligence applications).
Organization	Business strategy based on fierce competition. Existing models: Organizational, functional, economic, games and artificial life.	Political agenda based on incumbent majority and leadership priorities. Complex consortia between administration, universities and companies.

governments are to close geographic and social digital divides, with access to information and services everywhere and for all, to accelerate economic development, with business assistance, licenses and permits, and to make the governments of cities more efficient and accessible, for example with 24/7 only access to municipal services and multilinguism.

Existing models for digital cities are organizational, functional, economic, games or artificial life. Multi-agent systems are a promising methodology to develop digital cities, because they can bridge the gap between eGovernment concepts and system development. Moreover, the autonomy of users is central in digital cities and can be modeled using the autonomy of agents. Finally, interaction between artificial and human agents, and sometimes the distinction between them is unclear as the use of intelligent agents in some cities, or the use of avatars in second life.

The success factors for digital cities consist in achieving the participation of institutions and communities, in balancing top-down direction needed for technical infrastructure and bottom-up grass-roots initiatives necessary to insure citizens' cohesion and finally in finding equilibrium between economic and civic motivations. Research in this field addressed such issues in the proceedings of digital cities 2000 [7], 2002 [8] and 2005 [9] by focusing on concepts such as eDemocracy, digital divide and conviviality.

3   Legal and Institutional Norms in Digital Cities

In their introduction to normative multi-agent systems, Boella et al. give the following definition: "A normative multi-agent system is a multi-agent system together with normative systems in which agents on the one hand can decide whether to follow the explicitly represented norms, and on the other the normative systems specify how and in which extent the agents can modify the norms" [10]. We first discuss the distinction among various kinds of norms, we then discuss the implicit versus the explicit representation of norms, and finally the violation of norms. We illustrate our discussion with examples from digital cities.

3.1   Different Kinds of Norms

Several kinds of norms are usually distinguished in normative systems. Within the structure of normative multi-agent systems [11] distinguish "between regulative norms that describe obligations, prohibitions and permissions, and constitutive norms that regulate the creation of institutional facts as well as the modification of the normative system itself". A third kind of norms called procedural norms, have long been considered a major component of political systems, particularly democratic systems; Lawrence defines them as "rules governing the way in which political decisions are made; they are not concerned with the content of any decision except one which alters decision-making procedures" [12].

Constitutive norms combine several aspects, among which the intermediate concept known as *count as* such as in "X counts as a presiding official in a wedding ceremony", "this bit of paper counts as a five euro bill" and "this piece of land counts as somebodys private property" [13]. As per Searle, "the institutions of marriage, money, and promising are like the institutions of baseball and chess in that they are systems of such constitutive rules or conventions" [14]. In digital cities, an example of constitutive norm is *voting* in the sense that going through the procedure counts as a vote.

However, the role of constitutive rules "is not limited to the creation of an activity and the construction of new abstract categories. Constitutive norms specify both the behavior of a system and the evolution of the system" [11]. The dynamics of normative systems is here emphasized as in *norm revision*, certain actions count as adding new norms for instance amendments: "The normative system must specify how the normative system itself can be changed by introducing new regulative norms and new institutional categories, and specify by whom the changes can be done" [11]. In the US today, government agencies are required to invite public comment on proposed rules [2]. Citizens are therefore encouraged to propose their changes to regulations. This is done via the digital city governement interface that allows revisions to be traced and searched.

Two other aspects of constitutive norms are organizational, how roles define power and responsibilities, and structural, how hierarchies structure groups and individuals: New norms are introduced by the agents playing a legislative role, and ordinary agents create new obligations, prohibitions and permissions concerning specific agents [11].

Regulative Norms, like obligations and permissions are often used to model legal systems. However, "a large part of the legal code does not contain prohibitions and permissions, but definitions for classifying the common sense world under legal categories, like contract, money, property, marriage. Regulative norms can refer to this legal classification of reality" [13]. A regulative norm expressed as an obligation in the digital city of Luxembourg, is that citizens must use the file format PDF rather than Postscript in order to access the administration documents on the portal.

Regulative norms also express permission, rights and powers. For example, computer systems access rights and voting rights: In order to be allowed to vote in Luxembourg, an agent needs to prove it has been a resident for at least five consecutive years or was born in Luxembourg.

Regulative norms are not categorical, but conditional, they specify all their applicability conditions [11]. In the digital city of New York City, To renew online a Driver's License it is stipulated on New York digital city portal that you cannot change your address during this transaction, you must have completed form MV-619 (Eye Test Report) and read all the requirements before you begin the transaction [15].

Procedural norms are instrumental for individuals working in a system: Examples in digital cities, are back office procedures and processes designed for administrators to do their work. Lawrence distinguishes two kinds of procedural norms: Objective procedural norms are rules that describe how decisions are actually made in a political system and specify "who actually makes decisions, who can try to influence decision makers, what political resources are legitimate and how resources may be used". Subjective procedural norms are "attitudes about the way in which decisions should be made" [12].

3.2   Explicit vs. Implicit Representation of Norms

The first property of norms in the definition of normative multi-agent systems is that norms are explicitly represented; *explicite* meaning formalized and verbalized by some authorities, *implicite* meaning tacitely agreed upon, not specialized nor codified. Often, norms are given as requirements to computer systems but only implicitly represented. For example, you are filling out a census form and one question is whether you own a pet, but no explanation is given concerning the purpose of the information; assuming your answer is affirmative (you do own a pet), the outcome could be that either you are required to pay a pet license fee or the amount of the fee is directly deducted from your bank account. The digital city of Paris presents an example of explicit norm representation with the stipulation that, to create online library accounts you must be over 18 years old, otherwise an authorization of your parents is required.

Implicit representations are opaque to users and prevent governments to fulfill the democratic promise that transparency and explicit representations deliver. The representations of norms have to become more explicit and personalized to meet users' expectations as their needs for explanation and understanding of rules and regulations grows. Explicit representations of norms is also in the interest of governments and can be addressed with the development of mechanisms for knowledge representation and reasoning.

In digital cities, efforts are currently in-between implicit and explicit representations of norms by providing tools for text representation and retrieval, more advanced ontologies, semantic links and search capabilities. In 2006 for example, the US government added a branch to its business portal to help small businesses comply with Federal regulations; a need that was not being met by any other Federal government program [15].

3.3   Violations of Norms

The second property in the definition of normative multiagent systems, norms can be violated, is also seen as a condition for the use of deontic logic in computer science: "Importantly, the norms allow for the possibility that actual behavior may at times deviate from the ideal, i.e. that violations of obligations, or of agents rights, may occur" [16].

If norms cannot be violated then the norms are *regimented*. For example, if in access control, a service can only be accessed with a certificate, then this norm must be implemented in the system by ensuring that the service is only accessible when the certificate is presented. Regimented norms correspond to preventative control, as norm violations are prevented. When norm violations are possible, control is detective as behavior must be monitored and norm violations must be detected and sanctioned. "Social order requires social control, *an incessant local (micro) activity of its units*, aimed at restoring the regularities prescribed by norms. Thus, the agents attribute to the normative system, besides goals, also the ability to autonomously enforce the conformity of the agents to the norms, because a dynamic social order requires a continuous activity for ensuring that the normative systems goals are achieved. To achieve the normative goal the normative system forms the subgoals to consider as a violation the behavior not conform to it and to sanction violations" [13].

In digital cities, disincentive is often the mechanism used to prevent users from infringing the norms. For example, the digital city of Issy clearly stipulates that malicious intruders into the digital city will be prosecuted. There are normative multiagent systems in which norm violations are possible and can trigger new obligations, the so-called contrary-to-duty obligations. With contrary-to-duty obligations, there is not only a distinction between ideal and bad behavior, but there is also a distinction between various degrees of sub-ideal behaviors.

3.4 Dynamics of Norms

In many electronic institutions, norms are fixed and cannot be changed within the system, even though in many organizations there are roles defined within the system. The questions are whether digital cities are a collection of electronic institutions, whether manipulations and changes are allowed within the system. The US Regulations' office may be contributing to bring answers to this questions as it now provides on its site *Regulations.gov* a national forum for users to comment on existing and pending federal rules, therefore encouraging a more dynamic process for the modification and expliciteness of their rules and regulations.

4 Conviviality

First, we note that the many definitions of conviviality remain vague and not technical (table 2). We further note that the concept can be related to other non technical socio-cognitive concepts, such as trust and power, that have aquired more technical interpretation in multi-agent systems. We think current research is useful to develop *user-friendly* multi-agent systems.

4.1 Conviviality in Social Sciences

First used in a scientific and philosophical context [20], in 1964, as synonymous with *empathy*, conviviality allows individuals to identify with each other thereby experiencing each other's feelings, thoughts and attitudes. By extension, a community is convivial when it aims at sharing knowledge: Members trust each other, share commitments and interests and make mutual efforts to build conviviality and preserve it. A convivial learning experience is based on role swapping [21], teacher role alternating with learner role, emphasizing the concept of reciprocity

Table 2. Definitions of conviviality

Etymological and Domain Specific Definitions
15th century "convivial", from latin, convivere "to live together with, to eat together with". *French Academy Dictionary* [17]
Adj. Convivial: (of an atmosphere, society, relations or event) friendly and lively, (of a person) cheerfully sociable. *Oxford English Dictionary* [18]
Technology: Quality pertaining to a software or hardware easy and pleasant to use and understand even for a beginner. User friendly, Usability. By extension also reliable and efficient. *Grand Dictionnaire Terminologique* [19]
Sociology: Set of positive relations between the people and the groups that form a society, with an emphasis on community life and equality rather than hierarchical functions. *Grand Dictionnaire Terminologique* [19]

as key component and creating concepts such as learning webs, skill exchange networks and peer-matching communication, later expanded by Papert and the Constructionists with concepts such as *learning-by-making* [22].

Conviviality is then described as a social form of human interaction, a way to reinforce group cohesion through the recognition of common values. The sharing of habits and customs, for example the sharing of certain types of food or drinks, create and reinforce a community through a "positive feeling of togetherness"; individuals become part of the community which in turn, reinforces the community's awareness of its identity. The physical experience of conviviality is transformed into knowledge sharing experience: "To know is to understand in a certain manner that can be shared by others who form with you a community of understanding" [23].

Illich further develop the concept of conviviality with his notion of "individual freedom realized in personal interdependence" [24]; Conviviality should then be the foundation for a new society, one that gives its members the means, referred to as tools, for achieving their personal goals: "A convivial society would be the result of social arrangements that guarantee for each member the most ample and free access to the tools of the community and limit this freedom only in favor of another member's equal freedom". Conviviality is then seen by Putnam as an enhancement to social capital, a condition for the civil society where communities are characterized by political equality, civic engagement, solidarity, trust, tolerance and strong associative life [25], therefore tightly linking the performance of political institutions to the character of civil life [26]. These ideas are further developed by Lamizet who caracterizes conviviality as both "institutional structures that facilitate social relations and technological processes that are easy to control and pleasurable to use" [27]. An important use for conviviality today is for digital cities as a mechanism to reinforce social cohesion and as a tool to reduce mis-coordinations between individuals [28,1,29].

However, a negative side of conviviality emerges when it is instrumentalized, one group being favored at the expense of another. Ashby argues that "truth realities about minorities are built from the perspective of the majority via template token instances in which conflict is highlighted and resolution is achieved

Table 3. Different aspects of conviviality

Positive aspects (Enabler)	Grey aspects (Ignorance)	Negative aspects (Threat)
Share knowledge & skills	Ignore cultural diversity	Crush outsiders
Deal with conflict	Hide conflict	Fragmentation
Feeling of "togetherness"	Promote homogenization	Totalitarism
Equality	Political correctness	Reductionism
Trust	Non-transparent systematic controls	Deception

through minority assimilation to majority norms [...] Conviviality is achieved for the majority, but only through a process by which non-conviviality is reinforced for the minority" [30]. Taylor further add to this negative side the idea that conviviality can be used to mask the power relationships and social structures that govern communities. Taylor asks the question "whether it is possible for convivial institutions to exist, other than by simply creating another set of power relationships and social orders that, during the moment of involvement, appear to allow free rein to individual expression [...]. Community members may experience a sense of conviviality which is deceptive and which disappears as soon as the members return to the alienation of their fragmented lives" [31]. In table 3, we summarize the different aspects of conviviality.

4.2 Conviviality in Multi-Agent Systems

In multi-agent systems, "agents are capable of flexible (reactive, proactive, social) behavior" [32], this capability is crucial for the use of conviviality since it allows agents to cooperate, coordinate their actions and negotiate with each other. Following are examples of multi-agent systems applications that use different aspects of conviviality.

Embodied Conversational Agents (ECA) are autonomous agents with a human-like appearance and communicative skills. They have shown their potential to allow users to interact with the machine in a natural and intuitive human way: the conversation. To be able to engage the user in a conversation and to maintain it, the agents ought to have capabilities such as perceive and generate verbal and nonverbal behaviors, show emotional states and maintain social relationship [33]. In Cassell's Rea system, Embodied Conversational Agents are "specifically conversational in their behaviors and specifically human like in the way they use their bodies in conversation", they are capable of making content-oriented or propositional contributions to a conversation with human users [34]. Conversational Agents must be endowed with *conviviality*, that is "be rational and cooperative" [35] and the interaction with the agent is convivial if the agent presents, jointly and at all times, one or all of the following characteristics: Capacity for negotiation, contextual interpretation, flexibility of the entry language, flexibility of interaction, production of co-operative reactions and finally of adequate response forms. Conviviality is the essential and global characteristic that emerges from the intelligence of the system, not from a set of local characteristics that vary depending upon the application contexts and the types of users. Consequently a list of criteria will by itself not suffice to express conviviality, additional critical factors are the relations that bind the criteria together and the way these relations are perceived by individuals. Building on this work, Ochs et al. distinguish felt emotions from expressed emotions noting that "a person may decide to express an emotion different from the one she actually felt because she has to follow some socio-cultural norms" [36]. This is particularly relevant to the study of conviviality in multi-agent systems where agent communication distinguishes between private beliefs and goals and public opinions and intentions.

In the Intelligent Tutoring System proposed by Gomes et al., "convivial social relationships are based on mutual acceptance through interaction", on the reciprocity of students helping each other [37]. Students communicate through their agents: Each agent represents a student and has the function to pass information on the affective states of the student, this information can be inferred by the agent or adjusted by the student. A utility function takes as input a student's social profile and computes the student's affective states indicating if the student needs help, if it is the case, the system recommends a tutor. Remaining challenges are with defining utility function inputs to compute recommendations, presently a set of random values, and to automate inferences of students requiring help. This exposes the need for further research in evaluation methods and measures for concepts such as mood, sociability and conviviality. Further looking into interpersonal factors, Heylen et al. propose emotionally intelligent tutor agents that try to construct a model of the mental state of the student while being aware of the effects of the tutoring acts to determine the appropriate action sequences and the way to execute them [38].

Computational mechanisms for trust and reputation in artificial societies are widely researched [39,40] greatly relevant to conviviality. Reputation is the "indispensable condition for the social conviviality in human societies" state Casare and Sichman [41]. In this system, every agents are aware of every other agents' behavior and of their compliance, or not, to the rules of the group. A functional ontology of reputation is defined whereby "roles are played by entities involved in reputative processes such as reputation evaluation and reputation propagation." Concepts of the legal world are used to model the social world, through the extension of the concept of legal rule to social norm and the internalization of social mechanisms in the agent's mind, so far externalized in legal institutions. Reputation acts as a communication tool, ensuring complete social transparency throughout the system. However, the strict application of legal norms to reputation may suffer from rigidity, and one can wonder about ethical issues, such as privacy, raised by these types systems. Research addressing such issues are for example, Erickson and Kellog's socially translucent systems, characterized by visibility, awareness and accountability [42], and ter Hofte et al. [43] studies of place-based presence and trust evaluation.

5   Use of Norms for Conviviality

"Norms are cultural phenomena that prescribe and proscribe behavior in specific circumstances" state Hechter and Opp [44]. They are considered to be responsible for regulating social behavior: Interaction and exchange between strangers could hardly be imagined without norms. The law relies on norms as well but, as seen in section 3, legal norms differ form social norms. We summarized from various sources and present some excerpts in table 4.

Table 4. Legal norms versus social norms

Type	Legal Norms	Social Norms
Kinds of norms	Consitutive, regulative and procedural.	Consitutive and regulative; rarely procedural.
Norm representation	Exactly specified in written texts.	Unwritten, thus their content and rules are often imprecise.
Norm violation	Linked to distint sanctions, enforced by specialized bureaucracy.	Enforced informally, but can be a matter of life and death.
Norm modification	Created by design, generally through deliberative process.	Spontaneous, of uncertain origine.

5.1   Norms for Conviviality

There is no common definition of social norms and no agreement on how to measure them. A large body of research suggests that social norms regulate such diverse phenomena as cooperation [45], collective action [46] and social order [47]. Hechter and Opp [44] distinguish two types of definitions for social norms:

1. Norms that entail a moral imperative, a sense of oughtness, of duty; a social norm behavior that people believe must be performed without concern for its consequence for the agent. For example, a man who was engaging in duels was ready to die to save his honor. The sanction of an *oughtness norm* does not depend on the dectection of the violation because violators internalize this type of norm, therefore its violation entails some internal sanctioning: the experience of guilt or shame.
2. Norms that generate social expectations without any moral obligations, basically behavioral regularity; a certain behavior is identified as a social norm if deviating from that practice incurs a cost imposed on an agent. For example, a person questioned by a police officer is expected to behave respectfully otherwise he of she may be prosecuted.

In digital cities, a number of security issues like identity management, authentication and authorisa- tion can prevent users to *feel at ease*. Some problems are

new, for example, in contrast to the physical world, malicious users can create
new agents repeatedly to lure beginners, insult them and take advantage of them.
These unconvivial behaviors show mechanisms that differenciate social norms
from conviviality norms. From personal powers to social dependence, sociality
presupposes a *common world*, hence *interference*: the action of one agent can
favor (positive interference) or compromise the goals of another agent (negative
interference) [47].

5.2   Representation of Conviviality

Conviviality facilitates and regulates agent interactions, and therefore contri-
butes to agent coordination. For example, digital cities can separate systems for
beginners and experienced users, since beginners are frightened by the complexi-
ties of the real system, whereas experienced users are bored by the simplifications
developed for beginners. However, since beginners and experienced users have
to participate to the digital city at the same time, this introduces various challenges: when civil servants working for the digital city are confronted with a user,
they have to adapt their behavior with respect to the experience of the user.

Dynamic aspects of conviviality , such as the emergence of conviviality, occur
from the sharing of properties or behaviors whereby each members perception
is that their personal needs are taken care of.

5.3   Violation of Conviviality

It is always possible to violate social norms and therefore conviviality. Ignoring
cultural and social diversity is violating conviviality as it creates conviviality for a
group at the expense of others. In digital cities, as in physical cities, being ignored
when asking advices to a city administrator represents a conviviality violation
as it breaks the bilateral form expected from these communication acts to only
allow for unilateral communication. Excluding, ostracizing, an agent that does
not comply to the norms of the city when interacting with other agents from the
city is a ditributed mechanism that enforce the norms as in [48].

Other violations would be to promote homogenization, fragmentation, totali-
tarism, reductionism, deception, to enforce exclusion and to crush outsiders.

6   Conclusion

In this paper we contrast norms for conviviality with legal and institutional
norms in digital cities. We consider the following issues. First, the kinds of norms
typically distinguished in legal systems can be distinguished for norms of conviviality too. Second, norms for conviviality are often implicit, and we believe it
is an important question when such norms should be made explicit. Third, the
issue of violation of conviviality and ways to deal with it is of central concern in
web communities like digital cities. Fourth, norms concerning conviviality should
be able to change over time. Fifth, norms for conviviality can come from a wide
variety of sources.

References

1. Caire, P.: Designing convivial digital cities. In Nijholt, A., O.S., Nishida, T. (eds.) Proceedings of the 6th Workshop on Social Intelligence Design (SID 2007), pp. 25–40 (2007)
2. Lau, G.T., Law, K.H., Wiederhold, G.: Analyzing government regulations using structural and domain information. IEEE Computer 38(12), 70–76 (2005)
3. Weyrich, C.: Orientations for workprogramme 2000 and beyond. Information society technologies report, Information Society Technologies Advisory Group (1999)
4. Caire, P.: A critical discussion on the use of the notion of conviviality for digital cities. In: Proceedings of Web Communities 2007, pp. 193–200 (2007)
5. Van den Besselaar, P., Melis, I., Beckers, D.: Digital cities: Organization, content, and use. [7], pp. 18–32
6. Ishida, T.: Understanding digital cities. [7], pp. 7–17
7. Ishida, T., Isbister, K. (eds.): Digital Cities 1999. LNCS, vol. 1765. Springer, Heidelberg (2000)
8. Tanabe, M., van den Besselaar, P., Ishida, T. (eds.): Digital Cities 2001. LNCS, vol. 2362. Springer, Heidelberg (2002)
9. van den Besselaar, P., Koizumi, S. (eds.): Digital Cities 2003. LNCS, vol. 3081. Springer, Heidelberg (2005)
10. Boella, G., van der Torre, L., Verhagen, H.: Introduction to normative multiagent systems. Computational & Mathematical Organization Theory 12, 71–79 (2006)
11. Boella, G., van der Torre, L.W.N.: Regulative and constitutive norms in normative multiagent systems. In: Knowledge Representation, pp. 255–266 (2004)
12. Lawrence, D.G.: Procedural norms and tolerance: A reassessment. The American Political Science Review (1976)
13. Boella, G., van der Torre, L.W.N.: Constitutive norms in the design of normative multiagent systems. In: CLIMA VI, pp. 303–319 (2005)
14. Searle, J.R.: Speech Acts: An Essay in the Philosophy of Language. Cambridge University Press, Cambridge (1970)
15. Caire, P.: Conviviality for digital cities: A normative multi-agent systems approach. In: Dastani, M., de Jong, E. (eds.) Proceedings of The 19th Belgian-Dutch Conference on Artificial Intelligence (BNAIC 2007), pp. 73–80 (2007)
16. Jones, A., Carmo, J.: Handbook of Philosophical Logic. In: Deontic logic and contrary-to-duties, pp. 265–344. Kluwer Academic Publishers, Dordrecht (2002)
17. Dictionnaire de l'academie francaise. Neuvieme Edition, Version Informatisee (2000)
18. Oxford english dictionary. Oxford University Press, Oxford (2007)
19. Le grand dictionnaire terminologique. Office Quebecois de la Langue Francaise (2007)
20. Polanyi, M.: Personal Knowledge: Towards a Post-Critical Philosophy. University Of Chicago Press, Chicago (1974)
21. Illich, I.: Deschooling Society. Marion Boyars Publishers, Ltd. (1971)
22. Papert, S., Harel, I.: 1. In: Constructionism, MIT Press, Cambridge (1991)
23. Schechter, M.: Conviviality, gender and love stories: Plato's symposium and isak dinesen's (k. Blixen's) babette's feast. Trans, Internet journal for cultural sciences 1(15) (2004)
24. Illich, I.: Tools for Conviviality. Marion Boyars Publishers (1974)
25. Putnam, R.D.: Bowling alone: The collapse and revival of american community. In: Computer Supported Cooperative Work, p. 357 (2000)

26. Putnam, R.D.: Diplomacy and domestic politics: The logic of two-level games. International Organization 42(3), 427–460 (1988)
27. Lamizet, B.: Culture – commonness of the common? Trans, Internet journal for cultural sciences 1(15) (2004)
28. Caire, P.: Conviviality for ambient intelligence. In: Olivier, P., Kray, C. (eds.) Proceedings of Artificial Societies for Ambient Intelligence, Artificial Intelligence and Simulation of Behaviour (AISB 2007), pp. 14–19 (2007)
29. Caire, P.: A normative multi-agent systems approach to the use of conviviality for digital cities. In: Noriega, P., Padget, J. (eds.) Proceedings of The International Workshop on Coordination, Organization, Institutions and Norms in Agent Systems (COIN), pp. 15–26.
30. Ashby, W.: Unmasking narrative: A semiotic perspective on the conviviality/non-conviviality dichotomy in storytelling about the german other. Trans, Internet journal for cultural sciences 1(15) (2004)
31. Taylor, M.: Oh no it isn't: Audience participation and community identity. Trans, Internet journal for cultural sciences 1(15) (2004)
32. Wooldridge, M.: An introduction to multi-agent systems. J. Artificial Societies and Social Simulation 7(3), 16–23 (2004)
33. Pelachaud, C.: Multimodal expressive embodied conversational agents. In: ACM Multimedia, pp. 683–689 (2005)
34. Cassell, J.: Embodied conversational interface agents. Commun. ACM 43(4), 70–78 (2000)
35. Sadek, M.D., Bretier, P., Panaget, E.: ARTIMIS: Natural dialogue meets rational agency. In: International Joint Conferences on Artificial Intelligence, vol. 2, pp. 1030–1035 (1997)
36. Ochs, M., Niewiadomski, R., Pelachaud, C., Sadek, D.: Intelligent expressions of emotions. In: Affective Computing and Intelligent Interaction, pp. 707–714 (2005)
37. Gomes, E.R., Boff, E., Vicari, R.M.: Social, affective and pedagogical agents for the recommendation of student tutors. In: Proceedings of Intelligent Tutoring Systems (2004)
38. Heylen, D., Nijholt, A., op den Akker, R., Vissers, M.: Intelligent expressions of emotions. In: Affective Computing and Intelligent Interaction, pp. 707–714 (2005)
39. Sabater, J., Sierra, C.: Review on computational trust and reputation models. Artif. Intell. Rev. 24(1), 33–60 (2005)
40. Boella, G., van der Torre, L.W.N.: Normative multiagent systems and trust dynamics. In: Falcone, R., Barber, S., Sabater-Mir, J., Singh, M.P. (eds.) Trusting Agents for Trusting Electronic Societies. LNCS (LNAI), vol. 3577, pp. 1–17. Springer, Heidelberg (2005)
41. Casare, S., Sichman, J.: Towards a functional ontology of reputation. In: AAMAS 2005: Proceedings of the fourth international joint conference on Autonomous agents and multiagent systems, pp. 505–511. ACM Press, New York (2005)
42. Erickson, T., Kellogg, W.A.: Social translucence: an approach to designing systems that support social processes. ACM Trans. Comput.-Hum. Interact. 7(1), 59–83 (2000)
43. ter Hofte, G.H., Mulder, I., Verwijs, C.: Close encounters of the virtual kind: A study on place-based presence. AI Soc. 20(2), 151–168 (2006)
44. Hechter, M., Opp, K.D.: Social Norms. Russell Sage Foundation, Thousand Oaks (2001)
45. Conte, R., Castelfranchi, C.: Cognitive and Social Action. UCL Press (1995)

46. Ros, R., Veloso, M.M., de Mántaras, R.L., Sierra, C., Arcos, J.L.: Beyond individualism: Modeling team playing behavior in robot soccer through case-based reasoning. In: AAAI, pp. 1671–1674. AAAI Press, Menlo Park (2007)
47. Castelfranchi, C.: The micro-macro constitution of power. Protosociology 18, 208–269 (2003)
48. de Pinninck, A.P., Sierra, C., Schorlemmer, M.: Distributed Norm Enforcement Via Ostracism. In: Sichman, J.S., Padget, J., Ossowski, S., Noriega, P. (eds.) COIN 2007. LNCS(LNAI), vol. 4870, pp. 301–315. Springer, Heidelberg (2008)

On the Multimodal Logic
of Normative Systems

Pilar Dellunde

Universitat Autònoma de Barcelona and
Artificial Intelligence Research Institute (IIIA-CSIC)
Campus UAB, 08193-Cerdanyola del Valles, Catalonia, Spain
pilar.dellunde@uab.cat

Abstract. We introduce Multimodal Logics of Normative Systems as
a contribution to the development of a general logical framework for
reasoning about normative systems over logics for Multi-Agent Systems.
Given a multimodal logic L, for every modality $\Box_i$ and normative system
η, we expand the language adding a new modality $\Box_i^\eta$ with the intended
meaning of $\Box_i^\eta \phi$ being "ϕ is obligatory in the context of the normative
system η over the logic L". In this expanded language we define the
Multimodal Logic of Normative Systems over L, for any given set of normative systems N, and we give a sound and complete axiomatisation for
this logic, proving transfer and model checking results. The special case
when L and N are axiomatised by sets of Sahlqvist or shallow modal
formulas is studied.

Keywords: Fusions of Logics, Multimodal Logics, Normative Systems,
Multi-Agent Systems, Model Theory, Sahlqvist Formulas.

1 Introduction

Recent research on the logical foundations of Multi-Agent Systems (MAS) has
centered its attention in the study of normative systems. The notion of electronic
institution is a natural extension of human institutions by permitting not only
humans but also autonomous agents to interact with one another. Institutions
are used to regulate interactions where participants establish commitments and
to facilitate that these commitments are upheld, the institutional conventions
are devised so that those commitments can be established and fulfilled (see [1] for
a general reference of the role of electronic institutions to regulate agents interactions in MAS). Over the past decade, normative systems have been promoted
for the coordination of MAS and the engineering of societies of self-interested
autonomous software agents. In this context there is an increasing need to find
a general logical framework for the study of normative systems over the logics
for MAS.

   Given a set of states S and a binary accessibility relation R on S, a normative
system η on the structure (S, R) could be understood as a set of constraints
$\eta \subseteq R$ on the transitions between states, the intended meaning of $(x, y) \in \eta$

J.S. Sichman et al. (Eds.): COIN 2007, LNAI 4870, pp. 261–274, 2008.
© Springer-Verlag Berlin Heidelberg 2008

being "the transition from state x to state y is not legal according to normative system η". Several formalisms have been introduced for reasoning about normative systems over specific logics. Two examples are worth noting: Normative ATL (NATL), proposed in [2] and Temporal Logic of Normative Systems (NTL) in [3]. NATL is an extension to the Alternating-Time Temporal Logic and contains cooperation modalities of the form $<< \eta : C >> \phi$ with the intended interpretation that "C has the ability to achieve ϕ within the context of the normative system η". NTL is a conservative generalization of the Branching-Time Temporal Logic CTL. In NTL, the path quantifiers A ("on all paths...") and E ("on some path...") are replaced by the indexed deontic operators O_η ("it is obligatory in the context of the normative system η that..") and P_η ("it is permissible in the context of the normative system η that...").

The Multimodal Logic of Normative Systems introduced in this article is a contribution to define a general logical framework for reasoning about normative systems over logics for MAS. For this purpose we generalize to arbitrary logics the approaches taken in [2] and [3]. At the moment, we are far from obtaining a unique formalism which addresses all the features of MAS at the same time, but the emerging field of combining logics is a very active area and has proved to be successful in obtaining formalisms which combine good properties of the existing logics. In our approach, we regard the Logic of Normative Systems over a given logic L, as being the fusion of logics obtained from L and a set of normative systems over L. This model-theoretical construction will help us to understand better which properties are preserved under combinations of logics over which we have imposed some restrictions and to apply known transfer results (for a general account on the combination of logics, we refer to [4] and [5], and as a general reference on multimodal logic, to [6]). There are some advantages of using these logics for reasoning about MAS: it is possible to compare whether a normative system is more restrictive than the other, check if a certain property holds in a model of a logic once a normative system has restricted its accessibility relation, model the dynamics of normative systems in institutional settings, define a hierarchy of normative systems (and, by extension, a classification of the institutions) or present a logical-based reasoning model for the agents to negotiate over norms.

This paper is structured as follows. In Section 2 we present an example in order to motivate the introduction of the general framework. In Section 3 we give a sound and complete axiomatisation for the Multimodal Logic of Normative Systems, proving transfer results and we address a complexity issue for model checking. In Section 4 we restrict our attention to logics with normative systems that define elementary classes of modal frames. We have called them *Elementary Normative Systems (ENS)* and we prove completeness and canonicity results for them. Elementary classes include a wide range of formalisms used in describing MAS, modelling different aspects of agenthood, some temporal logics, logics of knowledge and belief, logics of communication, etc. Finally, in Section 5 we come back to our first example in Section 2, showing how our framework can be applied to multiprocess temporal structures, Section 6 is devoted to future work.

2   Multiprocess Temporal Frames and Normative Systems

In a multi-agent institutional environment, in order to allow agents to success-fully interact with other agents, they share the dialogic framework. The expres-sions of the communication language in a dialogic framework are constructed as formulas of the type $\iota(\alpha_i : \rho_i, \alpha_j : \rho_j, \phi, \tau)$, where ι is an illocutionary particle, α_i and α_j are agent terms, ρ_i and ρ_j are role terms and τ is a time term. An scene is specified by a graph where the nodes of the graph represent the different states of the conversation and the arcs connecting the nodes are labelled with illocution schemes.

Several formalisms for modelling interscene exchanges between agents have been introduced using multimodal logics. For instance, in [7] the authors provide an alternating offers protocol to specify commitments that agents make to each other when engaging in persuasive negotiations using rewards. Specifically, the protocol details, how commitments arise or get retracted as a result of agents promising rewards or making offers. The protocol also standardises what an agent is allowed to say or what it can expect to receive from its opponent. The multimodal logic presented in [7] introduces modalities $\Box_\phi$ for expressions ϕ of the communication language.

More formally, given a finite set of propositional atomic formulas, we could define the set of formulas of such a multimodal communication language in the following way:

$$\phi ::= p \mid \top \mid \bot \mid \neg\alpha \mid \alpha \wedge \alpha \mid \Box_{\phi_1}\alpha \mid \ldots \mid \Box_{\phi_k}\alpha$$

where p is an atomic propositional formula, α is a propositional formula and $\phi_1, \ldots, \phi_k$ are formulas of the communication language.

The standard Kripke semantics of these logics can be given by means of mul-tiprocess temporal frames. We say that $\Xi = (S, R_{\phi_0}, \ldots, R_{\phi_k})$ is a *multiprocess temporal frame* if and only if S is a set of states and for every $i \leq k$, R_{ϕ_i} is a binary relation on S such that $R = \bigcup_{i \leq k} R_{\phi_i}$ is a serial relation (that is, for every $s \in S$ there is $t \in S$ such that $(s, t) \in R$). A *multiprocess temporal model* is a Kripke model with a multiprocess temporal frame.

Let M be a multiprocess temporal model and $w \in M$, the satisfiability relation for the modalities $\Box\phi_i$ is defined as usual:

$$M, w \models \Box_{\phi_i}\alpha \text{ iff for all } w' \in M \text{ such that } wR_{\phi_i}w'$$

$$M, w' \models \alpha$$

Some examples of the protocols introduced in [7] can be formalised by formulas of the following form: $\Box_{\phi_1} \ldots \Box_{\phi_l}\bot$. For instance, with the formula

$$\Box_{Offer(i,x)}\Box_{Offer(i,y)}\bot$$

with $x \neq y$, we can express that it is not allowed to agent i to do two differ-ent offers one immediately after the other. Let us see now how formulas like $\Box_{\phi_1} \ldots \Box_{\phi_l}\bot$ can be understood as sets of constraints on the transitions between states. Given a multiprocess temporal frame $\Xi = (S, R_{\phi_0}, \ldots, R_{\phi_k})$, consider the following set of finite sequences of elements of S:

$$\Delta_\Xi = \{(a_0, \ldots, a_m) : \forall j < m, \exists i \le k \text{ such that } a_j R_{\phi_i} a_{j+1}\}$$

Then, a *normative system* η on the frame Ξ could be defined as a subset of Δ_Ξ. Intuitively speaking, a sequence $(a_0, \ldots, a_m) \in \eta$ if and only if this sequence of transitions is not legal according to normative system η. In our previous example, given a frame, the formula $\Box_{Offer(i,x)} \Box_{Offer(i,y)} \bot$, can be regarded as the following normative system (that is, the following set of finite sequences of the frame):

$$\{(a_0, a_1, a_2) : \text{ such that } a_0 R_{Offer(i,x)} a_1 \text{ and } a_1 R_{Offer(i,x)} a_2\}$$

Thus, any model satisfying the protocol introduced by $\Box_{Offer(i,x)} \Box_{Offer(i,y)} \bot$ can not include such sequences.

When defining an scene in an electronic institution we could be interested in comparing different protocols in order to show which of them satisfy some desired properties. In order to do so we could extend our multimodal language with additional modalities $\Box_{\phi_i}^\eta$, one for each normative system we want to consider. Next section is devoted to the study of the logical properties of these languages and later on, we will come back to our example applying this general framework.

3   Multimodal Logics of Normative Systems

We introduce first some notation and basic facts about multimodal languages. A *finite modal similarity type* $\tau = \langle F, \rho \rangle$ consists of a finite set F of modal operators and a map $\rho : F \to \omega$ assigning to each $f \in F$ a finite arity $\rho(f) \in \omega$. Finite propositional modal languages of type τ are defined in the usual way by using finitely many propositional variables, the operators in F and the boolean connectives $\wedge, \vee, \neg, \to, \leftrightarrow, \top, \bot$. For monadic modalities we use the usual notation $\Box_f$.

A *modal finitary structural consequence relation* $\vdash$ of similarity type τ is a relation between sets of formulas and formulas of the finite propositional modal language of type τ satisfying:

- $\phi \in \Gamma \Rightarrow \Gamma \vdash \phi$
- If $\Gamma \subseteq \Delta$ and $\Gamma \vdash \phi$, then $\Delta \vdash \phi$
- If $\Gamma \vdash \Delta$ and $\Delta \vdash \phi$, then $\Gamma \vdash \phi$
- $\Gamma \vdash \phi \Rightarrow s\Gamma \vdash s\phi$, for all substitutions s
- If $\Gamma \vdash \phi$, then there exist a finite subset Γ_0 of Γ with $\Gamma_0 \vdash \phi$
- $\vdash \phi$, for every classical tautology ϕ
- $p, p \to q \vdash q$
- For every $f \in F$,

$$p_0 \leftrightarrow q_0, \ldots, p_{\rho(f)} \leftrightarrow q_{\rho(f)} \vdash f(p_0, \ldots, p_{\rho(f)}) \leftrightarrow f(q_0, \ldots, q_{\rho(f)})$$

For a general account on consequence relations we refer to [8] say that a subset Λ of modal formulas is a *classical modal logic* of similarity type τ iff there exists a modal finitary structural consequence relation $\vdash$ of similarity type τ such that $\Lambda = \Lambda(\vdash)$, where $\Lambda(\vdash) = \{\phi : \emptyset \vdash \phi\}$. It is said that that Λ is *consistent* if $\perp \notin \Lambda$.

Given a type $\tau = \langle F, \rho \rangle$, a *Kripke frame* of type τ is an structure $(S, R_f)_{f \in F}$, where S is nonempty and for every $f \in F$, R_f is a binary relation on S.

Definition 1. *A normative system over a Kripke frame $(S, R_f)_{f \in F}$ is a subset of the following set of finite sequences of S:*

$$\{(a_0, \ldots, a_m) : \forall j < m, \exists f \in F \text{ such that } a_j R_f a_{j+1}\}$$

Observe that Definition 1 extends to the multimodal setting the definition of normative system introduced in Section 2 of [3]. Examples of classical modal logics with semantics based on Kripke frames are Propositional Dynamic Logic (PDL), Alternating-Time Temporal Logic (ATL) and Computational Tree Logic (CTL), but CTL*, the Full Computational Tree Logic is not a classical modal logic because it is not closed under uniform substitution.

Now we introduce in the language a new finite set of symbols N to denote normative systems. Given a finite propositional modal language of type $\tau = \langle F, \rho \rangle$, for every normative system $\eta \in N$, let τ^η be the type whose modalities are $\{f^\eta : f \in F\}$ and $\tau^N = \bigcup_{\eta \in N} \tau^\eta$. For every set of formulas Γ, let us denote by Γ^η the set of formulas of type τ^η obtained from Γ by substituting every occurrence of the modality f by f^η. The monadic operators $\Diamond_f$ are defined in the usual way as abbreviations $\Diamond_f \phi \equiv \neg \Box_f \neg \phi$ and we have also the corresponding $\Diamond_f^\eta$.

Given a classical modal logic L with semantics based on Kripke frames, we define the *Multimodal Logic of Normative Systems* over L, denoted by L^N, as being the smallest classical modal logic in the expanded language τ^N which contains L and L^η, for every $\eta \in N$.

Theorem 2. *Let L be a consistent classical modal logic axiomatised by a set Γ of formulas. Then,*

1. *$\Gamma^N = \Gamma \cup \bigcup \{\Gamma^\eta : \eta \in N\}$ is an axiomatisation of L^N.*
2. *L^N is a conservative extension of L.*
3. *If L is a decidable logic, then L^N is decidable.*

Proof. Since we have introduced a finite set of disjoint similarity types

$$\{\tau^\eta : \eta \in N\}$$

we can define the fusion $\bigoplus < L^\eta : \eta \in N >$ of disjoint copies of the logic L. Observe that, so defined, $L^N = \bigoplus < L^\eta : \eta \in N >$ and Γ^N is an axiomatisation of L^N. Then, by an early result of Thomason [9], L^N is a conservative extension of L. Finally we can apply Theorem 6.11 of [10], to obtain the corresponding transfer result.

In [11] a weak notion of normality is introduced to prove some additional transfer results for the fusion of logics. Let us assume that our classical modal logics satisfy the two conditions of Definition 2.5 of [11]:

1. For every $f \in F$, the semantics of $f(p_0, \ldots, p_{\rho(f)})$ is a monadic first-order formula.
2. For each R_f, there is a derived connective $\square_f$ such that the formula $\square_f p$ expresses $\forall x(y R_f x \to P x)$ and is closed under the necessitation rule: If $\phi \in \Lambda$, then $\square_f \phi \in \Lambda$.

This second condition corresponds to the notion of normality, but it is weaker than the usual normality requirement. Observe that the operators U and S (until and since) of Temporal Logic are only normal in the first position and not in the second. However, they satisfy conditions 1. and 2., the binary ordering $<$ can be associated with U and the binary ordering $>$ can be associated with S, thus condition 1. is satisfied. The monadic modalities H and G are derivable connectives, that satisfy the requirement of condition 2.

Following the lines of the proof of Theorem 2, by using Theorems 3.6 and 3.10 of [11], we can obtain the following transfer theorem:

Theorem 3. *Let L be a consistent classical modal logic axiomatised by a set Γ of formulas and such that satisfies conditions 1. and 2. above. Then, If L is complete and sound over the class of frames C, then L^N is also complete and sound over the class of frames $\bigoplus < C^\eta : \eta \in N >$.*

As an application of Theorems 2 and 3 we obtain that the Multimodal Logic of Normative Systems over the logics CTL and PDL, has a sound and complete axiomatisation, is decidable and has the Finite Model Property, because CTL and PDL are decidable and complete over the class of finite frames.

We end this section by introducing a model checking result. Given a frame $\Xi = (S, R_f)_{f \in F}$, we say that a subset of S is *connected* if for every $s, t \in S$, $(s, t) \in (\bigcup \{ (R_f \cup R_f^{-1} : f \in F \})^*$, where for any relation R, R^* denotes the transitive closure of R. We say that the frame Ξ is connected if its domain S is a connected set. Observe that, for every classical modal logic L that satisfies conditions 1. and 2. stated above and it is complete with respect to a class of connected frames, by Theorem 3, the Multimodal Logic of Normative Systems over L is also complete with respect to a class of connected frames.

Theorem 4. *Let L be a classical modal logic in a finite similarity type $\tau = \langle F, \rho \rangle$ and let $(S, R_f^\eta)_{f \in F, \eta \in N}$ be a finite model of the Multimodal Logic of Normative Systems over L such that the restriction of the model $(S, R_f^\eta)_{f \in F, \eta \in N}$ to the similarity type τ^η is connected. Then, the complexity of model checking a formula ϕ of type τ^N is*

$$O(\textstyle\sum_{\eta \in N} m_\eta + n \cdot k) + \sum_{\eta \in N}((O(k) + O(n)) \cdot C_L(m_\eta, n, k))$$

where $m_\eta = \sum_{f \in F} \left| R_f^\eta \right|$, $n = |S|$, k is the length of the formula ϕ and $C_L(m_\eta, n, k)$ is the complexity of model checking for logic L as a function of m_η, n and k.

Proof. By Theorem 2, L^N is a conservative extension of L and for every $\eta \in N$ the restriction of the model $(S, R_f^\eta)_{f \in F, \eta \in N}$ to the similarity type τ^η is a model of L and is connected by assumption. This fact allows us to generalize the result on temporal logics of Theorem 5.2 of [12]. We can express the complexity of a combined model checker for L^N in terms of a model checker for L.

For example, in the case of the Multimodal Logic of Normative Systems over CTL, the overall cost of the model checker for this logic is linear in the size of the model and in the length of the formula.

4   Elementary Normative Systems

There are some advantages of using Multimodal Logics of Normative Systems for reasoning about MAS: it is possible to compare whether a normative system is more restrictive than the other, check if a certain property holds in a model of a logic once a normative system has restricted its accessibility relation, model the dynamics of normative systems in institutional settings, define a hierarchy of normative systems (and, by extension, a classification of the institutions) or present a logical-based reasoning model for the agents to negotiate over norms. Up to this moment we have introduced an extensional definition of normative system (see Definition 1), in this section we present our first attempt to classify normative systems, we restrict our attention to normative systems defined by certain sets of first-order formulas, but only over some class of normal multimodal logics with standard Kripke semantics.

The choice of Sahlqvist formulas in this section is due, on the one hand, to the fact that a wide range of formalisms for MAS can be axiomatised by a set of such formulas (see next section). On the other hand, for the good logical properties of these logics (canonicity, transfer results, etc.). In Section 3 we have presented a general setting for dealing with any classical modal logic. Now, we focus only on some particular kind of logics. We want to study the specific properties of their normative systems that can be proved by using only the fact that these logics are axiomatised by sets of Sahlqvist formulas.

Given a set of modal formulas Σ, the *frame class defined by* Σ is the class of all frames on which each formula in Σ is valid. A frame class is *modally definable* if there is a set of modal formulas that defines it, and it is said that the frame class is *elementary* if it is defined by a first-order sentence of the frame correspondence language (the first-order language with equality and one binary relation symbol for each modality). An *Elementary Normative System* (ENS) is a propositional modal formula that defines an elementary class of frames and a normative system in any frame.

Throughout this and next section we assume that our modal languages have standard Kripke semantics and their modal similarity types have only a finite set of monadic modalities $\{\Box_f : f \in F\}$ and a finite set of propositional variables. Given a classical modal logic L and a set of Elementary Normative Systems N over L, for every $\eta \in N$ we generalize the notion introduced in Section 3 by defining the *Multimodal Logic of Normative Systems* over L and N, denoted by L^N, as being the smallest normal logic in the expanded language which contains L, N and every L^η. We now present a sound and complete axiomatisation and prove some transfer results in the case that L is axiomatised by a set of Sahlqvist formulas and N is a set of Sahlqvist formulas. We denote by $L(\eta)$ the smallest normal logic of similarity type τ^η which includes $L^\eta \cup \{\eta\}$.

Definition 5 (Sahlqvist formulas). *A modal formula is* positive (negative) *if every occurrence of a proposition letter is under the scope of an even (odd) number of negation signs. A* Sahlqvist antecedent *is a formula built up from* $\top, \bot$, *boxed atoms of the form* $\Box_{i_1} \ldots \Box_{i_l} p$, *for* $i_j \in I$ *and negative formulas, using conjunction, disjunction and diamonds. A* Sahlqvist implication *is a formula of the form* $\phi \to \varphi$, *when* ϕ *is a Sahlqvist antecedent and* φ *is positive. A* Sahlqvist formula *is a formula that is obtained from Sahlqvist implications by applying boxes and conjunction, and by applying disjunctions between formulas that do not share any propositional letters.*

Observe that $\bot$ and $\top$ are both Sahlqvist and ENS formulas. Intuitively speaking, $\bot$ is the trivial normative system. In $\bot$ every transition is forbidden in every state and in $\top$ every transition is legal. In the sequel we assume that for every set N of ENS, $\top \in N$.

Theorem 6. *Let L be a classical normal modal logic axiomatised by a set Γ of Sahlqvist formulas and N a set of ENS Sahlqvist formulas, then:*

1. $\Gamma^N = \Gamma \cup N \cup \bigcup \{\Gamma^\eta : \eta \in N\}$ *is an axiomatisation of L^N.*
2. L^N *is complete for the class of Kripke frames defined by Γ^N.*
3. L^N *is canonical.*
4. *If L and L^η are consistent, for every $\eta \in N$, and $\boldsymbol{P}$ is one of the following properties:*
   - *Compactness*
   - *Interpolation Property*
   - *Halldén-completeness*
   - *Decidability*
   - *Finite Model Property*[1]
   then L^N has $\boldsymbol{P}$ iff L and $L(\eta)$ have $\boldsymbol{P}$, for every $\eta \in N$.

Proof. 1–3 follows directly from the Sahlqvist's Theorem. The main basic idea of the proof of 4 is to apply the Sahlqvist's Theorem to show first that for every $\eta \in N$, the smallest normal logic of similarity type τ^η which includes $\Gamma^\eta \cup \{\eta\}$ is $L(\eta)$, is a complete logic for the class of Kripke frames defined by $\Gamma^\eta \cup \{\eta\}$ and is canonical (observe that this logic is axiomatised by a set of Sahlqvist formulas). Now, since for every Elementary Normative System $\eta \in N$ we have introduced a disjoint modal similarity type τ^η, we can define the fusion of the logics $\bigoplus <$ $L(\eta) : \eta \in N >$. It is enough to check that $L^N = \bigoplus < L(\eta) : \eta \in N >$ (remark that $L^\top = L$) and using transfer results for fusions of consistent logics (see for instance [13] and [11]) we obtain that L^N is a conservative extension and that decidability, compactness, interpolation, Hállden-completeness and the Finite Model Property are preserved.

---

[1] For the transfer of the Finite Model Property it is required that there is a number n such that each $L(\eta)$ has a model of size at most n.

We study now the relationships between normative systems. It is interesting to see how the structure of the set of all the ENS over a logic L (we denote it by $N(L)$) inherits its properties from the set of first-order counterparts. A natural relationship could be defined between ENS, the relationship of being one *less restrictive* than another. Let us denote it by $\preceq$. Given η, η', it is said that $\eta \preceq \eta'$ iff the first-order formula $\phi_{\eta'} \rightarrow \phi_\eta$ is valid (when for every $\eta \in N$, ϕ_η is the translation of η). The relation $\preceq$ defines a partial order on $N(L)$ and the pair $(N(L), \preceq)$ forms a complete lattice with least upper bound $\perp$ and greatest lower bound $\top$ and the operations $\wedge$ and $\vee$.

Now we present an extension of the Logic of Elementary Normative Systems over a logic L with some inclusion axioms and we prove completeness and canonicity results. Given a set N of ENS, let I^{N^+} be the following set of formulas:

$$\left\{ \Box_{i_1} \ldots \Box_{i_l} p \rightarrow \Box_{i_1}^\eta \ldots \Box_{i_l}^\eta p : i_j \in I, \eta \in N \right\}$$

and I^{N^*} the set:

$$\left\{ \Box_{i_1}^{\eta'} \ldots \Box_{i_l}^{\eta'} p \rightarrow \Box_{i_1}^\eta \ldots \Box_{i_l}^\eta p : i_j \in I, \eta \preceq \eta', \eta, \eta' \in N \right\}$$

Corollary 7. *Let L be a normal modal logic axiomatised by a set Γ of Sahlqvist formulas and N a set of ENS Sahlqvist formulas, then:*

1. *$\Gamma^{N^+} = \Gamma^N \cup I^{N^+}$ is an axiomatisation of the smallest normal logic with contains L^N and the axioms I^{N^+}, is complete for the class of the Kripke frames defined by Γ^{N^+} and is canonical. We denote this logic by L^{N^+}.*
2. *$\Gamma^{N^*} = \Gamma^N \cup I^{N^*} \cup I^{N^+}$ is an axiomatisation of the smallest normal logic with contains L^N and the axioms $I^{N^*} \cup I^{N^+}$, is complete for the class of the Kripke frames defined by Γ^{N^*} and is canonical. We denote this logic by L^{N^*}.*
3. *If L^N is consistent, both L^{N^+} and L^{N^*} are consistent.*

Proof. Since for every $i_j \in I$ every $\eta, \eta' \in N$, the formulas $\Box_{i_1} \ldots \Box_{i_l} p \rightarrow \Box_{i_1}^\eta \ldots \Box_{i_l}^\eta p$ and $\Box_{i_1}^{\eta'} \ldots \Box_{i_l}^{\eta'} p \rightarrow \Box_{i_1}^\eta \ldots \Box_{i_l}^\eta p$ are Sahlqvist, we can apply Theorem 6. In the case that L^N is consistent, consistency is guaranteed by the restriction to pairs $\eta \preceq \eta'$ and for the fact that η and η' are ENS.

Observe that for every frame $(S, R_f, R_f^\eta)_{f \in F, \eta \in N}$ of the logic L^{N^*},

$$R_{i_1}^\eta \circ \ldots \circ R_{i_l}^\eta \subseteq R_{i_0} \circ \ldots \circ R_{i_l},$$

and for $\eta \preceq \eta'$, $R_{i_1}^\eta \circ \ldots \circ R_{i_l}^\eta \subseteq R_{i_1}^{\eta'} \circ \ldots \circ R_{i_1}^{\eta'}$, where $\circ$ is the composition relation.

We end this section introducing a new class of modal formulas defining elementary classes of frames, the shallow formulas. For a recent account of the model theory of elementary classes and shallow formulas we refer the reader to [14].

Definition 8. *A modal formula is* shallow *if every occurrence of a proposition letter is in the scope of at most one modal operator.*

It is easy to see that every closed formula is shallow and that the class of Sahlqvist and shallow formulas don't coincide: $\Box_1(p \vee q) \rightarrow \Diamond_2(p \wedge q)$ is an example of shallow formula that is not Sahlqvist. Analogous results to Theorem 6 and Corollary 7 hold for shallow formulas, and using the fact that every frame class defined by a finite set of shallow formulas admits polynomial filtration, by Theorem 2.6.8 of [14], if L is a normal modal logic axiomatised by a finite set Γ of shallow formulas and N is a finite set of ENS shallow formulas, then the frame class defined by Γ^N has the Finite Model Property and has a satisfiability problem that can be solved in NEXPTIME.

5   Some Examples

Different formalisms have been introduced in the last twenty years in order to model particular aspects of agenthood (temporal Logics, logics of knowledge and belief, logics of communication, etc). We show in this section that several logics proposed for describing Multi-Agents Systems are axiomatised by a set of Sahlqvist or shallow formulas and therefore we could apply our results to the study of their normative systems. Let us come back to our previous example of Section 2, the multiprocess temporal frames. We have introduced first this basic temporal logic of transition systems, not because it is specially interesting in itself, but because it is the logic upon which other temporal logics are built and because it is a clear and simple example of how our framework can work.

Remember that $\Xi = (S, R_0, \ldots, R_k)$ is a *multiprocess temporal frame* if and only if S is a set of states, for every $i \leq k$, R_i is a binary relation on S such that $R = \bigcup_{i \leq k} R_i$ is a serial relation (that is, for every $s \in S$ there is $t \in S$ such that $(s, t) \in R$). It is easy to see that $\Xi = (S, R_0, \ldots, R_k)$ is a multiprocess temporal frame if and only if the formula of the corresponding multimodal language

$$\Diamond_0 \top \vee \ldots \vee \Diamond_k \top \text{ (MPT)}$$

is valid in Ξ. Let us denote by $MPTL$ the smallest normal logic containing axiom (MPT). For every nonempty tuple $(i_1, \ldots, i_l)$ such that for every $j \leq l$, $i_j \leq k$, consider the formula $\Box_{i_1} \ldots \Box_{i_l} \bot$. Observe that every formula of this form is shallow and ENS. We state now without proof a result on the consistency of this kind of normative systems over $MPTL$ that will allow us to use the logical framework introduced in the previous section.

Proposition 9. *Let N be a finite set of normative systems such that for every $\eta \in N$, there is a finite set X of formulas of the form $\Box_{i_1} \ldots \Box_{i_l} \bot$ such that η is the conjunction of all the formulas in X, $\bot \notin X$ and the following property holds:*

If $\Box_{i_1} \ldots \Box_{i_l} \bot \notin X$, there is $j \leq k$ such that $\Box_{i_1} \ldots \Box_{i_l} \Box_j \bot \notin X$.

Then, the logic $MPTL^N$ is consistent, complete, canonical, has the Finite Model Property and has a satisfiability problem that can be solved in NEXPTIME.

In general, a normal multimodal logic can be characterized by axioms that are added to the system K_m. The class of *Basic Serial Multimodal Logics* is characterized by subsets of axioms of the following form, requiring that AD(i) holds for every i,

- $\Box_i p \rightarrow \Diamond_i p$ AD(i)
- $\Box_i p \rightarrow p$ AT(i)
- $\Box_i p \rightarrow \Box_j p$ AI(i)
- $p \rightarrow \Box_i \Diamond_j p$ AB(i,j)
- $\Box_i p \rightarrow \Box_j \Box_k p$ A4(i,j,k)
- $\Diamond_i p \rightarrow \Box_j \Diamond_k p$ A5(i,j,k)

An example of a Kripke frame of $MPTL$ in which none of the previous axioms is valid is $\Xi = (\{0, 1, 2\}, \{(0, 1), (2, 0)\}, \{(1, 2)\})$. In particular, our example shows that the Multimodal Serial Logic axiomatised by $\{AD(i) : i \leq k\}$, is a proper extension of $MPTL$. Observe that any logic in the class BSML is axiomatised by a set of Sahlqvist formulas, therefore we could apply the framework introduced before to compare elementary normative systems on these logics.

Another type of logic axiomatised by Sahlqvist formulas are many Multimodal Epistemic Logics. Properties such as positive or negative introspection can be expressed by $\Box_i p \rightarrow \Box_i \Box_k p$ and $\neg \Box_i p \rightarrow \Box_i \neg \Box_i p$ respectively. And formulas like $\Box_i p \rightarrow \Box_j p$ allow us to reason about multi-degree belief.

The Minimal Temporal Logic K_t is axiomatised by the axioms $p \rightarrow HFp$ and $p \rightarrow GPp$ which are also Sahlqvist formulas. Some important axioms such as linearity $Ap \rightarrow GHp \wedge HGp$, or density $GGp \rightarrow Gp$, are Sahlqvist formulas, and we can express the property that the time has a beginning with an ENS. By adding the nexttime modality, X, we have an ENS which expresses that every instant has at most one immediate successor.

6   Related and Future Work

Along this work, in Sections 4 and 5, we have dealt only with multimodal languages with monadic modalities, but by using the results of Goranko and Vakarelov in [15] on the extension of the class of Sahlqvist formulas in arbitrary polyadic modal languages to the class of inductive formulas, it would be possible to generalize our results to polyadic languages.

We will proceed to apply our results to different extended modal languages, such as reversive languages with nominals (in [15], the elementary canonical formulas in these languages are characterized) or Hybrid Logic (in [14], Hybrid Sahlqvist formulas are proved to define elementary classes of frames). Future work should go beyond Elementary Normative Systems and consider the study of sets of normative systems expressed by other formal systems.

Several formalisms have been introduced for reasoning about normative systems over specific logics. Two examples are worth noting: Normative ATL (NATL), proposed in [2] and Temporal Logic of Normative Systems (NTL) in [3]. NATL is an extension to the Alternating-Time Temporal Logic and contains cooperation modalities of the form $<< \eta : C >> \phi$ with the intended interpretation that "C has the ability to achieve ϕ within the context of the normative system η". NTL is a conservative generalization of the Branching-Time Temporal Logic CTL. In NTL, the path quantifiers A ("on all paths...") and E ("on some path...") are replaced by the indexed deontic operators O_η ("it is obligatory in the context of the normative system η that..") and P_η ("it is permissible in the context of the normative system η that..."). In our article we have extended these approaches to deal with arbitrary multimodal logics with standard Kripke semantics. Our definition of normative system is intensional, but the languages introduced permit to work with extensional definitions like the ones in [3] and [2].

Apart from these two articles, there are other previous works where we found intuitions and formalisations that motivated the introduction of our framework. Moses, Shoham, and Tennenholtz in [17]-[19] defined the notion of social laws for multiagent systems. They set up a basic formal framework within which computational questions about social laws could be formulated. These ideas were developed by Fitoussi and Tennenholtz, considering simple social laws, social laws that could not be any simpler without failing, see [20]. Moses and Tennenholtz developed in [16] a deontic epistemic logic for representing properties of multiagent systems with normative structures. Their logic did contain notions of socially reachable states of affairs, which essentially corresponds to our normative system operators. Lomuscio and Sergot introduced in [21] deontic interpreted systems. The basic idea was to interpret the deontic accessibility relation as linking states where the system is correctly functioning. They gave an axiomatization of their logic, and also investigated the epistemic properties of their system.

6.1   Related Papers in This Volume

The paper by Viganò and Colombetti in [22] enrich the modelling language FIEVel for institutions, with new constructs to describe norms and sanctions. This is a similar approach to ours, since they introduce also model checking results and their logic is an extension of Normative Temporal Logic. The article also focusses on the study of properties of artificial institutions, showing that when they reflect certain interpretations of norms of human institutions, it is not always possible to satisfy them.

Cliffe, De Vos and Padget propose in [23] a formalism capable to specify and reason about multiple interacting institutions. In the paper they explore the consequences of the correspondence between landmarks and the institutional states of their executable model. The essence of the landmark definition is a condition on a state in order for an action in some protocol to have effect.

The paper by García-Camino, Rodríguez-Aguilar and Vasconcelos introduces in [24] a distributed architecture and non-centralised computational model for norms. This is an interesting contribution dealing with MAS normative conflicts that may arise due to the dynamic nature of MAS. The notion of MAS, regulated by protocols, is extended with an extra layer called *normative structure*. AMELI is extended including a new type of agent, the *normative managers*. This artifact allows the propagation of normative positions as a consequence of agents' actions.

An innovative approach to the dynamics of normative systems is the formalisation of Thagard's Coherence Theory in [25]. In their paper, Joseph, Sierra and Schorlemmer introduce an agent model based on coherence theory, the reasoning process of the intentional agent permits the agent to drop beliefs or to violate norms in order to keep a maximal state of coherence.

Acknowledgements. The author wishes to express her thanks to Carles Sierra, Pablo Noriega and the reviewers of this paper for their helpful comments. Research partially supported by the Spanish projects "Agreement Technologies" (CONSOLIDER CSD2007-0022, INGENIO 2010) and Project TIN2006-15662-C02-01.

References

1. Noriega, P.: Fencing the Open Fields: Empirical Concerns on Electronic Institutions. In: Boissier, O., Padget, J.A., Dignum, V., Lindemann, G., Matson, E., Ossowski, S., Sichman, J.S., Vázquez-Salceda, J. (eds.) ANIREM 2005 and OOOP 2005. LNCS (LNAI), vol. 3913, pp. 82–98. Springer, Heidelberg (2006)
2. van der Hoek, W., Wooldridge, M.: On obligations and normative ability: towards a logical analysis of the social contract. Journal of Applied Logic 3, 396–420 (2005)
3. Ågotnes, T., van der Hoek, W., Rodríguez-Aguilar, J.A., Sierra, C., Wooldridge, M.: On the Logic of Normative Systems. Twentieth International Joint Conference on AI, IJCAI 2007, pp. 1175–1180. AAAI Press, Menlo Park (2007)
4. Gabbay, D.M.: Fibring Logics. Oxford Logic Guides, 38 (1999)
5. Kurucz, A.: Combining Modal Logics. In: Blackburn, P., van Benthem, J., Wolter, F. (eds.) Handbook of Modal Logic, vol. 15, pp. 869–928. Elsevier, Amsterdam (2007)
6. Blackburn, P., van Benthem, J., Wolter, F.: Handbook of Modal Logic, vol. 15. Elsevier, Amsterdam (2007)
7. Ramchurn, S.D., Sierra, C., Godo, L., Jennings, N.R.: Negotiating using rewards. In: Proceedings of the Fifth international Joint Conference on Autonomous Agents and Multiagent Systems. AAMAS 2006, Hakodate, Japan, May 08–12, 2006, pp. 400–407. ACM Press, New York (2006)
8. Gabbay, D.M.: What is a Logical System? Oxford University Press, Inc, Oxford (1994)
9. Thomason, S.K.: Independent Propositional Modal Logics. Studia Logica 39, 143–144 (1980)
10. Baader, F., Ghilardi, S., Tinelli, C.: A new combination procedure for the word problem that generalizes fusion decidability results in modal logics. Information and Computation 204, 1413–1452 (2006)
11. Finger, M., Weiss, M.A.: The Unrestricted Combination of Temporal Logic Systems. Logic Journal of the IGPL 10, 165–189 (2002)
12. Franceschet, M., Montanari, A., de Rijke, M.: Model Checking for Combined Logics with an Application to Mobile Systems. Automated Software Engineering 11, 289–321 (2004)
13. Wolter, F.: Fusions of modal logics revisited. In: Kracht, M., de Rijke, M., Wansing, H., Zakharyashev, M. (eds.) Advances in Modal Logic, CSLI, Stanford (1998)

14. Cate, B.D.T.: Model Theory for extended modal languages. Ph.D Thesis, Institute for Logic, Language and Computation, Universiteit van Amsterdam. ILLC Dissertation, Series DS-2005-01 (2005)
15. Goranko, V., Vakarelov, D.: Elementary Canonical Formulae: extending Sahlqvist's Theorem. Annals of Pure and Applied Logic 141, 180–217 (2006)
16. Moses, Y., Tennenholtz, M.: Artificial social systems. Computers and AI 14, 533–562 (1995)
17. Shoham, Y., Tennenholtz, M.: On the synthesis of useful social laws for artificial agent societies. In: Proceedings of the Tenth National Conference on Artificial Intelligence (AAAI 1992), San Diego, CA (1992)
18. Shoham, Y., Tennenholtz, M.: On social laws for artificial agent societies: Offline design. In: Agre, P.E., Rosenschein, S.J. (eds.) Computational Theories of Interaction and Agency, pp. 597–618. MIT Press, Cambridge (1996)
19. Shoham, Y., Tennenholtz, M.: On the emergence of social conventions: Modelling, analysis, and simulations. Artificial Intelligence 94(1–2), 139–166 (1997)
20. Fitoussi, D., Tennenholtz, M.: Choosing social laws for multi-agent systems: Minimality and simplicity. Artificial Intelligence 119(1–2), 61–101 (2000)
21. Lomuscio, A., Sergot, M.: Deontic interpreted systems. Studia Logica 75(1), 63–92 (2003)
22. Viganò, F., Colombetti, M.: Model Checking Norms and Sanctions in Institutions. In: Sichman, J.S., et al. (eds.) COIN 2007 Workshops. LNCS (LNAI), vol. 4870, pp. 261–274. Springer, Heidelberg (2008)
23. Cliffe, O., De Vos, M., Padget, J.: Embedding Landmarks and Scenes in a Computational Model of Institutions. In: Sichman, J.S., et al. (eds.) COIN 2007 Workshops. LNCS (LNAI), vol. 4870, pp. 262–275. Springer, Heidelberg (2008)
24. García-Camino, A., Rodríguez-Aguilar, J.A., Vasconcelos, W.: A Distributed Architecture for Norm Management in Multi-Agent Systems. In: Sichman, J.S., Padget, J., Ossowski, S., Noriega, P. (eds.) COIN 2007. LNCS(LNAI), vol. 4870, pp. 275–286. Springer, Heidelberg (2008)
25. Joseph, S., Sierra, C., Schorlemmer, M.: A coherence based framework for institutional agents. In: Sichman, J.S., Padget, J., Ossowski, S., Noriega, P. (eds.) COIN 2007. LNCS(LNAI), vol. 4870, pp. 287–300. Springer, Heidelberg (2008)

A Distributed Architecture for Norm Management in Multi-Agent Systems

Andrés García-Camino[1], Juan Antonio Rodríguez-Aguilar[1],
and Wamberto Vasconcelos[2]

[1] IIIA, Artificial Intelligence Research Institute
CSIC, Spanish Research Council, Campus UAB, 08193 Bellaterra, Spain
{andres,jar}@iiia.csic.es
[2] Dept. of Computing Science, University of Aberdeen, Aberdeen AB24 3UE, UK
wvasconcelos@acm.org

Abstract. Norms, that is, obligations, prohibitions and permissions, are useful abstractions to facilitate coordination in open, heterogeneous multi-agent systems. We observe a lack of distributed architectures and non-centralised computational models for norms. We propose a model, *viz.*, normative structures, to regulate the behaviour of autonomous agents taking part in simultaneous and possibly related activities within a multi-agent system. This artifact allows the propagation of normative positions (that is, the obligations, prohibitions and permissions associated to individual agents) as a consequence of agents' actions. Within a normative structure, conflicts may arise – one same action can be simultaneousely forbidden and obliged/permitted. This is due to the concurrent and dynamic nature of agents' interactions in a multi-agent system. However, ensuring conflict freedom of normative structures at design time is computationally intractable, and thus real-time conflict resolution is required: our architecture support the distributed management of normative positions, including conflict detection and resolution.

1   Introduction

An essential characteristic of open, heterogeneous multi-agent systems (MASs) is that agents' interactions are regulated to comply with the conventions of the system. Norms, that is, obligations, prohibitions and permissions, can be used to represent such conventions and hence as a means to regulate the observable behaviour of agents [3,18]. There are many contributions on the subject of norms from sociologists, philosophers and logicians (*e.g.*, [1,2]). Recently, proposals for computational realisations of normative models have been presented. Some of them operate in a centralised manner (*e.g.* [3,4,5]) which creates bottlenecks and single points-of-failure. Others (*e.g.* [6,7]), although distributed, aim at the regulation of communication between agents without taking into account that some of the normative positions (*i.e.*, their permissions, prohibitions and obligations) generated as a result of agent interaction may also affect other agents not involved in the communication.

The class of MASs we envisage consists of multiple, simultaneous and possibly related agent interactions, or *activities*. Each agent may simultaneously

J.S. Sichman et al. (Eds.): COIN 2007, LNAI 4870, pp. 275–286, 2008.
© Springer-Verlag Berlin Heidelberg 2008

participate in several activities, and may change from one activity to another. An agent's actions within one activity may have consequences – These are captured as normative positions that define, influence or constrain the agent's future behaviour. For instance, a buyer agent who ran out of credit may be forbidden from making further offers, or a seller agent is obliged to deliver the goods after closing a deal. Within a MAS normative conflicts may arise due to the dynamic nature of the MAS and simultaneous agents' actions. A normative conflict arises, for instance, when an action is simultaneously prohibited and obliged. Such conflicts ought to be identified and resolved. This analysis of conflicts can be carried out in each activity. However, ensuring conflict-freedom on a network of agent conversations (or activities) at design time is computationally intractable as shown in [8].

We propose means to handle conflicting normative positions in open and regulated MASs in a distributed manner. In realistic settings run-time conflict detection and resolution is required. Hence, we require a tractable algorithm for conflict resolution along the lines of the one presented in [8]. The only modification required for that algorithm is that it should return a list of updates (or *normative commands*), that is, the norms to be added and removed, instead of the resulting set of norms obtained from the updates.

We need an architecture to incorporate the previously mentioned algorithm. Among other features, we require our architecture to be distributed, regulated, open, and heterogeneous. These features are included in other architectures such as AMELI [6]. However, the propagation of normative positions to several agents or to an agent not directly involved in the interaction and the resolution of normative conflicts has not yet been addressed.

We thus propose an extension of the architecture presented in [6] fulfilling these features. We extend AMELI by including a new type of agent, *viz.*, the *normative managers*, also adding interaction protocols with this new type of agent, allowing for a novel conceptual differentiation of administrative (or "internal") agents. Thus, the main contribution of the paper is a distributed architecture to regulate the behaviour of autonomous agents and manage normative aspects of a MAS, including the propagation of normative positions to different conversations and the resolution of normative conflicts.

This paper is organised as follows. In Section 2 we present a scenario to illustrate and motivate our approach. Normative structures are introduced in Section 3. Section 4 presents our distributed architecture and, in Section 5, we comment on related work. Finally, we draw conclusions and report on future work in Section 6.

2   Scenario

We make use of a contract scenario in which companies come together at an online marketplace to negotiate and sign contracts in order to get certain tasks done. The overall transaction procedure may be organised as five distributed activities, represented as nodes in the diagram in Figure 1. The activities involve different participants whose behaviour is coordinated through protocols.

After registering at the marketplace, clients and suppliers get together in an activity where they negotiate the terms of their contract, *i.e.* actions to be performed, prices, deadlines and other details. The client will then participate in a *payment*

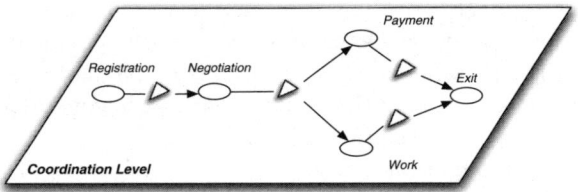

Fig. 1. Activity Structure of the Scenario

activity, verifying his credit-worthiness and instructing his bank to transfer the correct amount of money. The supplier in the meantime will delegate to specialised employees the actions to be performed in the *work* activity. Finally, agents can leave the marketplace conforming to a predetermined *exit* protocol. The marketplace accountant participates in most of the activities as a trusted provider of auditing tools.

3 Normative Structure

We address a class of MASs in which interactions are carried out via illocutionary speech acts [9] exchanged among participating agents, along the lines of agent communication languages such as FIPA-ACL [10]. In these MASs, agents interact according to protocols which are naturally distributed. We observe that in some realistic scenarios, speech acts in a protocol may have an effect on other protocols. Certain actions bring about changes in the *normative positions* of agents – their "social burden": what each agent is permitted, obliged and forbidden to do. We use the term normative command to refer to the addition or removal of a normative position. Henceforth we shall refer to the application of a normative command as the addition or removal of a given normative position. Occurrences of normative positions in one protocol may also have consequences for other protocols.

We propose to extend the notion of MAS, regulated by protocols, with an extra layer called *normative structure* (NS). This layer consists of normative scenes, which represent the normative state, i.e. the set of illocutions uttered and normative positions, of the agents participating in a given activity, and normative transitions, which specifies by means of a rule the conditions under which some normative positions are to be generated or removed in the given normative scenes. The formal definition of normative structure is presented in [8], and here we informally discuss it.

Fig. 2 shows an example of how a normative structure relates with the coordination level. A normative transition is specified between the negotiation and payment activities denoting that there is a rule that may be activated with the state of negotiation activity and that may modify the state of the payment activity. In our example, the rule would be that whenever a client accepts an offer of a supplier, an obligation on the former to pay the latter is created in the payment activity. The rule connecting the payment and the work activity would specify that whenever a client fulfils its payment obligation, an obligation on the worker to complete the contracted task is generated in the work activity.

We are concerned with the propagation and distribution of normative positions within a network of distributed, normative scenes as a consequence of agents' actions. In [8] the formal semantics of NSs was defined via a mapping to Coloured Petri Nets. Conflicts may arise after the addition of new formulae. Hence, if a new norm does not generate any conflict then it can be directly added. If a conflict arises, the algorithm presented in [11] is used to decide whether to ignore the new normative position or to remove the conflicting ones.

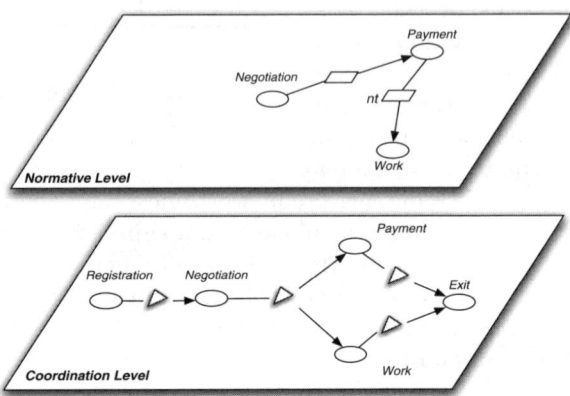

Fig. 2. Normative Structure and Coordination Level

4   Proposed Distributed Architecture

We propose an architecture to address the regulation of the behaviour of autonomous agents and the management of the normative state(s) of the MASs, including the propagation of normative positions and the resolution of normative conflicts. We assume the existence of a set of agents that interact in order to pursue their goals – we do not have control on these agents' internal functioning, nor can we anticipate it. We require the following features of our architecture:

Regulated. The main goal of our architecture is to restrict the effects of agent behaviour in the specified conditions without hindering the autonomy of external agents.

Open. Instead of reprogramming the MAS for each set of external agents, we advocate persistent, longer-lasting MASs where agents can join and leave them. However, agents' movements may be restricted in certain circumstances.

Heterogeneous. We leave to each agent programmer the decision of which agent architecture include in each external agent. We make no assumption concerning how agents are implemented.

Mediatory. As we do not control external agents internal functioning, in order to avoid undesired or unanticipated interactions, our architecture should work as a "filter" of messages between agents.

Distributed. To provide the means for implementing large regulated MAS, we require our architecture to be distributed in a network and therefore spreading and alleviating the workload and the message traffic.

Norm propagative. Although being distributed, agent interactions are not isolated and agent behaviour may have effects, in the form of addition or removal of normative positions, in later interactions possibly involving different agents.

Conflict Resolutive. Some conflicts may arise due to normative positions being generated as result of agent's behaviour. Since ensuring a conflict-free MAS at design time is computationally intractable, we require that resolution of normative conflicts would be applied by the MAS. This approach promotes consistency since there is a unique, valid normative state established by the system instead of a lot of different state versions due to a conflict resolution at agent's level.

To accomplish these requirements, we extend AMELI, the architecture presented in [6]. That architecture is divided in three layers:

Autonomous agent layer. It is formed by the set of external agents taking part in the MAS.

Social layer. An infrastructure that mediates and facilitates agents' interactions while enforcing MAS rules.

Communication layer. In charge of providing a reliable and orderly transport service.

External agents intending to communicate with other external agents need to redirect their messages through the social layer which is in charge of forwarding the messages (attempts of communication) to the communication layer. In specified conditions, erroneous or illicit messages may be ignored by the social layer in order to prevent them from arriving at their addressees.

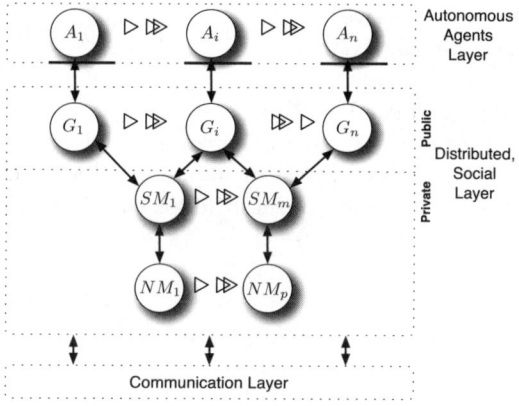

Fig. 3. AMELI$^+$architecture

The social layer presented in [6] is a multi-agent system itself and the agents belonging to it are called *internal agents*. We propose to extend this architecture by including a new type of agent , the normative manager (NM_1 to NM_p in fig. 3), and by adding protocols to accommodate this kind of agent. We call AMELI$^+$ the resulting architecture.

In AMELI$^+$, internal (administrative) agents are of one of the following types:

Governor (G). Internal agent representing an external agent, that is, maintaining and informing about its social state, deciding or forwarding whether an attempt from its external agent is valid. One per external agent.

Scene Manager (SM). Internal agent maintaining the state of the activity[1], deciding whether an attempt to communicate is valid, notifying any changes to normative managers and resolving conflicts.

Normative Manager (NM). This new type of internal agent receives normative commands and may fire one or more normative transition rules.

In principle, only one NM is needed if it manages all the normative transition rules. However, in order to build large MAS and avoid bottlenecks, we propose the distribution of rules into several NMs.

To choose the granularity of the normative layer, i.e. to choose from one single NM to one NM per normative transition, is an important design decision that we leave for the MAS designers. After choosing the granularity, the NMs are assigned to handle a possibly unary set of normative transitions. Recall that each normative transition includes a rule. The SMs

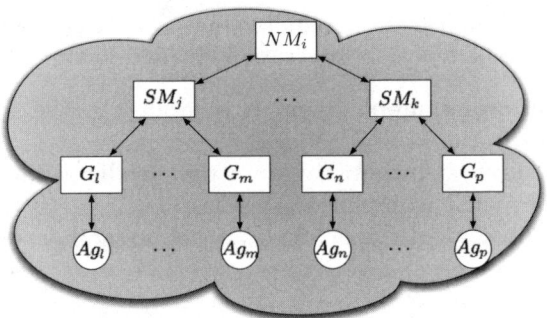

Fig. 4. Channels involved in the activation of a rule

involved in the firing of the rules are given a reference to the NM that manages the rule, i.e. its address or identifier depending on the communication layer. External agents may join and leave activities, always following the conventions of the activities. In these cases, its governor registers (or deregisters) with the SM of that scene.

4.1   Social Layer Protocols

Fig. 4 shows the communication within the social layer – it only occurs along the following types of channels:

Agent / Governor. This type of channel is used by the external agents sending messages to their respective governors to request information or to request a message to be delivered to another external agent (following the norms of the MAS). Governors use this type of channel to inform their agents about new normative positions generated.

---

[1] Hereafter, activities are also referred to as scenes following the nomenclature of AMELI.

Governor / Scene Manager. Governors use this type of channel to propagate unresolved attempts to communicate or normative commands generated as a result of such attempts. SMs use this type of channel to inform governors in their scenes about new normative commands generated as a result of attempts to communicate or conflict resolution.

Scene Manager / Normative Manager. This type of channel is used by SMs to propagate normative commands that NMs may need to receive and the ones resulting from conflict resolution. NMs use this channel to send normative commands generated by the application of normative transition rules.

Fig. 5 shows an enactment of a MAS in our architecture. Agents send attempts to governors (messages 1, 4 and 7) who, after finding out the normative commands attempts generate, propagate the new normative commands to SM_{s1} and SM_{s2} (messages 2, 5 and 8) who, in turn,

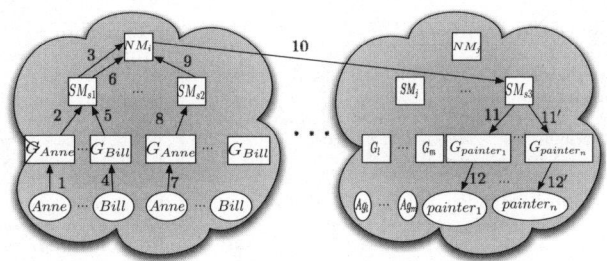

Fig. 5. Enactment of a normative transition rule

propagate them to the NM (messages 3, 6 and 9). As a normative transition rule is fired in the NM, a normative command is sent to SM_{s3} (message 10). After resolving any conflicts, SM_{s3} sends the new normative commands to all the involved governors (messages 11 and 11') who, in turn, send them to their represented agents (messages 12 and 12').

As the figure of the previous example shows, our architecture propagates attempts to communicate (and their effects) from agents (shown on the bottom of Fig 5) to the NMs (shown at the top of the figure). NMs receive events from several SMs whose managed state may be arbitrarily large. Since NMs only need the normative commands that may cause any of its rules to fire, NMs subscribe only to the type of normative commands they are supposed to monitor. For instance, if a rule needs to check whether there exists a prohibition to paint in a scene *work1* and whether there exists the obligation of informing about the completion of the painting job, then the NM will subscribe to all the normative commands adding or removing prohibitions to paint in scene work1 as well as all normative commands managing obligations to inform about the completion of the painting job.

In the following algorithms, Δ refers to essential information for the execution of the MAS, i.e. a portion of the state of affairs of the MAS that each internal agent is managing. As introduced above, depending on the type of the internal agent, it manages a different portion of the state of affairs of the MAS, e.g. a governor keeps the social state of the agent, and a scene manager keeps the state of a given scene. These algorithms define the behaviour of internal agents and

```
algorithm G_process_att(ag_i, msg)
input ag_i, msg
output ∅
begin
01 new_cmmds := get_norm_cmmds(msg, Δ)
02 foreach c ∈ new_cmmds do
03    Δ := apply(c, Δ)
04    sm := scene_manager(c)
05    send(c, ag_i)
06    send(c, sm)
07 endforeach
08 if new_cmmds = ∅ then
09    sm := scene_manager(msg)
10    send(msg, sm)
11 endif
end
```

(a) G response to an agent attempt

```
algorithm NM_process_cmmd(sm_i, msg)
input sm_i, msg
output ∅
begin
01 foreach cmmd ∈ msg do
02    Δ := apply(cmmd, Δ)
03    ncs := get_RHS_from_fired_rules(Δ)
04    foreach c ∈ ncs do
05       sm := scene_manager(c)
06       send(c, sm)
07    endforeach
08 foreach
end
```

(b) NM response to a command

```
algorithm SM_process_att(g_i, msg)
input g_i, msg
output ∅
begin
01 new_cmmds := get_norm_cmmds(msg, Δ)
02 foreach c ∈ new_cmmds do
03    Δ := apply(c, Δ)
04    send(c, g_i)
05    foreach ⟨nm, ev⟩ ∈ subscriptions do
06       if unify(c, ev, σ) then
07          send(c, nm)
08       endif
09    endforeach
10 endforeach
11 if new_cmmds = ∅ then
12    s := scene(msg)
13    c := content(msg)
14    send(rejected(s, c), g_i)
15 endif
end
```

(c) SM response to a forwarded attempt

```
algorithm SM_process_cmmd(nm_i, msg)
input nm_i, msg
output ∅
begin
01 Δ' := apply(msg, Δ)
02 if inconsistent(Δ') then
03    msg := resolve_conflicts(Δ, msg)
04 endif
05 foreach cmmd ∈ msg do
06    Δ := apply(cmmd, Δ)
07    foreach ⟨nm, ev⟩ ∈ subscriptions do
08       if unify(c, ev, σ) then
09          send(c, nm)
10       endif
11    endforeach
12    foreach g ∈ governors(cmmd) do
13       send(cmmd, g)
14    endforeach
15 endforeach
end
```

(d) SM response to a command

Fig. 6. Internal Agents Algorithms

are applied whenever a message msg is sent by an agent (ag_i), a governor (g_i), a SM (sm_i) or a NM (nm_i) respectively.

When an external agent sends to its governor an attempt to communicate (messages 1, 4 and 7 in Fig. 5), the governor follows the algorithm of Fig. 6(a). This algorithm checks whether the attempt to communicate generates normative commands (line 1), i.e. it is accepted[2]. This check may vary depending on the type of specification and implementation of the scenes: e.g. using Finite State Machines (FSM), as in [6], or executing a set of rules, as in [4].

If the attempt generates normative commands (line 2), they are applied to the portion of the state of affairs the governor is currently managing creating a new partial state (line 3). These normative commands are sent to the external agent (line 5) and to the scene manager (messages 2, 5 and 8 in Fig. 5) in charge of the scene where the normative command should be applied (line 6). Otherwise, the attempt is forwarded to the SM of the scene the attempt was generated in (line 10).

---

[2] In our approach, an ignored attempt would not generate any normative command.

If the governor accepts the attempt (after the check of line 1), it sends the SM a notification.The SM then applies the normative command received and forwards it to the NMs subscribed to that event (messages 3, 6 and 9 in Fig. 5).

However, if the governor does not take a decision, i.e. normative commands are not generated, the governor sends the attempt to the SM who should decide whether it is valid or not by following the algorithm of Fig. 6(c). This algorithm, like the one in Fig. 6(a), checks whether the received attempt generates normative commands in the current scene state, i.e. the portion of the state of affairs referring to that scene (line 1). If this is the case (line 2), they are applied to the current state of the scene (line 3) and forwarded to the governor that sent the attempt (line 4) and to the NMs subscribed to that normative commands (line 7). Otherwise (line 11), a message informing that the attempt has been rejected is sent to the governor mentioned (line 14).

In both cases, if the attempt is accepted then the normative manager is notified and it follows the algorithm of Fig. 6(b) in order to decide if it is necessary to send new normative commands to other scene managers. This algorithm processes each normative command received (line 1) by applying it to the state of the NM (line 2) and checking which normative transition rules are fired and obtaining the normative commands generated (line 3). Each of them are propagated to the SM of the scene appearing in the normative command (line 6, message 10 in Fig. 5).

If normative commands are generated, SMs receive them from the normative manager in order to resolve possible conflicts and propagate them to the appropriate governors. In this case, the SMs execute the algorithm of Fig. 6(d). This algorithm applies the normative command received on the scene state creating a temporary state for conflict checking (line 1), then checks if the new normative command would raise an inconsistency (line 2). If this is the case, it applies the conflict resolution algorithm presented in [8], returning the set of normative commands needed to resolve the conflict (line 3). Each normative command caused by the message sent by the NM or by conflict resolution, is applied to the scene state (line 6) and it is sent to the subscribed NMs (lines 7-11) and to the governors (messages 11 and 11' in Fig. 5) of the agents appearing in the normative command (lines 12-14).

NMs are notified about the resolution of possible conflicts in order to check if the new normative commands fire normative transition rules. If NMs receive this notification, they follow again the algorithm of Fig. 6(b) as explained above. When governors are notified by a SM about new normative commands, they apply the normative command received to the normative state of the agent and notify to its agent about the new normative command (messages 12 and 12' in Fig. 5).

In our approach, conflict resolution is applied at the SM level requiring all normative commands generated by a NM to pass through a SM who resolves conflicts and routes them. This feature is justified because SMs are the only agents who have a full representation of a scene and know the agents are participating in it and which role they are enacting. For example, if a prohibition for all painters to paint arrives at the work activity, a SM will forward this prohibition to the governors of the agents participating in that activity with the painter role and to the governors of all the new painters that join that activity while the prohibition is active. An alternative approach is to apply conflict resolution at the level of governor agents, curtailing some of the normative positions of its associated external agent. However, this type of conflict resolution is more limited since a governor only maintains the normative state of an agent. For example, a case that cannot be resolved with this approach is when all agents enacting a role are simultaneously prohibited and obliged to do something, i.e. when more than one agent is involved in the conflict.

Another approach would be if governors became the only managers of normative positions; in this case they would need to be aware of all normative positions that may affect its agent in the future, i.e. they would have to maintain all the normative positions affecting any of the roles that its agent may enact in every existing scene. For instance, a governor of an agent that is not yet enacting a painter role would also need to receive the normative positions that now applies to that role even if the agent is not in that scene or is enacting that role yet. This approach does not help with scalability since a large MAS with various scenes may generate a very large quantity of normative positions affecting agents in the future by the mere fact of their entering the MAS.

5 Related Work

The subject of norms has been studied widely in the literature (*e.g.*, [2,12,13]), and, more recently, much attention is being paid to more pragmatic and implementational aspects of norms, that is, how norms can be given a computational interpretation and how norms can be factored in the design and execution of MASs (e.g. [14,15,3,4,16]).

However, not much work has addressed the management of norms and reasoning about them in a distributed manner. Despite the fact that in [17,7] two languages are presented for the distributed enforcement of norms in MAS, in both works each agent has a local message interface that forwards legal messages according to a set of norms. Since these interfaces are local to each agent, norms can only be expressed in terms of actions of that agent. This is a serious disadvantage, *e.g.* when one needs to activate an obligation to one agent due to a certain message of another agent.

In [18] the authors propose a multi-agent architecture for policy monitoring, compliance checking and enforcement in virtual organisations (VOs). Their approach also uses a notion of hierarchical enforcement, i.e. the parent assimilates summarised event streams from multiple agents and may initiate further action on the subordinate agents. Depending on its policies, a parent can override the functioning of its children by changing their policies. Instead of considering any notion similar to our scene (multi-agent protocol where the number of participants may vary) and assigning an agent exclusively dedicated to the management of one scene, they assign another participant in the VO as parent of a set of agents. Although the parent would receive only the events it needs to monitor, it may receive them from *all* the interactions their children are engaging in. This can be a disadvantage when the number of interactions is large converting the parents in bottlenecks. Although they mention that conflict resolution may be accomplished with their architecture, they leave this feature to the VO agent thus centralising the conflict resolution in each VO. This can also be a disadvantage when the number of interactions is large since the VO agent has to resolve all the possible conflicts. This would require either all the events flowing through the VO agent or the VO agent monitoring the state of the whole VO in order to detect and resolve conflicts. The main theoretical restriction in their approach is that all the agents involved in a change in a policy must share a common parent in the hierarchy of the VO. In an e-commerce example, when a buyer accepts a deal an obligation to supply the purchased item should be added to the seller. However, as they are different parties, their only common parent is the VO agent converting the latter in a bottleneck in large e-commerce scenarios.

6   Conclusions and Future Work

We base the architecture presented in this paper in our proposal of normative structure and conflict resolution of [8]. The notion of normative structure is useful because it allows the separation of normative and procedural concerns. We notice that the algorithm presented in that paper is also amenable to the resolution of normative conflicts in a distributed manner.

The main contribution of this paper is an architecture for the management of norms in a distributed manner. As a result of the partial enactment of protocols in diverse scenes, normative positions generated in different scenes can be used to regulate the behaviour of agents not directly involved in previous interactions. Furthermore, conflict resolution is applied at a scene level meaning that resolution criteria involving more than one agent are now possible.

We want to extend normative structures [8], as we use them in our architecture, along several directions: (1) to handle constraints as part of the norm language, in particular constraints related with the notion of time; (2) to capture in the conflict resolution algorithm different semantics relating the deontic notions by supporting different axiomations (*e.g.*, relative strength of prohibition versus obligation, default deontic notions, deontic inconsistencies, etc.).

We also intend to use analysis techniques for Coloured Petri-Nets (CPNs) in order to characterise classes of CPNs (*e.g.*, acyclic, symmetric, etc.) corresponding to families of Normative Structures that are susceptible to tractable off-line conflict detection. The combination of these techniques along with our online conflict resolution mechanisms is intended to endow MAS designers with the ability to incorporate norms into their systems in a principled way.

Acknowledgements. This work was partially funded by the Spanish Education and Science Ministry as part of the projects TIN2006-15662-C02-01 and 2006-5-0I-099. García-Camino enjoys an I3P grant from the Spanish National Research Council (CSIC).

References

1. Habermas, J.: The Theory of Communication Action, 1st edn. Reason and the Rationalization of Society. Beacon Press (1984)
2. von Wright, G.H.: Norm and Action: A Logical Inquiry. Routledge and Kegan Paul, London (1963)
3. Fornara, N., Viganò, F., Colombetti, M.: An Event Driven Approach to Norms in Artificial Institutions. In: AAMAS 2005. Workshop: Agents, Norms and Institutions for Regulated Multiagent Systems (ANI@REM). Utrecht (2005)
4. García-Camino, A., Rodríguez-Aguilar, J.A., Sierra, C., Vasconcelos, W.: A Distributed Architecture for Norm-Aware Agent Societies. In: Baldoni, M., Endriss, U., Omicini, A., Torroni, P. (eds.) DALT 2005. LNCS (LNAI), vol. 3904, pp. 89–105. Springer, Heidelberg (2006)
5. Ricci, A., Viroli, M.: Coordination Artifacts: A Unifying Abstraction for Engineering Environment-Mediated Coordination in MAS. Informatica 29, 433–443 (2005)
6. Esteva, M., Rosell, B., Rodríguez-Aguilar, J.A., Arcos, J.L.: AMELI: An agent-based middleware for electronic institutions. In: Procs of 3rd Int'l Conf on Autonomous Agents and Multiagent Systems (AAMAS 2004), 236–243 (2004)
7. Minsky, N.: Law Governed Interaction (LGI): A Distributed Coordination and Control Mechanism (An Introduction, and a Reference Manual). Technical report, Rutgers University (2005)
8. Gaertner, D., García-Camino, A., Noriega, P., Rodríguez-Aguilar, J.A., Vasconcelos, W.: Distributed Norm Management in Regulated Multi-agent Systems. In: Procs of 6th Int'l Conf on Autonomous Agents and Multiagent Systems (AAMAS 2007), pp. 624–631, Hawai'i (2007)
9. Searle, J.: Speech Acts, An Essay in the Philosophy of Language. Cambridge University Press, Cambridge (1969)
10. Foundation for Intelligent Physical Agents (FIPA): FIPA-ACL: Message Structure Specification (2002)
11. Kollingbaum, M.J., Vasconcelos, W.W., García-Camino, A., Norman, T.J.: Conflict resolution in norm-regulated environments via unification and constraints. In: Baldoni, M., Son, T.C., van Riemsdijk, M.B., Winikoff, M. (eds.) DALT 2007. LNCS, vol. 4897, pp. 158–174. Springer, Heidelberg (2008)
12. Shoham, Y., Tennenholtz, M.: On Social Laws for Artificial Agent Societies: Off-line Design. Artificial Intelligence 73(1–2), 231–252 (1995)
13. Sergot, M.: A Computational Theory of Normative Positions. ACM Trans. Comput. Logic 2(4), 581–622 (2001)
14. Artikis, A., Kamara, L., Pitt, J., Sergot, M.: A Protocol for Resource Sharing in Norm-Governed Ad Hoc Networks. In: Leite, J.A., Omicini, A., Torroni, P., Yolum, p. (eds.) DALT 2004. LNCS (LNAI), vol. 3476, Springer, Heidelberg (2005)
15. Cranefield, S.: A Rule Language for Modelling and Monitoring Social Expectations in Multi-Agent Systems. Technical Report 2005/01, University of Otago (2005)
16. García-Camino, A., Noriega, P., Rodríguez-Aguilar, J.A.: Implementing Norms in Electronic Institutions. In: Procs of 4th Int'l Conf on Autonomous Agents and Multiagent Systems (AAMAS 2005), Utrecht, pp. 667–673 (2005)
17. Esteva, M., Vasconcelos, W., Sierra, C., Rodríguez-Aguilar, J.A.: Norm consistency in electronic institutions. In: Bazzan, A.L.C., Labidi, S. (eds.) SBIA 2004. LNCS (LNAI), vol. 3171, pp. 494–505. Springer, Heidelberg (2004)
18. Udupi, Y.B., Singh, M.P.: Multiagent policy architecture for virtual bussiness organizations. In: Proceedings of the IEEE International Conference on Services Computing (SCC) (2006)

A Coherence Based Framework for Institutional Agents

Sindhu Joseph, Carles Sierra, and Marco Schorlemmer

Artificial Intelligence Research Institute, IIIA Spanish National Research Council, CSIC
Bellaterra (Barcelona), Catalonia, Spain
{joseph,sierra,marco}@iiia.csic.es

Abstract. We introduce in this paper an agent model based on coherence theory. We give a formalization of Thagard's theory on coherence and use it to explain the reasoning process of an intentional agent that permits the agent to drop beliefs or to violate norms in order to keep a maximal state of coherence. The architecture is illustrated in the paper and a discussion on the possible use of this approach in the design of institutional agents is presented.

1   Introduction

Artificial institutions are multiagent system models inspired by human institutions [10] and used to create technological extensions of human societies [12]. These devices are designed to help agents cope with the uncertainty on the environment and in some cases to increase their individual utility. They are important due to the bounded nature of human and software rationality (global maximization of individual utility cannot be guaranteed in a complex society). If two or more persons exchange goods with one another, then the result for each one will depend in general not merely upon his own actions but on those of the others as well [8]. Therefore, to make these exchanges possible, behavioral rules that govern the way in which individuals can cooperate and compete are required [7]. Behavioral rules translate the social objectives into executable permissions, prohibitions, and obligations. These modalities are collectively called *norms*. Thus, institutions are role based normative systems representing a collective intention[1]. This is the case in general, but we do acknowledge the fact that institutions need not always represent a collective intention. But such institutions almost always undergo periodic revolutions as an attempt to reinforce collective intention.

Human institutions tend to adapt when the group conscience shifts or is in conflict with the current institutional definition. It is thus important to know and be able to verify at any point in time, that the institutional definition in *coherence* with its norms and social objectives and the objectives of the individuals in the group. Thus an institution to be sustainable almost always needs to continuously strive to achieve this coherent state, here we call it *equilibrium*. We say an institution is in a state of equilibrium when it has no incentive to change the institutional definition. When an *incoherence* or a deviation from equilibrium is detected, it is also important to identify the candidates that cause this incoherence to be able to bring the institution back into equilibrium.

---

[1] Collective intention here refers to the explicit expression of the intention and do not refer to the mental state.

J.S. Sichman et al. (Eds.): COIN 2007, LNAI 4870, pp. 287–300, 2008.
© Springer Verlag Berlin Heidelberg 2008

An autonomous agent is motivated to join an institution when it believes that the individual goals of the agent can be satisfied within the institution. And that happens in our opinion when the beliefs or goals of the agent are *coherent* with the institutional objectives. For simplicity, here we assume that all institutional objectives are realized through norms. Thus being incoherent with a norm is equivalent to being incoherent with a corresponding institutional objective. An agent will hence need to continuously re-evaluate the alignment of its beliefs and goals with that of the norms of the institution. Thus, it is important for an agent to know whether there is an incoherence among the beliefs and the norms, and how the decision is made on what needs to be changed to bring the coherence back. This incoherence among other things drives the agent to violate a norm, revise a belief or both. The individual state of equilibrium is achieved when the coherence between individual beliefs and goals, those of the group and those of the institution is maximized.

We use the theory of coherence and the theory of cognitive dissonance to ground our framework. The *theory of coherence* [11] has been well studied in the field of cognitive science and as a general theory to describe the world. Coherence theory is about how different pieces fit together to make a whole. It assumes that there are various kinds of associations between the pieces or the elements of a set. These are primarily positive or negative where a positive association suggests that the two elements support each other while a negative association indicates their mutual exclusion. Thagard views these associations as constraints between elements and proposes a theory of coherence as globally maximizing the satisfaction of these constraints. He proposes to partition the set of elements into accepted or rejected so that the overall coherence is achieved, or constraint satisfaction maximized. We use the theory to reason between the cognitions of an agent and its external associations such as institutions or social relations.

The *theory of dissonance* [5] in social psychology is closely related to the theory of coherence. Leon Festinger calls dissonance as the distressing mental state in which people feel they "find themselves doing things that don't fit with what they know, or having opinions that do not fit with other opinions they hold." The tension of dissonance motivates us to change either our behavior or our belief in an effort to avoid a distressing feeling. The more important the issue and the greater the discrepancy between behavior and belief, the higher the magnitude of dissonance that we will feel. We use the dissonance theory to motivate an action once the coherence theory identifies elements causing a reduction in coherence.

In this paper we propose an institutional agent architecture based on the theory of coherence. This architecture permits us to talk about the coherence of the individual beliefs, desires and intentions[2], coherence among these cognitions, and the coherence among the cognitions and institutional norms or social commitments. In particular when there is an incoherence between any of these elements, the agent often needs to choose between a norm violation or a belief revision to maximize its internal coherence. That is, the theory of incoherence helps us to model autonomous agents who can reason about obeying or violating institutional norms. From the institutional point of view, the same tools can be used to reason about an institution, coherence of an institution with respect to the conscience of the group and how to evolve norms to stay in alignment

---

[2] In the paper we discuss beliefs, the extension to desires and intentions is straight-forward.

with the objectives. While coherence theory helps to find the maximally coherent state, dissonance theory helps to decide how much of incoherence an agent or an institution can tolerate and which of the actions to chose from to reduce incoherence.

In Sections 2 and 3 we introduce our coherence-based framework and the reasoning of a coherence-maximizing agent. In Section 4 we illustrate with the help of an example, how this framework can be used to reason about norm violations. We conclude with related work in Section 5 and discussion and future work in Section 6. We use the example of a car agent in a traffic control institution. Here we give an intuitive summary of the example, for the reader to follow the coherence framework introduced in Section 2. In Section 4, we detail the example further.

The car agent in our example has personal beliefs and intentions. Where-as the traffic control institution has a set of objectives which it implements through a number of norms. The car agent initially starts with the belief that the traffic control is efficient, and is in a maximally coherent state with his beliefs, intentions and institutional norms. But when the car agent reaches a crossing of two lanes and is made to stop at the signal, where as the crossing lane has no cars waiting to go, it builds up a certain incoherence with its other beliefs and intentions such as the intention to reach the destination in time and the belief that the traffic control is efficient. As part of the constraint maximization, the agent identifies that the adopted intention *to obey the traffic norms* should be rejected to restore coherence. Further it finds that the dissonance is high enough to actually reject this intention. After the rejection of the intention means a potential norm violation as it no longer considers to obey the traffic norms.

2   Coherence Framework

In this section we introduce a number of definitions to build the coherence framework. Our primary interest is to put the theory in relation to an institutional agent context and to provide a formal representation and some computing tools. We do this for the belief cognition of an agent and for the norms of an institution.

2.1   Coherence Graph

To determine the coherence of a set of elements, we need to explore their associations. We shall use a graph to model these associations in order to compute coherence of various partitions of a given set of elements, and to determine its maximally coherent partition as well as to study other related aspects of coherency.

We shall define a coherence graph over an underlying logic. Given a set of propositional formulae PL, a *logic* over PL is a tuple $\mathcal{K} = \langle \mathcal{L}, A, \vdash \rangle$, with language $\mathcal{L} \subseteq PL \times [0, 1]$, i.e., a set of pairs formed by a proposition and a confidence value between 0 and 1, a set of *axioms* $A \subseteq \mathcal{L}$, and a *consequence relation* $\vdash \subseteq 2^{\mathcal{L}} \times \mathcal{L}$.

The nodes of a coherence graph are always elements of $\mathcal{L}$. The consequence relation determines the relationship between these elements, and thus puts constraints on the edges of a coherence graph. Furthermore, propositions that are assumed to be true belong to the axioms A of the logic.

A coherence graph is therefore a set $(\in V)$ of nodes taken from $\mathcal{L}$ and a set E of edges connecting them. The edges are associated with a number called the *strength of the connection* which gives an estimate of how coherent the two elements are[3]. The strength value of an edge (φ, γ), noted $\sigma(\varphi, \gamma)$, respects the strength values that it has with other connected edges. It is important to note that a coherence graph is a *fully connected graph* with a restriction that for every node $\varphi^4 \in \mathcal{L}$, $\sigma(\varphi, \varphi) = 1$ and if there are two nodes φ and, ψ that are not related, then $\sigma(\varphi, \psi) = 0$. Further α is a projection function defined from the set V to $[0, 1]$ which projects the confidence degrees associated with elements of $\mathcal{L}$. The role of this function is to make the confidence degrees explicit in the graph for ease of explanation.

Definition 1. *Given a logic* $\mathcal{K} = \langle \mathcal{L}, A, \vdash \rangle$ *over a propositional language* PL, *a coherence graph* $\langle V, E, \sigma, \alpha \rangle$ *over* $\mathcal{K}$ *is a graph for which*

- $V \subseteq \mathcal{L}$
- $E = V \times V$
- $\sigma : E \to [-1, 1]$
- $\alpha : V \to [0, 1]$

and which satisfies the following constraints:

- $A \subseteq V$
- $\forall v \in V, \sigma(v, v) = 1$
- $\sigma(v, w) = \sigma(w, v)$

We write $\mathcal{G}(\mathcal{K})$ *for the set of all coherence graphs over* $\mathcal{K}$.

Given this general definition of a *coherence graph*, we can instantiate two specific families of coherence graphs namely the *belief coherence graphs* $\mathcal{BG}$ and the *norm coherence graphs* $\mathcal{NG}$, which are of interest to us. $\mathcal{BG}$ represents graphs where the nodes are beliefs of an agent and the edges are association between beliefs. And $\mathcal{NG}$ represents nodes which are the possible norms defined in an institution. In this paper, we do not discuss the desire and the intention cognitions, but these can be defined similarly. And when defining the norm logic, we only talk about permissions and obligations, whereas norms may include prohibitions, too. Also for clarity we have kept the structure of the norms simple, but we intend to include objectives and values associated with a norm. The work by Atkinson and Bench-Capon [1] is indicative. We now define the belief and the norm logic to express the nodes of these graphs and their interconnections.

In our representation, beliefs are propositional formulas φ which are closed under negation and union with an associated confidence degree d. We may borrow the axioms and the consequence relation $\vdash$ from an appropriate belief logic. Then for example we have the following definition for the belief logic.

Definition 2. *Given the propositional language* PL, *we define the* belief logic $\mathcal{K}_B = \langle \mathcal{L}_B, A_B, \vdash_B \rangle$ *where*

---

[3] This value is fuzzy and is determined by the type of relation between the edges. For an *incoherence* relation, tends toward -1, for *coherence* a positive value tending toward 1.

[4] This should be understood as $\langle \varphi, d \rangle$, whenever it is understood from the context, we omit the d part of the element for better readability.

- *the belief language $\mathcal{L}_B$ is defined as follows:*
  - *Given $\varphi \in PL$ and $d \in [0, 1]$, $\langle B\varphi, d \rangle \in \mathcal{L}_B$*
  - *Given $\langle \theta, d \rangle, \langle \psi, e \rangle \in \mathcal{L}_B$, $\langle \neg\theta, f(d) \rangle \in \mathcal{L}_B$ and $\langle \theta \wedge \psi, g(d, e) \rangle \in \mathcal{L}_B$ where f and g are functions for example as in [3]*
- *A_B as axioms of an appropriate belief logic.*
- *$\vdash_B$ is a consequence relation of an appropriate belief logic.*

We need a number of additional constraints that we want the Belief coherence graphs to satisfy. They are constraints on how the strength values have to be assigned. A constraint that we impose on this number is that if two elements are related by a $\vdash$, then the value should be positive and if two elements contradicts then then there is a negative strength[5]. And here we define α more concretely as the projection function over the belief degree. Then we have

Given the belief logic $\mathcal{K}_B$, the *set of all belief coherence Graphs is* $\mathcal{G}(\mathcal{K}_B)$ satisfying the additional constraints:

- Given $\varphi, \psi \in V$ *and* $\Gamma \subseteq V$ *and* $\Gamma \vdash \varphi$
  - $\forall \gamma \in \Gamma, \sigma(\varphi, \gamma) > 0$
  - $\forall \gamma \in \Gamma$ *and* $\psi = \neg\varphi, \sigma(\psi, \gamma) < 0$
- $\forall \langle B\varphi, d \rangle \in V, \alpha(\langle B\varphi, d \rangle) = d$

We can similarly derive the set of all norm coherence graphs $\mathcal{G}(\mathcal{K}_N)$ corresponding to norms. In our definition, norms define obligations and permissions associated with a role. We use *deontic logic* to represent the norms, with the difference that we use modalities subscripted with roles. Thus O_r and P_r represent deontic obligations and deontic permissions associated with a role $r \in R$, the set of all roles. In this paper we assume the confidence degrees associated with norms to be 1. Thus we have the following definition for a norm logic $\mathcal{K}_N$.

Definition 3. *Given the propositional language PL and the set of roles R, we define the Norm logic $\mathcal{K}_N = \langle \mathcal{L}_N, A_N, \vdash_N \rangle$ where*

- *$\mathcal{L}_N$ is defined as:*
  - *Given $\varphi \in PL$ and $r \in R$, then $\langle O_r\varphi, 1 \rangle, \langle P_r\varphi, 1 \rangle \in \mathcal{L}_N$*
  - *Given $\langle \varphi, d \rangle$ and $\langle \psi, e \rangle \in \mathcal{L}_N$ then $\langle \neg\varphi, f_1(d) \rangle$ and $\langle \varphi \wedge \psi, g_1(d, e) \rangle \in \mathcal{L}_N$*
- *A_N following the standard axioms of deontic logic.*
- *$\vdash_N$ using the standard deduction of deontic logic[6]*

Given the norm logic $\mathcal{K}_N$ the set of all norm coherence graphs is $\mathcal{G}(\mathcal{K}_N)$ satisfying the additional constraints:

- Given $\varphi, \psi \in \mathcal{L}$ *and* $\Gamma \subseteq \mathcal{L}$ *and* $\Gamma \vdash \varphi$
  - $\forall \gamma \in \Gamma, \sigma(\varphi, \gamma) > 0$
  - $\forall \gamma \in \Gamma$ *and* $\psi = \neg\varphi, \sigma(\psi, \gamma) < 0$
- $\forall \langle \varphi, d \rangle \in V, \alpha(\langle \varphi, d \rangle) = 1$

---

[5] This relates to Thagard's *deductive coherence*, though in this paper, we limit our discussion to the general coherence relation.

[6] For an introduction to deontic logic, see [13] and in the context of institutions see [6].

2.2   Calculating Coherence

We can now define the coherence value of a graph, the partition that maximizes coherence and the coherence of an element with respect to the graph. These values will help an agent to determine whether to keep a belief or drop it, whether to obey a norm or violate it to increase coherence and which of the beliefs or norms need to be dropped to maximize coherence. This will also help an institution decide whether to accept a proposed norm change and to determine the gain in coherence when accepting or rejecting a change.

We use the notion of coherence as maximizing constraint satisfaction as defined by Thagard [11]. The intuition behind this idea is that there are various degrees of coherence/incoherence relations between nodes of a coherence graph. And if there is a strong negative association between two nodes, then the graph will be more coherent if we decide to accept one of the nodes and reject the other. Similarly when there is a strong positive association, coherence will be increased when either both the nodes are accepted or both are rejected. Thus we can construct a partition of the set of nodes, with one set of nodes in the partition being accepted and the other rejected in such a way to maximize the coherence of the entire graph. Such accepted sets are denoted by $\mathcal{A}$ and the rejected sets by $\mathcal{R}$. The coherence value is calculated by considering positive associations within nodes of $\mathcal{A}$ and within nodes of $\mathcal{R}$ and negative associations between nodes of $\mathcal{A}$ and $\mathcal{R}$. This criteria is called *satisfaction of constraints*. More formally we have the following definition:

Definition 4. *Given a coherence graph* $g \in \mathcal{G}(\mathcal{K})$ *and a partition* $(\mathcal{A}, \mathcal{R})$ *of V, we define the* set of satisfied associations $C^+ \subseteq E$ *as*

$$C^+ = \left\{ \forall (v_i, v_j) \in E \; \middle| \; \begin{array}{l} v_j \in \mathcal{A} \leftrightarrow v_i \in \mathcal{A} (\text{or } v_j \in \mathcal{R} \leftrightarrow v_i \in \mathcal{R}) \text{ when } \sigma(v_i, v_j) \geq 0 \\ v_j \in \mathcal{A} \leftrightarrow v_i \in \mathcal{R} \text{ when } \sigma(v_i, v_j) < 0 \end{array} \right\}$$

In all other cases the association is said to be unsatisfied.

To define coherence, we first define the total strength of a partition. The total strength of a partition is the sum of the strengths of all the satisfied constraints multiplied by the degrees (the α values) of the nodes connected by the edge. Then the coherence of a graph is defined to be the maximum among the total strengths when calculated over all its partitions. We have the following definitions:

Definition 5. *Given a coherence graph* $g \in \mathcal{G}(\mathcal{K})$, *we define the total strength of a partition* $\{\mathcal{A}, \mathcal{R}\}$ *as*

$$S(g, \mathcal{A}, \mathcal{R}) = \sum_{(v_i, v_j) \in C^+} | \, \sigma(v_i, v_j) \, | \cdot \alpha(v_i) \cdot \alpha(v_j) \tag{1}$$

Definition 6. *Given a coherence graph* $g = \langle V, E, \sigma, \alpha \rangle \in \mathcal{G}(\mathcal{K})$ *and given the total strength* $S(g, \mathcal{A}, \mathcal{R})$ *for all partitions of V (denoted as $\mathcal{P}(V)$), we define the* coherence *of g as*

$$C(g) = \max\{S(g, \mathcal{A}, \mathcal{R}) \mid \mathcal{A}, \mathcal{R} \in \mathcal{P}(V)\} \tag{2}$$

and we say that the partition with the maximal value divides the set of nodes into an accepted set $\mathcal{A}$ and a rejected set $\mathcal{R}$.

Given the coherence $C(g)$ of a graph, *the coherence of an element* $C(\varphi)$ is the ratio of coherence when φ is in the accepted set with respect to φ not being in the accepted set. That is if the acceptance of the element improves the overall coherence of the set considered, than when it is rejected, then the element is said to be coherent with the set. Then we have the definition:

Definition 7. *Given a coherence graph* $g \in \mathcal{G}(\mathcal{K})$, *we define the* coherence *of an element* $\varphi \in V$ *as*

$$C(\varphi) = \frac{\max_{\substack{\mathcal{A}, \mathcal{R} \in \mathcal{P}(V) \\ \varphi \in \mathcal{A}}} S(g, \mathcal{A}, \mathcal{R})}{\max_{\substack{\mathcal{A}, \mathcal{R} \in \mathcal{P}(V) \\ \varphi \notin \mathcal{A}}} S(g, \mathcal{A}, \mathcal{R})} \tag{3}$$

Similar to the coherence definitions of a graph, we now define the dissonance of a graph. We define dissonance as the measure of incoherence that exists in the graph. Deducing from the theory of dissonance [5] an increase in dissonance increases in an agent the need to take a coherence maximizing action. We use the dissonance as a criteria to chose among the number of alternative actions an agent can perform such as belief revision, norm violation or commitment modification for example. The dissonance of a graph is computed as the difference between the total strength of the graph and the coherence of the graph. Thus we have the following definition:

Definition 8. *Given a coherence graph* $g \in \mathcal{G}(\mathcal{K})$, *we define the* dissonance *of* g *with respect to a partition* $(\mathcal{A}, \mathcal{R})$ *as*

$$D(G, \mathcal{A}, \mathcal{R})^7 = \begin{cases} \infty \text{ if } C(G) = 0 \\ \frac{C(G) - S(G, \mathcal{A}, \mathcal{R})}{C(G)} \text{ otherwise} \end{cases} \tag{4}$$

2.3 Graph Composition

For an agent that is part of an institution and has social relations, it not only needs to maximize the internal coherence between its beliefs, but also needs to maximize the *social coherence* which is the coherence between the beliefs and the commitments made in the context of his social relations. Similarly, an agent which belongs to an institution, needs to maximize the *institutional role coherence*, that is the coherence between the projection of the norms onto the role he plays in the institution and his beliefs. This leads naturally the notion of graph composition, which will allow us to explore the coherence or incoherence that might exist between nodes of one graph and those of the other.

The nodes of a composite graph are always the disjoint union of the nodes of the individual graphs. The set of edges contains at least those edges that existed in the individual graphs. In addition a composite graph may have new edges between nodes of one graph to the nodes of the other graph.

---

[7] When $C(G) = 0$, $S(G, \mathcal{A}, \mathcal{R}) = 0$ and hence the dissonance is maximum. $D(G, \mathcal{A}, \mathcal{R}) = \infty$.

Definition 9. *Let $\mathcal{K}_1 = \langle \mathcal{L}_1, A_1, \vdash_1 \rangle$ and $\mathcal{K}_2 = \langle \mathcal{L}_2, A_2, \vdash_2 \rangle$ be logics over propositional language PL_1 and PL_2. Let $g_1 = \langle V_1, E_1, \sigma_1, \alpha_1 \rangle \in \mathcal{G}(\mathcal{K}_1)$ and $g_2 = \langle V_2, E_2, \sigma_2, \alpha_2 \rangle \in \mathcal{G}(\mathcal{K}_2)$. The set of composite graphs $g_1 \odot g_2 \subset \mathcal{G}(\mathcal{K})$ is the set of those coherence graphs $\langle V, E, \sigma, \alpha \rangle \in \mathcal{G}(\mathcal{K})$ over logic $\mathcal{K} = \langle \mathcal{L}, A, \vdash \rangle$—where $\mathcal{L}$ is the disjoint union of $\mathcal{L}_1$ and $\mathcal{L}_2$, A is the disjoint union of A_1 and A_2, and $\vdash$ is the smallest consequence relation containing both $\vdash_1$ and $\vdash_2$[8]— such that*

- $V = \{\mathcal{L}_1/\varphi \mid \varphi \in V_1\} \cup \{\mathcal{L}_2/\varphi \mid \varphi \in V_2\}$[9]
- $E = V \times V$ such that
    - if $(\varphi, \psi) \in E_1$ then $(\mathcal{L}_1/\varphi, \mathcal{L}_1/\psi) \in E$
    - if $(\varphi, \psi) \in E_2$ then $(\mathcal{L}_2/\varphi, \mathcal{L}_2/\psi) \in E$
- $\sigma : E \to [-1, 1]$ such that
    - $\sigma(\mathcal{L}_1/\varphi, \mathcal{L}_1/\gamma) = \sigma_1(\varphi, \gamma)$
    - $\sigma(\mathcal{L}_2/\varphi, \mathcal{L}_2/\gamma) = \sigma_2(\varphi, \gamma)$

These properties state that the nodes of the composite graph are the disjoint union of the original graphs. When making the composition, the existing edges and strength values are preserved.

3   A Coherence Maximizing Agent

In this section we describe some of the reasoning performed by a coherence maximizing agent. Consider an agent a having a belief coherence graph b, intention coherence graph i and role coherence graph n_r. At any moment in time the agent aims at coherence maximization. When the coherence cannot be further maximized, a does nothing, or has no incentive to act. For an agent who has no social commitments, nor is part of any institution, nor has any unfulfilled intentions, the accepted set $\mathcal{A}$ is the entire belief set, as he is not likely to have an incoherence.

We consider an agent that is part of an institution, has social commitments and is in the state of equilibrium. Below we show one of the possible algorithms that a coherence agent a can go through when it encounters a new belief (either communicated to the agent by others, by observation, or internally deduced).

Input: a new belief $\langle B\varphi, d \rangle$; a belief coherence graph $g = \langle V, E, \sigma, \alpha \rangle$, a composition graph $g_{bin} = g \odot g_i \odot g_{n_r}$ with the corresponding coherence measures C_{bin} along with $\mathcal{A}_{bin}$ and $\mathcal{R}_{bin}$, S_{bin}, D_{bin}, and a dissonance threshold D_T.

1: $V_b \leftarrow V \cup \{B\varphi\}$
2: $\alpha_b(B\varphi) \leftarrow d$
3: **for** $B\psi \in V$, $\Gamma \subseteq V$ **do**
4:     **if** $B\psi, \Gamma \vdash B\varphi$ or $B\varphi, \Gamma \vdash B\psi$ **then**
5:         $\sigma_b(B\psi, B\varphi) = 1$
6:         **for** $B\gamma \in \Gamma$ **do**

---

[8] For the moment we assume that the properties that make $\vdash_1$ and $\vdash_2$ a consequence relation as the same.

[9] We write $\mathcal{L}_i/\varphi$ for those elements of $\mathcal{L}$ that come form $\mathcal{L}_i$ in the disjoint union, with $i = 1, 2$.

```
 7:          σ_b(Bγ, Bφ) = 1
 8:       end for
 9:     end if
10:     if Bφ, Bψ ⊢ ⊥ then
11:          σ_b(Bφ, Bψ) = −1
12:     end if
13:   end for
14: g_bin ← g_b ⊙ g_i ⊙ g_{n_r}
15: S ← S_bin(g_bin, V_bin, ∅) using eq(1)
16: C ← C_bin(g_bin) using eq(2)
17: D ← D_bin(g_bin, V_bin, ∅) using eq(4)
18: if D ≥ D_T then
19:     A ← A_bin
20:     R ← R_bin
21: end if
```

The lines from 1 to 13 updates the belief graph by adding nodes, edges and their strength values. Here the algorithm does not fully determine the strength values but specify certain constraints on how the strength values are determined. Here we assume that a human user will provide them while respecting the constraints though we envision many semi automatic methods worth exploring (see section 6). The line 14 updates the composition graph considering the modified belief graph. The lines from 15 to 17 recalculate the strength, coherence and dissonance values of the new composite graph. Lines 18 and 19 check whether the dissonance value exceeds the threshold and if it does, the agent acts by removing the nodes causing the incoherence from the accepted set. To keep the discussion simple in this algorithm, we have simply removed the nodes. But in reality, the reaction to an incoherence can vary greatly. For instance a mildly distressed agent may choose to ignore the incoherence, may be satisfied with lowering the degree associated with a particular belief, may still choose to follow a norm. Where as a heavily distressed agent may not only chose to violate a norm, but initiate a dialogue to campaign for a norm change.

4   An Example

The main entities in our example are a car agent a having the role c in a traffic control institution and the institution itself T. We take a very simplified version of the objectives of T as

- minimizing the probability of collisions
- increasing the traffic handling capacity

To meet these objectives, the traffic control system has a signal at the crossing of the lanes along with specific norms of use. The norms of the traffic control system for the car agents belong to the set N_c.

The traffic is controlled using the norms given below and the corresponding norm coherence graph is shown in Figure 1. Note that all the coherence graphs in this example

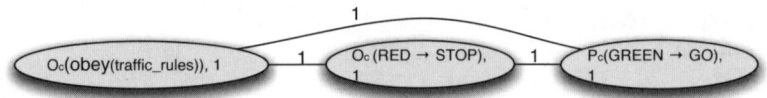

Fig. 1. Norm Coherence graph of the traffic control institution

have additional self loops which are not drawn for the sake of readability. But it is included in the coherence calculations.

- $O_c(\text{RED} \rightarrow \text{STOP}), 1 \rightarrow$ *It is obligatory to STOP, when the signal is RED*
- $P_c(\text{GREEN} \rightarrow \text{GO}), 1 \rightarrow$ *It is permitted to GO, when the signal is GREEN*

Here we illustrate the model with one of the most simple cases, namely the crossing between a major and a minor lane. The major lane has more traffic than minor lane. Due to the fixed time control, and due to ignoring to assign priority to the lanes, the signal durations are the same for both major and minor lanes. Thus there are situations when there are no cars waiting to cross at the minor lane and there is a "RED" light at the major lane. So the car agents at the major lane sometimes experience an incoherence when trying to follow the traffic norms. We now show the evolution of the coherence of an agent situated at the major lane with the help of the some figures.

A car agent a of role c at the major lane has the intention to reach destination X at time T. He holds a number of beliefs which support this intention. A few relevant beliefs of a for this intention are *can reach destination X in time t* and *traffic control is efficient* and a generic belief that *It is good to reduce pollution*. The composite graph $b \odot i$ is shown in Figure 2.

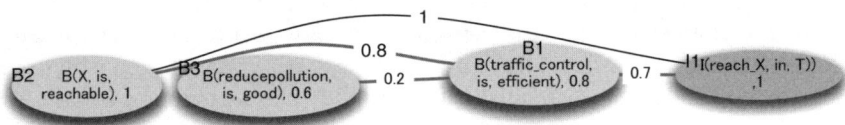

Fig. 2. $b \odot i$ Coherence graph of the car agent

We use Equations 1, 2, 4 of Section 2 for calculating the various coherence values of all the graphs of the example[10].

The coherence of the graph is $C(b \odot i) = 5.296$ with $\mathcal{A} = \{B1, B2, B3, I1\}$ and $D(b \odot i) = 0$. As a is part of the traffic control system, having a role c, the projection of the norms n_c to the beliefs graph of a with an additional intention *to stop at RED signal* is as given in Figure 3. This additional intention is due to the fact that a intends to follow the norms of the institution. Now the coherence of the composite graph is $C(b \odot i \odot n_c) = 17.716$ with $\mathcal{A} = \{B1, B2, B3, I1, I2, N1, N2\}$ and dissonance $D(b \odot i \odot n_c) = 0$, still staying 0.

When a encounters the "RED" signal, and observes the traffic, its belief graph gets enriched with new information, and due to this addition of new beliefs, the strengths get

---

[10] The strength values and the degrees on beliefs and intentions are given manually respecting the constraints on the graph definition.

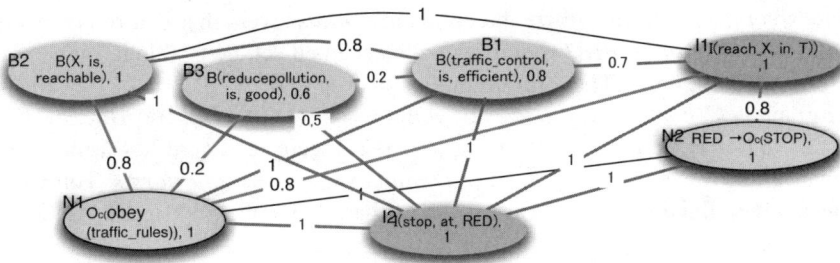

Fig. 3. Belief Coherence graph of the car agent with projected norms

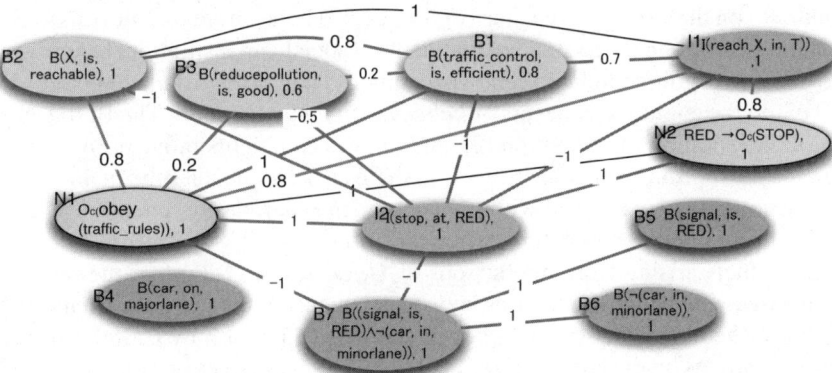

Fig. 4. Modified coherence graph

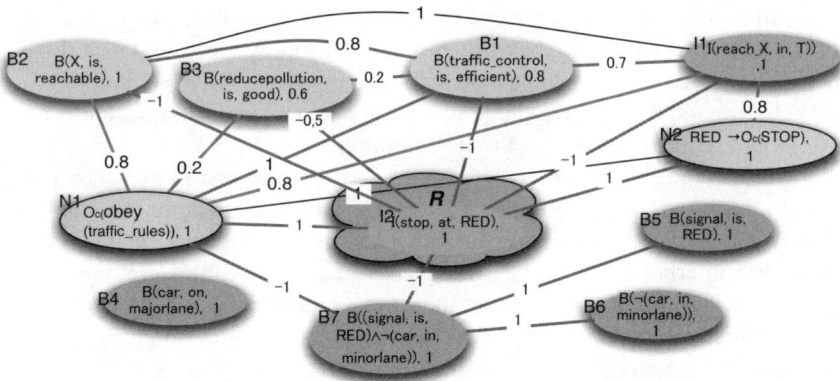

Fig. 5. Maximizing coherence - $\mathcal{A} = b \odot i \odot n \setminus \{I2\}$

modified. The new beliefs added to b are *a is at the Major lane*, *The signal is "RED"* and that *there are no cars on the minor lane*. The modified coherence graph is shown in Figure 4.

Now when trying to maximize the coherence, a discovers that if it removes the intention $I2 \rightarrow$ *to stop at RED signal* from the accepted set, he is able to maximize the coherence as in Figure 5. The total strength is $S(b \odot i \odot n_r, V, \emptyset) = 15.516$, Coherence of the graph is $C(b \odot i \odot n_r) = 23.716$ with $\mathcal{A} = \{B1, B2, B3, B4, B5, B6, B7, I1, N1, N2\}$ and dissonance $D(b \odot i \odot n_r) = 0.35$. Here the agent has a high enough dissonance[11] to reject the intention $I2$(*intention to obey the traffic norms*. This example though simple, illustrates how an agent can act based on coherence maximization.

5   Related Work

BDI theory is the most popular of the existing agent architectures. This architecture concentrates on the deliberative nature of the agent. There are several add ons to BDI architecture considering the recent developments in social and institutional agency, where the traditional cognitive model seems inadequate. They primarily include the addition of *norms* to the cognitive concepts of *belief, desire, and intention*. The BOID architecture with the addition of obligation [2], and the work on deliberative normative agents [4] are the most prominent among them. In the BOID architecture the main problem is conflict resolution between and within the modules belief, desire, intention and obligation. Their focus is on architecture, while they do not specify any means to identify or resolve conflicts arising from interactions of B, O, I and D. Further the modules are flat structured where the associations between elements in the modules are not exposed making it difficult to identify and analyze conflicts. The work by Castelfranchi in [4] again concentrates on the architecture. Their main contribution is the emphasis on agent autonomy. While most literature assume the strict adherence to the norms, they insist that it is an agent's decision whether to obey norms or not. As in the BOID architecture, they do not provide any mechanism by which an agent can violate a norm or reason about a norm violation. Another work by Lopez et al. [14] discusses how norm compliance can be ensured while allowing autonomy, using rewards and sanctions. Such mechanisms, while certainly complimenting our approach, only handle the issue at a superficial level and do not give the power to an agent to understand what it means to obey or violate a norm with respect to its cognitions.

On the other hand, the work of Pasquier et al. [9] is the first to our knowledge that attempts to unify the theory of coherence with the BDI architecture. The authors propose the theory as a reasoning mechanism to initiate a dialogue. DIalogue is initiated so that agent's internal incoherence is reduced. At each step of this argumentation process coherence is reevaluated. However there are a number of ways our approach differ from theirs. First we treat the coherence framework from a more fundamental perspective by making coherence graphs corresponding to BDI modalities elementary. Thus we now have a clear way of studying the interactions among and between the cognitions whereas they have a very problem specific formulation of coherence. This also implies we can derive the associations between elements (constraints) from the properties of the underlying logic whereas they have no way of deriving these constraints. And at a broader level, we try introduce agent autonomy which is lacking in the current BDI

---

[11] Assuming a dissonance threshold $D_T = 0.20$.

models. Finally there is no work which gives a coherence framework to reason about agents and institutions, individually and together.

And finally the collection of works by Thagard who proposed the coherence theory as constraint satisfaction [11]. He has applied his theory to explain many of the natural phenomena. But so far has not given a formal specification of coherence nor integration into other theories.

6   Discussion and Future Work

In this paper, we have formally defined the basic coherence tools for building institutional agents. We aim to further develop this theory in the following directions.

An important question we have left unanswered in the paper is given the beliefs or norms how their corresponding coherence graphs can be created. Evaluating the association between two atomic beliefs looks more like a human task, yet we can use similarity measures extracted from other repositories like ontologies, Wordnet or search results. Whereas evaluating associations between complex beliefs, we can use the underlying logic. Composing coherence graphs is another important aspect that we have dealt only superficially. The composition is important as it is the coherence measures of the graph compositions that normally identifies conflicts. We plan to explore these ideas in more detail in our future work.

In this paper we also limit our framework to logical systems whereas coherence can be applied to arbitrary graphs. In the future work we plan to make the coherence graphs more general so that non-logical agents can use coherence measures.

In the present work, we have provided the basic reasoning tools for a norm aware agent. We have shown when and how an autonomous agent could violate a norm. From the institutional perspective, a series of norm violations should trigger further actions, such as an analysis of why the norm is being violated. This could lead to a norm revision leading to an institutional redefinition. Our future work involves further exploration into questions related to norm violation from an institutional perspective.

We have simplified the representation of norms in the present work. In the future, we plan to have a more expressive representation of norms which includes the state of action when the norm is applicable, objectives behind the norm and the values promoted by the norm, borrowing the ideas developed in [1].

And finally, a coherence maximization may not only lead to a norm violation, but can also trigger a belief update, leading to the process of evolution of cognition. There are no widely accepted theories on how a cognitive agent can be evolved. The proposed theory helps to understand when a belief revision is profitable. In the future work, we propose to further explore cognitive revision in an institutional agent.

Acknowledgments. This work is supported under the OpenKnowledge[12] Specific Targeted Research Project (STREP), which is funded by the European Commission under contract number FP6-027253. Schorlemmer is supported by a *Ramon y Cajal* research fellowship from Spain's Ministry of Education and Science, which is partially

---

[12] http://www.openk.org

funded by the European Social Fund. Special acknowledgments to all the reviewers of COIN@DURHAM07 for their detailed reviews and insightful comments.

References

[1] Atkinson, K.: What Should We Do?: Computational Representation of Persuasive Argument in Practical Reasoning. PhD thesis, University of Liverpool (2005)

[2] Broersen, J., Dastani, M., Hulstijn, J., Huang, Z., van der Torre, L.: The BOID architecture: Conflicts between beliefs, obligations, intentions and desires. In: AGENTS 2001 (2001)

[3] Casali, A., Godo, L., Sierra, C.: Graded BDI models for agent architectures. In: Leite, J.A., Torroni, P. (eds.) CLIMA 2004. LNCS (LNAI), vol. 3487, Springer, Heidelberg (2005)

[4] Castelfranchi, C., Dignum, F., Jonker, C.M., Treur, J.: Deliberative normative agents: Principles and architecture. In: Jennings, N.R. (ed.) ATAL 1999. LNCS, vol. 1757, Springer, Heidelberg (2000)

[5] Festinger, L.: A theory of cognitive dissonance. Stanford University Press (1957)

[6] Goble, L., Meyer, J.-J.C. (eds.): DEON 2006. LNCS (LNAI), vol. 4048. Springer, Heidelberg (2006)

[7] Lin, J.Y.: An economic theory of institutional change: Induced and imposed change. Cato Journal 9(1) (1989)

[8] Neumann, J.V., Morgenstern, O.: Theory of Games and Economic Behavior. Science Editions, J. Wiley, Chichester (1964)

[9] Pasquier, P., Chaib-draa, B.: The cognitive coherence approach for agent communication pragmatics. In: AAMAS 2003 (2003)

[10] Searle, J.R.: The Construction of Social Reality. Free Press (1997)

[11] Thagard, P.: Coherence in Thought and Action. MIT Press, Cambridge (2002)

[12] Vigan, F., Fornara, N., Colombetti, M.: An operational approach to norms in artificial institutions. In: AAMAS 2005 (2005)

[13] von Wright, G.H.: An Essay in Deontic Logic and the General Theory of Action: With a Bibliography of Deontic and Imperative Logic. North-Holland Pub. Co, Amsterdam (1968)

[14] López y López, F., Luck, M., d'Inverno, M.: Constraining autonomy through norms. In: AAMAS 2002 (2002)

Distributed Norm Enforcement Via Ostracism

Adrian Perreau de Pinninck, Carles Sierra, and Marco Schorlemmer

IIIA – Artificial Intelligence Research Institute
CSIC – Spanish National Research Council
Bellaterra (Barcelona), Catalonia, Spain
{adrianp,sierra,marco}@iiia.csic.es

Abstract. An agent normative society has to deal with two main concerns: how to define norms and how to enforce them. Enforcement becomes a complex issue as agent societies become more decentralized and open. We propose a new distributed mechanism to enforce norms by ostracizing agents that do not abide by them. Our simulations have shown that, although complete ostracism is not always possible, the mechanism substantially reduces the number of norm violations.

1 Introduction

In a normative Multi-Agent System (MAS) a set of norms are added to restrict the set of available actions in order to improve the coordination between agents. An autonomous agent has the choice whether or not to support a norm. It is up to the agent to decide if it is convenient for it to abide by it. For a utility maximizer agent if following a norm is profitable, it is in the agent's own interest to act as the norm establishes. But this is not always the case, as some norms are profitable even when not all agents abide by them. For example, a norm that dictates that owners must clean the common areas. Cleaning entails a cost, and a clean area is a benefit to all. If an owner does not clean the common area (*i.e.*, a norm violator) thus not bearing its cost, but the others do, the area is still clean.

The aim of this paper is to introduce a new distributed mechanism that attains norm compliance by ostracizing norm violating agents. Our scenario allows agents to interact with each other. An agent can interact with the agents it is linked to directly or indirectly through a path of links (*i.e.*, agents can interact with direct neighbors, with neighbors of neighbors, and with their neighbors and so on...). An initiator agent will search for a path in the society to find a partner agent with which to interact. All the agents in the path that are not the initiator or the partner agent will be called mediator agents (*i.e.*, agents mediating the interaction).

We use a game-theoretic approach to interactions, which we model as a two-player game with two possible strategies; cooperate and defect. The utility function will be that of a prisoner's dilemma (see Figure 1).

The norm in this scenario is for all agents to cooperate, thus attaining the maximum utility for the society. Nonetheless, agents can choose to ignore the norm and defect (*i.e.*, violate the norm) thus gaining more utility. In order to

J.S. Sichman et al. (Eds.): COIN 2007, LNAI 4870, pp. 301–315, 2008.
© Springer-Verlag Berlin Heidelberg 2008

PD	Cooperate	Defect
Cooperate	3,3	0,5
Defect	5,0	1,1

Fig. 1. Prisoner's Dilemma Payoff Matrix

attain norm enforcement, some agents (we will call them enforcer agents) are given the ability to stop interacting with violators, and to stop them from interacting with the enforcer's own neighbors. When enough agents use this ability against a violator, it is ostracized. An agent is ostracized when it cannot interact with anyone else in the society, in this case it is a consequence of defecting in the interaction with many different agents.

The motivation behind using ostracism comes from the study of norm enforcement in primitive societies [11]. When a member of a community repeatedly ignored its customs, it was forced to leave. No one in the community would interact with the ostracized member from then on. Ostracism is achieved in human societies through force and physical constraint. In order to achieve ostracism of electronic entities, which interact through a network, we seek inspiration from the network security area. The most commonly used component in this case is a firewall, which blocks those communications which appear to be harmful. While firewalls are usually set up by humans through complex rules, enforcer agents will use gossip as a way to inform each other about malicious agents.

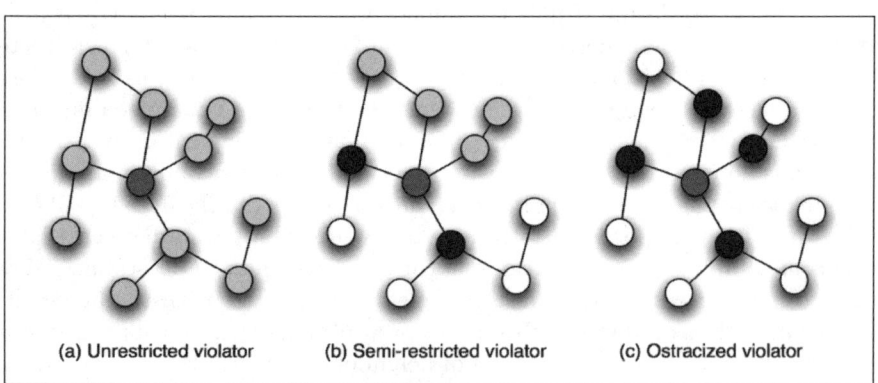

(a) Unrestricted violator   (b) Semi-restricted violator   (c) Ostracized violator

Fig. 2. Ostracizing a violator

The ostracism process can be seen in Figure 2. At first an undetected violator in the network (the dark gray node) can interact with all the other agents (light gray nodes are liable to interact with the violator). When the violator interacts, and defects, it can be detected by enforcer agents which will block it (black nodes are blocking agents, and white nodes are agents that the violator cannot interact with). When all the violator's neighbors block it, it is ostracized.

Gossip is essential to find out information about other agents in a distributed environment. We will use gossip as part of the enforcement strategy to ostracize agents. Information is gossiped only to agents mediating the interaction, to minimize the amount or resources it takes. If agent ag_v violates the norm when interacting with agent ag_1, ag_1 may spread this information to all mediator agents so they may block ag_v in the future.

By running a set of simulations, we study under which conditions the mechanism works, and give measures of its success (such as the violations received or the utility gained). Our hypotheses are:

- **H1** - Norm violations can be reduced by applying a local blocking rule.
- **H2** - The society's structure influences its enforcement capabilities.
- **H3** - The choice of blocking strategy influences the number of violations received.
- **H4** - Enforcement makes norm-abiding a rational strategy.

Section 2 describes related work in the area of norm enforcement. Section 3 presents a detailed description of the scenario we employ in the simulations. Section 4 describes the simulations and analyzes the resulting data. Finally, section 5 presents future work.

2   Related Work

The problem of norm enforcement has been dealt with in human societies through the study of law, philosophy, and the social sciences. Recently it is being dealt with in computer science, where norms are studied as a coordination mechanism for multi-agent systems. Axelrod [1] first dealt with the application of norms from an evolutionary perspective. Enforcement is seen by Axelrod as a sort of meta-norm to punish agents that do not punish violators. The norm game is often modeled as an N-Player Iterated Prisoner's Dilemma [1,8]. In these cases the norm is to cooperate and ways are sought to ensure that agents prefer cooperation. Other research studies norms that avoid aggression or theft [4,7,12,15]. In these cases agents gain utility by either finding items or receiving them as gifts. But these items can be stolen by other agents through aggression. An agent that abides by the possession norms will not steal food possessed by another agent, therefore avoiding aggression.

Two enforcement strategies have been studied to attain norm compliance: the use of power to change the utilities through sanctions or rewards [2,3,8,14], and the spread of normative reputation in order to avoid interaction with violators [4,6,7,12,15]. Both strategies have the goal of making norm adopters better off than norm violators. But this is not always accomplished [4,7], since all agents benefit from the norm while only enforcers agents bear its cost.

Norm enforcement models in [2,6] show how violating the norm becomes an irrational strategy when punishment is possible. But these models assume the following: (i) agents are able to monitor other agents' activities; and (ii) agents have the ability to influence the resulting utility of interactions. Assumption (i) can be materialized by having a central agent mediate all interactions [2], or by having agents recognize violators through direct interaction with them, or through gossip with other agents [4]. The first solution does not scale, since the mediator agent would be overwhelmed in a large system. The second scales because no agent is the enforcement bottleneck, but it is less efficient since in a distributed environment not all violations will be known to everyone. Assumption (ii) can be carried out through third-party enforcement [2], or self-enforcement [6] in which each agent carries out sanctions to agents it interacts with. Third party does not scale since it can easily be overwhelmed in a large system. For self-enforcement, all agents must have the ability to affect the outcome utility of interactions.

Axelrod [1] defines the "shadow of the future" as a mechanism to affect an agent's choice in iterated games. An agent is deterred from defecting when the probability of interacting with the same agent in the future is high, and agents will defect in future interactions with known violators. Nonetheless, this mechanism makes enforcers violate the norm as they also defect. Another method is the threat of ostracism or physical constraint. By not interacting with violators, an agent can interact with another agent and achieve a higher payoff. Younger has studied [15] the possibility of avoiding interaction with norm-violators, but does not prevent norm-violators from interacting with anyone else.

Kittock [9] was the first to study how the structure of a multi agent system affected the emergence of a social norm. He studied regular graphs, hierarchies, and trees. In [5] Delgado studied emergence in complex graphs such as scale-free and small-world, and in [10] studied the relationship between a graph's clustering factor and emergence.

Using the scenario presented in this paper, agents can monitor other agents' activities, and influence future interactions. The spread gossip, and sanctioning norm-violators with ostracism via blockage are the techniques used to achieve this influence. We have studied norm enforcement using these techniques in societies with differing structures.

3   The Scenario

We model our multi-agent system as an undirected, irreflexive graph: $MAS = \langle Ag, Rel \rangle$, where Ag is the set of vertices and Rel the set of edges. Each vertex models an agent and each edge between two vertices denotes that the agents are linked to each other. We have chosen three kinds of graphs for their significance: Tree, Random, and Small-World. We define a tree as a graph in which each node has one parent and some number of children; one node, the root node, has no parent, and the leave nodes have no children. Nodes are linked to their parents and children. In a random graph any node can be linked to any other one with a given probability. A small-world graph is created by starting with a regular graph[1], and adding enough random edges to make the average distance between any two vertices significantly smaller [13]. A small-world graph is highly clustered (*i.e.*, if

---

[1] $C_{N,r}$ is a regular graph on N vertices such that vertex i is adjacent to vertices $(i + j)\ mod\ N$ and $(i - j)\ mod\ N$ for $1 \leq j \leq r$.

a node has two neighbors, the probability of them being linked is high), and there are some links between distant parts of the graph that make the average distance between any two vertices small. A small-world network is small in the sense that one can always find a short path connecting any two vertices. The graph structures have been generated with a similar average number of links per node.

We use a game-theoretic approach by modeling interactions as a two-player prisoner's dilemma game. The norm is that agents ought to cooperate (*i.e.*, an agent disobeys the norm by defecting). In order for two agents to interact, there must be a path in the graph between the two. One agent will search for a path that leads to another agent with which to interact. We call the searching agent *initiator agent*, the agent chosen to interact *partner agent*, and the remaining agents in the path *mediator agents*. The partner finding process is explained below, but first we need to formally describe some terms.

We define the set of neighbors of an agent a_i as the set of agents it is linked to directly in the graph: $N(a_i) = \{a_j \in Ag \mid (a_i, a_j) \in Rel\}$. Each agent also has a set of agents it blocks (an agent cannot block itself): $B(a_i) \subseteq Ag \setminus \{a_i\}$. An agent a_i can query another agent a_j for a list of its neighbors. We call the set of agents that a_j returns, reported neighbors: $RN(a_i, a_j) \subseteq N(a_j)$. The set of reported neighbors depends on the blocking strategy of a_j. The strategies used in our simulations are explained below. A path is the route (without cycles) in the graph structure through which interaction messages are delivered. We represent a path as a finite (ordered) sequence of agents $p = [a_1, a_2, \ldots, a_n]$ such that for all i with $1 \leq i \leq n-1$ and $n \geq 2$ we have that $a_{i+1} \in N(a_i)$, and for all i, j with $1 \leq i, j \leq n$ and $i \neq j$ we have that $a_i \neq a_j$. The agent a_1 of a path is the initiator agent, agent a_n is the partner agent, the remaining ones are mediator agents.

In order to find a partner, the initiator agent a_i creates a path $p = [a_i]$ with itself as the only agent in it. A path with one agent is not valid, since an agent cannot interact with itself. Therefore, the initiator agent will query the last agent in the path (the first time it will be itself) to give it a list of its neighbors. It will choose one of them randomly[2] (a_j) and add it to the end of the path $p = [a_i, ..., a_j]$. At this point, if agent a_j allows it, the initiator agent can choose agent a_j as the partner. Otherwise, it can query agent a_j for its neighbors and continue searching for a partner. In our scenario this choice is taken randomly: with probability $p = 0.3$ a_j becomes the partner, and with probability $1 - p$ it becomes a mediator and a_i asks it for its neighbors.

If the path's last element is an agent a_n that refuses to interact with the initiator agent, and a_n returns an empty list of agents when queried for its neighbors, backtracking is applied. Agent a_n is removed and a different agent is chosen from the list of a_{n-1}'s neighbors and added to the end of the list.

Once the partner is chosen, a prisoner's dilemma game is played between the initiator and the partner. The game results and the path are known by both playing agents. Playing agents can choose to send the game results to all the mediators in the path. This is what we call *gossip*, which formally speaking is a tuple that contains the agents' names and their strategy choices for the given

---

[2] To avoid loops, an agent that is already part of the path cannot be chosen again.

game: $Gossip = \langle ag_i, ch_i, ag_j, ch_j \rangle$, where ch_i and ch_j are either *cooperate* or *defect*.

During the whole process agents can execute any of the following actions:

- Return a list of neighboring agents when asked for its neighbors.
- Accept, or reject, an offer to interact.
- Choose a strategy to play in the PD game when interacting.
- Inform mediators of the outcome of the interaction.

The society of agents is composed of three types of agents, each one characterized by a different strategy for the actions it can execute. A *meek agent* is a norm-abiding agent that always cooperates. It will always return all its neighbors to any agent that asks. A meek agent will always accept an offer to interact, it will always cooperate in the PD game, and it will never gossip. A *violator agent* follows the strategy of a meek agent, except that it always defects when playing a game, therefore it is not a norm-abiding agent. Violator agents in our simulations are very naive, they never model the other agents, or treat them differently depending on their actions. In short, they cannot change the strategies. Future work will look into more sophisticated norm-violators.

Finally, an *enforcer agent* has the ability to block violators, which is essential in order to achieve their ostracism. An enforcer agent shares the same strategies with meek agents with the following exceptions: It will add agents that have defected against it to its set of blocked agents, and will gossip to all mediators when defections happen. If an enforcer is informed of the results of a game it was mediating, it will act as if it had played the game itself. An enforcer agent will never choose an agent in its blocked set as a partner, and will not allow an agent in its blocked set to choose it as a partner. Therefore, a violator agent cannot interact with an enforcer who is blocking it. When an enforcer agent a_m is asked to return a list of its neighbors by an agent a_i who is not in its blocked set, two different strategies are possible. The Uni-Directional Blockage (UDB) strategy, where all its neighbors will be returned ($RN(a_i, a_m) = N(a_m)$). Or the Bi-Directional Blockage (BDB) strategy, where only those neighbors not in its blocked set are returned ($RN(a_i, a_m) = N(a_m) \setminus B(a_m)$). When the querying agent is in the enforcer agent's blocked set, it always returns an empty set.

The choice of enforcement strategy entails a trade off. Intuitively, one can see that enforcer agents are better off with the UDB strategy, since they will be able to use violator agents as mediators to reach other parts of the society. Enforcers will not be tricked by a violator more than once, so they are sure not to interact with them. Therefore, using violators as mediators benefits enforcers. Meek agents, on the other hand, do not learn to avoid violators. They may choose one unknowingly as their partner repeatedly. BDB is a better strategy for meek agents, it reduces their chances of choosing violator agents. Furthermore, a structure with a violator as a cut vertex, may be split into two different societies when the BDB strategy is used, and the violator is ostracized. If the UDB strategy is used, the society stays connected, since the ostracized violator can still be used as a mediator.

In order to focus on the most relevant aspects in our simulations, we made the following limiting assumptions:

– Agents cannot change their strategy (*i.e.*, a violator is always a violator).
– Agents cannot lie when sending gossip.
– There are no corrupt enforcer agents.
– There is no noise (*i.e.*, an agent knows its opponent's chosen strategy).

These assumptions imply that modeling agents' reputation is simple. Being informed once about an agent's strategy is enough, since information will never be contradictory. Therefore, there is no place for forgiveness, and sanctions are indefinite. Relaxation of these assumptions will be studied in future work.

4   Simulations

The simulations have been run using the scenario specified in Section 3. Each simulation consists of a society of 100 agents. The society will go through 1000 rounds, in a round each agent tries to find a partner with which to interact. If the agent finds a partner a prisoner's dilemma with the utility function of Figure 1 is played.

The parameters that can be set in each simulation are:

– Percentage of Violators (V) - from 10% to 90% in 10% increments.
– Percentage of Enforcers (E) - from 0% to 100% in 10% increments[3].
– Type of Graph (G) - either tree, small world, or random.
– Enforcement Type (ET) - Uni-Directional Blockage (UDB), or Bi-Directional Blockage (BDB).

An exhaustive set of simulations have been run with all the possible values for each parameter. Each simulation has been run 50 times in order to obtain an accurate average value. The metrics that have been extracted are: the mean violations received per agent, and the mean utility gained per agent. The metrics have been calculated for the whole society and for each agent type. The data gathered from the simulations supports our hypotheses.

(H1) Norm violations can be reduced by applying a local blocking rule. The graph in Figure 3 shows that the higher the percentage of norm-abiding agents that use a blocking rule, the lower the average number of norm violations received by any agent in our system. There are five different lines in the graph, each one stands for a different percentage of violating agents. In all cases a higher enforcer to meek agent ratio (*x*-axes) leads to lower violations received in average by any agent (*y*-axes). When the ratio of enforcers is high, violators end up interacting with each other. Therefore, the *y*-axes measures the violations received by "any" agent, the reduction in violations in Figure 3 is not significant. The data referring to the violations received only by norm-abiding

---

[3] The percentage of meek agents is computed through the following formula: $M = 100\% - V - E$. Therefore, $V + E$ cannot be more than 100%.

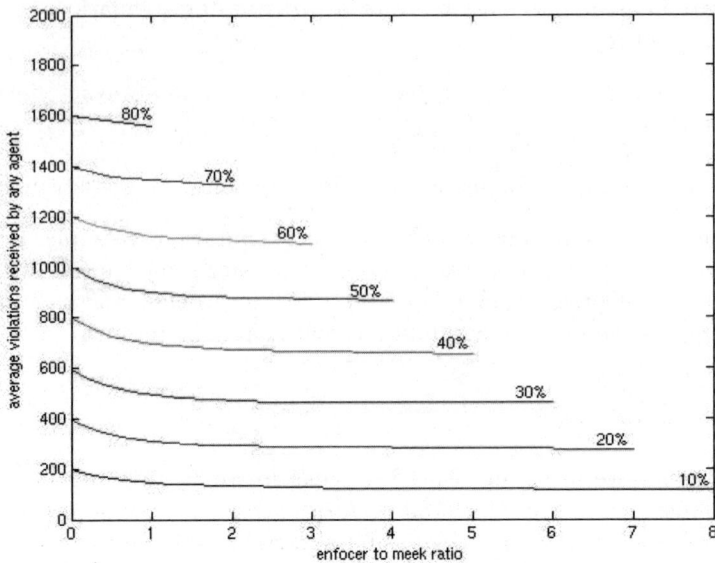

Fig. 3. Local blocking rule reduces violations to all agents

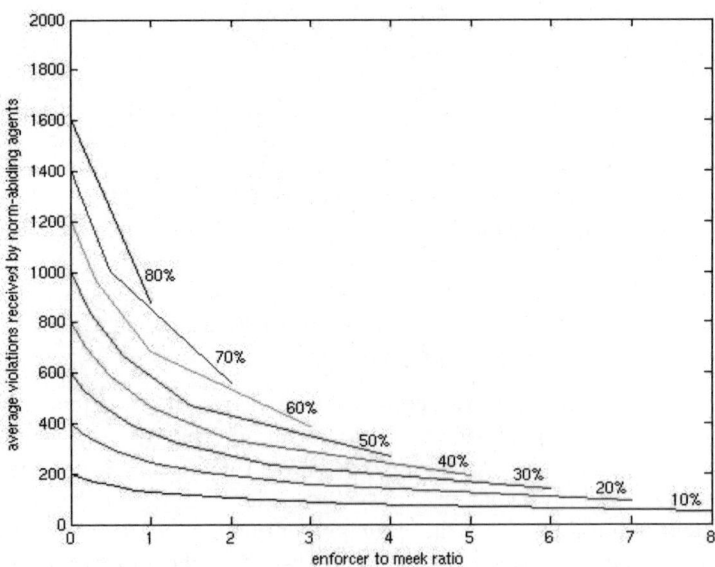

Fig. 4. Local blocking rule reduces violations to norm-abiding agents

agents shows a larger reduction (see Figure 4). Enforcer agents can perceive a norm violation at most once per violator agent. But if we look at the violations received by meek agents, we see that they experience an increment of violations

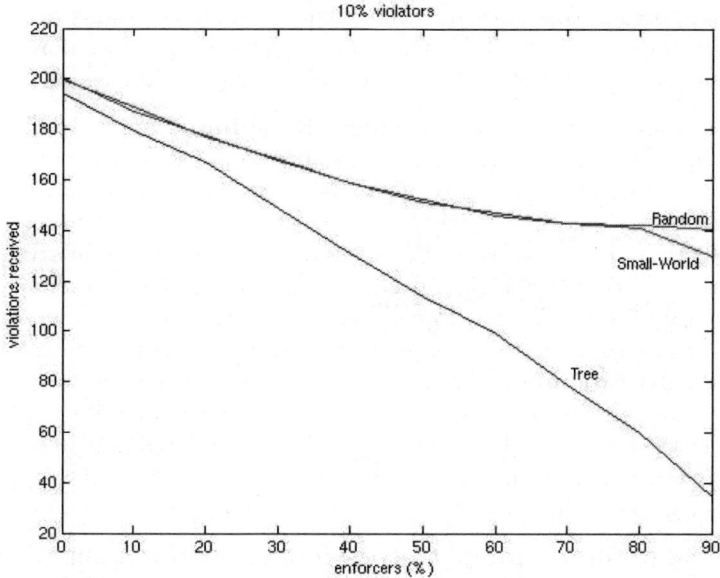

Fig. 5. Enforcement capabilities vary depending on structure (10% violators)

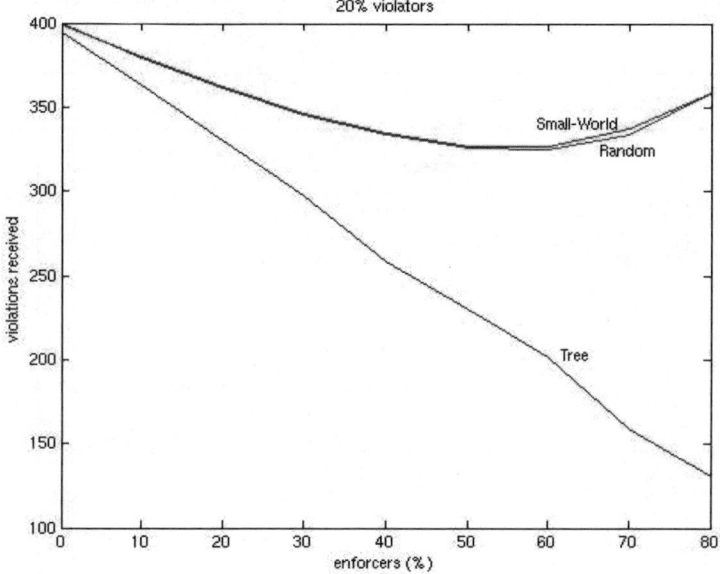

Fig. 6. Enforcement capabilities vary depending on structure (20% violators)

when the ratio of enforcers is high (see Figure 10). This means that enforcer agents have blocked violator agents, which are forced to interact with the small number of meek agents left unprotected. Since the meek are a small portion of the norm supporters, this does not influence the total violations perceived by norm supporters as a whole. Therefore, the higher the ratio of enforcer agents, the lower the average of violations perceived by norm-abiding agents.

(H2) The society's structure influences its enforcement capabilities. It is also seen from the data that different organizational structures in the multi-agent system influence norm enforcement. In Figure 5 and 6 we have extracted the average norm violations (y-axes) for each of the different structures tested: Random, Small World, and Tree. We have only shown the simulations where violator agents account for 10% and 20% of the population, therefore at most there will be 90% or 80% of enforcers, respectively. The x-axes contains the different percentages of enforcer agents tested. It can be seen that both random and small world networks have an almost identical graph line. On the other hand the tree structure has shown to improve the enforcement capabilities. The main difference between a tree and the other structures studied is that in a tree there is only one path between any two agents. In random and small world graphs, many paths can be usually found between any two agents.

(H3) The choice of blocking strategy influences the number of violations received. The data in Figure 7 supports this hypothesis. The x-axes shows the enforcer to meek agent ratio. The y-axes contains a metric for the increment in efficiency at protecting meek agents from violations. Efficiency is the difference (calculated in percentage) in violations received by meek agents for each of the

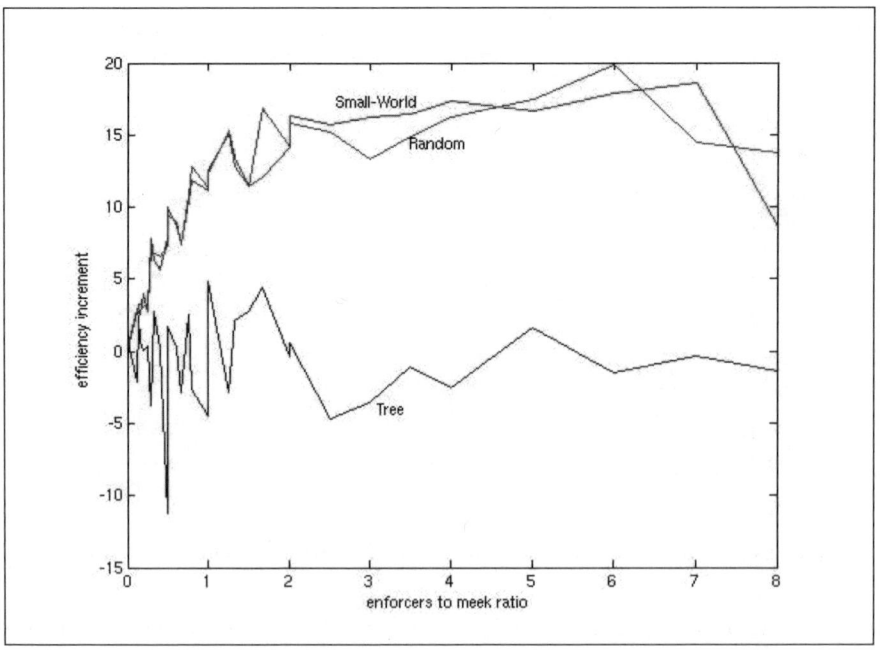

Fig. 7. Enforcement strategy influences received violations

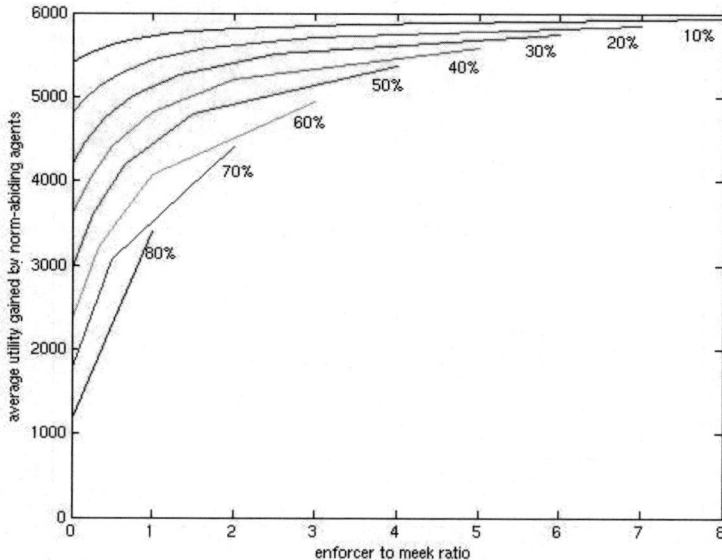

Fig. 8. Utility gained by norm-abiding agents

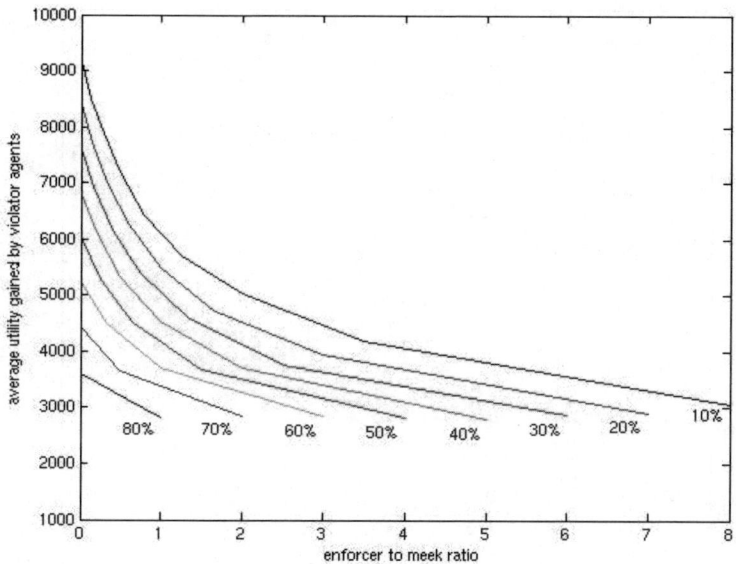

Fig. 9. Utility gained by norm-violating agents

two different enforcement strategies $\Delta E = ((V_{UDB}/V_{BDB}) - 1) \times 100$. ΔE calculates the increase in violations received by agents when using uni-directional blockage in respect to bi-directional blockage.

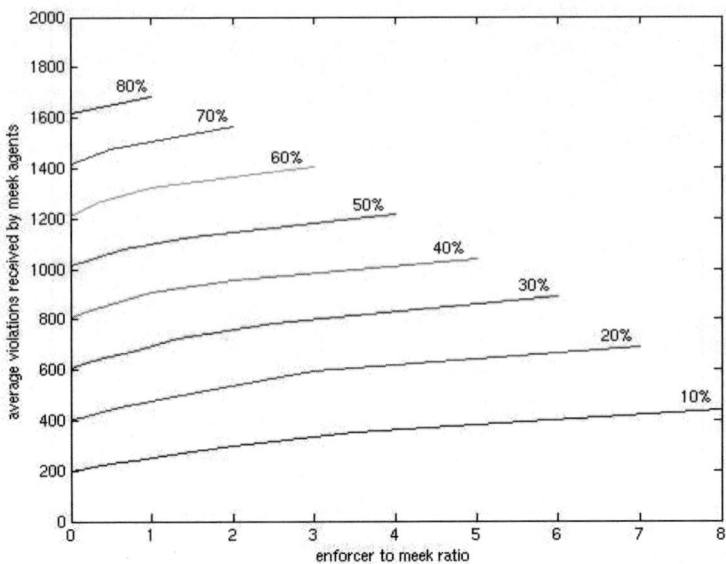

Fig. 10. Local blocking rule increases violations received by meek agents

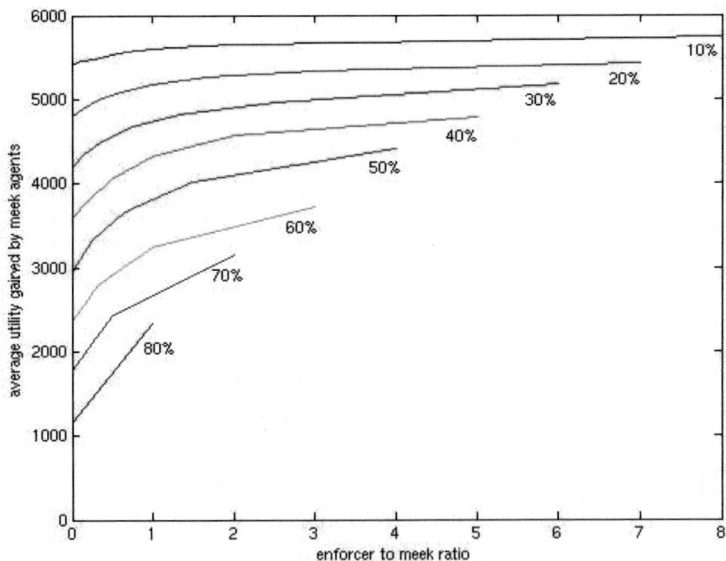

Fig. 11. Local blocking rule increases utility gained by meek agents

Figure 7 shows that for random and small world networks the efficiency is positively correlated with the enforcer to meek agent ratio. We can conclude that Bi-Directional Blockage has a higher efficiency at protecting meek agents from violator agents. This is not observed in the tree network. In this case the efficiency stays along the 0% line with some deviations. We argue that in networks organized as trees, the choice of enforcement strategy does not have a significant influence in the outcome. The tree network is already good for ostracizing offenders, and the blockage strategy does not improve it.

(H4) Enforcement makes norm-abiding a rational strategy. This hypothesis is supported by the utility gained by agents. A strategy is rational if it maximizes the agent's utility. What has been tested is whether following the norm maximizes the agent's utility, and in which conditions. Figure 8 shows the utility gained (y-axes) by norm supporting agents, its x-axes shows the enforcer to meek agent ratio. Figure 9 instead shows the utility gained by norm violating agents. In both figures each line represents the amount of violating agents in the system. As the number of enforcers increases there is a tendency for norm supporters to gain more utility, while the opposite tendency is observed for violator agents. When the number of enforcer agents is low, the utility gained by violator agents is much higher than the one gained by norm supporters. As the number of enforcer agents grows the roles are reversed. The inflection point depends on the amount of violator agents in the system. For simulations with 10% of violator agents, supporting the norm becomes rational when the enforcer to meek ratio is higher than 1.25. For simulations with 50% of violator agents, the ratio needs to be higher than 0.7. The rest of simulations have inflection points between those two values.

It is interesting to note that even though meek agents receive more violations as the number of enforcer agents grows (see Figure 10), the utility gained by them surprisingly increases (see Figure 11). This is due to the fact that meek agents are still able to interact with other norm-abiding agents. Since violators are being blocked the ratio of defection to cooperation is lowered and the utility is increased.

5   Future Work

This paper is part of ongoing research on norm enforcement. Future work will relax the set of assumptions about agents, by giving them the ability to change their strategies in time, to lie, and to allow enforcer agents to violate the norm (*i.e.*, corrupt enforcers). The assumption of perfect information will be relaxed by adding uncertainty and noise. For these cases elaborate gossip techniques and reputation management will allow agents to enforce the norm. In future work the agent's reputation will be modeled not through gossip but through interaction overhearing. Mediating agents could overhear the interactions instead of waiting for interacting agents to report the outcome. More so, other conservative blocking strategies can be studied; such as blocking off agents that mediate norm violators, or blocking agents until they are shown to be norm-abiders.

Furthermore, the impact of other network parameters and dynamic networks will be analyzed. New links between agents could be added dynamically and test how this affects norm enforcement. New enforcement techniques will be studied to take advantage of dynamic networks.

Finally, other studies have shown that the efficiency of enforcement diminishes when enforcement conveys a cost to the enforcing agent [1,8]. In future work there will be cost associated to blockage. One way to associate cost to enforcers is by removing their ability to stop agents from interacting with them. In this case, enforcers can withhold information from known violators, but if asked will have to interact with them and endure the norm violation.

Acknowledgments

This work is supported by the Generalitat de Catalunya under the grant 2005-SGR-00093, and the FP6-027253 OpenKnowledge[4] Project. A. Perreau de Pinninck is supported by a CSIC predoctoral fellowship under the I3P program, and M. Schorlemmer is supported by a *Ramón y Cajal* research fellowship from Spain's Ministry of Education and Science, both of which are partially funded by the European Social Fund.

References

1. Axelrod, R.: An evolutionary approach to norms. The American Political Science Review 80, 1095–1111 (1986)
2. Boella, G., van der Torre, L.: Enforceable social laws. In: AAMAS 2005: Proceedings of the Fourth International Joint Conference on Autonomous Agents and Multiagent Systems, pp. 682–689 (2005)
3. Carpenter, J., Matthews, P., Ong'ong'a, O.: Why punish: Social reciprocity and the enforcement of prosocial norms. Journal of Evolutionary Economics 14(4), 407–429 (2004)
4. Castelfranchi, C., Conte, R., Paoluccci, M.: Normative reputation and the costs of compliance. Journal of Artificial Societies and Social Simulation 1(3) (1998)
5. Delgado, J.: Emergence of social conventions in complex networks. Artificial Intelligence 141(1), 171–185 (2002)
6. Grizard, A., Vercouter, L., Stratulat, T., Muller, G.: A peer-to-peer normative system to achieve social order. In: AAMAS 2006 Workshop on Coordination, Organization, Institutions and Norms in agent systems (COIN) (2006)
7. Hales, D.: Group reputation supports beneficent norms. Journal of Artificial Societies and Social Simulation 5(4) (2002)
8. Heckathorn, D.D.: Collective sanctions and compliance norms: A formal theory of group-mediated social control. American Sociological Review 55(3), 366–384 (1990)
9. Kittock, J.E.: The impact of locality and authority on emergent conventions: Initial observations. In: AAAI 1994. Proceedings of the Twelfth National Conference on Artificial Intelligence, vol. 1, pp. 420–425. AAAI Press, Menlo Park (1994)
10. Pujol, J.M., Delgado, J., Sangüesa, R., Flache, A.: The role of clustering on the emergence of efficient social conventions. In: IJCAI 2005: Proceedings of the Nineteenth International Joint Conference on Artificial Intelligence, pp. 965–970 (2005)

---

[4] http://www.openk.org

11. Taylor, M.: Community, Anarchy & Liberty. Cambridge University Press, Cambridge (1982)
12. Walker, A., Wooldridge, M.: Understanding the emergence of conventions in multi-agent systems. In: Lesser, V. (ed.) Proceedings of the First International Conference on Multi-Agent Systems, San Francisco, pp. 384–389. MIT Press, Cambridge (1995)
13. Watts, D.J., Strogatz, S.H.: Collective dynamics of small-world networks. Nature (393), 440–442 (1998)
14. López y López, F., Luck, M., d'Inverno, M.: Constraining autonomy through norms. In: AAMAS 2002: Proceedings of the First International Joint Conference on Autonomous Agents and Multiagent Systems, pp. 674–681. ACM Press, New York (2002)
15. Younger, S.: Reciprocity, sanctions, and the development of mutual obligation in egalitarian societies. Journal of Artificial Societies and Social Simulation 8(2) (2005)

Model Checking Norms and Sanctions in Institutions*

Francesco Viganò[1] and Marco Colombetti[1,2]

[1] Università della Svizzera italiana, via G. Buffi 13, 6900 Lugano, Switzerland
{francesco.vigano,marco.colombetti}@lu.unisi.ch
[2] Politecnico di Milano, piazza Leonardo Da Vinci 32, Milano, Italy
marco.colombetti@polimi.it

Abstract. In this paper we enrich FIEVeL (a modelling language for institutions amenable to model checking) with new constructs to describe norms and sanctions. Moreover, we present a specification language to reason about the effectiveness of norms and sanctions in shaping agent interactions. Finally we show that when properties of artificial institutions reflect certain interpretations of norms of human institutions, it is not always possible to satisfy them. As a consequence, regimentation of norms is not always a viable solution.

1 Introduction

Rules defined by *artificial institutions* and enforced by their software implementations, named *electronic institutions* [5], have been put forward as means to regulate open multiagent systems. Institutions define two kinds of rules [17]: *norms* (also named *regulative rules* [17]), which regulate existing activities, and *constitutive rules*, which create the very possibility of certain institutional actions.

Artificial institutions are often designed to reflect constitutive and regulative rules defined by human institutions in artificial systems [10,9,7], and model checking can play an important role to evaluate the compliance of artificial institutions with rules of human institutions and to compare design alternatives arising from different interpretations of such rules.

In general, when we map human rules only onto constitutive rules of artificial institutions, we obtain systems where violations cannot occur (they are regimented [10,9]). Instead, when we introduce regulative rules into artificial institutions, we obtain systems where violations may occur due, for instance, to the agents' autonomy. As a consequence, when we analyze results obtained by a model checker, it is important to consider how rules of human institutions have been mapped onto rules of artificial institutions: if a norm of a human institution has been mapped onto a set of constitutive rules of an artificial institution and a property that reflects it does not hold, then the artificial institution is incorrect. Instead, when a norm n has been mapped onto regulative rules of the artificial institution, we have to analyze whether: (i) norms of the artificial institution are correct, that is, a property reflecting expected effects of norm n holds over paths compliant with norms, and (ii) sanctions applied when norms are violated enforce desirable effects of norm n over all other possible evolutions.

---

* Supported by the Swiss National Science Foundation project 200020-109525, "Artificial Institutions: specification and verification of open distributed interaction frameworks."

J.S. Sichman et al. (Eds.): COIN 2007, LNAI 4870, pp. 316–329, 2008.
© Springer-Verlag Berlin Heidelberg 2008

The main contributions of this paper are threefold: first, we extend FIEVeL [19], a modelling language for institutions amenable to model checking, with new constructs to describe norms and sanctions, exemplifying how norms can be defined and enforced with our language; second, we present a flexible specification language which provides temporal operators that select paths compliant with certain sets of norms, showing that existing proposals (e.g. [12,16,1]) can be reduced to particular patterns of specification of our language; finally, we contribute to the ongoing debate about *regimentation* and *enforcement* of norms [10,9,6,8], showing that when human institutions impose a specific interpretation of norms, it may be the case that properties that reflect them cannot be satisfied by artificial institutions under the assumption that agents are autonomous. As a consequence, *regimentation* of norms is not always a viable solution.

The remainder of this paper is structured as follows: Section 2 introduces the OMS-FOTL logic which is used to define the semantics of FIEVeL and to state properties of institutions in Section 3, where we provide an overview of our framework by resuming results discussed in our previous works. Section 4 presents how norms can be described with FIEVeL, while Section 5 introduces a language to define properties which consider only evolutions of institutions that comply with certain sets of norms. Section 6 explains how to formalize sanction mechanisms with FIEVeL and finally Section 7 provides a comparison of our approach with related works and presents some conclusions.

2 Ordered Many-Sorted First-Order Temporal Logic

An ordered many-sorted first-order temporal logic (OMSFOTL) is a many-sorted first-order logic [13] enriched with temporal operators and hierarchies of sorts. The signature of an OMSFOTL logic consists of a finite nonempty set of *sort symbols* Σ, a *hierarchy of sorts* $\leq_\Sigma$ (where $\sigma_1 \leq_\Sigma \sigma_2$ means that sort σ_1 is a *subsort* of sort σ_2), finite sets of *constants* (C), *function symbols* (F), and *predicate symbols* (P), and a denumerable set of *variables* (V). Moreover, an OMSFOTL signature defines function ξ which assigns a sort to every variable and every constant, and a signature (i.e. a sequence of sorts) to every function and predicate symbol. Given sorts Σ, the set T_σ of *terms of sorts* σ is the smallest set such that:

- $v \in T_\sigma$ if $v \in V$ and $\xi(v) \leq_\Sigma \sigma$;
- $c \in T_\sigma$ if $c \in C$ and $\xi(c) \leq_\Sigma \sigma$;
- $f(t_1, ..., t_n) \in T_\sigma$ if $f \in F$, $\xi(t_i) \leq_\Sigma [\xi(f)]_i$ for $1 \leq i \leq n$ and $[\xi(f)]_0 \leq_\Sigma \sigma$

where $[\xi(q)]_i$ refers to the i-th sort of the signature of a predicate or function symbol q. The set T of *terms* is the union of the sets T_σ for all $\sigma \in \Sigma$ and the set A of *atomic formulae* is the smallest set such that:

- $(t_1 = t_2) \in A$ if there exists sort σ such that $\xi(t_1) \leq_\Sigma \sigma$ and $\xi(t_2) \leq_\Sigma \sigma$;
- $p(t_1, ..., t_n) \in A$ if $p \in P$ and $\xi(t_i) \leq_\Sigma [\xi(p)]_i$ for $1 \leq i \leq n$.

The set of *formulae* is defined according to the following grammar:

$$\varphi ::= \alpha \mid \neg\varphi \mid \varphi \wedge \varphi \mid \exists\varphi \mid \mathbf{X}\varphi \mid \varphi\mathbf{U}\varphi \mid \mathbf{E}\varphi$$

where α is an atomic formula.

The semantics of OMSFOTL is given with respect to a Kripke structure M, a path π (i.e., a sequence of states $\pi = s_0, s_1, s_2, \ldots$ of M), and an interpretation function I which, given a state s and an atomic formula $\alpha \in A$, returns a value in $\{0, 1\}$. In the sequel we use π_k to denote the k-th state of path π and π^k for the suffix of π starting at state π_k. A formula φ is true in a model M over a path π in M ($M, \pi \models \varphi$) when:

$M, \pi \models \alpha$ iff $I(\alpha, \pi_0) = 1$;

$M, \pi \models \neg\varphi$ iff $M, \pi \not\models \varphi$;

$M, \pi \models \varphi \wedge \psi$ iff $M, \pi \models \varphi$ and $M, \pi \models \psi$;

$M, \pi \models \exists x \varphi$ iff there exists a constant c of sort $\xi(x)$ such that $M, \pi \models \varphi_c$, where φ_c is obtained from φ by replacing all unbounded occurrences of variable x with constant c;

$M, \pi \models \mathbf{X}\varphi$ iff $M, \pi^1 \models \varphi$;

$M, \pi \models \varphi \mathbf{U} \psi$ iff exists an $i \geq 0$ such that $M, \pi^i \models \psi$ and for all $0 \leq j < i$ $M, \pi^j \models \varphi$;

$M, \pi \models \mathbf{E}\varphi$ iff there exists a path π' such that $\pi'_0 = \pi_0$ and $M, \pi' \models \varphi$

assuming, for the sake of presentation, that for each state s of M: (i) for each constant c of sort σ there exists an individual i such that $I(c, s) = i$, and (ii) that for each individual i there exists a constant c such that $I(c, s) = i$. Expressions *true*, *false*, $(\varphi \vee \psi)$, $(\psi \rightarrow \varphi)$, $(\varphi \leftrightarrow \psi)$, and $\forall x \varphi$ are defined in terms of $\neg$, $\wedge$, and $\exists$ in the conventional manner, and temporal operators $\mathbf{F}$, $\mathbf{G}$, and the path quantifier $\mathbf{A}$ are introduced as abbreviations as usual [3] to state that eventually φ holds ($\mathbf{F}\varphi \equiv true\mathbf{U}\varphi$), φ is satisfied by all states of a path ($\mathbf{G}\varphi \equiv \neg\mathbf{F}\neg\varphi$), and that all paths satisfy φ ($\mathbf{A}\varphi \equiv \neg\mathbf{E}\neg\varphi$).

In [20] we have shown that if we assume that each sort σ is associated to a finite domain D_σ, then OMSFOTL is as expressive as CTL* [4,3] and its models can be encoded with a finite number of atomic propositions. Despite it, we adopt OMSFOTL for two main reasons: (i), it represents an abbreviated form for long and complex formulae and (ii), institutions describe rules that typically are independent of the cardinality of domains and which can be naturally expressed by allowing quantification over sorts.

3 Modelling, Specifying, and Verifying Institutions

In [19] we proposed a metamodel of institutions based on the notion of an agent status function, which can be interpreted as a position involving a (possibly empty) set of institutionalized powers [11], obligations, prohibitions, etc. To formalize status functions and related concepts, we map them onto sorts, functions, and predicates of an OMS-FOTL signature and define a set of axioms to capture their interrelations and temporal evolution. For instance, common aspects of status functions are represented by introducing sort σ_{sf}, which also defines the function $subject$ denoting the agent (σ_{aid}) the status function has been assigned to. Sort σ_{sf} also induces the two predicates $assigned$ and $modified$, which respectively represent if a status function is currently assigned (or revoked) and if it has been modified by the occurrence of an institutional event. Finally, the metamodel defines a set of axioms based on such symbols, for instance requiring that if a status function is not affected, then its subject does not change:

$$\mathbf{AG}\forall f(\neg\mathbf{X}modified(f) \rightarrow \exists a(subject(f) = a \wedge \mathbf{X}subject(f) = a)) \qquad (A.1)$$

```
 1  basic-sorts:
 2    σ_resources;
 3    σ_reqState = {answ, notAnsw};
 4  base-events:
 5    message giveResource(rec:σ_aid, res:σ_resources);
 6    ...
 7  institution resourceManagement {
 8    status-function member() {...}
 9    status-function requested(reqRes:σ_resources, ag:σ_aid,
10      sta:σ_reqState){...}
11    status-function holder(resource:σ_resources){
12    key resource;
13    powers give ← (∃ r:σ_requested (assigned(r)∧ag(r)=rec∧
14      reqRes(r)=resource(f)∧sta(r)=answ)∧res=resource(f));
15  }
16    ...
17    institutional-events:
18      institutional-action give(rec:σ_aid, res:σ_resources)
19      pre ∃ x:σ_member(assigned(x)∧subject(x)=rec
20        ∧¬subject(x)=actor);
21      eff r:σ_requested revoke (reqRes(r)=res),
22        k:σ_holder assign (subject(k)=rec, resource(k)=res);
23      ...
24    conventions
25      exch-Msg(giveResource) [true]=c=> give
26        [rec=c=>rec res=c=>res]
27      ...
28  }
```

Fig. 1. Fragments of the Resource Management institution

An institution evolves because events (σ_{ev}) occur or agents perform actions (σ_{act} $\leq_\Sigma \sigma_{ev}$). Each event-type e induces a sort σ_e and three predicates, $happens_e$, $prec_e$, and eff_e, which express when an event of type e happens and what conditions must be satisfied before and after its occurrence. In contrast with *base-level events* (e.g., *exchange-message* events), the occurrence of an *institutional event* (σ_{ie}) requires that another event conventionally associated to it occurs and that, in the case of institutional actions, the actor must be empowered to perform it:

$$\mathbf{AG}\forall\overline{x}((prec_{ia}(\overline{x}) \wedge \exists f(subject(f) = x_1 \wedge empowered_{ia}(f,\overline{x}) \wedge assigned(f)$$
$$\wedge \bigvee_{a\in\sigma_{act}} \mathbf{X}(conv_{a-ia}(\overline{x}) \wedge happens_a(\overline{x}'))) \leftrightarrow \mathbf{X}happens_{ia}(\overline{x}))$$

$$(A.2)$$

where: $\overline{x}$ is a set of variables determined by predicate $happens_{ia}$; the first variable of $\overline{x}$ refers to the actor of action ia; predicate $empowered_{ia}$ states when status functions are empowered to perform institutional action ia; predicate $conv_{a-ia}$ represents the existence of a convention among action a and institutional action ia; and $\overline{x}'$ reflects how arguments of ia are mapped over arguments of action a.

To model institutions in terms of the concepts described by our metamodel, in [19] we introduced FIEVeL, a modelling language for institutions, whose syntax is exemplified in Figure 1 and whose semantics is given by providing a translation of its constructs into a set of symbols and formulae of an OMSFOTL logic. According to Figure 1, in the Resource Management institution a *member* can request a *holder* to *give* the control of one of its resources. When an agent accepts to satisfy the request, it is empowered to give a resource to the agent that has requested it, which becomes its new *holder*. More precisely, line 2 of Figure 1 induces sort $\sigma_{resources}$, which represents a set of resources, while lines 8-10 introduce status functions *member* (σ_{member}) and *requested* ($\sigma_{requested}$), which represent respectively the status that an agent should have to request the control over a resource and the status acquired after having successfully performed a request to an *holder*. Resources are hold by agents through status function *holder* (declared at line 11 of Figure 1), which defines sort $\sigma_{holder} \leq_{\Sigma} \sigma_{sf}$ and function *resource* of signature $\xi(resource) = \langle \sigma_{resources}, \sigma_{holder} \rangle$. According to lines 13 and 14, an *holder* is empowered to *give* a resource *res* when an agent has requested it and the *holder* has already acknowledged to transfer the control over the requested resource as required by the following axiom:

$$\mathbf{AG} \forall s \forall actor \forall rec \forall res(empowered_{give}(s, actor, rec, res) \leftrightarrow \exists f(f = s \wedge$$
$$(\exists r(\mathtt{assigned(r)} \wedge \mathtt{ag(r)} = \mathtt{rec} \wedge \mathtt{reqRes(r)} = \mathtt{resource(f)} \wedge$$
$$\mathtt{sta(r)} = \mathtt{answ} \wedge \mathtt{res} = \mathtt{resource(f)})))) \quad (A.3)$$

where $\xi(actor) = \xi(rec) = \sigma_{aid}, \xi(res) = \sigma_{resources}, \xi(s) = \sigma_{sf}, \xi(f) = \sigma_{holder}$, and $\xi(r) = \sigma_{requested}$.

According to FIEVeL semantics, lines 18-22 define institutional action *give* such that: (i) it can be performed only if the *receiver* is a *member* and if it is not the *actor*, and (ii) it revokes status function *requested* to the receiver and assigns status *holder* to it. More precisely, institutional action *give* induces predicates $happens_{give}$, $prec_{give}$, and eff_{give} ($\xi(happens_{eff}) = \langle \sigma_{aid}, \sigma_{aid}, \sigma_{resources} \rangle$) such that predicates $prec_{give}$ and eff_{give} satisfy the following axioms:

$$\mathbf{AG} \forall actor \forall rec \forall res(prec_{give}(actor, rec, res) \leftrightarrow (\exists x(\mathtt{assigned(x)} \wedge$$
$$\mathtt{subject(x)} = \mathtt{rec} \wedge \neg \mathtt{subject(x)} = \mathtt{actor}))) \quad (A.4)$$

$$\mathbf{AG} \forall actor \forall rec \forall res(eff_{give}(actor, rec, res) \leftrightarrow \mathbf{X}(\forall r(reqRes(r) = res \rightarrow$$
$$(\neg assigned(r) \wedge modified(r))) \wedge \forall k(resource(k) = res \rightarrow$$
$$(assigned(k) \wedge modified(k) \wedge subject(k) = rec))) \quad (A.5)$$

where $\xi(actor) = \xi(rec) = \sigma_{aid}, \xi(res) = \sigma_{resources}, \xi(x) = \sigma_{member}, \xi(r) = \sigma_{requested}$, and $\xi(k) = \sigma_{holder}$.

Finally, lines 25 and 26 define a convention such that the exchange of a message of type *giveResource* counts-as the performance of action *give* when the sender is empowered and preconditions of action *give* are satisfied. As a consequence, axiom (A.2) is instantiated as follows:

$$\mathbf{AG}\forall actor \forall rec \forall res((prec_{give}(actor, rec, res) \wedge \exists f(subject(f) = actor \wedge$$
$$assigned(f) \wedge empowered_{give}(f, actor, rec, res) \wedge$$
$$\mathbf{X}(happens_{giveResource}(actor, rec, res) \wedge conv_{giveResource-give}(actor, rec, res))) \leftrightarrow$$
$$\mathbf{X}happens_{give}(actor, rec, res))$$
$$(A.6)$$

where $\xi(actor) = \xi(rec) = \sigma_{aid}$, $\xi(res) = \sigma_{resources}$, and $\xi(f) = \sigma_{sf}$.

In our framework, also properties are specified in terms of OMSFOTL formulae such that temporal operators ($\mathbf{X}$, $\mathbf{G}$, $\mathbf{F}$, and $\mathbf{U}$) are always preceded by a path quantifier ($\mathbf{E}$ or $\mathbf{A}$). One of the main advantages of our approach resides in the fact that any symbol introduced by our metamodel or by an institution can appear in a property. Furthermore, to increase the flexibility of the language, occurrences of events are referenced with a generic predicate *happens* and we write "$x : \sigma$" to say that variable x is of sort σ. For instance, the following property requires that whenever an agent receives a positive answer to its requests, it will eventually become the *holder*:

$$\mathbf{AG}\forall act : \sigma_{aid} \forall rec : \sigma_{aid} \forall res : \sigma_{resources}(happens(accept, act, rec, res)$$
$$\rightarrow \mathbf{AF}\exists h : \sigma_{holder}(subject(h) = rec \wedge resource(h) = res)) \quad (P.1)$$

Analogously, we can also check if whenever a holder accepts to give a resource, it will eventually do so:

$$\mathbf{AG}\forall act : \sigma_{aid} \forall rec : \sigma_{aid} \forall res : \sigma_{resources}(happens(accept, act, rec, res)$$
$$\rightarrow \mathbf{AF}happens(give, act, rec, res)) \quad (P.2)$$

In [20] we presented a symbolic model checker specifically developed to verify FIEVeL institutions. Given an institution and a set of properties, our tool proceeds as follows: (i) it converts the institution into a set Φ of OMSFOTL formulae by considering the semantics of FIEVeL constructs and axioms determined by our metamodel (see axioms (A.3), (A.4), and (A.5)); (ii) formulae Φ are translated into propositional logic and subsequently converted into a formula in conjunctive normal form (CNF); (iii) given the set of assignments satisfying the CNF (whose disjunction constitutes the transition relation of a Kripke structure) and a formula φ_0, representing a set of initial states, a symbolic representation of an institution is built and is exploited to verify properties by applying standard symbolic algorithms [3]. According to our model checker, properties (P.1) and (P.2) do not hold: since constitutive rules reported in Figure 1 define possible actions that agents can carry out, but do not ensure that empowered agents will necessarily perform them, it may be the case that agents accept to give their resources but do not perform action *give*.

4 Norms

To define the semantics of norms, our metamodel assumes the existence of sort σ_o, whose individuals reify norms of institutions. Sort σ_o is used to express prohibitions and obligations characterized by certain deadlines (not necessarily a time expression), and we consider that a state of affairs is permitted if it is reached without violating any norm. In particular, for the sake of conciseness, in this paper we focus only on norms which are considered fulfilled or violated only *once* after a given status function is imposed on an agent and certain conditions are met. Given sort σ_{state}, which introduces constants *unfired*, *activated*, and *inactive*, sort σ_o is characterized by function *state* ($\xi(state) = \langle \sigma_{state}, \sigma_o \rangle$), which keeps trace of the temporal evolution of a norm, a set of timers (e.g., function *activation* which counts how many time events have occurred since a norm has been activated), and by a set of predicates (*start*, *fulfillment*, and *violation* of signature $\xi(violation) = \langle \sigma_{sf}, \sigma_o \rangle$). Agents are subject to norms when certain status functions are imposed on them: to model the interdependency among norms and status functions, we introduce function *ofStatus* ($\xi(ofStatus) = \langle \sigma_{sf}, \sigma_o \rangle$) which denotes the status function an obligation is associated to. When a status function is not assigned, then its norms are considered to be *inactive* and cannot be violated: we represent this fact by the following axiom, which states that norms of a revoked status function are always *inactive*:

$$\mathbf{AG}\forall o\forall f((ofStatus(o) = f \land \neg assigned(f)) \rightarrow state(o) = inactive) \quad \text{(A.7)}$$

where $\xi(o) = \sigma_o$ and $\xi(f) = \sigma_{sf}$. Similarly, Axiom (A.8) requires that when a status function is imposed on an agent, then the state of a norm is set to *unfired* if predicate *start* is not satisfied, otherwise it is set to *activated*:

$$\mathbf{AG}\forall o\forall f((ofStatus(o) = f \land \mathbf{X}(assigned(f) \land modified(f))) \rightarrow ((\neg start(o, f)$$
$$\land \mathbf{X}state(o) = unfired) \lor (start(o, f) \land \mathbf{X}state(o) = activated)))$$
$$\text{(A.8)}$$

Axioms (A.7) and (A.8), as well as other axioms omitted here for the sake of brevity, describe the temporal evolution of functions *state* and *activation*, which in combination with predicates *fulfillment* and *violation*, determine when an obligation should be considered to be infringed. In particular, given predicate *violated* of signature $\xi(violated) = \langle \sigma_o \rangle$, a norm is violated if and only if it was *activated*, the associated status function is not modified, *violation* holds while *fulfillment* is false:

$$\mathbf{AG}\forall o\forall f(ofStatus(o) = f \rightarrow (\mathbf{X}violated(o) \leftrightarrow (state(o) = active \land$$
$$(violation(o) \land \neg fulfillment(o) \land \neg \mathbf{X}modified(f))))) \quad \text{(A.9)}$$

Norms are described in FIEVeL according to the following syntax:

```
norm ::= symbol start fulfillment violation ;
start ::= "start" "<->" expression ";" ;
fulfillment ::= "fulfillment" "<->" expression ";" ;
violation ::= "violation" "<->" expression ";" ;
```

where expression is an OMSFOTL formula which does not contains $\mathbf{U}$, $\mathbf{E}$, $\mathbf{G}$, or nested occurrences of $\mathbf{X}$. Moreover, given that a norm is described within a status function σ_s, free occurrences of a variable f of sort σ_s may appear in any formula used to describe a norm's condition. A norm *symbol* induces sort $\sigma_{symbol} \leq_\Sigma \sigma_o$ and defines under what conditions predicates $fulfillment, violation$, and $start$ hold when are evaluated over an obligation of sort σ_{symbol}, as exemplified by the following axiom schema:

$$\mathbf{AG}\forall o\forall f(fulfillment(o,f) \leftrightarrow (ofStatus(o) = f \wedge \texttt{expression})) \qquad (A.10)$$

where $\xi(o) = \sigma_{symbol}$ and $\xi(f) = \sigma_s$. Combining instances of Axiom Schema (A.10) (and similarly for predicates $violation$ and $start$) with Axiom(A.9), it is possible to automatically classify states with respect to each norm defined by an institution. In contrast with other approaches (e.g., [16] and [1]), in our framework designers can describe norms at a high-level in terms of institutional concepts, ignoring the actual number of states and transitions admitted by an institution. For instance, the following norm, named $h1$ and associated to the *holder* status function, states that once a holder accepts to give the control of a resource, then it ought to do so before a certain time interval elapses:

```
h1  start<->X ∃ ag:σaid ∃ rec:σaid ∃ res:σresources (subject(f)=ag ∧
            resource(f)=res ∧ happens(accept,ag,rec,res));
    fulfillment<->∃ ag:σaid ∃ rec:σaid ∃ res:σresources (subject(f)=ag
            ∧ res=resource(f) ∧ X happens(give,ag,rec,res));
    violation<->(activation(o)=1 ∧ X happens(time));
```

Without proper sanction mechanisms, the introduction of norms typically does not change the set of properties satisfied by an institution, given that autonomous agents may not comply with such norms [5,2,9,18,7]: as a consequence certain properties may not hold in an institution even if its rules are correctly stated. For instance, properties (P.1) and (P.2) do not hold in the new model of the Resource Management institution obtained by adding norm $h1$, despite this correctly requires that a *holder* gives a resource after it has positively answered to an agent. This is due to the fact that norms regulate existing activities, describing what evolutions of an institution should be considered as legal, but do not change the temporal evolution admitted by an institution.

5   Normed Temporal Operators

To analyze whether an institution may lead a system into certain states when its norms are respected, we can exploit predicate $violated$ and the fact that in our framework norms are reified as norm individuals. Therefore, it is possible to quantify over sort σ_o (and its subsorts induced by each norm), investigating how norms condition the evolution of an institution. In particular, in this paper we define operators that allow designers to reason about what properties are satisfied by an institution when a set of norm individuals are not violated. More precisely, given a set of norms which constitute the extension of formula φ_o (an open formula in which variable o of sort σ_o occurs free), *normed temporal operators* are defined as follows:

- $\mathbf{EG}^{\varphi_o}\varphi =_{def} \mathbf{EG}(\forall o : \sigma_o(\varphi_o \rightarrow \neg violated(o)) \wedge \varphi)$;
- $\mathbf{EX}^{\varphi_o}\varphi =_{def} \mathbf{EX}(\forall o : \sigma_o(\varphi_o \rightarrow \neg violated(o)) \wedge \varphi)$;
- $\mathbf{E}\psi\mathbf{U}^{\varphi_o}\varphi =_{def} \mathbf{E}(\forall o : \sigma_o(\varphi_o \rightarrow \neg violated(o)) \wedge \psi)\mathbf{U}(\forall o : \sigma_o(\varphi_o \rightarrow \neg violated(o)) \wedge \varphi)$;

Since the satisfaction of CTL temporal operators (with the exception of **EX**) refers to the initial state π_0 of a path π [4,3], then also their normed counterparts refer to state π_0. As a consequence, if state π_0 violates norms φ_o, then the normed operators **EG**$^{\varphi_o}$ and **EU**$^{\varphi_o}$ are trivially falsified. This may occur when the system is inconsistent or because normed temporal operators are nested and external operators do not ensure compliance with norms considered by internal operators. While in the former case we would conclude that our system is irrational, in the latter case we may get counter-intuitive results. To avoid this, we can prefix internal operators with **EX**$^{\varphi_o}$, ensuring that the initial state is not considered and only paths compliant with norms of internal operators are taken into account. Despite this problem may be avoided by different definitions of normed temporal operators, we consider more relevant the fact that normed and unnormed operators are evaluated over the same set of states and are expressed in terms of the standard semantics of CTL [4,3]. In doing so, if formula φ_o refers to an empty set of obligations, then normed temporal operators are equivalent to their temporal counterpart (e.g., **EG**$^{false}\varphi \equiv$ **EG**φ), and **EG**$^{\varphi_o}$, **EX**$^{\varphi_o}$, and **EU**$^{\varphi_o}$ constitute an adequate set of operators, since we have the following equivalences:

- $\textbf{EF}^{\varphi_o}\varphi \equiv \textbf{E}true\textbf{U}^{\varphi_o}\varphi$;
- $\textbf{AG}^{\varphi_o}\varphi \equiv \neg\textbf{EF}^{\varphi_o}\neg\varphi \wedge \textbf{EG}^{\varphi_o}true$;
- $\textbf{AX}^{\varphi_o}\varphi \equiv \neg\textbf{EX}^{\varphi_o}\neg\varphi \wedge \textbf{EX}^{\varphi_o}true$;
- $\textbf{A}\psi\textbf{U}^{\varphi_o}\varphi \equiv \neg(\textbf{E}\neg\varphi\textbf{U}^{\varphi_o}(\neg\varphi \wedge \neg\psi)) \wedge \neg\textbf{EG}^{\varphi_o}\neg\varphi \wedge \textbf{EF}^{\varphi_o}\varphi$;
- $\textbf{AF}^{\varphi_o}\varphi \equiv \neg\textbf{EG}^{\varphi_o}\neg\varphi \wedge \textbf{EF}^{\varphi_o}\varphi$;

It is worth observing that by definition, the consistency of norms represents a necessary condition for the satisfaction of normed temporal operators universally quantified over paths, otherwise they would be trivially satisfied by an inconsistent normative system. In contrast with other specification languages characterized by a normative flavor (e.g. [14,16,1]), which assume that the normative system is consistent (i.e., there exists a legal outward transition for every state) either by assuming axiom D [14] or as an explicit hypothesis on the transition system [16,1], in our approach the absence of contradictory norms represents a desirable property that a rational institution ought to satisfy and that can be verified by our model checker. To exemplify the use of normed temporal operators, we modify Property (P.2) such that if holders respect all norms of the institution and they perform action *accept*, then they will *give* their resources:

$$\textbf{AG}\forall act : \sigma_{aid}\forall rec : \sigma_{aid}\forall res : \sigma_{resources}(happens(accept, act, rec, res) \rightarrow$$
$$\textbf{AF}^{\exists h:\sigma_{holder}\exists f:\sigma_{sf}(subject(h)=subject(f)\wedge ofStatus(o)=f)}happens(give, act, rec, res))$$
$$\text{(P.3)}$$

We can also rewrite property (P.1) to investigate whether norm $h1$ is capable of directing the behavior of holders in such a way that when an agent has requested a good and has received a positive answer, it will eventually become the holder of the good:

$$\textbf{AG}\forall act : \sigma_{aid}\forall rec : \sigma_{aid}\forall res : \sigma_{resources}((happens(accept, act, rec, res)$$
$$\rightarrow \textbf{AF}^{\exists w:h1(w=o)}\exists h : holder(subject(h) = rec \wedge resource(h) = res))) \quad \text{(P.4)}$$

To conclude this section we compare the expressiveness and the flexibility of our approach to the specification languages proposed in [1] and [12]. In [1] the authors proposed *Normative Temporal Logic* (NTL), a language similar to CTL with the exception that operators **A** and **E** are replaced by O_η and P_η, which intuitively can be read as "for all paths compliant with the normative system η" and "there exists a path compliant with the normative system η". Given the semantics provided in [1] and assuming that η represents a set of norms, NTL operators are equivalent to normed temporal operators characterized by a formula φ_η representing all individuals of sorts belonging to η. For instance, formula $O\Box_\eta\varphi$ of NTL corresponds to $\mathbf{AX}^{\varphi_\eta}\mathbf{AG}^{\varphi_\eta}\varphi$, where φ_η is defined as follows: $\varphi_\eta \equiv \bigwedge_{\sigma_n \in \eta} \exists k : \sigma_n(k = o)$.

In [12] Lomuscio and Sergot presented a modal operator $O_a\varphi$ which expresses the fact that φ holds over reachable states where agent a complies with its protocol. Assuming that a is an agent, $O_a\varphi$ is equivalent to $\mathbf{AX}^{\exists f(ofStatus(o)=f \wedge subject(f)=a)}\varphi$. While NTL does not provide any construct to reason about agents, in [12] it is possible to investigate only the compliance of agents with the whole set of norms (described as a protocol): instead, normed temporal operators allow us to reason about subsets of norms and agents, and to express complex interdependencies among them as exemplified by Property (P.3).

6   Sanction Mechanisms

To guarantee that those agents that follow norms are not damaged by those who do not, institutions should provide rules that describe what kind of sanctions are applied when agents violate norms. According to [17], the imposition of status functions constitutes a necessary condition for the application of sanctions, since "with that new status come the appropriate punishment" [17, pag. 50]. Such status functions not only may provide new powers and new obligations (prohibitions), but may also revoke or change existing powers or norms: for instance, the exclusion of an agent from an interaction ruled by an institution (e.g., an auction) means that powers and norms defined by such institution have been revoked. Analogously, officials can apply sanctions only if they have the necessary powers, and certain obligations (prohibitions) may further regulate how such powers ought to be exerted. Therefore, given that sanctions modify the powers and norms of agents, we propose to model sanction mechanisms as rules that impose or revoke status functions when a norm is violated.

In our framework sanction mechanisms are defined according to the following grammar:

```
sanction ::= "sanction" symbol "pre" expression ";" "eff" post
    ("," post)* ";" ;
precondition ::= expression;
post ::= (selection "-X->")? effects
selection ::= var ("," var)* "(" expression ")"
effects ::= var ("assign"|"revoke") "(" term "=" term
    ("," term"=" term)* ")";
```

where `expression` is an OMSFOTL formula which does not contain temporal operators or path quantifiers, and `post` is constituted by (i) an (optional) *selection expression* and (ii) an expression describing what statuses are assigned or revoked when the sanction mechanism is activated. As we will see, effects must hold when a violation is detected, while the selection expression is evaluated in the previous state. For this reason, we separate the selection expression from the effects through symbol -X->.

For instance, the following sanction mechanism describes that when a norm $h1$ is violated, then the resource is assigned to the agent that has requested the good and powers and obligations associated to status function $requested$ are revoked:

```
sanction h1
pre true;
eff r2:σ_requested revoke (reqRes(r2)=resource(f)),
    r1:σ_requested res:σ_resources a:σ_aid (res=resource(f)∧reqRes(r1)=res
        ∧ a=requester(r1)) -X->
        r2:σ_holder assign(resource(r2)=res,subject(r2)=a)
```

Before continuing with our presentation, it is worth remarking that in our approach sanction mechanisms reflect what powers, obligations, and prohibitions are assigned to agents when violations are observed, which does not necessarily means that sanctions (like fines) are automatically enforced by the system. Despite designers may decide to enforce norms through automatic reactions of the system, FIEVeL allows to model scenarios where sanction mechanisms confer powers to certain agents to punish violations: for instance, when an agent violates a norm, an officer may be empowered to impose a fine and obliged to do so before a certain time instant.

Sanction mechanisms do not induce any new sort: instead, each of them introduces two predicates, pre_{san_i} and eff_{san_i}, which respectively represent a condition that must be satisfied before a violated obligation activates the i-th sanction mechanism, and its effects. Predicates pre_{san_i} (and analogously predicates eff_{san_i}) are determined by the obligation sort that must be sanctioned (σ_{symbol}) and the status function that defines it (σ_s). Furthermore, predicate pre_{san_i} must satisfy the following axiom schema:

$$\mathbf{AG}\forall o \forall f(pre_{san_i}(o, f) \leftrightarrow \text{precondition}_i) \qquad (A.11)$$

where $\xi(o) = \sigma_{symbol}$ and $\xi(f) = \sigma_s$. Similarly, each sanction mechanism instantiates the following axiom schema which defines what status functions are imposed or revoked when a sanction mechanism is activated:

$$\mathbf{AG}\forall o \forall f(eff_{san_i}(o, f) \leftrightarrow (\bigwedge_{k=0}^{K_i} \forall \bar{s}_{k_i}(\text{expression}_{k_i} \rightarrow \mathbf{X}\exists t_{k_i}$$

$$([\neg]assigned(t_{k_i}) \wedge \bigwedge_{l=1}^{N_{k_i}} term_{k_i,l,1} = term_{k_i,l,2})))) \qquad (A.12)$$

where variables $\bar{s}_{k_i}$ is a set of variables defined by the k-th effect expression of the i-th sanction mechanism and t_{k_i} represents status functions that will be assigned or revoked. Finally, the following axiom schema states that the i-th sanction mechanism brings about its effects when it is activated by the violation of an obligation and its preconditions are met:

$$\mathbf{AG}\forall o \forall f((ofStatus(o) = f \wedge pre_{san_i}(o, f) \wedge \mathbf{X}violated(o)) \rightarrow eff_{san_i}(o, f))$$
$$(A.13)$$

Axiom Schema (A.13) suggests that, as institutional events, also sanction mechanisms concur to the definition of predicate *modified*, which ensures that a status is not assigned (revoked) when no institutional event or sanction mechanism affects it (see Section 3). Moreover, Axiom Schema (A.13) describes the main difference among institutional events and sanction mechanisms: while the former happen because other events occur and certain conditions are satisfied (see Axiom (A.2)), the latter are fired only by violations. To some extend, we can interpret Axiom Schema (A.13) as defining a single convention for the activation of any sanction mechanism.

Properties (P.1) and (P.2) can be regarded as two different interpretations of the human norm "when agents accept to give a resource, then requesters ought to become the new holders", where the latter property explicitly refers to the actor and the action that ought to be performed. Norm $h1$ introduced in Section 4 reflects such rule and the introduction of a sanction mechanism for norm $h1$ changes the set of constitutive rules in such a way that Property (P.1) is satisfied by the Resource Management institution. Observing Figure 1, we can notice that the violation of norm $h1$ forces the effects of action *give*, but not the performance of the action itself: therefore, we can expect that Property (P.2) still does not hold, which is confirmed by our model checker. As it has been formulated and unless we introduce a convention such that *accept* counts as *give* (which may be incompatible with the rules of a human institution), we think that it is impossible to devise a mechanism to satisfy Property (P.2), since it would mean that we are capable of forcing an autonomous agent to act.

7 Discussion and Conclusions

In this paper we have extended FIEVeL with new constructs to model normative aspects of institutions and we have introduced a flexible specification language to define properties regarding paths that are compliant with norms. We have also exemplified how an institution can be developed by using our approach, verifying that it satisfies certain requirements and modifying its constitutive and regulative rules to comply with them. We have also shown that when properties stem from norms of human institutions that artificial institutions should reflect, it is not always possible to satisfy them, at least under certain interpretations of the human institutions.

In [9] Grossi et al. presented an overview of the role of norms and sanctions in institutions. According to [9] it seems that every norm can be either regimented or enforced, while we think that the viability of such mechanisms depends on the meaning attributed by designers to norms. As we have seen, certain interpretations may exclude the possibility of regimenting them and, generally speaking, regimentation of norms regarding institutional aspects can be achieved only by converting regulative rules into constitutive rules. More precisely, prohibitions can be regimented by revoking powers [6,7] while obligations can be enforced by changing the interpretation of certain terms. For instance, norm "all yes/not questions should be answered" can be trivially regimented by assuming that silence counts as a positive (negative) answer. Instead, assuming that only a message sent by an agent counts as a communicative act (like in [7]) it is impossible to regiment such norm.

In [6] sanctions are considered only as rules which *create* new obligations (commitments) and powers, while in this paper we have claimed that sanctions may also *delete* obligations and powers by revoking status functions. Moreover, the approach discussed in [6] is based on an intuitive semantics, which does not allow the development of a framework to verify properties guaranteed by institutions. Analogously, the correctness of protocols modelled in terms of institutional concepts by Artikis et al. [2,15] is only guaranteed by systematic executions. Despite the terminologies used in this paper and in [2] are quite similar, in [2] *physical actions* can be performed only by agents playing a specific role, suggesting that such actions are actually institutional. Furthermore, the formalism used in [2,15] does not provide any abstraction to describe that every institutional action must be empowered in order to be successfully executed. Instead, the authors have to specify this fact for every single action and for every role.

In [8] a rule language is introduced to model norms and to represent the effects of concurrent events. The author proposed the notion of *enforcing events*, which means that obligatory events are considered as if they were executed even when agents do not perform them. In our opinion, events' enforcement transforms regulative rules into constitutive rules, by defining when time events count as obligatory events, and represents an effective mechanism to describe automatic updates of institutions. In general, we believe that it is not possible to enforce all kinds of events, especially those (like actions) that can only be performed by autonomous agents.

The constructs presented in Section 4 constitute a high-level description of norms, and our tool automatically classifies transitions and states as compliant with each norm of the system. In this respect, our approach is similar to the one presented in [18]. Instead, the input language of the model checker described in [16] requires designers to explicitly list the set of states that each agent may reach, and to classify them as *red* (an agent violates the protocol) or *green*. Although red states are such only because they violate a protocol [12,16], such classification is not inferred from the protocol but must be manually provided independently from it: therefore designers may introduce discrepancies among the protocol and the classification of states. Similarly, in [1] systems are described with a low-level language which requires to associate a name to each transition, and norms can be defined only by listing under what conditions a set of transitions is considered legal.

In the future we plan to define a translation of axioms stemming from our metamodel and from FIEVeL models into Prolog, providing a single framework for the definition, verification, and monitoring of institutions.

References

1. Ågotnes, T., van der Hoek, W., Rodríguez-Aguilar, J.A., Sierra, C., Wooldridge, M.: On the logic of normative systems. In: Proceedings of the 20th International Joint Conference on Artificial Intelligence, pp. 1175–1180 (2007)
2. Artikis, A., Kamara, L., Pitt, J., Sergot, M.J.: A Protocol for Resource Sharing in Norm-Governed Ad Hoc Networks. In: Leite, J.A., Omicini, A., Torroni, P., Yolum, p. (eds.) DALT 2004. LNCS (LNAI), vol. 3476, pp. 221–238. Springer, Heidelberg (2005)
3. Clarke, E.M., Grumberg, O., Peled, D.: Model Checking. MIT Press, Cambridge (1999)

4. Emerson, E.A., Halpern, J.Y.: "Sometimes" and "not never" revisited: on branching versus linear time temporal logic. Journal of the ACM 33(1), 151–178 (1986)
5. Esteva, M., Rodríguez-Aguilar, J.A., Sierra, C., Garcia, P., Arcos, J.L.: On the Formal Specification of Electronic Institutions. In: Sierra, C., Dignum, F.P.M. (eds.) AgentLink 2000. LNCS (LNAI), vol. 1991, pp. 126–147. Springer, Heidelberg (2001)
6. Fornara, N., Colombetti, M.: Specifying and Enforcing Norms in Artificial Institutions. In: Omicini, A., Dunin-Keplicz, B., Padget, J. (eds.) Proceedings of the 4th European Workshop on Multi-Agent Systems (2006)
7. Fornara, N., Viganò, F., Colombetti, M.: Agent Communication and Artificial Institutions. Autonomous Agents and Multi-Agent Systems 14(2), 121–142 (2007)
8. García-Camino, A.: Ignoring, Forcing and Expecting Concurrent Events in Electronic Institutions. In: Sichman, J.S., et al. (eds.) COIN 2007 Workshops. LNCS (LNAI), vol. 4870, pp. 316–329. Springer, Heidelberg (2008)
9. Grossi, D., Aldewereld, H., Dignum, F.: Ubi lex, ibi poena: Designing norm enforcement in e-institutions. In: Noriega, P., Vázquez-Salceda, J., Boella, G., Boissier, O., Dignum, V., Fornara, N., Matson, E. (eds.) COIN 2006, vol. 4386, pp. 110–124. Springer, Heidelberg (2007)
10. Jones, A., Sergot, M.J.: On the characterization of law and computer systems: The normative systems perspectives. In: Deontic Logic in Computer Science: Normative Systems Specification, pp. 275–307 (1993)
11. Jones, A., Sergot, M.J.: A formal characterisation of institutionalised power. Journal of the IGPL 4(3), 429–445 (1996)
12. Lomuscio, A., Sergot, M.: A formulation of violation, error recovery, and enforcement in the bit transmission problem. Journal of Applied Logic 1(2), 93–116 (2002)
13. Manzano, M.: Introduction to many-sorted logic. In: Many-sorted logic and its applications, pp. 3–86. John Wiley, Chichester (1993)
14. Meyer, J.-J., Wieringa, R.J.: Deontic Logic: A Concise Overview. In: Deontic Logic in Computer Science: Normative Systems Specification, pp. 3–16. John Wiley, Chichester (1993)
15. Pitt, J., Kamara, L., Sergot, M., Artikis, A.: Formalization of a voting protocol for virtual organizations. In: Proceedings of the 4th Conference on Autonomous agents and Multi-Agent Systems, pp. 373–380 (2005)
16. Raimondi, F., Lomuscio, A.: Automatic Verification of Deontic Interpreted Systems by Model Checking via OBDD's. In: Proceedings of the 16th European Conference on Artificial Intelligence, pp. 53–57 (2004)
17. Searle, J.R.: The construction of social reality. Free Press, New York (1995)
18. Sergot, M.J., Craven, R.: The Deontic Component of Action Language nC+. In: Goble, L., Meyer, J.-J.C. (eds.) DEON 2006. LNCS (LNAI), vol. 4048, pp. 222–237. Springer, Heidelberg (2006)
19. Viganò, F., Colombetti, M.: Specification and Verification of Institutions through Status Functions. In: Noriega, P., et al. (eds.) COIN 2006. LNCS (LNAI), vol. 4386, pp. 125–141. Springer, Heidelberg (2007)
20. Viganò, F., Colombetti, M.: Symbolic Model Checking of Institutions. In: Proceedings of the 9th International Conference on Electronic Commerce (ICEC 2007), pp. 35–44. ACM Press (2007)

Author Index

edes-Druck, Berlin
Lehmann, Berlin

Lecture Notes in Artificial Intelligence (LNAI)

Vol. 4737: B. Berendt, A. Hotho, D. Mladenic, G. Semeraro (Eds.), From Web to Social Web: Discovering and Deploying User and Content Profiles. XI, 161 pages. 2007.

Vol. 4733: R. Basili, M.T. Pazienza (Eds.), AI*IA 2007: Artificial Intelligence and Human-Oriented Computing. XVII, 858 pages. 2007.

Vol. 4724: K. Mellouli (Ed.), Symbolic and Quantitative Approaches to Reasoning with Uncertainty. XV, 914 pages. 2007.

Vol. 4722: C. Pelachaud, J.-C. Martin, E. André, G. Chollet, K. Karpouzis, D. Pelé (Eds.), Intelligent Virtual Agents. XV, 425 pages. 2007.

Vol. 4720: B. Konev, F. Wolter (Eds.), Frontiers of Combining Systems. X, 283 pages. 2007.

Vol. 4702: J.N. Kok, J. Koronacki, R. Lopez de Mantaras, S. Matwin, D. Mladenič, A. Skowron (Eds.), Knowledge Discovery in Databases: PKDD 2007. XXIV, 640 pages. 2007.

Vol. 4701: J.N. Kok, J. Koronacki, R. Lopez de Mantaras, S. Matwin, D. Mladenič, A. Skowron (Eds.), Machine Learning: ECML 2007. XXII, 809 pages. 2007.

Vol. 4696: H.-D. Burkhard, G. Lindemann, R. Verbrugge, L.Z. Varga (Eds.), Multi-Agent Systems and Applications V. XIII, 350 pages. 2007.

Vol. 4694: B. Apolloni, R.J. Howlett, L. Jain (Eds.), Knowledge-Based Intelligent Information and Engineering Systems, Part III. XXIX, 1126 pages. 2007.

Vol. 4693: B. Apolloni, R.J. Howlett, L. Jain (Eds.), Knowledge-Based Intelligent Information and Engineering Systems, Part II. XXXII, 1380 pages. 2007.

Vol. 4692: B. Apolloni, R.J. Howlett, L. Jain (Eds.), Knowledge-Based Intelligent Information and Engineering Systems, Part I. LV, 882 pages. 2007.

Vol. 4687: P. Petta, J.P. Müller, M. Klusch, M. Georgeff (Eds.), Multiagent System Technologies. X, 207 pages. 2007.

Vol. 4682: D.-S. Huang, L. Heutte, M. Loog (Eds.), Advanced Intelligent Computing Theories and Applications. XXVII, 1373 pages. 2007.

Vol. 4676: M. Klusch, K.V. Hindriks, M.P. Papazoglou, L. Sterling (Eds.), Cooperative Information Agents XI. XI, 361 pages. 2007.

Vol. 4667: J. Hertzberg, M. Beetz, R. Englert (Eds.), KI 2007: Advances in Artificial Intelligence. IX, 516 pages. 2007.

Vol. 4660: S. Džeroski, L. Todorovski (Eds.), Computational Discovery of Scientific Knowledge. X, 327 pages. 2007.

Vol. 4659: V. Mařík, V. Vyatkin, A.W. Colombo (Eds.), Holonic and Multi-Agent Systems for Manufacturing. VIII, 456 pages. 2007.

Vol. 4651: F. Azevedo, P. Barahona, F. Fages, F. Rossi (Eds.), Recent Advances in Constraints. VIII, 185 pages. 2007.

Vol. 4648: F. Almeida e Costa, L.M. Rocha, E. Costa, I. Harvey, A. Coutinho (Eds.), Advances in Artificial Life. XVI, 1215 pages. 2007.

Vol. 4635: B. Kokinov, D.C. Richardson, T.R. Roth-Berghofer, L. Vieu (Eds.), Modeling and Using Context. XIV, 574 pages. 2007.

Vol. 4632: R. Alhajj, H. Gao, X. Li, J. Li, O.R. Zaïane (Eds.), Advanced Data Mining and Applications. XV, 634 pages. 2007.

Vol. 4629: V. Matoušek, P. Mautner (Eds.), Text, Speech and Dialogue. XVII, 663 pages. 2007.

Vol. 4626: R.O. Weber, M.M. Richter (Eds.), Case-Based Reasoning Research and Development. XIII, 534 pages. 2007.

Vol. 4617: V. Torra, Y. Narukawa, Y. Yoshida (Eds.), Modeling Decisions for Artificial Intelligence. XII, 502 pages. 2007.

Vol. 4612: I. Miguel, W. Ruml (Eds.), Abstraction, Reformulation, and Approximation. XI, 418 pages. 2007.

Vol. 4604: U. Priss, S. Polovina, R. Hill (Eds.), Conceptual Structures: Knowledge Architectures for Smart Applications. XII, 514 pages. 2007.

Vol. 4603: F. Pfenning (Ed.), Automated Deduction – CADE-21. XII, 522 pages. 2007.

Vol. 4597: P. Perner (Ed.), Advances in Data Mining. XI, 353 pages. 2007.

Vol. 4594: R. Bellazzi, A. Abu-Hanna, J. Hunter (Eds.), Artificial Intelligence in Medicine. XVI, 509 pages. 2007.

Vol. 4585: M. Kryszkiewicz, J.F. Peters, H. Rybinski, A. Skowron (Eds.), Rough Sets and Intelligent Systems Paradigms. XIX, 836 pages. 2007.

Vol. 4578: F. Masulli, S. Mitra, G. Pasi (Eds.), Applications of Fuzzy Sets Theory. XVIII, 693 pages. 2007.

Vol. 4573: M. Kauers, M. Kerber, R. Miner, W. Windsteiger (Eds.), Towards Mechanized Mathematical Assistants. XIII, 407 pages. 2007.

Vol. 4571: P. Perner (Ed.), Machine Learning and Data Mining in Pattern Recognition. XIV, 913 pages. 2007.

Vol. 4570: H.G. Okuno, M. Ali (Eds.), New Trends in Applied Artificial Intelligence. XXI, 1194 pages. 2007.

Vol. 4565: D.D. Schmorrow, L.M. Reeves (Eds.), Foundations of Augmented Cognition. XIX, 450 pages. 2007.

Vol. 4562: D. Harris (Ed.), Engineering Psychology and Cognitive Ergonomics. XXIII, 879 pages. 2007.

Vol. 4548: N. Olivetti (Ed.), Automated Reasoning with Analytic Tableaux and Related Methods. X, 245 pages. 2007.

Vol. 4539: N.H. Bshouty, C. Gentile (Eds.), Learning Theory. XII, 634 pages. 2007.

Vol. 4529: P. Melin, O. Castillo, L.T. Aguilar, J. Kacprzyk, W. Pedrycz (Eds.), Foundations of Fuzzy Logic and Soft Computing. XIX, 830 pages. 2007.

Vol. 4520: M.V. Butz, O. Sigaud, G. Pezzulo, G. Baldassarre (Eds.), Anticipatory Behavior in Adaptive Learning Systems. X, 379 pages. 2007.

Vol. 4511: C. Conati, K. McCoy, G. Paliouras (Eds.), User Modeling 2007. XVI, 487 pages. 2007.

Vol. 4509: Z. Kobti, D. Wu (Eds.), Advances in Artificial Intelligence. XII, 552 pages. 2007.